GREAT ROCK DRUMMERS

SIXTIES

REVISED

THE BLUES PROJECT / PROJE

BY
BOB CIANCI

Author photo by Billy Jeansonne.

Published by Hal Leonard Corporation
7777 Bluemound Road
P.O. Box 13819
Milwaukee, WI 53213

Trade Book Division Editorial Offices
19 West 21st Street
Suite 201
New York, New York 10010

Library of Congress Control Number: 2006920460
ISBN 0634099256

Printed in the United States of America
Second Edition

7777 W. BLUEMOUND RD. P.O. BOX 13819 MILWAUKEE, WI 53213

Visit Hal Leonard online at **www.halleonard.com**

Hal Leonard books are available at your local bookstore, or you may order through
Music Dispatch at 1-800-637-2852 or www.musicdispatch.com

GREAT ROCK DRUMMERS OF THE SIXTIES

REVISED

by Bob Cianci

HAL•LEONARD®

CONTENTS

INTRODUCTION

Little did I realize sixteen years ago that I would be sitting at my PC revising *Great Rock Drummers Of The Sixties*. I thought the book would just fade out of print and remain a pleasant memory, a notable chapter in my life. To my surprise, it continues to generate interest from drummers worldwide and in the process has become an extremely rare and collectible book.

In fall 2004, I asked Harvey Finkel, owner of the Clinton Book Shop in Clinton, New Jersey to do an extensive search for a copy of *GRDOTS*, as I've come to call it. About a week later, Harvey called and told me his employee Ann Richardson, a crack "book finder," had located three copies. One was selling for $179, another for $225, and a third, in England, for $410! I was surprised and awed to learn it had become so valuable. Trouble was, neither the publisher nor I made money on the used copies. So the logical move was to revise the book and get it out there again.

We have reprinted the original book with a back-to-the-drawing-board revision of the Honorable Mentions, updates on each individual chapter, and a new introduction and epilogue.

You will find many interesting additions to the Honorable Mentions section. No matter how hard I tried to get it finished, drummers kept popping up that need to be included. You'll find the names of many members of Sixties garage-punk bands added to the section, as well as the most prominent R&B and funk drummers who worked at Motown and Stax Records and with James Brown. They influenced countless rock players worldwide.

When *GRDOTS* was published in 1989, a few critics blew it off with bad reviews. Ultimately, the slings and arrows of critics don't matter, and that comes from someone who has written his share of scathing reviews as a music journalist for more than thirty years. What's important is the reader, the person who shells out his or her hard-earned cash for a book and gains knowledge and enjoyment from it. That's all that really matters. The support and praise I have received over the years from pro and amateur drummers, industry professionals and Sixties music fans has been overwhelming and gratifying, to say the least.

When I conceptualized *GRDOTS*, my priority was to give some long-deserved recognition to drummers who had slipped between the cracks: Bobby Elliott, Jerry Edmonton, Dino Danelli, Johny Barbata, Barry Jenkins, Keith Webb, Don Stevenson, and many more. Included, of course, were the obvious stars like Appice, Moon, Starr, Mitchell, Watts and Baker, but there was never any question that providing much-needed recognition to deserving musicians was the goal. Over the years, I have come to the conclusion that I accomplished that goal beyond my wildest dreams. That alone made all the difficult work worthwhile. I might also add there were moments when I feared *GRDOTS* would never get finished, and there were times when I sweated its completion—we didn't have air conditioning at home back then, and I was working on a simple electric typewriter. Now, I have air conditioning throughout the house, a PC, and the Internet at my disposal.

But *GRDOTS* did get done, and for better or worse, even with its occasional faults, it seems as if everyone in the drum industry has read it, along with those fortunate people who still own the five thousand or so original copies. I continue to get e-mails from people all over the world who have owned *GRDOTS* for years or have just discovered it. Some want to know where they can find an original copy. The praise, support, and compliments continue to come in and never fail to make my day.

I would like to thank everyone who helped in getting this revision finished, including the well-known drummers themselves and their families. Thanks to everyone who bought *GRDOTS* over the years and continue to enjoy the original book. The drumming community is truly a cosmic fraternity, a brotherhood like no other. Ladies are welcome too.

Thanks also to John Cerullo and Belinda Yong of Hal Leonard for their cooperation, help and patience; Adam Budofsky of *Modern Drummer* for his help in locating Kenney Jones; Frank Annunziata for being a good friend and traveling companion; my wife, Maureen, and daughters Renae and Carianne for putting up with my frequent absences; cousins Catherine and Dimitri Karas for their love and assistance; my oldest friend, Neil "Rollo" Feltz for his constant encouragement; Vern Miller, my bass-playing partner for all these years, for his wisdom and down-to-earth common sense; and the almost endless list of Internet buddies I am blessed with from the now-defunct DCI forum and the new drumforum.org for their encouragement and support: Frogman Frank, JR, Mario, Paulie, Vinnie, Dan, Frankie, Rhys, Lucio, Alan, Steve, Rick P, Jim J. and the rest of you characters. You guys are the best. I value your friendship more than you realize. Now, can we all get together for some good Italian food? Special thanks to DCI host Harry Cangany for his much-appreciated compliments over the years.

To Billy, Bruce and Mary Anne Jeansonne of *Classic Drummer* magazine: thank you for bringing me into your publishing family and for giving me a classy title. I'm proud to be part of the fastest-growing adult drum magazine in the world.

To Garrison, John Good and Don Lombardi of DW; Steve Lobmeier and John D'Addario Jr. of Evans; and Pat Brown and Kevin Radomski of Pro-Mark: thank you for the opportunity to endorse your excellent products and for the years of good vibes and greeting cards. Thanks also to Bob Zildjian, Wayne Blanchard, Robert Mason, and Mark Love of Sabian Cymbals, for your kindness, generosity and great products.

To every hardworking man or woman who runs or works in an independent drum shop or music store: Hang in there. Don't succumb to the egregious "big box" competition. You're the real backbone of the musical instrument business and you deserve to make a living. We need you. Drummers…please support and patronize independent music retailers. Without you, they're history.

To George Sigler, the world's best drum-department manager, and Jim Riccio of Ritchie's Music in Rockaway, New Jersey—you guys are the bomb. Equal thanks to Jon Haberman at Alto Music in Middletown, New York. Thanks to all of you for the great gear deals over the years. "OK, what's the 'Bob' price?"

To my favorite World War II fighter pilot, former Captain Bill Hendrian, who flew blue-nosed P-51s in the 352nd Fighter Group in England and destroyed at least four German planes (and most likely more), thanks for your friendship and good advice.

To my friend, former drum teacher and spiritual father, the late Carl Wolf: Colombo, you taught much more than just rudiments and Ted Reed's *Syncopation*. The time I spent with you was a lesson in living. I miss you. I'm sorry we never really said goodbye. We'll meet again someday on the other side. Special thanks to my friend Scott Goldman for his friendship and encouragement.

And finally, I'd like to send a cosmic shout-out to my "soul parent," Adelaide Cianci, who passed away in 1991. She was the original inspiration for *GRDOTS* and never received credit first time around. About seven years before I thought about writing a book, she said to me, "You know so much about these drummers. Why don't you write a book?"

She was on to something. Thanks, Mom.

Bob Cianci
March 2006

PROFILES

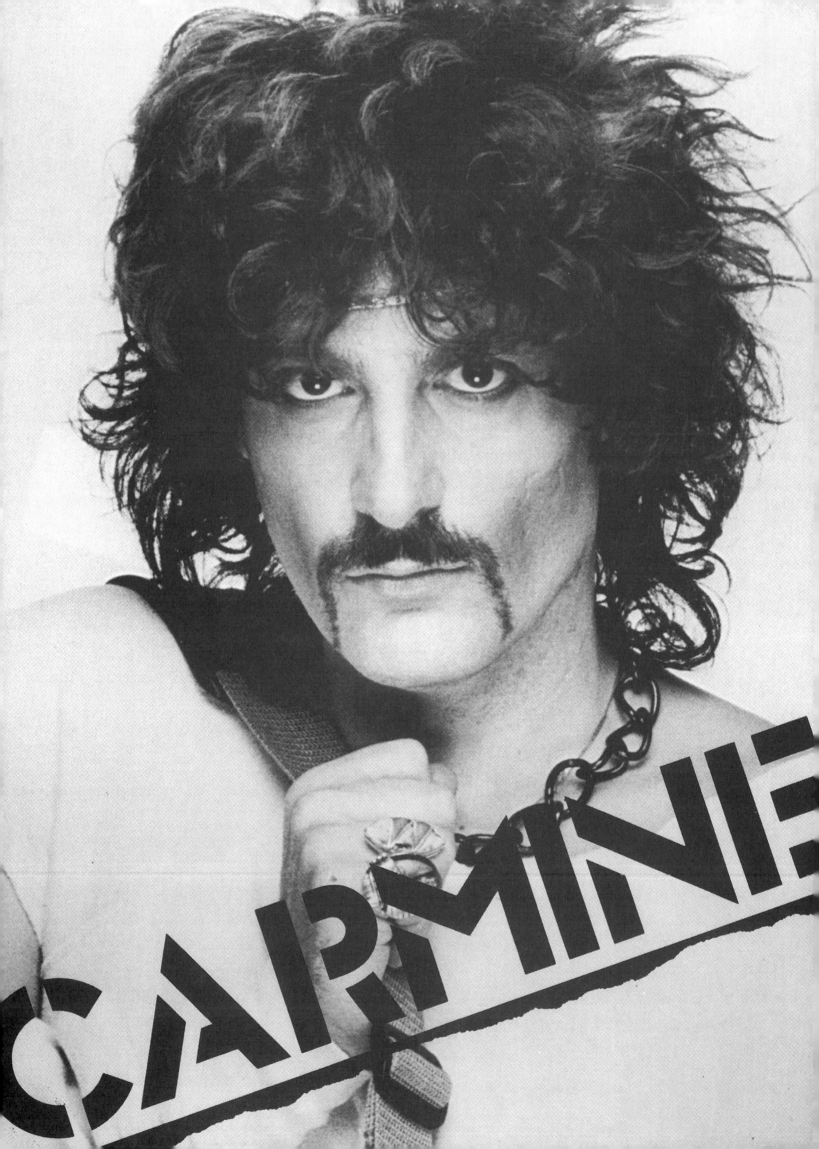

LET'S GET ONE THING STRAIGHT FROM THE BEGINNING.

The guy pronounces his name *Ap-Peace*. Not *Appa-See*, or *Appa-Chee*, or *Ap-Peachy*, or even *Appi-Chay*, although that's very close to the phonetically correct Italian way of saying it.

Now that we've gotten past the correct way to say the name, let's not forget to mention that Carmine Whatever-His-Name Is deserves a lot of credit for popularizing oversized drumsets, for being a consistently hard-hitting power drummer who is never content to rest on his laurels and has influenced countless young and not-so-young-anymore drummers. He is also a vocalist and songwriter, a highly active, visible, and stimulating clinician and teacher, an actor, philanthropist, arranger, producer, businessman, magazine columnist, and the author of five informative drum books, two videos, and a how-to-do-it cassette series on drumming. Good Lord, the man really is the "ultimate rock overachiever," as his manager calls him! He also plays in two bands, King Kobra and Blue Murder, and at this writing, is planning a reunion tour with The Vanilla Fudge and a book of Rock 'n' Roll road stories.

Doesn't this dude ever sleep?

APPICE

Carmine is a true Sixties survivor, someone whose philosophy has always been to go onstage, forget your troubles and kick ass.

CARMINE APPICE

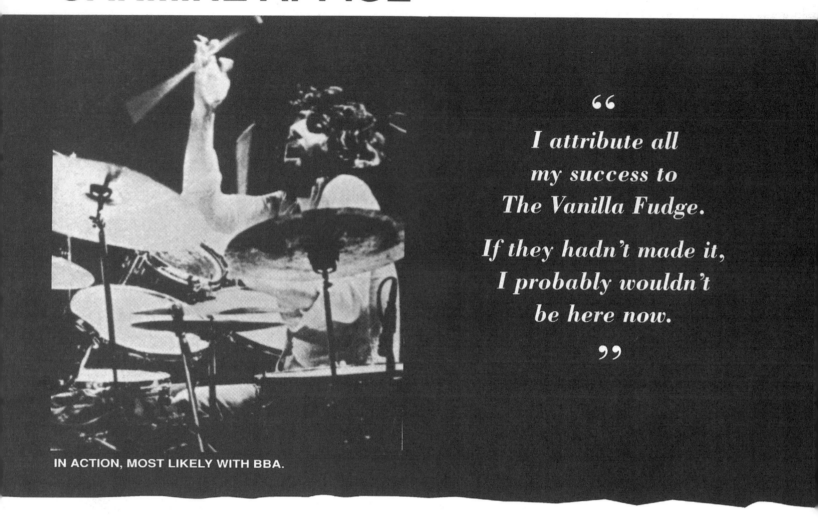

66

I attribute all my success to The Vanilla Fudge.

If they hadn't made it, I probably wouldn't be here now.

99

IN ACTION, MOST LIKELY WITH BBA.

Of course, Carmine will be the first to tell you about all his musical activities and accomplishments, but, he does it in a way that leaves one feeling it's not so much an over-stimulated ego, but that of an incredibly enthusiastic, well-focused and proud musician who is quite aware of his rightful place in rock drumdom. Carmine is a true Sixties survivor, someone whose philosophy has always been to go on-stage, forget your troubles and kick ass. Apparently, that's good advice, for in the late 1980's, Carmine Appice isn't just surviving, he's doing better than ever. Some have argued his claims of achievement, but whether they like it or not, he seems to have what it takes to back it all up.

Carmine was one of those talented drummers who really impressed me as a kid. His work on the first Vanilla Fudge album, especially on their rearranged version of The Supremes classic, "You Keep Me Hangin' On," was awesome. I recall trying to master his way of doing a splashy roll on the crash cymbal, only to catch it quickly. It was a very effective trick that added a lot of drama and tension to The Fudge's music, which was pretty dramatic in its own right. Although some critics accused the group of being heavy-handed and lumbering, they certainly were trendsetters, and Carmine himself was a visual genius. His twin bass drums were huge. He had what appeared to be a converted parade tenor drum mounted as a rack tom, and two of the largest floor toms you'd ever seen, like the one in that famous Slingerland ad from the late Fifties and early Sixties with Gene Krupa...an 18x20," or some ridiculous size. Behind him was a humongous gong, the first ever in rock music, Carmine twirled his

sticks, jumped up to his feet for effect, made wild faces and even then, seemed almost bigger than life, a drummer with his own special flair for music and showmanship. You knew this boy was going places. He did. And still is.

Life for Carmine began in Brooklyn, New York, on December 15 (he was reluctant to divulge the year), the son of Carmine Charles and Mary Appice. Around the age of eleven, Carmine realized a fondness for drums. His cousin, Joey, had a drumset and Carmine enjoyed banging away when the family would get together over the holidays. At thirteen, his parents agreed to drum lessons and Carmine studied for four years with a teacher named Dick Bennett, a fine player in the Buddy Rich tradition.

"My parents were very supportive. They paid for the lessons and when I had a gig, my father would drive me until I was old enough to take my own car."

Carmine studied from the Ted Reed books including *Syncopation* and the Charley Wilcoxon book. He later spent some time woodshedding the Reed Latin book as well. For practice, Carmine would usually spend an hour to an hour and a half doing his lessons on the pads and then do another hour or so playing along with records, as at the time, there were no rock drumming books available. He liked Gene Krupa and Buddy Rich, as well as Joe Morello, Philly Joe Jones, and Max Roach.

"I practiced along with the Krupa/Rich drum battle records and other jazz things. I also used to play with "Wipeout" and "Teen Beat" and things like that."

It wasn't long before Carmine joined a little band that consisted of his friends Harvey Citron on guitar and trumpeter Mario Vitale. They played weddings and Bar

THE ROAD CASES TELL CARMINE'S STORY OF TWENTY PLUS YEARS ON THE ROAD.

Mitzvahs and Carmine remembered earning the princely sum of $7.50 for one of his first gigs. He also studied theory and harmony and participated fully in all the musical organizations his high school had to offer, including the concert band, marching band, orchestra, jazz band, and percussion ensemble.

It was at this time, that Carmine became turned on to black rhythm and blues drummers like Bernard Purdie and the drummers who played with James Brown. These influences helped instill a strong sense of groove in his playing.

"Basically, I just took a little bit of everybody and put it together. I liked the power of the big band drummers and added the rock thing and came up with my style."

Carmine never worked with a metronome during his formative years.

"I always had pretty good time from the getgo.' I worked with my teacher and he had pretty good time as well, so I never owned a metronome until recently."

After graduating high school, Carmine worked with a few New York rock bands until he got a call from a group called The Pigeons, who were looking for a drummer.

"They had heard about me around New York. They heard that I had a good foot, a good feel and that I could sing, so I joined The Pigeons and ten months later, we had a single on the charts. *You Keep Me Hangin On'* was done as a demo and next thing you know, it was a hit single that did great all over the country and actually, all over the world."

To those unaware, The Pigeons were to become The Vanilla Fudge. In an interview from *Musician's Industry*

magazine, Carmine had this to say about The Fudge.

"Vanilla Fudge was the first classical, symphonic rock band." The Fudge specialized in performing and writing very complex, intense, and often slowed-down arrangements that deviated far beyond the average three chord Rock 'n' Roll tune. Carmine was given free reign in the studio and live, to play anything he wanted.

"I attribute all my success to The Vanilla Fudge. If they hadn't make it, I probably wouldn't be here now. We were different, we had good singing, good vocals, a great vibe in the band and we were really good at arranging and that's what made us happen."

The Fudge's first album, *Vanilla Fudge*, released in 1967, was the first LP to break into the national Top Ten without the benefit of a Top Ten single. On its second week on the *Billboard* charts, it jumped an amazing 167 points and eventually settled in the Top Five.

After five albums and countless live dates, The Fudge called it quits. Carmine had this to say from the aforementioned interview.

"If I had the head on my shoulders now back in the old Vanilla Fudge days, we'd still be together. We got bored and broke it up. What we should have done is kept the group together but done solo things, worked with (Jeff) Beck when we wanted to, and keep everything loose. When we broke up, we threw away a million dollars worth of gigs."

One of the factors that contributed to the Fudge's demise was bassist Tim Bogert and Carmine's new friendship with English guitar superstar Jeff Beck. It

CARMINE, ALWAYS THE ROCKER,
ADOPTS MAX HEADROOM-LIKE SHADES
FOR THIS MID EIGHTIES PROMO SHOT.

seems that Beck played some gigs with his band that included Rod Stewart and Ron Wood, with The Fudge. Seeing Beck literally blew both musicians away. Fudge guitarist Vinnie Martell was a competent player, but not in the same league as the sometimes erratic Beck. Tim and Carmine made their move and left The Fudge, with plans to put together a new band with Jeff, but unfortunately, just as the final details were being worked out, Beck, a hot rod enthusiast, was in a very serious car accident that temporarily cancelled all plans for the new band until he recuperated. Bogert and Appice then put together Cactus, with former Mitch Ryder guitarist Jim McCarty and ex-Amboy Dukes vocalist Rusty Day. Cactus toured and recorded with frequency from 1970 until 1972. The group was naturally guitar-based, whereas The Fudge had been centered around the Hammond organ of Mark Stein. When Jeff Beck came back in late '72, Carmine and Timmy again jumped again at the chance to play with him. One studio LP was produced, "Beck, Bogert and Appice,"

So, I said to myself, 'Damn it, I'll write a book, just for the hell of it.' I wrote it based on how I learned my first rock rhythms. My lawyer helped get it published, I got five hundred dollars as an advance, and boom, I'm an author. When I assembled *Realistic Rock*, I included pictures and things to make it more fun and appealing. I don't want it to be a dry, tutorial exercise book. The kids should have fun while they're learning. That is critical to sustaining your interest in an instrument."

Carmine's ideas on how to put together a successful rock drum book paid off. *Realistic Rock* has sold over *three hundred thousand* copies to date, has been translated into foreign languages, and is still going strong, having been revised and reprinted. Carmine followed it up with *Realistic Double Feet* (1974), *Realistic Hi-Hat* (1977), *Rudiments To Rock* (1977) and *Realistic Reggae Rock* (1983).

Itching to get back to performing as a member of a hot band, Carmine accepted an invitation to join Rod

"Hold a solid groove and throw another timing in and keep coming back. Play with a lot of energy and power."

and there was also a live album released in Europe and the Orient that is now a very highly prized collectible. Personality and musical differences sadly split BBA apart.

According to Carmine, the second BBA album, which was never released, contained quite a lot of fusion and jazz/rock, much of it in odd time changes. The LP was shelved, as Beck and Appice began work on what was to eventually become *Blow By Blow*. For some reason, Carmine's drum tracks were discarded and a session drummer re-recorded his parts. Appice wound up suing Beck over authorship of some of the material on the LP, but the case was settled out of court.

After the Beck debacle, Carmine left New York, moved to Los Angeles and joined a band called KGB, an ill-fated "supergroup" that also included singer Ray Kennedy, keyboardist Barry Goldberg, guitarist Mike Bloomfield and former Blind Faith bassist Rick Grech. Two forgettable LP's later, KGB bit the dust. Carmine considered it the low point of his career, calling KGB, "useless."

At this time, Carmine, who in 1972, had authored the excellent rock drum book, *Realistic Rock*, probably the first authentic rock drumming book, threw himself head-long into teaching and doing drum clinics as an endorsee of Ludwig drums and Paiste cymbals. He quickly established his name as one of great interest to young rock drummers, but more on that later.

Realistic Rock was originally written as a reaction to the lack of rock books for aspiring drummers. Carmine remarked in the *Musician's Industry* interview.

"It started when I went into a Sam Ash music store in New York and saw some drum books. I'd been reading and learning from them all my life and they seemed so out of touch with the new music scene. There'd be some short-haired asshole on the cover with the comment, 'Learn to play drums in five easy lessons' or some such shit. I looked at the rhythms and they were ten years old.

Stewart's new group, in 1976. Kenney Jones had originally been pegged as the drummer, but he backed out at the last minute. Rod had auditioned about thirty drummers, when one of his roadies called Carmine to see if he could recommend a replacement for Jones, to which Carmine replied that he would be interested in the gig himself. He went down to a rehearsal, played, and the drum chair was offered. Carmine took it.

Working with Stewart did have its drawbacks. Carmine was told to play simply and steadily and was forced to scale down his set to five pieces with a single bass drum. He also had to play a lot of ballads with Stewart, something that has always bored him silly. On record, a session drummer was brought in to handle the ballads. The gig did have its good points though. The money was nice, Carmine got to play with a lot of power and energy, and Rod consented to give him a drum solo to appease the growing legion of Appice fans. In the end, the five years Carmine spent with Stewart was a very positive experience. He got to play for the largest audiences of his life with Rod and the gig re-established him as a major rock drumming force. Carmine also expanded his songwriting credits on the hits" Do Ya' Think I'm Sexy" and "Young Turks," both written in conjunction with Stewart and both gigantic sellers.

Once again, Carmine resumed doing clinics and symposiums worldwide. In Europe and Japan, he used a translator to get his message across when speaking. When he played, no translation was necessary. His drumming said it all. For three years, he donated a portion of his proceeds from clinics to UNICEF, the well known children's relief organization. In recognition of his contributions, Los Angeles mayor Tom Bradley declared May 23, 1981, "Carmine Appice Day" in the City Of Angels. The honor was awarded during the "Second Annual Carmine Appice Drum Off," which featured a host of celebrity drummers including Carmine's hero, Buddy

CARMINE APPICE

Rich. It attracted a crowd of over 10,000 drumming enthusiasts and has now become an annual event all across the country, with the finals being held in Los Angeles. *MTV* and *Entertainment Tonight* have covered the event nationally.

After parting company with Rod, Carmine released his first solo album on Pasha Records, distributed by Epic, entitled *Carmine Appice-Rockers*, which featured more high-energy drumming, including two solo numbers, "Drum City Rocker," with his brother, Vinnie Appice, now drummer in Dio, and "Drums Drums Drums," which was co-written with Richie Podolor, who worked closely with Sandy Nelson on his famous drum solo records in the late Fifties and early Sixties (See Sandy Nelson's chapter). The album sold respectably and also featured Carmine as lead singer throughout.

Appice's next project was with primal guitarist Ted Nugent. He worked with Nugent in the spring and summer of 1982, cut the *Nugent* LP and toured with Ted nationwide.

In 1983, in an unexpected move, Carmine formed a band called DNA with ex-McCoys/Johnny Winter guitarist Rick Derringer. They recorded a seven song Lp titled *Party Tested*, that was released on Boardwalk Records. A video followed that received some airplay on MTV.

Through it all, Carmine kept up a steady schedule of clinics, tours with the likes of Ozzy Osbourne, and session work with artists as diverse as Paul Stanley of Kiss, Eric Carmen, fusion bassist Stanley Clarke, Pink Floyd, guitarist and Cher's ex-boyfriend, Les Dudek, and others.

"LET ME ADJUST MY COLLAR HERE..." CARMINE IN THE 1980'S

He even had the time to write a regular drumming column for *Circus* Magazine and run the Synsonics/1983 Carmine Appice National Drum Battle Tour, a 15-city amateur drumming competition sponsored by Mattel Electronics!. And if that wasn't enough, Carmine produced and released two video tapes, *Master Class* and *Drum Clinic* to help young drummers and later, as mentioned, put together an audio cassette, *Power Rock Drum System*, again for the student drummer. His dedication to the education of young drummers has been wide reaching to say the least.

1985 saw the formation of King Kobra, a commercially-viable heavy metal band. Two LP's on Capitol Records were released. They contributed to the sound-track of a moved called *Iron Eagle* and were eventually dropped by Capitol, which resulted in three of the band members leaving in 1987. Undaunted, Carmine reformed the band with three new members and started his own record company, Rocker Records, to release their next LP, *King Kobra III*, which has now begun to catch on with metal fans. Carmine had this to say about the project in a recent interview in *Rock* magazine.

"The new album is leaning more and more toward the first album as far as heaviness and energy. And I think the songs are better. I'm really happy with the result we achieved. *King Kobra III* is the best one we've done so far, and I'm really looking forward to getting that and Rocker Records off the ground. A year down the line, I want to see Blue Murder happening, and see King Kobra happening on Rocker Records. I'd like to see a Vanilla Fudge live album..."

Wait a minute! Back up. What's this Blue Murder? Blue Murder is Carmine's newest band, a power trio that also includes former Whitesnake guitarist Keith Sykes, and ex-Firm bassist, Tony Franklin.

The new band came about last fall in England. Carmine was there to see brother Vinnie perform with Dio and learned that Cozy Powell, the first drummer in Blue Murder, had backed out of the project. Carmine met with Sykes and Franklin, they jammed and it clicked immediately. He commented in *Metal Edge* magazine that, "We played like we'd been together for years. The rest is history. There's a real good vibe between us, and a lot of respect."

Carmine also related, "With Blue Murder, it's back to the days where I can play whatever I want."

"I tried to stay American when I went from Ludwig to Slingerland. I turned down a nice deal with Tama and I'm sorry I did."

Blue Murder's first album, which was recorded in Vancouver, Canada, will be released this summer, and Carmine is committed to tour in support of the LP. It also looks like The Vanilla Fudge will tour and do the live album Carmine envisioned. These varied projects, as well as more clinics, will keep our boy busy for the foreseeable future. But what about his personal life?

"Well, I've been married three times (laughs)! I've got a lovely girlfriend named Sarah, who I live with and it's great. We love each other, she understands where I'm coming from and where I'm going, and she takes good care of me. We're thinking about having a kid soon."

As a final note, Carmine has just completed a starring role in an upcoming horror/rock film called *Black Roses*. He played the part of a drummer in a band (natch) who turns into a zombie.

You just never know where the unpredictable Mr. Appice will turn up next.

Just answer one question for me if you would, Carmine...Do you ever stay home and just watch TV?

EQUIPMENT:

Carmine played on pots and pans as a child and later graduated to toy drumsets, which he constantly broke.

"In 1961, I got a bass drum. Jeez,' I don't even know what size it was, maybe a 22x10," with a 5x14" snare drum and a 10" cymbal. That was my first set and I got it for Christmas from my parents. My next set was Gretsch. It was red sparkle, with a 9x13" tom, 22" bass drum and a red sparkle snare drum, with a 20" Zildjian cymbal. Gradually, I added on to it and got a hi-hat, a floor tom and another cymbal. This was the set I used with The Vanilla Fudge on 'You Keep Me Hangin On.' I used Zildjian cymbals. That's all there was back then."

After The Fudge hit the charts, Carmine secured an endorsement deal with Ludwig drums and Paiste cymbals. It was at this time that he came up with the idea of large, oversized drums, and Ludwig, always a forward-thinking organization, was more than happy to put together a radical set for him.

"My Ludwig set had two 26" bass drums a 12x15" tom, which was the small tom, a 16x18" floor tom, and a 22" bass drum turned on its side and that was my big tom. I also had a 6 1/2" snare drum and a 36" gong, which was the first gong in rock."

"In the Seventies, I used the same Ludwig equipment, but different size drums. I used 10", 12", 13", 15", 16," and 18" toms, two 24x15" bass drums, and a 5 1/2" snare. That was the first Octa-Plus outfit Ludwig made. I also had the first maple wood set they ever made."

This setup remained basically the same throughout the decade, although Carmine occasionally added a 20" Ludwig tympani and two syndrums that were built into 8" and 10" melodic toms.

His Paiste cymbals included 15" Soundedge medium hi-hats, a 22" heavy ride, 20" medium crash, 18" medium crash, 18" China type medium, an 18" 1930's vintage China (actually made in China), and a 52" gong.

He used Paiste cymbals until 1980, at which time, he switched to the new Zildjian Amir cymbals. Carmine now endorses Sabian.

Does he use any electronic drums?

"Good Luck! I like real drums with real skins that you can dig into and kick ass."

In 1982, Carmine ended his long association with Ludwig and after turning down a "big money deal" with Tama, agreed to use and endorse Slingerland drums. At that time, Slingerland was on their last legs and someone of Carmine's stature should have helped the ailing company's fortunes, but it was not to be. Slingerland, one of the truly great names in the history of American drums, eventually went under, only to be purchased recently by Gretsch.

Carmine's black Slingerland set included two 24x15" bass drums, 6" and 8" single-headed toms, 10," 12," and 13" double-headed rack toms, 16x16" and 16x18" floor toms, and an 18x20" tom suspended in the air, plus a 5 1/2 x 14" brass shell snare, a 22" Tympani, and the Randy May E/A internal microphone system. He also had an identical Slingerland set in Violin Red. All hardware on both sets was solid brass.

His Zildjian Amir cymbals were the same sizes as the Paistes.

Carmine also used and endorsed Mattel Synsonics drums. His monitor system was made by Peavey and was capable of blowing up to 2,800 watts of power. He also had a specially-made "Wah-Wah" snare drum made.

A few years ago, Carmine gave up the Slingerland deal and went with Pearl.

"I like Pearl drums and hardware. They're very strong and they give good service (the company). It's a good drum company. The drums sound great. My Pearls are three-ply. I'm a believer in three-play kits 'cause they resonate more. I use two 24x15" black lacquer bass drums with brass hardware. I have 10," 12," and 13," 16x16," and 16x18" floor toms, and an 18x18" floor that's up in the air like an aerial tom. Those are all Ferrari Red lacquer with brass hardware. Then, I have what I call "pancake drums," which are 22" bass drums cut in half...22x7," with 24" heads on them. I use three of those, with Pearl chain drive pedals and hardware."

Carmine prefers Remo CS black dot heads on the snare and Pinstripes on the other drums for live work. In the studio, he goes back and forth between Ambassadors and CS black dots.

Regarding sticks, Carmine has always used Regal Tip nylon sticks, first in the 5A size. What he uses now, is a 5A/Carmine Appice Regal, with an extra tip on the butt end.

"I found that when you play with the butt end, you lose some of your bounce, so we put a tip on the butt end."

When asked whether he ever muffled the drums, he replied that he rarely does so.

Carmine has a drum roadie named Glenn Foster.

"He helps me set everything. He knows the way I like

CARMINE APPICE

THE CURRENT LINEUP OF KING KOBRA, 1988. CARMINE IS DEAD CENTER.

to have things set up. He tunes the drums, changes heads, all that stuff. Live, he shows me metronome settings for the next song to make sure the tune is in the right groove."

And how does he feel about Japan's place in the contemporary drum market?

"That's life, you know? American unions screwed everything up. Same thing with cars and every other product. I tried to stay American when I went from Ludwig to Slingerland. I turned down a nice deal with Tama and I'm sorry I did. I ended up going with Pearl anyway. A lot of the drums that are out today are pretty much the same. The Japanese drums are fantastic. They make them beautifully. Some of the old Ludwigs *do* sound fantastic. I must say, it's very hard to find drums that sound as good as my old Ludwigs did. As far as Ludwig, the crafts-manship was better in the Sixties, but who knows? Maybe old Pearl drums from that time sound great too."

Carmine worked very closely with Ludwig.

"I came up with the concept of big drums, like the 24x15' bass drum, which led them to develop the 24x16" bass. I invented the hi-hat anchor to hold the hi-hat onto the bass drum. I invented the aerial toms that my brother Vinnie is using. That's just some of the things."

STYLE AND TECHNIQUE:

To repeat a well-used cliche, Carmine Appice has never exactly been the shy, retiring type. He was and is such a commanding presence behind the drums, there was no way on earth you could miss him. Besides the visual impact of his showmanship, the stick twirling and tossing, there were the incredibly fast fills that hit with the power of a runaway freight train. Carmine certainly has some of the fastest hands and wrists in rock and is unafraid to use them wherever appropriate. Power drums...that's the key to Carmine. Hit 'em hard, hit 'em fast and hit 'em like you mean it each time, every time. Although he's never been what one might consider to be an overly subtle player and some even think his earlier work is a little busy, he's kept up with the times and is today, even more groove-bound and uncluttered, in order to coincide with current musical stylings.

You have to give him credit for daring to try things, like breaking up a shuffle rhythm let's say, to interject an explosive fill laden with sixteenths and double strokes. Inevitably, he'll land on his feet on the downbeat, leaving the listener to wonder, "How did he do that?" His style of playing is also amazingly distinctive. There's just nobody else who sounds quite like Carmine and no one that you could point to and say, "That's where he came from." He's a manifestation of his greatest influences-Gene Krupa, Buddy Rich, Joe Morello, Max Roach, and later, Keith Moon, Mitch Mitchell, Ginger Baker and yes, John Bonham. Even Carmine will admit that he stole licks from all of them and others (his British contemporaries mentioned above, all stole from him too) to forge his own way of playing.

One of Carmine's most distinctive tricks is the triplet-based riffing between the snare, multiple toms and double bass drums, like the end of the BBA version of *Superstition* (see Selected Cuts). To put it mildly, Carmine sounds like a one-man demolition team, and that's a compliment! He has such control, it's hard to believe he's really capable of pulling off these complex poly-rhythms, but he does it nonetheless. What may seem like a jumbled mass of beats is, in actuality, a very precise routine.

Carmine's left hand grip is radically different than any other player on the scene today. He holds the stick between the first and second finger rather than between the thumb and first finger. It is still considered a matched grip.

How does he feel about the current crop of Eighties drummers.

"There aren't that many drummers from Europe or Britain that really blow my mind, you know? In the Eighties especially. I used to like Bonzo a lot...Ian Paice too. I do like Simon Phillips. There are a lot of American Drummers I like. I like my brother Vinnie. I think he's great. I like Stewart Copeland a lot, Terry Bozzio, Gregg Bissonette, Billy Cobham, Lenny White, Tony Williams...you could go on and on and on. Why do I like them? They're original, they're really good, they've got good feels, good playing, good everything."

Carmine, through his years of experience, has definite feelings about the manner in which English and American drummers approach their instrument.

"The way I see it, unless you're playing real punk or pop, or something where you're using a metronome, British drummers have a feel that's definitely a little lazier than American drummers. American drummers play right on the beat, where a British drummer might play a little behind the beat. This is something I learned when I was with Rod Stewart."

He has barely succumbed at all to the electronic drum fad and does not trigger electronic percussion onstage.

'I've found the best sound for me is to plug my real drums into a Yamaha REV-7 or XBX-90 with gated reverb, and it sounds really good. I tried triggering and there was too much hassle involved. I don't care for it very much. And I don't like all the manuals."

He sees a world of difference in recording technology today versus the Sixties, as could be expected.

"It's unbelievably different. When I did *Vanilla Fudge*, it was on an eight track. Now, we can go up to forty-eight tracks and trigger things, punch in and out with drums. You can play with drum machines and overdub the drums later, so many different things. The technology doesn't intimidate me. I don't care. I can do whatever it takes. Sometimes I do the drums last and play to a drum machine. On the new King Kobra album, I played the drums last to a drum machine."

"I used to love recording. Now, I hate it! (laughs) I've been doing it too long. The biggest problem I ever had in the studio was wearing headphones. I now use tissue paper in my ears to cut down on the high frequencies that cause damage. Tissue paper also helps eliminate headaches in the studio."

Carmine does enjoy playing in odd time signatures.

"I love it. I can play in every one fluently, with no problem."

Although Carmine does not exercise in any way to prepare for drumming, he does so to lose weight.

"I exercise to keep my stomach down."

He similarly doesn't do much to mentally prepare himself either, preferring to practice for five or ten minutes before a show. At home, he practices an average of ten hours a week, going through what he called the "basic books."

As far as Carmine's drumming philosophy, he stated, "Hold a solid groove and be able to go outside the groove and throw another timing in and keep coming back. Play with a lot of energy and power. The attitude is to do your best all the time, be positive and go for it. That's what my attitude has always been. Especially before you go onstage, you can't sit around going, 'Oh, I got problems,' or 'I can't do this, I can't do that.' You've just got to go up and screw your problems and get up there with an attitude that 'I'm gonna' kick some butt now.' That's what I've always done, and it's worked for me."

When all is said and done, Carmine Appice would like to be remembered most as a trendsetter.

"I started the trend of playing power drums with oversized, weird sized drums. In 1968, I had the first oversized set of drums, the first maple set. In '70, I had the first Octa-Plus set. I've been trying to set trends through my whole career, you know? That's how I'd like to be remembered."

Was there any final advice he could impart to young, upcoming drummers?

"Yeah, I would suggest that they study. I think studying is a very important part of drumming today."

CARMINE APPICE

"You Keep Me Hanging On" (Atco LP #33-224, *Vanilla Fudge,* Vanilla Fudge)
Here it is, Carmine's first commercially-released performance, and it still sounds great. The famous and recognizable patterns-the immortal triplets with the dotted eighth feel, are just as intense and mind-destroying as they were over twenty years ago. Mix these with the painfully slow, dramatic groove and Carmine's riveting cymbal washes caught just in the nick of time, and what you get is a crystal clear picture of the drummer as a young evolving artist in the initial stages of developing a truly individual style. We're happy to present a partial drum transcription of "You Keep Me Hanging On" for the very first time, at the end of this chapter.

"Shotgun" (Atco LP #33-278, *Near The Beginning*, Vanilla Fudge)
"Shotgun" is this writer's favorite Fudge cut of all time–probably the most intensely heated performance they ever committed to vinyl. Carmine, whose drums dominate all the way, approaches the song with fire in his eyes and hands from the first note. The feel is nothing like the original Jr. Walker version, but it's still very gritty in its own way. Appice's energy level boils over, on the lightning-fast fills and numerous one bar breaks he trades with the rest of the band. Carmine and bassist Tim Bogert always had a very special relationship, a real musical empathy, and it's very evident on this cut. Listen to the way Appice brings the backbeat in on one and three instead of two and four after the drum break section ends.

"Need Love" (Atco LP #SD 33-303, *Rock 'N Roll*, Vanilla Fudge)
"Need Love," like "Shotgun," is one of The Vanilla Fudge's most passionately fervid Rock 'n' Roll cuts, in fact, it's barely controlled abandon personified. A simple shuffle rhythm opens it up for twelve bars, with Tim Bogert answering organist Mark Stein, and Carmine playing a very spare quarter note routine on snare, bass and hi-hat. This is followed by sixteen bars of thunderous, straight eighth note rock time that once again breaks into an accent-laden shuffle, that Carmine punctuates with effective snare/bass/cymbal accents. Check out the way he breaks out of the set rhythm pattern to interject a frenzied fill-in that slots right back into the groove comfortably. This has always been one of his best tricks.

"You Can't Judge A Book By The Cover" (Atco LP #33-340, *Cactus*, Cactus)
From the first Cactus album, Willie Dixon's famous blues is given a completely overhauled treatment, with several demanding feel and rhythm changes, all of which Carmine handles with consummate ease. His power drum concept comes to the fore during Jim McCarty's almost violent guitar solo and Carmine's use of dynamics is superb. We also hear the Appice gong in action right before the final rideout.

"No Need To Worry" (Atco LP # 33-304, *Cactus*, Cactus)
When the first Cactus album was recorded in 1970, many rockers felt it their patriotic duty to include the obligatory twelve bar slow blues on their LP's. Not that there's anything wrong with blues, by any means. What makes this so noteworthy is Carmine's personal stamp, which is rampant throughout this wrenching vocal performance by Rusty Day. The uniquely Appicean fills, cymbal washes, and subtleties, like the closed rolls leading into the verses, are masterfully done.

"Big Mama Boogie-Parts I and II" (Atco LP # SD 33-356, *One Way...Or Another*, Cactus)
Carmine sits out Part I completely on this John Lee Hooker-styled boogie. If you ever wondered just how fast the Appice hands were, listen to the one bar explosion that leads into Part II. Carmine kicks butt, period, right to the last drum flurry.

"Superstition" (Epic LP # 32140, *Beck, Bogert and Appice*, Beck, Bogert and Appice)
BBA's remake of Stevie Wonder's hit is much harder-edged and extremely funky, with Carmine supplying an elastic groove and murderous fills behind Beck's stabbing guitar and Bogert's blasting bass. The end belongs to Carmine alone, and his background vocals aren't too shabby either.

"Hot Legs" (Warner Brothers Lp # HS 3373, *Rod Stewart-Greatest Hits*, Rod Stewart)
"Hot Legs" could have been done convincingly by The Faces, owing to its Chuck Berry-like sound and feel. Carmine does what he must consider to be his best British imitation, and plays behind the beat all the while. His fills on the vocal breaks toward the end are spectacular. Also notable, are the accents he hits on the words "Hot Legs." Whether this was his idea or not, it's imaginative for sure.

"Drums, Drums, Drums" (Pasha LP # 3, *Carmine Appice-Rockers*, Carmine Appice)
Carmine liked Sandy Nelson's rock drum solo records as a teen and jumped at the chance to collaborate with Richard Podolor, Nelson's partner in crime, to come up with this modern-sounding drum solo extravaganza, an updated reworking of the Nelson sound. This is from Carmine's only solo album, and if you can find a copy (it's becoming hard to locate), pay attention to the Gene Krupa/Sandy Nelson-inspired tom tomming, mixed with droning chants, all wrapped up in a minor key.

"Redline" (Rocker LP # NRCD-26, *King Kobra III*, King Kobra)
This is 1988 commercial heavy metal, so never let it be said Carmine is stuck in the Sixties. His timekeeping is thrash-rock frantic, yet crisp and well-defined, and his cymbal work is clean, with a powerful backbeat on two and four. The drums are very well recorded, with a contemporary flair. This album was supposedly recorded on a shoestring budget after King Kobra lost their Capitol Records deal. When I spoke to Carmine in late June, 1988, it had already sold over twenty thousand copies just weeks after its release. The chaotic ending is pure, vintage Appice.

CARMINE APPICE TODAY

He still pronounces his name *ap-peace*, and at fifty-nine years old, he's still the odds-on favorite to be "rock's ultimate overachiever," as he was called in 1989. Carmine Appice just can't sit still. His date book is filled with arena tours and recording sessions, clinics, master classes, symposiums and even rock club dates. According to his Vanilla Fudge bandmate, frequent collaborator, and friend bassist Tim Bogert, Carmine's three-thousand-minutes-a-month cell-phone plan is hardly adequate for this active, personable man who knows his place in the world of rock drumming and doesn't mind telling anyone who cares to listen. He's down-to-earth, friendly and willing to talk to drummers anywhere, anytime. As the premier hard-rock drummer of his day, Carmine's achievements and innovations have been documented *ad infinitum* in many places. With that in mind, let's try and catch up to this "man of boundless energy."

Carmine has kept busy recording and boasts an impressive track record of albums released under his own name and as a session drummer. His own discs include *Guitar Zeus Vol. 1*, *Guitar Zeus Vol. 2* and *Guitar Zeus Japan*, all released in the mid- to late Nineties. The *Zeus* projects teamed the drummer with a core band and a who's who of great rock guitarists. *V8* is a jazz/rock fusion disc recorded in 1977, but released only recently.

"I cut that *V8* album in '77," says Carmine, "but it was never released because they [the record company] thought it was too confusing. There aren't many people who can go from rock to jazz and be successful in both. Usually you start and are known as a rock drummer and that's what you are."

Carmine also played on tribute discs to Alice Cooper, Queen and Aerosmith in the past few years as a session drummer. But the oddest tribute disc to feature the drummer was one for Garth Brooks in 2003. Sounds strange, but Brooks is actually a hard-rock fan that happened to hit it big playing country music. Other Appice session appearances have occurred on discs by Jeff Watson, Marty Friedman, Danny Johnson and others. Carmine remains in-demand in this role. Discs containing unreleased and live material featuring Carmine with King Kobra and Blue Murder were also released in the mid- to late Nineties.

In 1991, Carmine and bassist Bogert teamed with guitarist Rick Derringer for a one-off recording project called, appropriately called Derringer, Bogert & Appice, with the title *Doing Business As*, a clever play on words. In 1999, Carmine and Tim paired again with a hotshot Japanese guitarist in a band called Char, Bogert & Appice. Needless to say, Carmine and Tim enjoy working together. More on that later.

Carmine's legendary drum book, *Realistic Rock*, has now sold more than 300,000 copies over the years, is now available as a video, and was recently voted one of the top twenty-five books on drum of all time by *Modern Drummer* magazine. Carmine also issued a follow-up called *Realistic Rock For Kids*. On tap is another book entitled *The Children's Book Of Rhythm*. Carmine has also recorded regularly and toured with guitarist Pat Travers, and their new CD and video, both called *Travers-Appice Live*, will be released in summer 2006. Carmine has often hinted that he'd like to write a book about his life as a touring musician, but we'll have to wait and see.

In 1991, Carmine was honored in Los Angeles and four other US cities with a proclamation of "Carmine Appice Day" to honor his contributions to music, education and drumming. He has been presented with numerous awards over the years, including a Lifetime Achievement Award presented by the Sabian cymbal company, whose products he has endorsed since 1985.

One of the first drummers to hold clinics, Carmine continues to do them as his schedule allows, but sees problems with the manner in which they are presented.

"First of all, the clinics have all been done. You don't even see that many clinics today. It used to be, a clinic was made for a student or drummer to go there and learn something. But these guys today, they don't really teach you anything. They just do this crazy stuff. It's more self-indulgent, so the student thinks, 'I'll never do that! I might as well give up!' Joe Morello told me, 'Teach 'em, make 'em laugh and play for 'em, and you'll always have a great, successful clinic.' I've done that throughout my career and I've watched him do it and he's definitely right.

"A lot of these DVDs I'm seeing today from drummers don't really break it down to where you can understand it. The last DVD of Terry Bozzio, all the ostinatos, he broke them down. He showed you how to do it. You actually see what he is doing; you break it down and practice it slow like that.

"There are a lot of great drummers today, like Terry Bozzio. He's amazing. You've got Cobham, who's still amazing. Some of these new guys are pretty incredible in what they do. This Marco Minneman and Thomas Lang. These guys have taken it to another level. I call them 'scientists' now. I mean, some of the feet on these people—it's ridiculous!"

Carmine has been criticized over the years for "jumping ship" on endorsement deals, and perhaps the critics have a point. Like Buddy Rich, he has moved around a lot over the years for reasons known only to him. After his deal with Premier ended in 1992, Carmine went with Mapex and stayed for twelve years. Now he is back with Slingerland and was heavily involved with the development and design of the new Slingerland drums.

"My Slingerlands sound like the old ones. I think everybody knows that thin shells vibrate more. That's one of the reasons I wanted to go back to Slingerland, because I knew they were making the drums the old way by hand, so they're going to sound like they used to. I tell you, these kits sound so good. They sound so warm!"

Carmine has three Slingerland sets at his disposal, all in the same configuration: two bass drums, two rack toms, two floor toms and a current Slingerland copper shell snare. The sets are finished in yellow leopard, red leopard and white lacquer. His cymbals are Sabian all around.

Although some youngsters may no longer consider Carmine "cutting edge," he remains the man who laid the blueprint for hard rock drumming, a huge influence on today's drummers and a positive role model. With no end in sight to his activities, Carmine keeps up his hectic pace. He finds touring a little harder on occasion, but is managing just fine on the rock 'n' roll road.

As of this writing, Carmine is on tour with the original members of Vanilla Fudge, along with The Doors of the 21st Century, Steppenwolf and The Yardbirds. The tour is called the Strange Days Tour '05 and is now on its second leg in Canada, following sold-out US concerts, primarily in open-air "sheds."

Carmine's outlook remains upbeat. He even has a newly designed web site, www.carmineappice.net, that's loaded with merchandise, a forum section, photos and much more.

"I plan to keep on rockin' for a while. I was always trying to be the Gene Krupa of rock. Everything I've done was to bring the drums out front, including the drum-offs I did for five years to bring attention to the drums. So my philosophy has always been, if you're going to do something, do it all out. Be into it and do it to the best of your ability."

CARMINE APPICE WITH THE AUTHOR.

PHOTO COURTESTY OF BOB CIANCI

MICK

"When young bands are still recording and having hits with Kinks music, that speaks for itself "

PLAYING IN A ROCK BAND IS ALWAYS A GIVE-AND-TAKE SITUATION. Compromises, musical and personal must always be made and to be sure, there are ups and downs. Sometimes there are arguments. Occasionally, it gets even more ugly.

Mick Avory spent over twenty years as the authoritative, hard-hitting drummer with The Kinks, and in that long stretch of time, he experienced more peaks and valleys playing with this most checkered and quirky group of British Invasion survivors than one would care to believe.

Take for instance this famous tale of "group interaction" that occurred in 1965.

At a gig in Cardiff, England, Mick, enraged after guitarist Dave Davies spat at him and knocked over part of his drumkit for blowing the intro to *Beautiful Delilah*, crowned Dave over the head with the footboard end of his hi-hat stand and sent him crashing to the stage unconscious in front of a stunned audience. Ray Davies immediately burst into tears fearing his brother was dead and later, prevented the police from arresting Avory, by claiming the incident was part of the stage act. This had not been the first time blows had been exchanged between Dave and Mick. Avory had blackened Davies' eyes earlier on that tour.

This is in no way meant to imply that there weren't good times in the Kinks Kamp. The stormy periods should not obscure the fact that Michael Charles Avory, for years, has been a get-down-to-business, exceptional drummer who has, like a few others in this tome, never gotten his share of individual attention. The old axiom about the whole being greater than the sum of its parts sadly means that talented team players like Mick often get overlooked.

Mick was born February 15, 1944 in Hampton Court, a southwestern suburb of London, and became infatuated with drums at thirteen, while a member of the Sea Scouts. Mr. and Mrs. Avory were "puzzled but supportive," in Mick's words, but they agreed to drum lessons and later drove him to his earliest gigs before he had a car.

A V O R Y

MICK AVORY

STEREO
KINKS-SIZE
FEATURING
ALL DAY AND ALL OF THE NIGHT
TIRED OF WAITING FOR YOU

reprise
6158

THE LP FOR THEIR SECOND
LP. MICK, THIRD FROM
LEFT, LOOKS A BIT OUT OF
TOUCH WITH REALITY.

MICK, ON LEFT, CIRCA
1965, WITH EXECUTIVES
OF REPRISE RECORDS,
INCLUDING DEAN MARTIN
ON THE RIGHT

" In hindsight, I think learning to play in a jazzy style was a bit misleading for me when I started playing rock 'n' roll."

Mick's teacher, Chris Hewitt, taught him rudiments, rhythm patterns, timing, technique, and independence. They worked from the Buddy Rich/Henry Adler book and although Mick had originally been drawn to skiffle and trad (British dixieland) jazz, he soon realized a strong attraction for American jazz drummers Max Roach, Joe Morello, Art Blakey, Shelley Manne, Elvin Jones, and Philly Joe Jones. Mick used a metronome when doing his lessons and practiced routines his teacher wrote out for him. Chris Hewitt was a respected, local jazz drummer, so Avory had to pick up his Rock 'n' Roll chops on the street, in the clubs, and off records, as millions of other youngsters did then and today.

"In hindsight, I think learning a jazzy style was a bit misleading for me when I started to play Rock 'n' Roll, as I didn't fully realize what I was required to play at times. I was gaining Rock 'n' Roll experience playing with local bands and possibly, it gave me a slightly different approach."

His lessons with Hewitt lasted one year and in that time, Mick also gained a basic understanding of written music. Hewitt also built him some practice pads that he still has.

At this time, Mick was living in East Molesey, a bedroom suburb of London. After finishing school, he worked various jobs doing carpentry, drafting, and sheet metal labor. At eighteen, he decided music was more important.

Mick worked the London club circuit with a number of bands, including a group called The High-Lites, in 1961. In 1963, he played with The Rolling Stones for a few weeks and foolishly turned down the gig when they asked him to join on a permanent basis. Later regretting the decision, Mick answered an ad in *Melody Maker* and auditioned with The Kinks at a pub called the Camden Head, in Islington, north of London. They ran through some R&B and Chuck Berry numbers, and within a matter of minutes, the drum chair belonged to him. The Kinks, like The Stones and early Beatles, had had a very hard time finding a regular drummer their own age who wanted to play the music they liked, so Avory must have seemed like a God-send. One of the first gigs Mick played with them was at the Oxford Town Hall. After that, they secured a spot on a national package tour with The Dave Clark Five.

The Kinks first couple of singles had died miserably on the charts. One was a remake of Little Richard's "Long Tall Sally." For the third single, it was decided by the group and their management that they'd try a Ray Davies tune, "You Really Got Me," which featured the raunchy lead guitar of Dave Davies, who reportedly achieved the fuzzy guitar sound by slitting his amp speakers. The song had gone down well on the Dave Clark tour, and it was do-or-die time for The Kinks. This one had to be a hit, or else. You probably know the story from

there. "You Really Got Me" was a stone smash hit, in England, Europe, and in America as well. What few people don't know is that Mick did not play on the session. A studio drummer was used, a very common practice in those days. To set the record straight, Mick did play on all the subsequent hits that followed; "All Day And All Of The Night," "Till The End Of The Day," "Tired of Waiting For You," "Who'll Be The Next In Line," "See My Friends," "A Well Respected Man," and "Dedicated Follower Of Fashion." The first and last two were sizeable US hits also. It seemed like The Kinks were headed for major stardom in America, but a dispute with the US Musician's Union prevented them from playing more than a few live gigs here until 1969, a near tragedy for the group. Unable to capitalize on their US record sales, The Kinks kept to the British and European concert circuit until their differences with the union were resolved.

I was lucky enough to have had the chance to see The Kinks on their first bona fide US tour back then, at The Fillmore East. Onstage were four extremely nervous musicians, who essentially, were facing the demanding US public for the first time. Ray Davies looked like a ghost as he sang the hits. They performed quite a few numbers from their current LP at the time, *Arthur*, including the great track, "Victoria." Mick played confidently and steadily all night. I had watched The Kinks on TV several years prior, on *Shindig*, and had been very impressed with Mick's ability, especially on cuts like "I Gotta Move," with its frantic eighth note hi-hat riffing. I never figured out how he kept up the pace at such a fast tempo and in such an unceasing manner. Also, Mick had one of the deadliest snare drum sounds imaginable on those early hits.

Not surprisingly, Mick never enjoyed total freedom of expression within the group.

"My drumming days with The Kinks were quite vast, so lots of different ideas and methods of achieving things took place. On some songs, Ray would have a pretty fixed idea of what he wanted. On others, he would be more open to experiments, as long as they fit the situation. Some songs were developed by the group just jamming, but in the end, you had to select the important ideas and disregard the others, or it would end in a muddle."

He also had a bit of difficulty and frustration getting comfortable in the recording studio.

"When I first started to record, it felt really strange. Normally I was stuck in a corner away from everyone else while they worked out chords, etc. That made me feel really isolated. Also, nearly all the songs were worked out in the studio, so by the time the boys had the tune together and had a semblance of a song, I would still be in the dark. By this time, they were doing takes and I would be frantically trying to arrange my drumming into a song I didn't really know. I also found that not hearing a vocal when learning a song to be very difficult. My timekeeping was more of a problem for the rest of the band than me.

MICK AVORY

THE KINKS, LOOKING LIKE LORDS OF THE MANOR, ON BRITISH TV.

Seriously though, I was always quite reasonable at keeping straight time. Intros and endings were more of a problem for me."

What Mick liked most was touring.

"I used to enjoy the live gigs the best in those days, although The Kinks were reluctant to work all the gigs we could have done. The big package tours were usually a lot of fun to do. We certainly had our share of fan worship in the Sixties, but a lot of it happened more when we were working. We tended not to work the London area too much, so we weren't often mobbed on our leisure time, although we were recognized frequently."

Mick bases The Kinks lasting success on their individual musical and visual styles.

"When young bands are still recording and having hits with Kinks music, that speaks for itself."

He also admired quite a few contemporary English Sixties drummers.

"The Sixties rock drummers I liked all had distinctive styles. Bobby Elliott of The Hollies was always a favorite of mine. I liked Brian Bennett with The Shadows, John Bonham, Mitch Mitchell, who was with Riot Squad at the time, Aynsley Dunbar, Bobby Graham, and Clem Cattini, who mainly did sessions. It's difficult to remember how they all influenced me, but I used to watch them at situa-

tions I thought I was weak at and see how they dealt with it."

In the early Seventies, The Kinks signed with RCA Records and began to produce theme albums like *Preservation Act One, and Two, Muswell Hillbillies, Soap Opera,* and *Schoolboys In Disgrace.* They also did the music for a couple of minor film scores, including one called *Percy,* and added a brass section for certain live gigs to duplicate what was recorded on their current LP's. With hits like "Lola," "Ape Man," and "Celluloid Heroes," The Kinks experienced a new era of U.S. popularity. Their sound, once raw and raunchy, had now softened, as leader/songwriter Ray Davies became more and more foppish, mincing and introspective. It was also at this time, that the group became rather infamous for erratic and sometimes sloppy, unpredictable live shows. The old personality flare-ups again occurred and there were personnel changes. At one point, Ray Davies quit the group onstage and returned after a period of exhausted depression.

"The earlier part of the Seventies was actually quite satisfying with the hits and later, with the brass section that broadened our scope again. In turn, it gave me the opportunity to play something different from straight Rock 'n' Roll drumming."

The advent of punk rock in the mid to late Seventies once again rejuvenated The Kinks, as it did for many other bands. Disco even infiltrated the band's music with the track, "I Wish I Could Fly Like Superman." Ray Davies, as a writer, was influenced by musical trends, but on the whole, Mick considered punk to be a crude fashion based on some of the images of the Sixties. It reminded him of the rebellious trend of groups like The Stones and Pretty Things.

In 1977, The Kinks inked a deal with Arista Records and finally broke through in a very big way in the United States. On the liner notes of the LP, *Come Dancing With The Kinks, The Best Of The Kinks, 1977-86*, writer Mitchell Cohen elaborated on their success.

"In the years covered in this compilation, Our Heroes found themselves, to the delighted surprise of many, crossing the breadth and depth of the United States Of America, handily filling basketball arenas with members of the ever-expanding Loyal Order of Kinkphiles, while simultaneously selling cartloads of records. The perennial *bande 'a part* became a part of the rock mainstream. Shocking as it is to contemplate, the ranks of Kinks fans were swelled with youngsters who were learning the alphabet when "Waterloo Sunset" was bestowed on the world, who identify "You Really Got Me" with David Lee Roth. 1977-85 will go down in the annals of Kinkphilia as 'The American Years.' From the start of the band's association with Arista, the band reached out to the USA. Over in Britain, where punk was rearing its nasty head, The Kinks were consigned to oldhatdom, but meanwhile, back in the States, rock fans were finding The Kink's renewed vigor positively exhilarating. At the beginning of the band's Arista tenure, with everyone in agreement that honest-to-goodness songs should be on the agenda rather than the conceptual extravaganzas of the RCA epoch, Ray Davies responded with a new dedication to pop craft. The best songs on *Sleepwalker* (1977) and *Misfits* (1978) questioned the value of the very activity that Davies and The Kinks had been engaging in for (then) almost a decade and a half: making Rock 'n' Roll."

And finally, The Kinks live shows tightened up, as the band came out of their corner swinging.

Again from the liner notes of *Come Dancing With The Kinks*, Mitch Cohen reported.

"Despite their position as eminences of the British Invasion, ripe for tribute by the next generation, The Kinks showed all the young powerchord rowdies that the old men could match them point for point. Coming so belatedly in The Kinks' career, the multi-tiered roar of the crowd didn't ossify the band as it had many rockers who'd made an abrupt leap to arenas. There was simply so much *bon vivance* exuded from the stage, such an air of implausibility at seeing songs that once fell on unresponsive ears being greeted with the cheers of 18,000 Kinks converts, such gratification for the overdue vindication of everybody's favorite underband, that it was difficult to feel anything but a swell at a 1980's Kinks concert."

With FM radio hits like "Destroyer," "Juke Box Music," "Come Dancing," "Catch Me Now I'm Falling," "Low Budget," "Better Things," "Don't Forget To Dance," "Around The Dial," and the seasonal "Father Christmas," The Kinks enjoyed their greatest popularity ever and the financial rewards finally enabled them to cut down their touring activity, which had been frequent during the Arista years.

Near the end of The Kinks association with Arista, Mick finally decided that after over twenty years, it was time to call it a day to the crazy days as a performing member of The Kinks.

"My leaving was not a snap decision. It was rather something that had grown over a lot of years, and in the end, our playing and caring relationship had deteriorated to the point of making me feel uncomfortable and depressed. Although I left the band four years ago, we still share the business interest of our recording studio (Konk Studios), so it wasn't like severing myself completely. I'm still involved in the running of the studio."

"I was sad to leave the band after spending so much of my life in it, especially when I thought of the great times we had had. But, I would not gloat over the past. The mental release I got after I left made it the right thing to do."

"My life these days is a bit quieter and more settled than it used to be with The Kinks, which gives me a chance to do other things. My wife, Jackie and I, have a daughter, Jennifer. My career never caused too much of a family problem, particularly now, that I don't go on tour anymore. I'm only doing fringe things (gigs) at this time. I've got one regular gig at weekends and odd stuff I pick up. I don't think I'll ever give up playing in some way or another. It has become too much a part of me now to do so...so long as I'm able to, that is."

Mick enjoys listening to guitarists such as Robert Cray and Eric Clapton at the moment and also likes some of the music that is currently on the charts, like singer Paul Johnson.

"I have to listen to Madonna quite a lot, as my daughter likes her."

He looks back on his long tenure with The Kinks with great fondness.

"I'd like to be remembered as someone who played a part in drumming with a successful rock band spanning over twenty years, which is basically what I did."

EQUIPMENT

Some British drummers, when describing drum sizes, list width before depth, so a 9x13" will become a 13x9." This is what Mick has done and it was decided to leave his remarks as is.

Mick first played on an old Sea Scouts parade drum that was mounted crudely on a chair, using a scrub brush and a stick to keep time. He did his lessons at home on the homemade drum pads his teacher made for him.

His first kit was an unknown brand and must have been ancient.

"It had a very old marching bass drum, 28x12," a 14x8" snare, one temple block, one 18" cymbal mounted on a spring attachment on the bass drum, and also a 10" very thin tom with no tension rods, all in a lacquered wood finish. I got them in 1957. I believe a friend knew of someone that wanted to throw them out of his attic."

"From then, I bought a mixture of a drumkit, with money I saved from a paper and grocery round. It consisted of a new premier hi-hat with 14" Zyn cymbals, one Ajax 12x8" small tom tom mounted on the bass drum,

ON TOUR IN THE EARLY
1970S IN THE U.S.
NOTE THE BUTT END
TRADITIONAL GRIP

BEHIND HIS BLACK
GRETSCH SET, 1973-1974.
MICK STILL USES THIS KIT

which was a 20x14" Ajax. The large tom tom was a 16x16," had a batter head only and I can't remember the make. The snare drum was a thin shell Broadway, a 14x3 1/2."

"The kit also included 16" and 18" Zyn cymbals."

Mick used three sets in the Sixties. The first was an English Rogers kit made by Boosey and Hawkes.

"They claimed they were the same as the American Rogers drums, but they weren't and I didn't like them at all. They were blue mother of pearl. The snare was a 14x5 1/2," small tom 12x8," 16x16" floor tom, and a 22x14" bass drum."

The Rogers kit was quickly traded in for a silver sparkle Ludwig set. With the exception of the rack tom, which was a 9x13," the sizes were the same. This was the set-up Mick used primarily during The Kinks earliest days of stardom.

His next kit was Gretsch, again in silver sparkle, comprised of 20x14" bass drum, 12x8" and 14x14" toms, and a 14x6" snare.

Right after purchasing his first Ludwig set, Mick was offered an endorsement opportunity with Premier, but turned it down.

In the Seventies, he acquired another Ludwig outfit straight from the factory as an endorsee. This one was "grey/blue" mother of pearl, with 13x9" and 16x16" toms, a 24x14 bass drum and a 14x6 1/2" snare. He followed that set up with a British-built Hayman kit consisting of 22x14" bass, two rack toms, 12x8 and 14x9," a floor tom that was 16x16," and a 14x5 1/2" snare.

Mick's cymbal set-up was simple and basic; It was Zildjians all around, with 14" hi-hats, a 16" crash, 18" crash, and a 20" ride cymbal.

His next drum purchase was another Gretsch set in solid black, made up of a 22x14" bass, 13x9" and 14x10" rack toms, a 16x16 floor tom, and a 14x6 1/2 Ludwig snare. Mick has kept this kit and stores it in the current group's van for use on their regular Saturday night gig.

The next set was a Sonor in silver grey, with a 24x14" bass, 8x8," 10x8," 12x8," 13x9," and 15x15" rack toms, with 16x16" and 18x18" floor toms, and two snares, one a metal shell 14x6 1/2," and the other a 14x8" wood shell.

In the late Seventies, Mick's cymbal set-up changed slightly, although he stayed with Zildjian. The hi-hats were occasionally 15" and an 18" or 20" China was added.

"I liked Zildjian cymbals, but you had to select them carefully as they were all different, whereas the Paiste cymbals I've used since are more consistent in their particular type.'

Obviously a man of many drumsets, Mick recently acquired a Yamaha kit in a solid grey finish (he seems to like grey, doesn't he?). The sizes are 22x16" on the bass drum, with 12x10" and 13x11" rack toms, a 16x18" floor, and a 14x6 1/2" metal shell snare. Sometimes he uses an identically sized Pearl metal snare with this kit. The Yamahas stay at home and are used for any other gigs Mick might pick up.

Besides trying many different brands of drums, Mick has done the same with sticks over the years.

'I went from 5A Star sticks (Japanese Oak) in the Sixties, to Regal Tip 5B's, to Ringo Starr 5b's. Then I moved on to Regal 2B's, Pro-Mark 2B's, F, D & H 2B's, and then had my own made by the London Rock Shop, which are similar to the 2B size. Right now, I'm using their 5B model."

"As far as drumheads, I used Ludwig orchestral batters, or sometimes Remo Weather Kings. I've used Evans, which are a bit dull-sounding, but OK to mic' up with no bottom heads on. Mostly I use use Remo Ambassadors or Pinstripes on the snares, with the blasted (coated) finish, and Pinstripes everywhere else. I've also used Canasonic linen-type skins and Remo black and silver spots. Overall, I prefer the Pinstripe heads, as they are pretty durable and sustain the note slightly longer on the tom toms."

"The muffling of drums is sometimes necessary when miking them. I used to use things called Dead Ringers a lot on tour, which were just strips of adhesive foam that were stuck around the edge of the drumhead. Some drums have a built-in damper, but they usually work loose inside the drums and rattle and cause problems. Also, they dampen unevenly. Normally now, I just use tissue paper and gaffers tape to take any ring out of a drum. I put a cushion inside the bass drum and have an 8' diameter hole in the front skin. In the studio nowadays, the equipment is much more sophisticated than it used to be, so dampening and doctoring drums isn't so necessary, but years ago, I used to do all sorts of things to get a desired sound, like covering skins with newspaper on the toms, or putting a piece of a cigarette packet between the snare and the under skin."

As far as miking, Mick uses a Shure SM-57 for the snare on top, Sennheiser 451's for the toms, Beyer 201's for the cymbals and hi-hats, and two AKG 414's as ambient mic's.

He likes Japanese drums and feels their popularity is merited.

"They make great kits now, like all the hi-fi, video, radios, cameras, computers, and electronic stuff they produce. They've always been able to produce products at a very competitive price, which is usually people's first consideration when buying something. Not that Yamaha are very cheap. I don't think they (drum manufacturers) make drums any better today necessarily than they used to, but they've developed a few new ideas along the way and have made improvements to the sound. The hardware has improved greatly. I haven't made any direct comparisons with old and new drums, but I think I could buy any new drums to match old ones for sound and feel. Indeed, lots of drums are made now based on old styles. I should think there aren't as many handmade drums or parts as there used to be, but I don't think the sound has suffered because of this. A sturdily-made drum with inlaid mother of pearl would not necessarily have a good sound, which is the most important factor."

MICK AVORY

THE JACKET FROM THE KINKS' FOURTH U.S. ALBUM RELEASE.

STYLE AND TECHNIQUE:

"Understand yourself, then believe in yourself. Try and learn something new as often as possible. Be good at your own style."

Mick offered these words of encouragement to young players and it accurately describes his drumming philosophy, which he further expanded on.

"I think the main role of the drummer is the same today as it is always. That is, to beat time and be the foundation of the band along with the bass. I also consider it very useful if a young player can play another instrument. This gives him or her a better understanding of the musical side and also what the rest of the band requires. Positive attitude is a must for a good performance. To get that, you have to be properly prepared yourself and have a good mental rapport with the other musicians. And just plain enjoy yourself."

When putting together a volume of this type, it eventually becomes difficult to come up with descriptive adjectives to describe a drummers style (Thank you, Mr. Roget) without being redundant. But when talking about Mick Avory, keep in mind that he was and always has been a Rock 'n' Roll smasher and basher in the grand English tradition...but a basher with brains. The best words fitting to Avory are hard-driving, simple, economical, honest, and very reliable. He has always exhibited all these traits, even when The Kinks temporarily put away the chunky power chords in the late Sixties and early Seventies, in favor of a more subtle form of music. As the music became quieter and more introspective, so did the drumming. No matter what direction Ray Davies' songs took, be it British music hall, trad jazz, folky ballads, ersatz country/western, or punky hard rock in the 1980's, Mick was there, adding what was needed at all times, always with taste and enthusiasm, earning his living and doing his job correctly. He could always be relied upon to come up with something appropriate. His strongest suit was his uncompromisingly aggressive timekeeping and incendiary fills. Admittedly, he has a problem with intros and endings and spends much time getting them right. He approached each Ray Davies tune as a completely new and unique entity unto itself.

"Understand yourself, then believe in yourself. Try and learn something new as often as possible."

**A ROCK 'N' ROLL SURVIVOR.
MICK LOOKING YOUTHFUL IN THE 1980'S.**

Mick had no problem keeping up with trends in drumming and sounded every bit as contemporary as drummers many years his junior. With the changes in drumming, so too came changes in recorded drum sounds and the methods of which those sounds are obtained. Some of the current trends leave Mick a little reminiscent.

"Recording technology has taken a great step forward since the Sixties. You can more or less do anything in the studio today, but I think it has taken a lot of human element out of the records compared with the Sixties. I feel there is a place for electronic drumming which will be there forever, but it won't replace acoustic drummers. It's rather like the photograph and the painting. Our studio has a Simmons electronic kit, but I've only used it as an additional effect for recording, not onstage. It makes me feel a bit redundant sometimes with all the new technology, but I can lock myself in with a click usually, if it's necessary."

Mick does warming-up exercises with large sticks first. Sometimes he plays rudiments on a cushion or in the air for a few minutes in order to loosen up. To prepare mentally, he tries to think about how he'll handle things he's not too confident about, so he can approach it positively.

"Other than that, a couple of drinks works the best to relax me and curb any anxiety. I still practice three or four hours a week on the average. After a loosening exercise, I usually play stuff I use in my gig and random solo stuff, just to keep conversant with things I can't do. Then I work at other things I can't do, either from a book, something I've developed myself, or an interpretation of something I've heard."

Mick admittedly has had very little experience playing in odd time signatures, although he has tried things in three/four, six/eight, seven/four and five/four.

"I've quite enjoyed odd signatures once I've established what to play."

Like most drummers, Mick has suffered his share of aches and pains.

"I used to get terrible blisters at the start of a tour and would wear golf gloves sometimes. Also, I had tendinitis

MICK AVORY

MICK'S FIRST POST-KINKS BAND, THE CREATION, CIRCA 1985. THE CREATION WERE AN EXPERIMENTAL AND CONTROVERSIAL MID-SIXTIES MOD BAND THAT SELF-DESTRUCTED DUE TO INTERNAL PROBLEMS. SADLY, THE SAME THING HAPPENED IN THE EIGHTIES WHEN THEY TRIED TO REGROUP.

in my right wrist and a mysterious pain in my shoulder where I could hardly raise my arm. I took pain killers for these."

"Any emotional or personal problems I've had were gradual or consistently there, so they did not affect my playing noticeably."

Mick never experimented too much with drugs and had this to say about the subject.

"My per diems (the amount of money he received daily while on tour) wouldn't stretch to it. I did eat a rather large lump of hash one night, and don't recommend it to give a good drumming performance. The remedy was lots of vitamin C and black coffee."

Mick used to think that American drummers were better trained and dedicated to the technique aspect of drumming.

"Nowadays, I think the approach is much the same between British and American players, as they come into contact with each other much more now. The facilities for learning and learning techniques have greatly improved."

"I haven't seen a great deal of European drummers of late, but I was very impressed with Simon Phillips at a clinic I saw in London a couple of years ago. Jon Hiseman and Carl Palmer are also very good and I've seen them too, but I prefer Simon's style and approach. He's particularly good with his feet and left hand lead. There are obviously lots of American drummers that are brilliant, but again, I've seen relatively few. I've seen Billy Cobham and Steve Gadd who were very impressive, although their styles are different."

SELECTED CUTS:

"All Day And All Of The Night" (Reprise LP #R-6158, *Kinks-Size*)
When discussing Mick Avory and The Kinks, there's no better place to start than right here. From the first wail of Dave Davies' fuzz guitar intro to the final cymbal crash, "All Day And All Of The Night," is, without any shadow of a doubt, one of the greatest records to emerge from the British Invasion. It's joyously raw, raucous, wonderfully uninhibited and a timeless classic that sounds just as good today as it did twenty-three years ago when it was recorded. Mick's drumming sounds like an exposed nerve ending, fraught with tension and barely controlled abandon. His fills between the vocal lines on the second verse are incredible, as are the snare hits and cymbal accents into the wild guitar solo, that some think was actually played by Jimmy Page, then the number one rock guitar session man in England. Dave Davies has hotly denied that story for years.

"Got Love If You Want It" (Reprise LP #R-6143, *You Really Got Me*)
This old Slim Harpo blues tune starts out with Mick playing a restrained Latin-type beat and when Ray hollers, "All right boys, let's go!," the pace changes to a harmonica-dominated rave-up that sounds very much like something The Yardbirds might have done. It's also a signal for Mick to interject some very aggressive and strident fills in keeping with the freewheeling nature of the change. The final verse brings about a key change from F sharp to A flat and allows Mick to base his timekeeping off the snare drum, using the cymbals to punctuate the first and third beat of each bar in a triplet-infused attack.

"Tired Of Waiting For You" (Reprise LP #R-6158, *Kinks-Size*)
Lesson Number One on how to play a basic ballad with style and imagination. Mick's drag-like figures on the chorus are noteworthy, as are the fills and overall good feel of this Kinks klassic, an FM radio staple.

"I Gotta Move" (Reprise LP #R-6158, *Kinks-Size*)
Mick relentlessly pushes this number with his insistently syncopated straight time that reminds one of an oncoming steamroller. There's nary a fill-in to be heard. It's simply his attack alone that makes this one work so well.

"Deadend Street" (Reprise 45 #0540)
This little-known Kinks single features a jazz feel with a shuffle rhythm. Mick's fill-ins are primarily triplets, with action between the snare and small tom. Timekeeping is kept to the hi-hat for the verses with the ride cymbal for the choruses and lowdown trombone solo at the end. "Deadend Street" is an enjoyable slice of vintage Kinks and shows a different side of the Avory style that harkens back to his trad jazz roots.

"Celluloid Heroes" (RCA LP #6065, *Everybody's In Show-Biz*)
This is one of Ray Davies' and The Kinks greatest performances in my humble opinion, and Mick supplies one of the tastiest drum routines of his career. He knows exactly when to lay back and when to make his move. The overall pattern is quarter notes on the hi-hat with a two and four backbeat on the snare. On the choruses, Mick adds fills comprised primarily of eights and sixteenths. The final choruses feature him kicking the band left and right, all in a very appropriate way for a ballad nonetheless.

"(Wish I Could Fly Like)" Superman (Arista Lp #8300, *Low Budget*)
In the late Seventies everybody, or at least it seemed like almost everybody, was jumping on the disco bandwagon and The Kinks were no exception. Hungry for a hit record, they recorded "(I Wish I Could Fly Like) Superman." Naturally, the 12" dance mix single had Mick's drums way up-front and not coincidentally so. He supplies one of the strongest four on the floor bass drum parts extant, in those days before drum machines took over. Despite the song's disco flavor, the heavy guitars still win out, with help from the ever-present Mr. Avory.

"You Really Got Me" (Arista LP #8041, *One For The Road*)
Ok, so Mick didn't play on the studio version of this old Kinks warhorse, but his slam-bang drumming on this, the live version from 1980, makes up for his absence on the original. Just to show you he's human, Mick falters a little on the first chorus, dropping a beat by mistake, but who cares, it's only Rock 'n' Roll, right? The intensity Avory generates with his use of dynamics is memorable, as is his whole performance throughout this classic rocker.

"Do It Again" (Arista Lp #8264, *Word Of Mouth*)
Mick gets into a great rock groove on this all-out later Kinks classic, sounding like he did on the group's earliest records. The drum intro after the build is an eighth and sixteenth triplet and Mick uses this figure several times in different combinations. He also employs rudimental ruffs leading into the choruses a couple of times. Listen for the raucous sixteenth note fill before the last guitar break.

"Better Things" (Arista Lp #8328, *Give The People What They Want*)
Mick bashes away in the English tradition on this excellent Ray Davies tune, which has a very strong folk rock appeal. Listen closely for the snare/cymbal accent right before the choruses, as it is ideally placed. Mick's hits on the cymbal bell follow the lyrics in a musical way, and very effectively.

MICK AVORY TODAY

Former Kinks drummer Mick Avory still lives in England and currently plays with a Sixties revival band called The Class Of '64 that includes ex-Hollies bassist Eric Haydock and ex-Tremeloes guitarist and singer Chip Hawkes, plus two other members. The band plays extensively on the European oldies and festival circuit in England, Sweden, Holland, Germany, Italy, Malta and many other countries, and is available for private parties and affairs. Their song list consists of hits from The Kinks, Hollies and Tremeloes, as well as new originals and cover material. From all accounts, the band, which formed in the spring of 2004, is enjoying their gigs and has been going over well among audiences of all ages. The Class of '64 has released a CD, available at their live shows and through their web site, www.swinging60szone.net/theclassof64.html.

Mick is still a partner in Konk Studios in London, works occasional "pub" jazz gigs locally playing his vintage Gretsch drums, and enjoys golf in his spare time. He toured a few years ago with singers Brian Knight, Damien McCabe and Billy O'Hare. He supposedly does not own a computer and prefers not get involved with the Internet. Mick recently referred to The Kinks as "a bunch of misfits," but he's proud of his work with the group and the music they made over the years. Rumors persist of an original-member Kinks reunion, but as of this writing no plans have been made.

"I was sad to leave the band after spending so much time of my life in it. . . . The mental release I got after I left made it the right thing to do."

John

THIS PHOTO WAS TAKEN FOR PROMO LITERATURE
ACCOMPANYING THE L.A. GETAWAY ALBUM.

> **"**
> *The music made in the sixties was one of a kind. It's original and there's nothing else like it.*
> **"**

 TURTLES HAD BEEN AROUND SINCE 1965 or so and had had a couple of medium-sized hits like "It Ain't Me Babe" and "You Baby," but it wasn't until their 1967 monster smash, "Happy Together," that they became a household word, as it were. Dare I say the reason for that disc's and its follow-ups success was due to the infectious drumming? I think it may have been. The man behind the skins was an Italian-American kid originally from New Jersey named Johnny Barbata. His attack was strong and true. He hit the drums with extreme authority and somehow made quarter note triplets and other add fills fit within a strict musical form much the way the great Dino Danelli did with The Young Rascals. He had recently taken over the drum chair after the original drummer, Don Murray, left, and he seemed to fit right into The Turtles new, pop image, musically and visually. Maybe John was good luck, because the hit-hungry Turtles got the elusive Number One with "Happy Together."

It didn't take long for the word to spread among West Coast musicians; John Barbata could cut the mustard, both live and in the studio. The session work began to come in abundantly, as did other offers. John played with Crosby, Stills, Nash, and Young collectively and on their solo projects. He did his own album with Joel Scott Hill, Chris Ethridge, and others, the magnificent and now rare *L A Getaway*, and finally, played with Jefferson Airplane/Starship until 1978 when a serious car accident and conversion to Born Again Christianity changed his priorities and drew him away from the craziness of the rock world.

Born April 1, 1945 in Passaic, New Jersey, John spent his first seven years living in the neighboring towns of Clifton and Nutley, a mere stones throw from this writer's hometown of Bloomfield. His parents were Charles and Martina Barbata, whose professions were auto mechanic/carpenter/electrician/sheet metal worker, and registered nurse, respectively. Mr. Barbata was, in John's words, a "jack-of-all-trades," who moved his family to Saranac Lake, New York in 1952 and finally, to California, in 1960, where the Barbata's eventually settled in San Luis Obispo.

Barbata

John Barbata

THE SENTINALS, JOHN'S FIRST SERIOUS ROCK BAND, JUNE, 1964. (John on left)

FLOWER POWER, 1968.

Around the time of their move to New York state, John realized he wanted to play drums after watching a drummer on television. His parents encouraged him to pursue music, but worried that he'd be able to make the payments on the blue sparkle Rogers drumset he had bought on time payments.

John went to high school in San Luis Obispo, where he played in the marching and concert bands and a pep rally band. The experience was invaluable, for it taught him basic music reading and rudiments. He did not have private lessons at that time, but learned a great deal from playing along with his favorite records.

"I'm basically a self-taught drummer. I figured if I could copy things off records, I could do anything. I did have some lessons from Buddy Rich and from a couple of top LA session drummers later in my career."

One of John's first bands was called The Velvetones, a group that played Dixieland jazz and swing - no Rock 'n' Roll at all. From there, he joined a more successful band, The Sentinels, who scored a modest surf hit in California in the early Sixties, that provided them with some fairly prestigious gigs. They were a show band that played surf, rock, and R&B.

After graduating high school, John went to Hollywood to break into the music scene there. He played with Joel Scott Hill for a while. Musicians at the time spent their evenings (if they didn't have a gig) hanging out at two different clubs, The Whiskey A' Go Go and the Action Club, where John met Gene Clark, then a member of The Byrds, who told him that The Turtles were looking for a drummer. John wound up doing a session with the group and was hired because the recording engineer (and The Turtles) were impressed with his playing. The first single he recorded with them was, of course, "Happy Together," the first Number One hit for the band, as has been mentioned.

"That record really stylized me as a drummer because of the things I played on it. The Turtles had about ten hits and I played on seven or eight of them. I was always given the freedom to be creative, especially when I got with The Starship. I not only sang on the records and live, but got to do a drum solo."

His drumming on "Happy Together" was very tight, but his performances on the follow-up hits, ""Elenore," "She'd Rather Be With Me," You Showed Me," and "You Know What I Mean" were equally tasty.

John's initial reaction to recording was like, "Putting glasses on and going to college to study. When you're not playing in front of a big crowd, you have to play steady, you have to be creative, you have to be fast, and if you're not, you're not supposed to be there."

"I enjoyed all the touring because those were great days, back in the Sixties and into the Seventies, touring with The Turtles, The Starship, and the others. There was nothing else like it. It was a time when music was changing. Just being part of that was great, from being an opening act to being THE act."

"The Turtles was the first and last group I was in where the kids were still screaming and going crazy. I'll never forget the time we were headlining with The Young Rascals down in Montgomery, Alabama. We had to go about three hundred feet to get to the stage and there were girls on both sides of the runway, pulling at our hair, pulling buttons off, taking anything and everything they could get just to have a souvenir of The Turtles. It was pretty wild. Each one of us had a policeman behind us and we had to bend over like it was the longest football play of our lives going up to that stage. There were a few more times when that happened."

"That music really holds up today. A lot of the Sixties music, those styles, are coming back. The music made in the Sixties is one-of-a-kind, it's original and there was nothing else like it. It'll probably never happen again. I don't even like the music today. It's nowhere near what it was like in the Sixties and Seventies. It was more honest, more real, and more creative."

John professed a strong liking for and influence from Dino Danelli, drummer with The Rascals.

"I liked Dino for his stick twirling. He and I were the major stick twirling drummers from the Sixties. He was in a more R&B group than I was. I also liked Jim Keltner, Al Jackson, Bernard Purdie, and Ringo Starr, but from what I heard, Paul McCartney showed Ringo what to play on the drums a lot of times. Ringo wasn't great, he sped up the tempo, but he had a nice style. When I heard a drummer do something, some lick I liked, I just added it to my own style."

"As a studio drummer, I'd have to say that Hal Blaine was very influential to a lot of drummers. Otis Redding's drummer (Al Jackson) was by far the most dynamic."

John naturally looks back at the music scene in Hollywood during the Sixties, with a great deal of affection.

"When I first came to Hollywood, Lee Michaels and I were backing up Joel Scott Hill and we were living at this place called the Colonial West on Sunset Boulevard. Some of The Mamas and Papas were living there, Paul Butterfield's Blues Band…there must have been about fifteen bands living there and there was just nothing like it. I remember going up to see Paul Butterfield and he and the whole band were packing pistols! There was no place like Hollywood back then. The whole scene was just incredible."

In 1970, John left The Turtles and went with Crosby, Stills, Nash, and Young.

"What they did was fire Dallas Taylor and Greg Reeves because they wanted to sing and be part of the big four and Stephen and Crosby and the rest of them weren't going for that, so they fired 'em and got us (John and bassist Fuzzy Samuels). We were low-keyed and great musicians and they knew that we weren't going to try and sing and be part of their trip, so they made us part of the group, even though we didn't get a chance to sing, which was fine with me. That was the first time I'd had a chance to be with a gigantic supergroup, even though The Turtles had sold a lot of records and had been the biggest-selling group of 1967."

But how did the gig with C,S,N,&Y come together?

"The Turtles had done a lot of gigs with Buffalo Springfield, so I knew Neil and Stephen. By 1970, The Turtles were falling apart and I went up to northern California, where a friend, Leo Mackota, encouraged me to go after the job with C,S,N,&Y. I went back down and played with them for about an hour and a half in an audition situation and that was it–I got the gig."

"We did the *4 Way Street* album and it sold five million copies. We were the biggest group of 1971. Nobody else sold that many albums that year."

John's drumming on *4 Way Street* is nothing short of incendiary. If you have never listened to the LP, it is highly recommended if only for the drumming.

When not working with C,S,N,&Y together, John toured or cut sessions with all the individual members, including Graham Nash's *Songs For Beginners*, and *Wild Tales*, Stephen Stills' first LP, at least one album with David Crosby and Graham Nash, and Neil Young's *Time Fades Away*.

"I was up at my ranch and got a call from Neil Young, who was on tour with Kenny Buttrey (noted country/western drummer) and he wasn't making it. Neil asked me to out on the road, so I said sure. I went out there and he was paying me $7,500 a week for three months. Of course, the *Time Fades Away* album came out of that tour. There's a song called "LA" where I did some good stuff on the cymbal bell. I remember *Rolling Stone* saying that it was creative drumming."

At that time, John dove headfirst into sessions and played with Linda Ronstadt, Ry Cooder, Dave Mason, Johnny Rivers, Booker T. Jones, The Everly Brothers, David Blue, Judee Sill, John Sebastian, his old friend, Lee Michaels, Batdorf and Rodney, John David Souther, and Carole King. He also played on The Byrds reunion album, but was never credited on the jacket.

"That used to happen a lot back then. There were a lot of other records I played on–over one hundred albums total. I really can't remember all of them and some were really obscure, things that you may never have heard of. After *4 Way Street*, I cut about eighteen albums with different artists in sixteen weeks."

"There was only a handful of musicians from each caliber…guitar, bass, drums, and piano, that were doing all the sessions and they got all the work in the Sixties and Seventies. I was lucky to get in on that. You have to be fast and pull a session together. And you've got to be creative and tasty. It seems like only one out of thirty drummers even knows how to tune

John Barbata

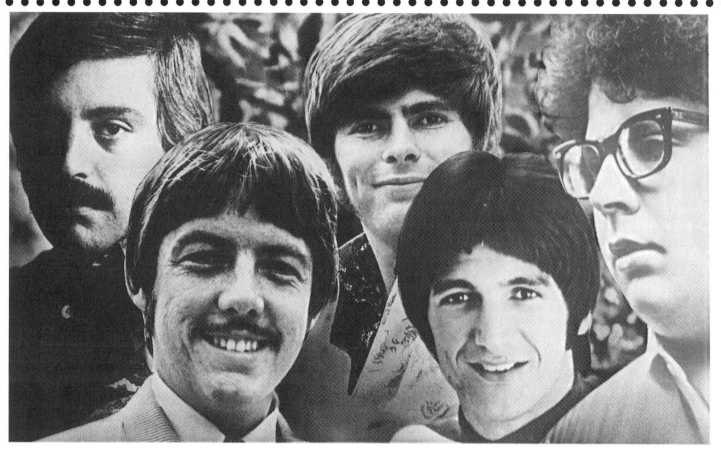

A PHOTO COMPOSITE OF THE TURTLES. JOHN IS IN THE LOWER RIGHT CORNER.

their drums. You've got to have good cymbals. Studios are expensive and you can't waste time. It was hard for me to get in at first. I used to watch Hal Blaine a lot and think, 'What is this guy doing that I can't do?' Then I realized, and you can tell this to anyone in the book, the whole secret to recording and being a good studio drummer is to learn to relax. If you listen to black artists, they all sound nervous. Most black artists like to push, and even live, they're edgy, because they like to be exciting. That's the way they play. But records don't lie. You've got to be right in the pocket all the time, 'cause if you're not, it'll sound nervous, and if it sounds nervous, it won't sound good. The tape recorder tells no lies."

"British drummers were good in their own way, but every British band and British drummer I ever saw, with the exception of a couple, always played nervous. They don't play relaxed and that's the secret to being great as far as I'm concerned. It's one thing to be a technician, but in the studio, they didn't want you to be a technician. They wanted you to play simple. If you didn't play relaxed, none of that mattered. Sure, you had to have great time, but if you couldn't play relaxed, they didn't want you. You can hear that in British musicians...they play nervous. I frankly don't like many British musicians."

"I'm definitely studio-prone. Being a studio musician is being one of the elite, playing with the best musicians in the world, down in Hollywood or Hollyweird, whatever you want to call it. That's just the way it is."

Before hooking up with C,S,N,&Y, John reunited with Joel Scott Hill (later a member of The Flying Burrito Brothers) and bassist Chris Ethridge in the only project that John could claim as his own (or part of his own), a group called Jerome, that recorded one LP on Atlantic Records called *LA Getaway*, now a very hard-to-find collectible. Piano player Mac Rebennack (Dr. John) played on the LP, as did a host of others.

"I had already joined C,S,N,&Y by the time that record came out, and Ahmet Ertegun (president of Atlantic Records) knew about it, so he killed the album and it never got any publicity. We thought we were doing a Cream kind of thing, a supergroup, but they pressed up so few copies and they didn't produce any more after the initial pressing was sold, so *LA Getaway* died. I only have two copies left and can't find anymore. I don't even think the name Jerome appears on the album jacket."

In 1973, with the help of David Crosby, John joined the then-deteriorating Jefferson Airplane and recorded two LP's with them, *Long John Silver*, and *Thirty Seconds Over Winterland*. His solo with bassist Jack Casady on the cut "Feel So Good," from the latter album, is particularly funky and well worth listening to.

John helped convince Grace Slick and Paul Kanter to ground The Airplane and reform the group into Jefferson Starship. Under this new name and musical persona, superstar status came with hit records like "Miracles," the song that signaled the return of Airplane vocalist Marty

THIS IS FROM JOHN'S ZILDJIAN CYMBAL ENDORSEMENT AD, CIRCA 1977.

church. I became a Born Again Christian and had no desire to go back on the road and subject her to that kind of existence. Rock 'n' Roll is a total drug scene and everyone comes on to everyone else. I love my wife too much to put her through that."

In the Seventies, when most of his contemporaries were "Putting their money up their noses," John invested his in real estate in northern California, where he bought about four hundred acres of prime land. Today, he has sold off most of that four hundred acres and as a result, is financially secure. He lives with his wife, Angie, and their infant daughter, Leah, in the same ranch house he has owned for years. Angie is a guitarist/vocalist and she and John have recorded together. He is still playing drums, doing sessions for gospel artists like Sandy Patty, and Priscilla and Linda Coolidge, sisters of well known singer, Rita Coolidge. He also plays in a group comprised of fellow church members called The Trinity Band.

"I think I'm going to come out of my shell soon. I've gone through some changes in the last few years and might even put a big band together. I've made a lot of money and am out of the Rock 'n' Roll scene. I'm not really that interested in it. If I get into anything, it'll be big band music or fusion."

"I was talking with Jim Keltner a while ago and he told me how much money session drummers are making these days, so I may try to get back into session work."

One detects a quiet restlessness in John Barbata. Despite his pleasant life with family, financial security, and strong religious beliefs, he is still very much a drummer who wants to contribute to music in a positive way. The more I spoke with him, the more apparent it became that John wants to be recognized not only for what he's done already done, but for whatever might lie ahead for him musically. Once you hear the roar of the crowd, it's hard to stay away from it for too long. Although he does a little part-time carpentry work on the side, the man is a drummer, first and foremost. He has also taught drums and participated in a few local drum clinics. John enjoys working with young kids and is very generous about showing them his style. He also spends time teaching them how to properly tune drums.

When I commented that he never really got the widespread recognition he deserved, John replied, "You're right. I never got the credit I should have gotten. Maybe my name was not as well known worldwide as some others, but for a while, I was the hottest drummer in Hollywood. That didn't last forever, because I didn't make my whole life and career as a

Balin to the fold. John was given a five to six minute solo at every concert, an impressive pyrotechnical display, that ended with him leaping out from behind the drums.

"I always wanted to be more than just a drummer."

He stayed with the Airplane/Starship for over five years until an incident occurred that forced him to reexamine his life in new ways.

On the evening of October 28, 1978, John had been drinking at a bar near his ranch, in the town of Elk, California, with a friend. On the way home, driving a brand new Datsun pickup truck he had just bought, John swerved off the road to avoid hitting a deer. He plowed squarely into a tree, broke his neck, right arm, and jaw. At first, the news went around that he had died.

"Everyone thought I was dead. Rona Barrett (gossip columnist) even did a thing on TV about the accident. I was laid up for nine months recuperating."

What happened with his Starship gig?

"They fired me because they knew it would take a long time for me to heal."

Ironically, John's replacement was Aynsley Dunbar, an English drummer.

The accident and resultant recuperative period gave John a chance to re-evaluate his life, his goals, and priorities.

"I was sitting up on the roof of my house about a year after the accident thinking about why I didn't die. I had just met my wife around that time and we started going to

John Barbata

● ●

studio drummer. I played with groups and that took up a lot of time."

John told me about a few of his "never-was."

"David Geffen was the biggest manager in Hollywood at the time. He called me into his office and said, 'John, there's this new group that is forming, and this guy, Glenn Frey, wants you and Chris Ethridge to be the drummer and bass player. They're going to be called The Eagles.' I said, 'The Eagles? I never heard of them. Who are they?' He said, 'They're going to be big.' I said, 'Well, I can't leave Crosby, Stills, Nash, and Young to do this. It's just too big of a group.'"

"That's one of my claims to fame."

"I had just come back off a Starship tour. I had made a quarter of a million dollars that year and had just blown off after the tour, when Linda Ronstadt called me up to do the *Blue Bayou* album. I was just too tired at the time, so I had to say no. The same week, Jackson Browne called me and wanted me to play on his album. Another time, Van Morrison, who I consider to be one of the top three songwriters of our time, came up to my ranch and wanted me to join his band. I was with Graham Nash at the time and we were really tight. I couldn't leave Graham, so I had to turn Van down."

"The last story happened while I was still touring with Graham Nash. I got a call from Elvis Presley's manager. He wanted me to play in Las Vegas with Elvis. It would have been nice to tuck that name under my belt, but I just couldn't do it."

John also has a few very memorable recollections that he shared.

"It was the last days of The Airplane and we did a free concert in Central Park on a Monday afternoon. They announced it the day before and there was something like 150,000 people there. There were all different kinds of people there...all ages. I ended up doing a drum solo and it was just a sea of people. There's something about a free concert that people like and they really get off on. There's a lot of energy in the air. That's one of the days I'll never forget."

"Another one was actually the last gig for Marty and me in The Starship. It was in England, the last gig of the tour. Grace had left the group a few days before. Paul Kantner was fighting with her and she quit because Paul pushed her husband down a flight of stairs or something like that. Anyway, we were headlining over Genesis, The Cars, Tom Petty, Devo, The Atlanta Rhythm Section, and a couple of other groups. That was a great show. There were about 150,000 people there too. It was real exciting."

"The other really memorable thing was when I went out with Johnny Rivers years ago on a tour and we did the Atlanta Pop Festival. Right in the middle of this concert, the lights went out. It was the Fourth of July. I just kept playing drums and did a sixteen minute solo and people went crazy. I remember distinctly, this old man who must have been sixty years old, sitting onstage drinking a beer, and he just couldn't believe it...the excitement of the people and the whole thing in general."

"Jamming in the studio with Eric Clapton was really incredible too."

John certainly is a man of strong likes and dislikes, who is very opinionated on subjects musical. His general dislike for the playing of English musicians has already been noted. He also disdains the use of electronic drums and absolutely detested the punk music boom of the late Seventies.

"I hated punk. I mean, I understand how it came about, with the world situation and the government and all, but the level of talent in most of the punk bands was very low. There were a few groups that came out then that were good. The Police were one. I came from the Love Generation and the punks were the Hate Generation. Most people felt like I did about punk. All it did was bring out a lot of energy. I like to listen to The Crusaders, Aretha Franklin, Van Morrison, and old R&B, and Rock 'n' Roll. I guess I'm just a product of the old times."

"I was very fortunate. I had a great career. Most drummers only go around once. I went around three times and played with the best musicians in the world."

STYLE AND TECHNIQUE

"I always considered myself a very unorthodox drummer."

"Well, maybe not unorthodox...I think stylish might be a better adjective. Stylish not in a fashion sense, but in an individualistic way. From a drumming viewpoint, of course."

The first time I saw Johnny, Johny, or John, as he's been known at various times, was on the Carson Show in 1967. Behind those Rogers drums was a real presence, a smiling, take charge, get-it-done player, who put it right in the pocket. You couldn't help notice John, he was so good. He radiated energy. Let's just say the guy made a very definite impression.

While some drummers like Kenney Jones play slightly behind the beat and others like Carmine Appice push it beyond, John Barbata lays his time squarely in dead center, and does it in such a way as to stimulate those around him to feel like playing.

John has always been a strict proponent of the use of the hi-hat for something like 90% of his timekeeping duties. When he does use a ride cymbal, it's very often done on the bell, with a decided Latin American flavor. Check out the cowbell on the bridge of "She'd Rather Be With Me."

"I totally turned that around in the middle of that song. I'm not big into Latin drummers, but my style has those elements in it. Fortunately, they (The Turtles) liked what I did, so they left it in."

He used the hi-hat in ways that were, at the time, very revolutionary. There was a great deal of left and right crossover interplay between the snare and hi-hat, usually involving combinations of eighths and sixteenths. He picked up on Bernard Purdie's *sips*, quickly opened and shut hats, for accenting purposes. In addition, John explored the many sounds obtainable when the hi-hats are played with varying degrees of pressure on the footboard.

Let us mention now that he was probably the first acclaimed drummer to use two sets of hi-hats, one foot-controlled and the other set stationary. This enabled him to have many different sounds at his disposal. Today, the double hi-hat is gaining wide acceptance.

"I probably should have patented that double hi-hat. I was the first person that I knew of who used it, but other guys enjoy using it now, so..."

John seemed to have a knack for making his effective, simple fills land right back on track after completion.

"I think if you can do a fill and come out of it and back in at the same tempo, you're good. Working with a metronome will help you with that. It'll teach you good time. Don't be afraid to practice with one."

Listening to John, one hears him often putting a strong edge on the final chorus on the end of whatever tune he happens to be playing. This trick was learned from the wise hands of Hal Blaine. Barbata also managed to pull off fills like quarter note triplets and rudimental ruffs and drags, placed in odd places. Maybe he was unorthodox at that.

John feels fortunate that he doesn't have to exercise much in order to keep fit for drumming.

"One time I didn't play for six months and went down to Malibu to do an album for Booker T. Jones. We recorded the whole thing in about two days and it was all first takes. I hadn't played in a long time. It's something you don't forget. It's just there."

He doesn't keep up any sort of rigid practice schedule. "I mainly just sit down and play beats. I do the rudiments and really, it's just a lot of jamming, with my wife and the local musicians around here."

"Of course, the drummer's role is to keep time, but as far as I'm concerned, the drummer is the backbone of the music, the most important member of the band. Obviously today, there's more drummers and bass players in contemporary music than anything else. Lets face it, a drummer uses both feet and both hands and sometimes even sings. Without a good drummer, the band isn't going to sound good. A drummer keeps the music together and makes the band sound tight. If you're fortunate enough to have other musicians who have time as good as he does, then you've really got something. Maybe I'm a little prejudiced, but that's the way I see it."

John discussed his feelings on developing the right attitudes to play music.

"Being a studio musician, if you didn't have a good attitude, they didn't want you in the studio. A bad attitude doesn't make for good surroundings. One thing I learned from Hal Blaine is that a good drummer can pull a recording session together and say, 'Come on you guys, let's do another take, I know we can get this a little better. Let's just get together on this. A lot of producers and engineers see that and when they see that in a musician, that's when they like to hire them. Once the word gets around town, it's good for you. Having the right attitude is very important. Some guys go a little too far. They kiss ass a little too much!" (laughs)

"I'll never forget the time when I was with C,S,N,&Y and Russ Kunkel came around. He was sniffing around trying to get as much work as he could, looking around trying to get gigs from people. But that didn't bother me much. He could barely do a double stroke roll, but he's a great studio drummer."

"If you're down or pissed off, you can really play bad. It's easy to do. The whole thing, especially on the road, was to be consistent. Consistency means greatness. If you can be consistent all the time, just like in sports, then you're gonna' be good. That's what I strived to do. I never drank alcohol on a night that I would play because drummers don't need alcohol. It only slows them down. Or drugs in general. I never really liked cocaine. I was so hyper and had so much energy that I didn't need it. As a matter of fact, I wouldn't even drink coffee because it would jack me up too much."

"I smoked pot for twenty years, but gave it up when I became a Born Again Christian. It relaxed me and helped me to play at times, but I wouldn't advocate that for anybody these days, because you really don't need it. I don't need it now and really didn't need it then. It was just part of the Sixties that grew into me. I wasn't addicted to it, but just enjoyed it. Pot was part of the society and everybody did it. It was just a way of life."

John's spiritual beliefs have, in his opinion, made him a more relaxed drummer.

"I can't emphasize enough that relaxation is the key to drumming. If you can play relaxed, that's the key."

I'd like to be thought of as an unorthodox, very tasty, creative drummer who played with some of the best people in the world ... and who was a funny guy and a show man on-stage. I really like to be an entertainer and give the people something more than just a musician onstage. Be a total all-around performer."

"Remember, a good drummer can make a bad band sound good!"

EQUIPMENT

John started as many of us did, with a practice pad. He went from there to a pieced-together drumset while a member of the pep rally band at school. His first professional set was a blue sparkle Rogers Holiday model, with 9x13" and 16x16" toms, 22" bass drum, and a 5x14" Powertone snare. He paid twenty dollars a month on time payments until the kit was paid off. That set served him through his earliest bands and into The Turtles, at which time, he procured a blue onyx four piece Rogers set, with the same size drums.

John secured an endorsement agreement with Rogers, who used him in a couple of well-circulated advertisements. He also endorsed Zildjian cymbals. (see photos)

By the end of the Sixties, John made the switch to Ludwig. His setup changed also. Gone was the 9x13". In its place was a 10x14", followed by a timbale, 16x16", and 16x18" toms, and a Ludwig brass shell snare, sized 5 1/2x14". The bass drum was a 24".

The 22" is good for recording, but I like the 24". It has a great sound to it."

There's no reason for him to consider any other brand of drum today.

"I feel like I've always used Ludwigs. To me, a recording session is Ludwig drums and a Fender bass. They've been proven too many times to be the best. I

45

John Barbata

● ●

"I'm basically a self-taught drummer. I figured if I could copy things off records, I could do anything."

know there are other drums out there, but there's something real raw-sounding about Ludwig drums, recording-wise, that sounds real good for some reason. I've always like the brass shell snare drums. I've got a couple of them and recently found out you couldn't get them anymore."

John uses Paiste cymbals in the studio and Zildjians live.

"Paiste's are quick, they don't hang on...they go *psshhh* and cut off, whereas Zildjians are great live. They don't break as easy. You can beat 'em up more live."

John's Paiste cymbals are smaller than his Zildjians, a brand he still endorses. His Zildjians are sized as follows; 16" crash, 18" crash, 21" ride, two sets of 14" hi-hats, and an 8" splash mounted on top of his 18" crash, something he picked up from Louie Bellson, legendary jazz drummer.

The Ludwig set John used in the Seventies is still in use today. It's a maple wood finish in the above sizes.

SELECTED CUTS

"Happy Together" (White Whale 45 #244, *The Turtles*)-"Happy Together" is, without a doubt, the most famous Barbata drum track, interestingly, the first major recording he played on. It almost single-handedly established his reputation as a hot, up-and-coming drummer. The basic feel is a lazy shuffle that picks up steam on the choruses. John's fill are all memorable and highly recognizable; the kicks between the snare and bass drum on the first verse, the eighth note triplets leading into the chorus, and the fantastic off-time cymbal bell figure, one of his trademarks.

"She'd Rather Be With Me" (White Whale 45 #249, *The Turtles*)-This could be John's tightest and finest drum performance with The Turtles. He propels the sunny tempo beautifully and adds his own special touches, with the aforementioned quasi-Latin tempo change on the bridge, to the flawlessly executed double strokes into the last verse. Simply an incredible performance.

"Elenore" (White Whale 45 #276, *The Turtles*)-"Elenore" is an example of the tasty, understated side of the Barbata style. Congas and only a very spare bass drum accompany the first verse, except for two nice snare/bass combinations that repeat on the second verse. An eighth/quarter triplet fill brings in the first chorus and the drums come on strong, only to quiet down again for the second verse. He uses the quarter note triplet fill again to usher in the second chorus and hits the same riff two more times on this appealing slice of California good time rock. Listen to John's kinetic bass drum pattern on all the choruses.

"I'm Chief Kamanawanalea (We're The Royal Macadamia Nuts)" (White Whale LP #WWS-7118, *The Turtles, The Turtles Present The Battle Of The Bands*)-At 1:30, this is the humorous side of John Barbata. "I'm Chief Kamanawanalea" (which really means, 'Come on, I wanna' lay ya') is a call and response chant with John adding jungle-like tom toms and is one of the only examples of a drum solo he ever recorded. Yeah, it's silly and ridiculous to listen to today, but then again, the album on which it appeared was a goof, with The Turtles impersonating eleven different bands, costumes and all!

"Bring It To Jerome" (Atco LP #SD13357, *LA Getaway*)-"Bring It To Jerome," an old Bo Diddley chestnut, is a rolling, nasty blues shuffle. John gets into the over-all groove and pushes his fellow musicians admirably. He opens it up a little more during the all-too-short guitar solo.

"I've played around with drum computers a little bit, but not electronic drums. They just don't have what it takes to be great. I like real drums."

John uses Regal Tip Rock model sticks, Remo heads and primarily Ludwig hardware, and that doesn't mean heavy duty.

"I like lightweight hardware and never used the heavy stuff. Being in the studio, you want to be able to set up and break down quick and it's just too much to carry around."

Concerning heads specifically, John recommended trying a thicker head on the bottom, like a Remo Emperor, and a thinner one, a Diplomat, on top.

"It gives a more round sound...a very interesting sound."

As far as muffling the bass drum, John uses another trick from Hal Blaine; take two handkerchiefs and tape them completely up on either side of the bass drum pedal. Then John tunes the bass drum to a low G and the toms in fourths. His cymbals are in thirds. The tuning of the snare is dependent on the situation. Tighter for R&B, looser for rock.

John feels that craftsmanship on current drums is very high, whether they're Japanese or American, but prefers his older Ludwigs to anything else he has tried.

"The Ludwigs are proven and they're what I'm used to."

Although John reads music, he never had to read a chart once throughout his career as a studio drummer.

"I used to make up lead sheets like; Intro/Verse/Verse/Chorus/Bridge/Verse/Chorus/Out. That's all I ever used."

"Promised Land" (Atco LP #SD13357, *LA Getaway*)-Chuck Berry time here and John's contribution again is a spectacular groove, alternating from the hi-hats to the ride cymbal. The whole track and the drum part in particular, has a very loose, off-the-cuff feel. Could it have been a first take or something that just "happened" in the studio?

"Carry On" (Atlantic LP #SD2-902, Crosby, Stills, Nash, & Young, *4 Way Street*)-"Carry On," a Stephen Stills song, gives John the opportunity to stretch out on an extended jam. That's not to imply that his playing within the general framework of the song isn't excellent. Far from it. His over-all attack is strong, true, and very authoritative, with much use of funky bass drum patterns and Purdie-like hi-hat accents. On the jam, his use of dynamics is superb, as is the tune's basic groove, well set up with the help of bassist Calvin "Fuzzy" Samuels. The whole thing builds to a droning climax with Stills and Young fighting for domination, as John knocks it right on the head, until "Carry On" grinds to a halt. David Crosby introduces John by saying, "The drummer, his name is Johnny Barbata. He played his ass off!"

"Long Time Gone" (Atlantic LP #SE2-902, C,S,N,&Y, *4 Way Street*)-John settles into a relaxed R&B feel on this David Crosby classic and employs another trademark; sixteenth note fills interplayed between the snare and hi-hat, a signature riff he used for years.

"LA" (Reprise LP #MS-2151, Neil Young, *Time Fades Away*)-One of John's favorite drum tracks, this medium tempo cut, one of Young's lesser known songs, features imaginative use of the cymbal bell in a spot where the music hangs for a moment, a very creative and well-thought out idea. His fills are also tasteful and just a little out there

"Feel So Good" (Grunt/RCA LP # BFL 1-1047, Jefferson Airplane, *Thirty Seconds Over Winterland*)-One of the better cuts off the last Airplane album, "Feel So Good" spotlights lead vocals by Jorma Kaukonen and offers a clear picture of the bluesy, jamming direction electric Hot Tuna would later take. John keeps the time on the hats on the verses and the ride on the choruses and jam. He provides the right accents and fills in all the appropriate places. The zenith, however, is John's solo workout with bassist Jack Casady. These two push each other into rhythmic nirvana, as John alternates back and forth from both sets of hi-hats and adds some spectacular fills.

JOHNY BARBATA TODAY

It's "Johny" Barbata now. For years, it was "John," "Johnny," or "Jonny," but just for the record, the drummer prefers "Johny."

Johny Barbata, wife Angie and daughter Leah pulled up stakes several years ago and moved from Comptche, California, to Ada, Oklahoma, to get away from the air pollution caused by large chemical companies in the area. Johny sold the rest of their land and the family settled on a ninety-acre ranch with a 2,700-foot log home that they remodeled. The land is situated more than a thousand feet above sea level and the Barbata's have the best panoramic view in the area. Johny built a twenty-four-track recording studio in the house and he engineers and produces rock, country, blues and gospel sessions, but steers clear of hip-hop and disco, which understandably turn him off. Johny is still musically active in a blues-rock trio called Barbata, Ellison & Sanders and spends less time these days playing Christian music. He describes lead guitarist Scott Ellison as a "great guitar player, singer and frontman."

JOHNY BARBATA TODAY.

Johny reports, "This power trio really smokes. It is one of the best bands I have ever played in. We have played in some of the best blues clubs in America, like Buddy Guy's, Chicago Dave's and The Green Parrot in Key West, Florida, to name a few."

Johny began making redwood coffee tables years ago as a hobby, and discovered he could sell them for a tidy profit. He continues to make and sell them today. If you visit his web site, www.johnybarbata.com, you can purchase T-shirts, Johny's compilation CD of drumming twenty hit singles, drum instruction videos and more. You can also check out two CDs of original rock and country-rock Johny made with his wife and various distinguished musical friends, *Oklahoma The Heartland* and *California*.

Barbata's most recent project is his book, *Johny Barbata: The Legendary Life Of A Rock Star Drummer*. The book recounts the drummer's story from his childhood in New Jersey and New York, to his teen years in California, and details his drumming career from start to present, with many interesting stories of his personal life and much more. It's a vanity-published book available for sale on Johny's site.

As with many of today's drummers, Johny's drums of choice are DW. He plays a six-piece set in black satin lacquer with gold hardware. His cymbals are still Paiste and he uses Pro-Mark sticks. The famous stationary bass drum-mounted hi-hat cymbals, a supposed Barbata invention, are still there. Johny and his family maintain a healthy lifestyle, eating organic foods, drinking clean water, taking vitamin supplements and getting plenty of rest. He's thankful he came through the drug lifestyle and survived. Johny's born-again Christian faith remains strong.

"When I was a young boy and found out that one day I would die and that life doesn't last forever, I was devastated. But when I found out you can have eternal life through Jesus Christ, I went forward and dedicated my life to God. I thank God for delivering me. I am very thankful for having an illustrious career. I have had a very blessed life and hope to continue on…my story has only just begun."

(All quotes from *Johny Barbata: The Legendary Life Of A Rock Star Drummer*.)

dino

I OWE A REAL DEBT OF GRATITUDE TO BILL SCOTTI. Bill, who was known as Billy back then, was a friend of mine, although when we were younger, he used to beat me up all the time. One day, I finally mustered some strength from somewhere and got the upper fist. He never picked on me again. We remained friends.

Several years later, we both became interested in playing drums at about the same time, but he beat me to it by a few months, had started lessons, and had talked his parents into buying him a cheap, Japanese drumset that we both used to bang on. We were talking on the telephone one day and the conversation went something like this.

Bill: "Have you heard this new group called The Young Rascals yet?"

Bob: "Nah, who are they?"

Bill: "I've seen them on TV a couple of times, I think on *Where The Action Is*. Wait til you see their drummer! His name is Dino and he's gotta' be the coolest drummer I've ever seen in my whole life. He makes these really cool faces when he plays and he twirls drumsticks better than anybody I ever saw. He twirls 'em in his left hand between every beat on the snare drum. He's just *so* good! You're really gonna' like Dino a lot."

Well, I was interested to find out more about this Dino, so I watched *Hullabaloo* when The Young Rascals were on and Bill was right. Sitting behind the silver sparkle Ludwig drumset was Dino Danelli, twirling sticks, moving his head from side to side in time with the music and playing some of the best drums I had heard anywhere. I had the gut feeling that this was a phenomenal player, a guy who could play jazz as well as rock, a guy who had street sense and had played in a lot of different bands. Needless to say, I was floored by Dino Danelli. He was definitely one of the most dynamic drummers to emerge from the Sixties. He's still a great player. And yes, he twirled those sticks better than anyone. Here was a guy who had it all; tremendous talent, flashy showmanship, good looks and a hot band.

Born in July, 1944 in Jersey City, New Jersey, Dino's early home life was hardly happy. His parents had a rocky marriage, to say the least.

"It was a fighting situation with my parents. The kids would go down into the street until the police came and took my father away. Then he'd come home the next day and it would start all over again."

danelli

A CURRENT PUBLICITY STILL OF DINO, TAKEN SPRING, 1988.

dino danelli

DINO AROUND 1968, WITH THE SILVER AND BLACK LUDWIG SET.

"I guess morals were pretty loose back then. My friends and I broke into a school and stole a few parade drums and cymbals"

At approximately ten years of age, Dino saw Gene Krupa and Buddy Rich in a drum battle on television. It was the major turning point of his life.

"That changed my whole life, seeing Gene and Buddy on TV. There's no doubt that I was headed for a life of crime on the streets of Jersey City until then. Once I saw them, I knew I was going to play drums."

So, how does a poor boy acquire a drumset in Jersey City in the 1950's? Simple, he steals them.

"I guess morals were pretty loose back then. My friends and I broke into a school and stole a few parade drums and cymbals. They were locked up, but not too well, so we just took them. The bass drum was huge and the snare was the deepest I'd ever seen, like a big tom tom with snares on the bottom, a parade drum for sure. I played them on blocks, with just enough room for the snares to vibrate. It was a crude setup, but they were good enough to get me started."

He took to the drums right away.

After Dino "appropriated" the drums, he cleaned out some coal bins under his apartment house, built a stage, set up a hi-fi record player, got a few tables and chairs and called the place Dino's Casino, playing his drums with records. Kids from the neighborhood would come down and listen, and eventually, guys started bringing their dates in and there was some drinking going on as well. Dino never charged admission, although he could have done so. Musician's began showing up to jam and the place became so popular, a local newspaper ran a cover story. Then the police raided and closed it down due to the underage boozing.

Around 1956, the battling Danelli household just became too much for Dino to handle, so he quit school and moved out. He began taking the train into Manhattan to the Metropole Club on Seventh Avenue and 48th Street. Too young to go in, he'd stand outside and listen to and watch musicians playing inside. The Metropole is now a topless joint, but in the Fifties, jazz players like Louis Armstrong, Henry "Red" Allen, Jack Teagarden and Lionel Hampton played there regularly. Gene Krupa and his trio played there too.

"The guy who worked at the door of the Metropole would always chase me away. I got so I could time Gene's sets, when he'd start and finish. I'd leave after his first set and come back in time for his next one. The doorman wasn't a very pleasant person, but I was there so much, he just couldn't do anything about kicking me out anymore."

It was at a bar in Union City, New Jersey, called the Transfer Station, that Dino hooked up with an Elvis Presley-styled rock band originally from Knoxville, Tennessee, called Ronnie Speakes and The Elrods. Their drummer was leaving. Even though Dino had never played Rock 'n' Roll before, he joined the band. They went back to Tennessee for some gigs and Dino got to meet another drummer there who influenced him, a crippled man named Bobby Coleman, who, despite paralysis, taught Dino the basics of rock drumming; a heavy backbeat, rock fill-ins, and bass drum patterns. Coleman had a special bass drum pedal that raised his leg up higher than normal. He would use the right elbow to hit his leg down on the pedal and according to Dino, he never missed a beat. Coleman's sparse bass drum patterns and the other licks he showed him were a tremendous help to the teenaged Dino, who prior, had listened only to jazz drummers.

When Speakes and his band returned to New York, the group managed to get an afternoon gig at the Metropole. They had decided to bring in Rock 'n' Roll on a trial basis. Dino, who earlier was considered that-pest-of-a-kid-who-wouldn't-leave, was now taken in by the staff of the Metropole, and was accepted as the club mascot.

"The owners really got to like me and they let me live upstairs in one of the dressing rooms. Before that, I was living in this wild rooming house in Jersey City with Ronnie and the rest of the guys in the Speakes band. There were old widowed women, mechanics, a hillbilly steel guitar player, just a strange combination of people."

And it was at the Metropole that Dino became friends with his idol, Gene Krupa.

"He took a liking to me. I used to dress like him. I used to look a little like him when I was younger and I combed my hair like him. Gene was such a pleasant person and a real gentleman. He went out of his way to be nice to me. He'd call my name from the stage and say hello to me in (front) of the whole audience. He'd say, 'Come see this guy in the afternoon here at the Metropole.' It made me feel great. I'd go upstairs into his dressing room. He was having heart problems then and would lay down between sets and just relax. We'd talk a little bit. I would ask him questions, but I was pretty shy. Looking back on it, I wish I had been able to really talk to him a lot more because I had the opportunity, but it was really kind of a surface thing where I never got into any real depth with him."

When Dino decided to leave home, his mother, Theresa Danelli, despite her maternal misgivings, supported and encouraged her son's musical aspirations.

"She was my backbone. She knew about all that swing era stuff. She had been a bobby-soxer herself and had gone to the Paramount to see Frank Sinatra and Benny Goodman with Gene on drums. She used to tell me how great it all was. That was her Rock 'n' Roll time. Everything I wanted to do, she was totally behind me all the way. She told me about all those songs from that era too. I still don't know a lot about that music, but she told me about Roy Eldridge and Anita O'Day and the records they made with Gene's band. I'd go out and hunt down those records like 'Drum Boogie' and 'Drummin' Man'."

While speaking with Dino, one question kept coming up in my head. Just how did a youngster support himself living on the streets of Jersey City and Manhattan?

"I don't even know, Bob, when I think back how I made it, but I did. There wasn't much money. You ate, you lived, you had clothes, you just did it. It wasn't really struggling. You didn't think about struggling then. You just thought about making it and doing it. You didn't think about making ends meet. Kids couldn't do it today. Drugs, teenage prostitution and rip-offs were around then, but it wasn't as rampant as it is now. It was just a great environment, a total musical environment. I was working two gigs, at the Metropole in the afternoon and in Hoboken at night. I'd take the train over to Manhattan and work from one to six, take two hours off, take the train to Hoboken, work from nine to three in the morning, pack my kit and go back on the train, set up at the Metropole and then go upstairs and go to sleep. To think of doing that today, you would say to yourself, 'How could I do that?' but you just did it!"

After his gig with Ronnie Speakes ran its course, Dino gigged constantly with various musicians, usually playing what he termed an early form of jazz-rock.

"There was a lot more going on than just the Metropole. There were places all over the Village that were happening. It was the time of Lenny Bruce, the comedian and Greenwich Village was really happening, really wild. It was the end of the beat generation. There was a lot or rhythm and blues. Ray Charles was happening. There was a lot of work, a lot of one night gigs. An agent would call me and I'd get three or four guys and go down to Trude Heller's and work there at night, the Cinderella Club, the Cafe Wha, the Night Owl. Richard Pryor was down there. Jimi Hendrix was playing around. Bob Dylan was at Folk City. There were plenty of places to play. It was right before the Beatles caught on."

dino danelli

Dino frequently mentions Count Basie's former drummer, the late Sonny Payne, as the man who taught him showmanship.

"I first saw Sonny Payne at Birdland (the legendary jazz club), which was on 50th Street, a fabulous place, where musicians would get up and jam with each other late at night. One night, Sonny Payne came in, and I had never heard of him before that. He sat in and just blew me away. He was really fancy, doing a lot of tricks, twirling the sticks. I wasn't really into Count Basie, but nobody ever swung that band the way Sonny did. Not even Jo Jones. Sonny Payne did something to that band that was amazing. He had this magic about him. I've heard different things about Sonny...that his timing wasn't perfect, that he'd forfeit that for doing all of this fancy stuff, but that band just came alive when Sonny played. I saw the Basie band one night when both Sonny and Jo Jones played and the difference between the two was like night and day. The showmanship he had, the moves he had! He'd move his body, his head, twirl sticks. I got the twirling from guys like him and I brought it into rock. Sonny had great flash. There was something about his showmanship that drew you in more than Gene. I think of Gene as more of a stylish guy. Lionel Hampton was another great showman. He always played a little drums. He used to have a floor tom with cast iron legs and he'd jump up on it and tap dance!'

"Those guys were just so great! I heard they got a lot of that stuff from Cab Calloway, the singer. Even James Brown got those dance steps from him. Cab used to do a step that looked like Michael Jackson's moonwalk.'

In 1963, Dino took a year and spent it soaking up the rich musical experience that is the city of New Orleans. He claims he hardly slept for the year he was there. The rhythm and blues tradition was unlike anything Dino had ever heard before. It was a valuable education that changed the way he thought about music and Rock 'n' Roll specifically.

In 1964, he returned to New York and put together an R&B show band with horns called The Showstoppers.

"A real original name!," Dino said in jest.

The Showstoppers played a lot of Ray Charles/Otis Redding-type soul material and toured around the Midwest with a little success, but they didn't last and Dino once again found himself living at the Metropole. The twist was the craze at the Peppermint Lounge. It was here that he met Felix Cavaliere, the future vocalist/organist of The Rascals.

"Felix had heard about me and came around to see me at the Metropole. We had known the same girls...the same little clique of girlfriends. We got together and got a gig with a female singer named Sandy Scott, who took us to Vegas. It was a weird job. To make it in those days was to play Vegas...you were really doing well. They paid you well, but there was nowhere else to go. You could record and I had done some sessions, but nothing spectacular, so Felix and I took this gig with this

actress/singer. She got dressed up and did costume changes, told jokes and sang. She wasn't great, but she put on a good show and always gave us a couple of songs so we could do our own thing. The Beatles had just happened and we were blown away by them. Just the idea of four guys writing their own songs and doing it the way they did knocked us out. We had both gotten drafted at the same time, but I had gotten out by taking a bunch of diet pills, staying up for a long time and going to a shrink. Back then, people weren't doing that, so the government didn't catch on, but Felix had to go back east and get out, so we agreed that once he took care of that, he would call me and we would put together a band."

"While Felix was home, he hooked up with Eddie Brigati and Gene Cornish. He knew them from playing the same circuit of clubs. We all knew Eddie from New Jersey when he used to sing with all the bands that played the Choo Choo Club in Garfield, his hometown. Felix called me and said he had Gene and Eddie and these were the guys we needed, so I came home and we just got together, the four of us, and learned about forty songs in a day or two and went to work at the Choo Choo Club in early 1965."

"Felix and I took a trip up to Harlem and went to a couple of record shops, because we needed material fast so we could work. I remember going through the racks and finding 'Good Lovin' and 'Mustang Sally'. We put them into the act."

After a short spell at the Choo Choo Club, the band, who were dubbed The Young Rascals, began attracting the attention of some businessmen who were opening a club out in East Hampton, Long Island called the Barge. They hired the group to play on Monday and Tuesday nights.

"A lot of people had started to come over to see us play in Jersey, but nothing serious happened until we got to the Barge. A lot of record executives had summer homes there. Ahmet Ertegun (president of Atlantic Records) came to see us, heard 'Good Lovin' and knew immediately that it was a hit. We signed with Atlantic, and Ahmet put us together with Arif Mardin and Tom Dowd, who produced us."

Somewhere along the way, The Young Rascals began wearing the infamous Lord Fauntleroy costumes they initially became known for. The question of how the costumes came about is one that people have been asking Dino for years.

"Everybody always asks me that question (laughs). The guy who thought of it was a friend of ours who used to help out with the equipment, kind of a road manager. Everybody was wearing outfits in those days. You had to have a gimmick. He knew we were street kids, so he suggested we try those costumes. It seemed to fit at the time."

Atlantic, as mentioned, teamed The Young Rascals up with producers Arif Mardin and Tom Dowd, who had spent time watching the band live at the Barge. From the

WITH THE YOSEMITE SAM KIT, 1969.

outset, they did not attempt to change The Rascals sound in any way, imperfections and all.

"Tommy and Arif had this sense about them. They knew when to get involved and when not to. We couldn't have done it without them. If someone had tried to take the band and shape it into something different and take the raw edges out, it wouldn't have worked. They had the sense to accept the rawness, all the things that were wrong. They would choose takes when the time wasn't perfect or where there were mistakes, but if there was something on them that had that magical feel, they'd use that take. 'Good Lovin' was like that. It's not a perfect record as far as tempo or sound, but, there's something on that particular track, that particular take, that had that magical thing that made it work. You can't define what it is. We'd go to them and say, 'It's wrong.' We were hard to convince, because we wanted to do it better. They taught us a lot about making records."

The band's first single, "I Ain't Gonna Eat Out My Heart Anymore," only rose to about fifty on the national

charts, but it got them known. The second single, "Good Lovin' " rocketed straight to number one in April, 1966. With the fame came fan worship.

"The fans were great. There was a part of you that loved it and a part that hated it because it had nothing to do with music. We got caught up in it. Everything happened for The Rascals so fast, we couldn't see what we were sacrificing at the time. You just had to go with it. Your time wasn't your own. We were caught up in the Rock 'n' Roll world."

Was it difficult to walk down the streets of New York?

"Yeah, for a time there it was. You couldn't go anywhere. It was silly. Girls would stay outside your house."

The hits just kept coming for The Rascals, who dropped the "Young" after a short period of time: "You Better Run," "Come On Up," and the very soulful "People Got To Be Free," and "Lonely Too Long," the light and breezy smash," Groovin," the jazz-inspired "A Girl Like You," "How Can I Be Sure," and the psychedelically-flavored "It's Wonderful." As The Rascals matured, their

dino danelli

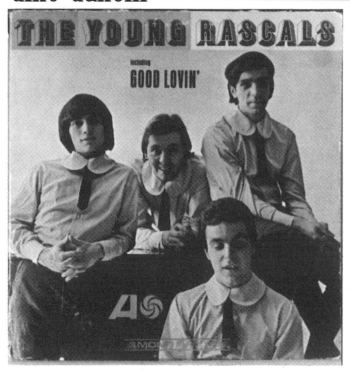

THE FIRST RASCALS LP, 1966.

COLLECTIONS WAS THE RASCALS SECOND ALBUM ON ATLANTIC RECORDS.

music did too. Although they toured extensively in the early days, as the hits increased, the group cut down their road work drastically to spend more time in the studio. The results were not always to Dino's liking.

"Felix and Eddie wrote some great songs, so what I'm trying to say isn't meant to denigrate their work. They wrote some classic records. It was the recording that gets to my ear. I would be tired of a song even before it came out. After recording, editing, mixing, and doing all that, I was tired of it. I've always been like that. Listening back, there are certain things on those records that I don't like. 'How Can I Be Sure' is a great song with a beautiful melody, and Eddie did a great job with his vocal, but there's a part in the middle of the song where Eddie and Dave (Brigati, Eddie's brother, who sang background on most of The Rascals' hits, more or less a fifth member of the band) did this backup vocal that's mixed too far in front in the mix and it destroys the whole thing for me. Those things become more and more exaggerated over the years. Most of those records have parts like that and a lot of them are too busy. There are things on there that shouldn't be there. 'Good Lovin' stands up, 'Lonely Too Long' stands up. 'Groovin' ' will always work, 'People Got To Be Free' will always work. Those are the ones I can still listen to today. No one is as critical as yourself about your own records."

The Rascals never had a bass player live (Felix played bass pedals), but they usually used famed session bassist Chuck Rainey in the studio.

"We got away with not using a bass player live until guys like Larry Graham and the other Motown guys made heavy bass necessary and the music became much more bass-bottom-orientated. Up to that point, bass wasn't a big thing that people were tuned in to."

With all the financial and personal success The Rascals achieved, problems began to arise. Drugs infiltrated the group's ranks and they fell victim to the crank-

out-the-hits corporate rock trip. It was the age of the dynamic lead guitarist and Gene Cornish, while a solid rhythm guitar player, never adjusted his approach. The Rascals had always been an organ-based band and music was changing rapidly. The Rascal's recording process became formalized. People just showed up on their own, did their parts and left. The camaraderie was gone. Tempers flared and egos were overblown. The end was coming fast.

"We never changed over during that psychedelic era in 1968. Gene wasn't into that kind of music, so he didn't pick up on it. Our writing took a different turn at that time due to people's experimentation with drugs. It slowly disintegrated into nothing. The magic stopped. Making records became a drag. You had a hit, so you had to go in and make another hit. Business pressures set in. Felix and Eddie started going different ways in their writing. They couldn't connect anymore and it all just dissolved. We weren't playing as much as we used to either. When we became successful, we spent a lot of time enjoying the pleasures that came with making a lot of money, so we didn't tour like we should have. Eddie wanted more artistic freedom and wasn't getting it, so he left in 1969. He and Felix had a falling out over something and I'm not even sure what it was about. Once that writing team was broken up, everything changed."

Gene Cornish also left the group at that time, so Felix and Dino reformed with new personnel, all jazz musicians, secured a deal with Columbia Records, and turned out two jazz LP's, *Peaceful World* and *Island of Real*.

"We gave Clive Davis (Columbia Records president) a nervous breakdown! He thought he was signing The Rascals and we were going to turn out Rascals records. What he got was two jazz albums that didn't sell. Our audiences weren't leaning in a jazz direction. They were becoming younger and younger, so that concept just didn't work."

In 1971, The Rascals called it quits.

1973 brought the formation of a new band with Dino and Gene Cornish called Bulldog. A Top Forty hit, "No," almost did it for the Bulldog, but it was not a big enough hit to guarantee the band's future.

"Gene and I had this idea to put together another street-orientated rock band and we found this guy who was a tremendous singer with great street sense. Our hearts weren't totally into it like they should have been. It just didn't jell music-wise or personality-wise. "No" needed about fifteen or twenty more radio stations to be a national breakout, but it didn't happen. It stopped at thirty-something. We probably would have survived if we had broken through with that song."

Dino and Gene went from Bulldog to a production project with the Canadian group, April Wine. The LP they did with the band went gold in Canada, but didn't do anything in the States. They next produced an album by Michael Bruce, former guitarist with Alice Cooper, but the record was never released.

Realizing that production was not going to be his life's work, Dino and Gene returned to New York in 1977 and put together a new band, Fotomaker, a vocally-dominated, English-sounding rock band, that included ex-Raspberries lead guitarist, Wally Bryson.

"We were Beatles-influenced, with strong lead vocalists, but the problem with that band was that it lacked vocal direction. We had Lex Marchese, who was a very polished singer. Our keyboard player sang lead too and so did Wally, who had a much rougher vocal style. No one could focus in on just what the band was. Also, it was not the right time for a band like that. Punk was happening really strong then and we weren't like that at all. It was more subtle. The music that was going on was just totally raw shit. We had a Top Forty hit, "Miles Away," but didn't stick it out. We put out two albums on Atlantic and recorded a third, but never released it. The record company was pretty fed up because they were advancing us all this money and not making any of it back. We tried to do a Fleetwood Mac, but very few bands can make that concept work...not having one focal point."

Around this time, Dino began pursuing his long time interest in graphic design and art as a new career. He had always dabbled in art, had designed some of The Rascals album covers and had even won an award for his innovative work. At one point, Dino left music entirely and moved to Germany to live in an artists colony. After several months, he returned to America to resume his music.

In 1981, Dino joined Little Steven and The Disciples of Soul, Miami Steve Van Zandt's group, that he formed right before leaving Bruce Springsteen's E Street Band. He stayed with them for four years, spending most of his time in Europe, where the band was very popular. He left Steven's ranks in late 1984 due to the illness of his mother. Mrs. Danelli died about a year and a half later, a victim of cancer. While with Steven, Dino recorded two cuts on their debut album and the entire second LP. His experiences doing the second album didn't sit well with him.

"That second album was a troublesome record from the beginning. It took so long to record and Steven kept mixing and re-mixing until there was hardly anything left from the way it originally was. Also, there were hardly any drums on that record. Steven didn't want any fill-ins anywhere. We were recording and a roadie came in and started taking away all my drums. He said, 'Steven doesn't want you to play any fills,' so there I was, sitting there with a snare, bass drum and hi-hat. I had to talk to Steven and I told him I wouldn't do any fill-ins, just give me the drums back because I feel naked sitting there without them."

"There were problems too with Steven...it was hard to understand what he was singing and he didn't want to use a producer, because he thought he could do it all himself. You need someone to bounce ideas off of in the studio, but Steven didn't have that. I'm still doing Steven's artwork for his album covers. He has one more record left to go on EMI, but after that, who knows, unless he has a hit."

Today, Dino spends about half of his time doing graphic design and art work and the rest with music. He even formed a short-lived ska band a few years ago called Modo.

Dino's last recorded project was with a Boston-based called Frontier Blue, whose sound he compared to that of Simple Minds. He produced some of their LP and played on several tracks. Due to problems within the band and with their management, the album had not been released as of this writing.

Right at this moment, the only musical project that Dino is thinking about is the reunion of The Rascals, first, for Atlantic Records Fortieth Anniversary Show, scheduled for May, 1988, and if that goes well, there are serious plans for the band to tour in the summer of 1988. In the works also, is a live album and possibly a videotaped concert film, most likely for cable television.

"I talked to the promoters this morning and the contracts for the tour should be in the mail in a day or two. We've been to this stage at least a half a dozen times already, so I just take it with a grain of salt. Everybody's gearing up for it. It will be Felix, Gene and me, and we'll probably have to get another guitarist and keyboardist, and definitely a bass player. The promoters are the same guys who did the Tyson/Spinks fight and they've got a lot of money to invest in it. So far, there are about thirty-five dates booked, mostly in indoor-outdoor venues like the Garden State Arts Center and places like that. I want to see sixty to seventy solid dates, a live album and a video. If we're going to do it, it's got to be right."

What about Eddie Brigati?

"I don't see Eddie taking part. If he decided to do a few gigs with us, that's fine, but I doubt that he'll participate. There's talk about doing a big thing at Nassau Coliseum and for that show, we'd probably bring in a brass section and really do it up."

"I feel two ways about it. I'm into it with just the three of us, but I'm not as into it as I would be if it was the original band with everyone."

Would you consider using Dave Brigati to replace Eddie for these gigs?

"You know, I thought about that, but under the circumstances, I don't think he would do it. It would be a weird situation, unless Eddie just told him to go ahead and do it. That would work if it came about. Dave would be the best replacement for Eddie, for sure."

dino danelli

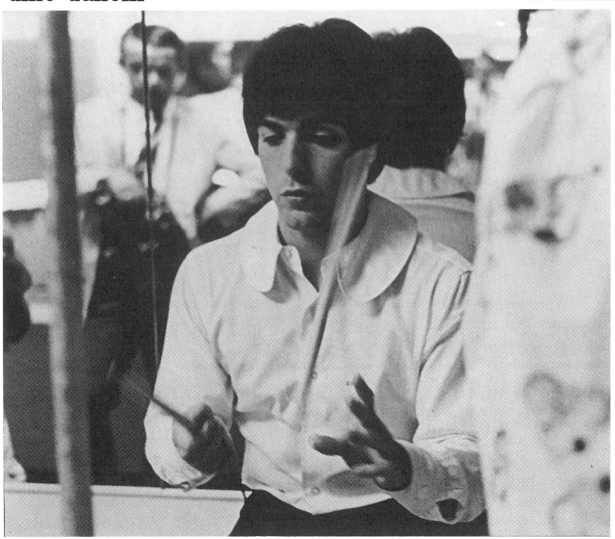

THE FAMOUS DANELLI STICK TOSS.

"I don't know what's out there anymore for The Rascals. Older people will remember us, but what about younger people? It just remains to be seen how we'll draw. The promoters said there will be a lot of publicity. Shelley Finkel (one of the promoters) kind of grew up with us and he feels there might be a mass audience again for this band. Maybe not recording-wise, but playing-wise, like The Beach Boys."

And what about the possibility of The Rascals going into the studio to record some new material?

"We haven't talked about it because there's so many problems with that. You get older, you learn more, and everybody would want certain things. The thing you've got to do is get a record label interested. Very few people have come back like that. The only band that has been able to come back on record has been The Monkees. They had a hit. If there was serious interest in The Rascals by a record company...Atlantic isn't interested. They own the old catalog and will probably re-release it all. I would take the shot at doing something new...going into a studio with the guys and doing some recording, but it would have to be material that had the same kind of energy as the old stuff. It would have to have that urban intensity to it. I don't know if everybody still has the head to do that. It's been a lot of years. It would be easier for me than the other guys. I still attack the drums the way I

did then. My intensity never let down, but I have no idea if Felix or Gene would approach recording the same way."

"I don't know how I'm going to feel playing the old music. Sometimes I practice along with the old records and I think it might be good to rearrange some of them, change them around so they sound fresh without losing the classic feel of the old arrangement."

Dino has been a New Yorker for many years and can't conceive of living anywhere else. He has a small but comfortable apartment on the fashionable Upper East Side of Manhattan, very close to Central Park, that he shares with his girlfriend.

His living room is stark white, with one chair, a table, a small couch, a phone, a chest of drawers and a modest television in one corner.

"I like that cold, hospital feel. Some people don't care for it, but I like the open space."

There are no gold records on the walls, no pictures of The Rascals, no reminders that a famous rock drummer lives here.

"You don't know how many hours I've spent doing art-work on that table. Art is great, but it's such a solitary, lonely thing at times."

"My essence is still to do something with music."

Dino Danelli is still a drummer, first and foremost.

THE RASCALS, 1988.

EQUIPMENT: A CONVERSATION WITH DINO

AUTHOR' NOTE: Although this is a deviation in the format used throughout the book, I think you'll find this conversation with Dino very interesting and entertaining.

BC: Once you got rid of the parade drums, what kind of kit did you get?

DD: Well,I used to do a lot of sitting in with bands then and I'd go and play with King Curtis and his band in Union City. He was really helpful...he loved me! I'd play "Drum Boogie" and "Caravan" with him. His drummer had some extra pieces of equipment and he helped me put together a set of different color sparkle finish drums. There was a black sparkle drum, one was white...the ugliest-looking drumset you ever saw, but they worked.

BC: Heinz 57 Varieties?

DD: Exactly!

BC: Do you remember what brand of drums they were?

DD: All different brands. I used those for a while and got into them. Then I started working at the Metropole and got the set from Cozy Cole.

BC: The red sparkle Rogers set?

DD: Yeah, that was a killer drumset. Cozy asked me what I wanted, so I told him three tom toms, two snare drums...as much equipment as I could get (laughs). He got me everything I wanted. Did you ever see the set Cozy played?

BC: No.

DD: He had a massive amount of drums (laughs)! He had a set that had floor toms surrounding him on both sides, plus the traditional two toms on the bass drum, but he had these floor toms all around, high and low, tilted, plus massive amounts of cymbals. It was the ultra-ultra heavy metal drumset for back then. I used those Rogers right up through The Rascals, in fact, I used them to record the entire first album. The toms were all ripped off over the years, but I still have the snare and bass drum. I think it was the first 24" bass drum in rock. Carmine Appice saw that and went out and got a bigger bass drum. That Rogers bass drum was always killer in the studio.

BC: After you retired the Rogers, you went with Ludwig.

dino danelli

DD: Right, I became friends with Danny, the drum guy at Manny's Music. Those guys used to come around the corner and see me at the Metropole. Everybody knew that I was going to do something with music, so they all helped me out. With Danny,anything I needed, he'd make arrangements with Ludwig to get it . Equipment was never a problem.

BC: The sets I remember you using with The Rascals were the champagne sparkle and silver sparkle sets and later, the silver sparkle set with the black band running through it. You were the first guy I ever saw who put a rack tom on a floor stand.

DD: I started doing that when I had the parade drums because there was no tom holder on the bass drum. I got used to the freedom of that setup and it was easier to deal with.

BC: That's what I do and I copied it from you! It's so much better than using one of those old rail/mount tom holders that used to come on the old drums. All you could do was slide it up and down and not really do anything with it. Putting the tom on a floor stand is THE way to go.

DD: I got that silver sparkle Ludwig set from Manny's.

BC: (Looking at a picture of the set) It looks like a 22" bass drum, 13" rack and a 16" floor tom.

DD: I had two silver sparkle bass drums, a 22" a 24."

BC: This one (looking at the *Collections* album cover) looks like a 24."

DD: That could very well be a 24" on the champagne set.

BC: You said you've given away all those sets over the years?

DD: Yeah, that set went to Willie Davis, who used to play with Joey Dee's band. Terrific drummer. He fell into hard times and started living on the street. I saw him one day in a studio and he needed drums, so I gave him that set. In those days, I had four or five of each set. I gave one set to Pete Bunetta, the record producer that did Smokey Robinson. That set was painted up with Yosemite Sam and other cartoon characters in Day-Glo.

BC: What happened to the silver sparkle set with the black band?

DD: God knows what happened to them!

BC: I know you used an electronic set for a while, but you mentioned that now you usually rent a Tama or Pearl set when you play.

DD: Right. I've more or less gone back to traditional drums while using a Simmons kit with it. I love certain aspects of electronic drums and will include them if we do The Rascals tour. I might have two different drums set on a high and low riser.

BC: Didn't you build that electronic set you used while you were with Steven?

DD: Yeah, that didn't work out. There were problems with it because the triggers weren't working properly and would short out once in a while. It was horrendous actually...very embarrassing. Embarrassing Moment Number One took place in Italy.

BC: Of all places!

DD: Yeah, (laughs). When the electricity goes out, you can always depend on the drummer to do a solo, but with the electric kit I had, when the electricity went out, and it went out four or five times during that show, the drums were like this (taps on table). I was over! I didn't have a traditional drumkit with me.

BC: You never carried an acoustic set as a backup?

DD: No.

BC: I'm interested enough in electronic drums that I'd like to go out and do a gig with my band using Simmons just to see how it would be, but I think I'd keep my acoustic drums in the car just in case.

DD: Good idea, Bob! (laughs)

BC: Or, I'd keep a spare brain.

DD: We always had an extra brain.

BC: The playing surfaces were plastic weren't they?

DD: Yes. I went down to Canal Street and got the plastic tubes and fiberglass parts and actually built every piece of that set.

BC: You had been playing on real drumheads for years. What was it like playing on plastic sheets after that?

DD: I got used to it. In some ways, it was more comfortable than playing on real heads. When I first learned how to play, I didn't have drums, so I played on tables. It was much more responsive. I could do faster things on the hard surfaces. As long as it would respond properly, it was fine. Sometimes, the triggers would delay just a little and that's death. Some nights that delay would come back in my monitor and it would be really hard to keep the time going. It was the beginning era of drum detonators and they weren't perfected yet.

BC: How big was that set?

DD: I had a flat screen as the bass drum and three tom toms, all long tubes, and a snare drum that was also a plastic tube. I only used two cymbals and a hi-hat. I loved the way it looked. It was clear plastic and my riser was clear also. There were lights under the riser, so they would shine up under the drums. That's how we would open the show. It looked like something out of *Star Wars*.

BC: When you go out now do a gig, do you use a five piece set?

DD: I'm thinking about using something really big this time…two bass drums, but one of them will probably be a Simmons. I don't actually play two bass drums. I saw what Rick Allen of Def Leppard did with foot switches and may try to something like that. I definitely want a big set, a massive amount of drums.

BC: Will you buy a new set or do you think you'll be able to get an endorsement deal?

DD: I'll probably try and hook up with a drum company. With what I've got coming up with The Rascals, I should be able to get an endorsement deal.

BC: Which company would you like to go with?

DD: Probably Pearl or Tama. I love the sturdiness of their stuff.

BC: This leads to another question…having used Ludwig and Rogers drums for years, we now have to talk about Japan's almost total domination of the drum market. Although I recognize their stuff is very good, all my sets are old American-made drums. I have Gretsch, Rogers and Slingerland sets and Ludwig and Leedy snare drums. How do you feel about that?

DD: Not having that stuff anymore, I don't know. I haven't liked the new Ludwig drums I've played lately, so I don't care about it. Pearl and Tama make really heavy-duty hardware and drums and I've just adapted to all their stuff. I have no preference about drums. I like Pearl or Tama, but if I look around and find something else, I'll try them.

BC: How about Yamaha?

DD: Their drums are terrific. There are some other small, Japanese drum companies who are unknown over here. There's a Japanese drum magazine that I pick up occasionally and although it's all written in Japanese, the pictures of some of these lesser known sets are beautiful.

BC: How about cymbals? What do you like these days?

DD: I've always liked Zildjians. I want to try those Meinl cymbals again. I did one endorsement ad for them and still have some of them left, so I might use those. It just depends on what kind of deal I can get. I've always had total faith in Zildjian.

BC: Do you have any preference in sticks?

DD: I like marching sticks, but not heavy ones. I don't even know who makes the sticks I use, but they're long and thick, but not heavy, with wooden tips. I never liked plastic tip sticks for rock. For jazz, they're OK.

STYLE AND TECHNIQUE:

To call Dino strictly a "self-taught' " drummer is by no means accurate. Probably more than anyone else in this book, Dino Danelli learned his profession on the street, "just doing it," as he is fond of saying. His home life was intolerable, so he split, without thought as to how he would survive. His influences early on were Gene Krupa, Buddy Rich, Cozy Cole, Sonny Payne, and many other jazz drummers, some of whom he had the pleasure and privilege of knowing intimately. They were his teachers. Others he met along the way helped him also, like Bobby Coleman, the otherwise unknown, crippled drummer from Tennessee, who gave Dino the basics of Rock 'n' Roll drumming.

Most of all, Dino learned to play the way he did by simply living, eating, and breathing drums and music for years. He "just did it." Of course, this would not have been possible had he not had a tremendous amount of God-given talent at his disposal. One must consider the times and environment in which he developed his musical skills. He ingratiated himself to others who gave him encouragement, free equipment and a place to live. Today, it would be all but impossible for a youngster to do what he did, living in New York City. With the explosion of drugs, crime, social disease, rip-off artists, and all the other evils of contemporary city life, a modern-day Dino would stand very little chance of succeeding.

It should be noted that at one time, Dino did take a few drum lessons from Sam Ulano, the well-known New York teacher, and supposedly contacted my former teacher, Carl Wolf, about lessons during the mid-Sixties.

According to Dino, the lessons with Sam Ulano, "never worked out."

Obviously, Dino had the common sense to absorb and take to heart all the advice and training people gave him in his early years. Without that abundant common sense, he might have been lost. He freely took whatever people were willing to give. Perhaps that is why Dino has been so generous in helping others over the years. When was the last time someone gave you a set of drums?

Stylistically speaking, Dino came from three different areas; jazz, rock, and rhythm, and blues.

Early on, Dino was influenced by the rock drumming of Gary Chester and Hal Blaine. He later listened closely to some of his British counterparts in the Sixties.

"I always liked Ringo a lot and felt he was in a class by himself. He had a nice feel although I've heard John and Paul had a lot do to with what he did on record."

"Charlie Watts with The Stones was great, because he stumbled in all the right places. New Orleans drummers did the same thing. Charlie did it in the English sense. He made mistakes, but always pulled out right."

"Keith Moon was a unique player, but I think a lot of his success with The Who had a lot to do with Pete Townshend. There were a lot of holes in the music for Keith to fill up. I used to hear Keith jam down at Steve Paul's Scene in the Sixties and he didn't play the way he did with The Who. Sometimes when he played with other people, it didn't work out."

From an R&B standpoint, Dino copped licks from Al Jackson, Bernard Purdie and many others. He was groove-oriented and cuts like 'Mustang Sally' and 'In The

dino danelli

"With Steven, I had to use a click track on the second album, but live, it was totally different, I could really play like I always do."

One question that Dino is inevitably asked is exactly what he played on "Good Lovin'."

"There was no set pattern. It was a combination of different beats I had played over the years. There was a Latin flavor, mixed with the 'Turn On Your Lovelight' feel. There was a bit of Ray Charles in there. If you listen to the song, there's no set thing. On other takes we did, there was a pattern, but on the take that became the record, I deviated from it totally and we just happened to use that one. The take that was the record was much more free."

"It goes back to Arif and Tommy and their intuition about picking takes that had that magic feel. I don't think The Rascals could have had the success we had without them. We owe them a lot."

Dino always had total freedom to create interesting and innovative drum parts with The Rascals.

"All our records were like that. I could always do what I wanted. No one tried to change what I was doing. Felix and I always locked in around each other. We knew what the other guy would do before he'd do it. It was a special kind of thing that made the band solid."

Midnight Hour' from the first Rascals album attest to this.

If you are a Rock 'n' Roller like me, you might tend to skip over ballads and go straight to the rockers. In The Rascals case, it pays the Danelli fan to go back and listen to the slow numbers, for they contain some of Dino's most dynamic work. Tunes like "Since I Fell For You," "Baby Let's Wait," and "More" all begin with Dino playing in a very restrained manner, in one case, with brushes. Both songs reach a point where Dino interjected explosive fills, sometimes double stroke rolls and occasionally triplets. A lesser-skilled drummer might not be able to pull these off. His jazz influence is all over cuts like these. Another trick that Dino used not only on the ballads, but on "Slow Down" from the first album, was a quickly-caught cymbal roll, a lick that Carmine Appice also used throughout his tenure with The Vanilla Fudge.

Live, Dino has always had a charismatic presence behind the drums that shines brighter than the average rock drummer, however competent. With The Rascals, Dino's drums were rarely set up in back of Gene, Felix, and Eddie, but to the right of the stage in front. He worked very closely with Eddie, who played "the toys," or percussion instruments such as maracas and tambourines. Like Dino's description of the effect that Sonny Payne's showmanship had upon him, Dino exuded the same. He drew the listener in with his showmanship; twirling sticks with his left hand between each backbeat on the snare, bouncing sticks off the floor, bouncing sticks off the floor tom, never missing a beat, standing up to catch a crash cymbal and choke it. Although he considers the twirling corny these days, he still does it once in a while.

Dino's latest studio projects have presented a very simple 1980's approach, but live, he still gets creative with fills.

ADDENDUM:
DINO DANELLI June 25, 1988

Last night, The Rascals headlined a concert at the Brendan Byrne Arena in East Rutherford, New Jersey. Felix Cavaliere, Gene Cornish and Dino, along with a lcontingent of backup musicians and singers, tore thre every hit and such Rascals classics as "In The Midnight Hour," "Mustang Sally" and an extended version of "Good Lovin." Dino's playing was tight and muscular and had all the magic of the Sixties. And yes, did twirl those sticks!

The tour will last all sumer and there will probably be a live album and video.

After the show, Dino and I had a chance to chat amidst the backstage confusion. He was happy with the group's performance, but thought they would be able to tighten it up as the tour progressed.

Dino looked great. He had lost some weight and was dressed in black with his characteristic Ninja headband.

His set for the tour is a six piece, blak Pearl outfit, with three Power rack toms, floor tom, chrome snare and bass, with two 16" crash cymbals, an 18" ride, and 16" and 18" Chinas. All the cymbals were Sabian. He also had one Simmons pad, but didn't use it.

It was great to see Dino and The Rascals together again after eighteen years.

SELECTED CUTS

"I Ain't Gonna' Eat Out My Heart Anymore" (Atlantic LP #8123, *The Young Rascals*)
The Rascals first single, "I Ain't Gonna Eat Out My Heart Anymore" starts with a steadily building two bar snare roll. Dino keeps time on the ride cymbal during the verses, choruses, and guitar solo, but brings it down to the hi-hat for the bridge. His short, eighth note lick right before the last chorus is strong, as are the sixteenth note fills to the fade-out.

"Slow Down" (Atlantic LP #8123, *The Young Rascals*)
Dino kicks out this flat-out rocker with insistent ride cymbal time, the kind you rarely hear anymore, at least on records. Listen to his sixteenth note fills, accents and quarter note triplets during the organ solo. The high point, however, occurs in the third verse after Felix shouts, "cool it." Dino brings the volume down with a snare/hi-hat shot and a quickly-caught cymbal roll that comes in from nowhere, an amazing, but slightly off-the-wall riff.

"Good Lovin' " (Atlantic LP #8123) *The Young Rascals*)
Probably the most well-remembered Rascals hit because it was their first big one. As Dino explained earlier in this chapter, "Good Lovin' " has no set drum pattern. What he played on this take was the *Lovelight* riff, with shades of Ray Charles, mixed with a Latin feel. The timing fluctuates a little here and there and it's hardly perfect from an Eighties point of view, but it feels great and that's what counts.

"What Is The Reason" (Atlantic LP #SD 8134, *Collections*)
The high points of "What Is The Reason" are Dino's one bar drum breaks, all of which are spectacular. The first is an odd combination of eights and sixteenths unlike anything this scribe has ever heard before. The second and fourth sound like double strokes between the snare and small tom and are very crisply executed, with great control. The third one is straight sixteenths around the set. Listen also for the quarter notes triplet fill on the crash cymbal and bass drum on the final chorus, another favorite Danelli trick. On the stereo version of *Collections*, the drum breaks pan from left to right.

"Nineteen Fifty Six" (Atlantic LP #SD 8134, *Collections*)
An obscure track from *Collections*, this tune is most notable for the Chuck Berryish, Chicago blues shuffle groove Dino lays down with the help of guitarist Gene Cornish. Dino, who co-wrote the song with Gene, digs in and hits that nasty sweet spot right on target.

"Come On Up" (Atlantic LP #SD 8134, *Collections*)
One of the hardest, guitar-dominated raveups The Rascals ever recorded, with supposed druggy lyrics, "Come On Up" also featured heavy drumming with a very sparse bass drum lick and a well-placed hi-hat *sip* on the last verse. Dino's sixteenth note fill on Felix's scream is thunderous.

"Since I Fell For You" (Atlantic LP #SD 8134, *Collections*)
This is a prime example of the Danelli ballad style. Dino is such a presence behind the kit, that ballads always featured his individual stamp. This cut starts out relaxed and quiet, but Dino gradually brings the pace and dynamics up as the song progresses, climaxing with a bluesy ending, punctuated with an enthusiastic drum riff.

"A Girl Like You" (Atlantic LP #SD 8148, *Groovin'*)
This is The Rascals jazzy side and Dino gives the tune a bouncy, tasteful drum track. All his accents and fills are well-placed and economical. He uses cross-stick rimshots on the verses and bridge, snare hits on the choruses. Very well thought out drumming!

"Groovin' " (Atlantic LP #SD 8148, *Groovin'*)
Dino played congas and a woodblock on this cut, another of their biggest hits. There is no drumkit per se, on this track and it's not missed at all. What was played, worked...no more, no less.

"How Can I Be Sure" (Atlantic LP #SD 8148, *Groovin'*)
Another very big Rascals hit, "How Can I Be Sure" is in three/four, with a distinct French sound and feel, complete with accordion. It gives Dino the opportunity to work within a time signature some drummers find very confining. His playing, naturally, is very jazz-oriented, with a very light, free-flowing quality. He seems very much at home working within the framework of the tune.

"You Better Run" (Atlantic LP #SD 8148, *Groovin'*)
Our final cut is back to hard rock again and it's one of The Rascals best and most fondly remembered tracks. Pat Benatar covered it a few years back and scored a hit with it as well. On the original version, Dino plays a rigid, militaristic pattern on the verses, but on the choruses, using dotted eights and sixteenths on the toms for the lead-in, changes the rhythm over to a shuffle, playing triplets on the ride cymbal with a backbeat of two and four on the snare. Listen closely to the oddly-placed bass drum offbeats on the verse. All told, "You Better Run" contains cuts of Dino's most savage drumming.

DINO DANELLI TODAY

Today, Dino Danelli lives in the same Upper East Side Manhattan studio apartment he has occupied for many years. Dino makes his living primarily playing with The New Rascals, a band he leads with guitarist Gene Cornish. His graphic art, which supplemented his living as a musician over the years, is on the back burner.

"I found that mixing art with music wasn't working anymore as a profession. I still draw and paint for myself, but don't do it for a living anymore. There are so many phonies and charlatans in the art world. You have no idea how bad it is. There are forgeries everywhere you turn and people who want to rip you off and take advantage of you.

"The New Rascals are active mostly during the spring and summer months. We play in the Midwest a lot and do the casinos, Sixties rock festivals and some clubs, and we do very well. We're kind of low-key. We don't have a web site or anything, but we sell out all the

DINO DANELLI IN 2001.

time. The Indian casinos love us. Gene and I still have that fire and intensity playing the hits and we've found some musicians who are total professionals and are able to recreate The Rascals' sound very accurately onstage. Neither Felix [Cavaliere] or Eddie [Brigati] are involved at all. Those two are still at odds with each other over songwriting credits, royalties and I'm not even sure what else. There are personality issues involved. It seems like every time Gene and I and the various lawyers and businessmen try and do something positive for The Rascals, Felix and Eddie cause problems."

In 1988, Dino, Gene and Eddie thwarted Felix's plans to freeze the rest of the band out of royalties by rerecording Rascals hits for use in television commercials.

"That's typical of the stuff that happens. We got that straightened out before he actually did anything. I don't know why he wanted to do that to us. Maybe it was bad advice he got from someone."

Tentatively scheduled for the spring 2006 is a Rascals tribute CD and a tribute concert in New York City. Dino has been involved with the planning of both projects.

"A lot of people have said it's about time we did something like this. Sid Bernstein, our original manager, is involved. We're going to have some serious names on this CD and we're still trying to get commitments from certain people. I'd love to get Sting involved. I know Bruce Springsteen and Steve Van Zandt are included; there are other names I can't mention right now, but it's going to be a great CD and concert."

Is there any possibility of getting the four original members there and playing onstage?

"Who knows? What we need is a powerful businessman like Irving Azoff or someone like that to mediate and try to get Felix and Eddie to participate. Gene and I want a full-blown Rascals reunion at least for that show, but there are so many years of problems and issues to overcome."

Dino is also heavily involved in music production these days. He's always looking for good new bands to record.

"There's such a healthy music scene downtown. There are so many clubs with live music happening. I go downtown almost every night and check out new bands. These kids aren't making any money; they're playing for the door, basically, but there's some great music down there. I've taken several bands into the studio and I've come very close to having a hit a couple of times, but it hasn't happened yet. Gene and I got involved with record production years ago and it grew on me."

Dino is also looking for a publisher for a book he has written called *A Rascals Odyssey*. It's Dino's story, but it's not the "same old rock autobiography" you might expect.

"When I decided to write the book, I went to Barnes & Noble and other bookstores and checked out the rock music books. At first, I wondered if there was even a market for a book like mine, but after looking around, I saw there was. My book isn't like the others; it's more of an erotic novel and auto-biography. It's my story before and after The Rascals and about the women I had relationships with. It's very graphic. I didn't pull any punches, but I did change the names of some of the women, because a few of them are famous actresses now and they have families, and I wouldn't want to embar-rass them. If they give me permission to use their names, that's one thing, but I won't divulge their names otherwise.

There are photos and reproductions of some of my artwork too. Right now, the book is a shell at just over one hundred pages, but once I get a deal with a publisher, I'll expand it so there's more for the reader. The time we were inducted into the Rock and Roll Hall of Fame would be a whole chapter unto itself! I think it's going to be a very cool book. Some of it is reality and there are fantasy sections too. I wanted to get The Rascals' story out there before I leave this planet."

As far as equipment, it's provided for him at every venue in which The New Rascals play.

"I go to gigs with a stick bag. The drums, cymbals and hardware are provided all the time. It's a rider in our con-tract. I still prefer Yamaha, Pearl or Tama drums and hard-ware. I prefer Japanese hardware because it's strong and less complicated to deal with."

"Every time Gene and I try to do something positive for The Rascals... Felix and Eddie cause problems."

JERRY EDMONTON, 1969, IN A
DUNHILL RECORDS PROMO SH[O]

JERRY EDMONTON

"Within about twenty minutes, we had worked up the whole arrangement of 'Born To Be Wild', with everyone playing just what they felt like playing."

1968 WAS A PRETTY GOOD YEAR.

I got my driver's license, the garage band I was in was working pretty regularly, and on my seventeenth birthday, I bought Steppenwolf's first album on Dunhill Records simply because I liked the way the group looked on the cover. Back then, record prices were still cheap enough that you could take a chance on something you had never heard.

I slapped that sucker on my Magnavox portable stereo phonograph and was immediately knocked out by the band's tough stance, their fuzz-drenched guitar sound and swirling Hammond organ. However, what caught my attention was, as could be expected, the drummer; a straight-ahead, get-the-job-done player, whose fill-ins always seemed to work in the right places, at a time when mine sometimes didn't. The drums were not only played well, the sounded superb and were obviously well recorded. The bass drum was punchy and the snare cracked beautifully.

The drummer's name was Jerry Edmonton.

Throughout Steppenwolf's days of rock success, Jerry always delivered, song after song, album after album, a master of taste, feel, and workmanlike musicianship. He was always reliable, right on top of things, laying it straight down. This studious-looking Canadian was capable of rising to prodigious heights. Later on, he even wrote or co-wrote some of the band's best known material like *Monster* and *For Ladies Only*.

The music business is a funny animal. Hit records and financial success don't automatically guarantee lasting or even temporary notoriety. For some strange reason, even after all the gold records, sellout shows and glory days, Jerry never received the credit among fellow musicians and rock fans alike that he deserves. No one has ever mentioned his name to me when the discussion revolves around Sixties drummers. No one seemingly has ever publicly cited his influence. None have acknowledged his talent.

JERRY EDMONTON

FROM "THE ED SULLIVAN SHOW", 1969.

Sometimes, it seems that I am the only person out there who liked Jerry's playing. Where are the other Edmonton fans out there?

In this author's opinion, Jerry was one of the unsung drumming greats of the Sixties.

Born in Oshawa, Ontario, Canada in 1946, Jerry, whose real last name is McCrohan, was the son of Owen and Margaret McCrohan. Mr. McCrohan managed and booked a large ballroom on the shores of Lake Ontario, called the Jubilee Pavillion, that featured big bands and later, Rock 'n' Rollers like Bill Haley and The Comets. Jerry got his first exposure to music and the music business through his father's work, as he spent quite a bit of time listening to the various groups that played at the Pavillion. Piano lessons early on soured him in terms of learning music from a formal viewpoint.

"The elderly woman who gave us all piano lessons was not a very enjoyable person to be around,' he said.

"I used to go by the bandroom at school and see these people bashing cymbals together and beating on tympani's, trying to play their version of classical music and marches, and it didn't do anything for me. I'd go home and listen on Jimmy Reed, Elvis Presley, and Little Richard. That was more exciting than school music."

Consequently, Jerry never had any formal training whatsoever on drums.

His musical taste revolved heavily around bluesmen like Jimmy Reed, and R&B artists such as Booker T. and The MG's, Sam and Dave and many others.

Jerry actually wanted to learn saxophone before drums, but buck teeth and his orthodontist's refusal to let him play sax pushed him to try drums instead. He began by working out on someone else's drumset. Brother Dennis was playing guitar by this time and had organized a band called Jack London and The Sparrows. London was a local singer/lyricist. When their drummer quit, Jerry joined. Mr. and Mrs. McCrohan, who always encouraged their son's musical aspirations, bought Jerry his first drumset at age fifteen. Dennis and Jerry had full run of the family basement to play music anytime, day or night. Mr. McCrohan was delighted with his sons' choice of careers.

After much rehearsing, the band began gigging around the Oshawa/Toronto area, including an appearance at a local radio station. A tape, recorded from that radio show, secured the band a contract with Capitol Records of Canada. A single, "If You Don't Want My Love," shot straight to Number One on the Canadian charts, and an album followed, entitled, *Presenting Jack London and The Sparrows*. The single and LP were never released in the United States, and both are highly collectible today. It was at this time that the McCrohan

1969, JERRY ON DRUMS, "THE ED SULLIVAN SHOW."

"There's always someone who feels they were 'born to be wild'. I'm sure the next generation will feel they were too."

The Sparrow's management took them down to New York and secured the group a deal with Columbia Records. Three singles were released, none of which did much. The Sparrow recorded enough songs for an album, one that was finally released long after Steppenwolf had become well known. They gigged around the New York area for a while and later left for California to play at the Whiskey A Go Go and other local LA nightspots without a lot of success. At this point, they decided to give San Francisco a try, moved north and played at the Ark in Sausalito, The Avalon Ballroom and Winterland, both in Frisco. With little happening in terms of work or recording, The Sparrow split up. Jerry and John Kay stayed together and moved back to Los Angeles. Brother Dennis changed his name to Mars Bonfire and decided to become a songwriter (he later wrote "Born To Be Wild" and many other tunes for Steppenwolf and himself).

Back in LA, John and Jerry hooked up with producer Gabriel Mekler, who was looking for a band to work with. He had contacts with Dunhill Records, who were also anxious to sign a rock band at the time. Keyboardist Goldy McJohn, who had been in The Sparrow, was re-recruited, and bassist Rushton Moreve and guitarist Michael Monarch were added and that was the birth of Steppenwolf. In a matter of a few weeks, the new band had put together over an hour's worth of material, including the soon-to-be-classic, "Born To Be Wild."

"Within about twenty minutes, we had worked up the whole arrangement of *Born To Be Wild*, with everyone playing just what they felt like playing. I couldn't have been in either The Sparrow or Steppenwolf without the freedom to play the way I felt. Vice versa for the rest of the members. It was a very open policy. You came up with your parts and played. If someone had a suggestion, that was a help, but you were never told, 'play it this way, or else.' It was an equal situation. No one was considered the leader, and that made it much more democratic. I pretty much had the freedom to influence the band as far as tempos. John sometimes wrote tunes that were a little folksier-sounding due to his background and I'd get him to pick the tempo up and make it rock a little more. Those things always worked out well. That freedom also allowed me to get the band to experiment with tempo and feel changes. It's really obvious on the first few albums. The producers we worked with, Gabriel Mekler and later, Richie Podolor, were very understanding of the way Steppenwolf worked and never really pushed too hard to change the natural feeling of the way we played our instruments. They were very open-minded about it."

brothers decided to change their last name to Edmonton, undoubtedly from the city of the same name. They felt that being the sons of a prominent booking agent and promoter would hurt them in terms of getting gigs with their dad's competitors.

Jack London and The Sparrows then moved to the Yorkville Village district of Toronto after their record hit and played all the local clubs, usually for a piece of the door.

"We got the doorknob, about six inches of wood off the bottom (laughs), all the lemonade you could drink and beer later, if you were old enough. We'd be lucky if we walked out of the Chez Manique or El Patio clubs with $45.00 for the whole band, sometimes even as little as $15.00, to go home to our one room where we all pretended to live."

After the royalties from their hit record came in, London pocketed the cash himself. This led the others to oust him as lead singer. They continued as a four piece band for a little while and then met John Kay, who was working the coffeehouse and club circuit. Kay was doing a blues gig, accompanying himself on guitar and harp. The band liked what they heard and saw. A friendship was struck and John Kay joined the band, now christened The Sparrow. He added a lot of new material to the band, including "The Pusher," an anti-drug anthem written by Hoyt Axton.

JERRY EDMONTON

*" The first time
I sat down behind
the Simmons and
kicked the kick drum
and hit the snare,
I said, 'Right,
this is it.'"*

JERRY LOOKING VAGUELY MYSTICAL
IN THIS 1976 PUBLICITY SHOT

THE LAST STEPPENWOLF LINEUP, 1976. JERRY IS IN THE BOWLER HAT.

Steppenwolf's laissez-faire attitude in the studio certainly paid off. "Born To Be Wild" went on to become their first bona fide hit record, a Sixties rock classic, an anthem to every young person who has ever considered him or herself to be just a little on the rebellious side. It's a song that has meaning to every generation of rock devotees and will undoubtedly continue that way for many years. It was also the first time the term *heavy metal* appeared in a rock song. Little did Dennis Edmonton know what he was creating back in 1967, when the song was written.

Jerry not only enjoyed the recording process, but became hooked on the technological end of it also. He spent invaluable time working with the engineers doing mixdowns and mastering.

The studio, however, was not without its difficulties.

"Because we were set up so we couldn't see each other in the studio, we'd have sloppy endings, and in the early days, it was almost impossible to hear each other, as the equipment was not sophisticated. I used to move around a lot when I played drums and the old headphones they used to use would fall off in the middle of a take. Another inconvenience that went with the territory of being the drummer, and every drummer knows, is that it used to take forever to get a good drum sound in the studio. You were the first guy there, the first guy to set up, then they· say, 'let's get a drum sound.' For what seems like hours, you're pounding on your drums and playing routines and by the time they get the drum sound, everybody else has set up in about ten minutes and are ready to do the take. By that time, you're kinda' burned out, because you've been getting a drum sound for the last century. I never enjoyed that too much! After a while, working with the same producers and the same drum kit, it became easier."

Jerry enjoyed the grind of roadwork.

"It was fun, I must admit. There's nothing like leaving school and going on the road with the boys. It was tough once in a while. The travel arrangements left a lot to be desired; cramming everyone into a station wagon with a U-Haul trailer and not being able to afford more than one hotel room for five guys. In the later stages, when Steppenwolf started to tour, conditions were a lot better. We were on a bus and that was fun. If you got tired out from too many long gigs in a row, you could always sleep on the bus, do a little sightseeing, see the country, write tunes, whatever. Going overseas was a total gas. I love traveling and feel fortunate that at a young age, I got exposed to a lot of countries, different people. I miss it. The audiences make it all worthwhile. Touring with other good bands made it all a great experience."

Jerry attributes Steppenwolf's success to the fact that the band did it their way. They never compromised and were never consciously aware of trying to please anyone. They played the way they felt and sang about things they felt were substantive. And, they happened to be at the right place at the right time.

"Steppenwolf had a sound, and I give John Kay a lot of credit for that. If you hear John's vocal coming over the radio, you immediately say, 'that's Steppenwolf.' The rawness of Michael Monarch's guitar, Goldy's organ playing, Rushton's bass, my drumming, together, made a recognizable sound."

"We were a very efficient band and were not at all nervous about auditioning for Dunhill. Our first album was recorded in three days at a cost of $8,000.00, which is unheard of today!"

"The youth of the world were ready to hear music with some meaningful lyrical content. Kids seemed able to identify with a lot of our lyrics. There's always someone who feels they were *born to be wild.* I'm sure the next generation will feel they were too. Pick up a lyric sheet not only from Steppenwolf, but almost anyone back in the late Sixties, and there's real content. Good lyrics. Thoughtful, meaningful lyrics, things that are consistent and will be around for a long time."

One thing Jerry would like to do is remix the old Steppenwolf tracks, to give them more of an Eighties sound.

"I'd love to do that, but at this point, I don't think the record company would go for it," he laughed.

"Back then, I used to think the kick and snare were really punchy, but compared to the drum sounds today, and particularly on dance records, the drums now dominate the mix. I wouldn't mind hearing my early tracks with that kind of projection."

"Music-wise, content-wise, arrangement-wise, I think our stuff holds up really well, in fact, I think it sounds better than a lot of music today. How many bands actually go into a studio and record together today? Not too many. The recording process has become rather sterile."

"When I look back at the Sixties, I realize it was a great scene with the invasion of all the British bands. I think it really kicked a lot of American artists in the butt. Of course, the whole world was watching The Beatles next move. The Sixties changed the world; attitudes, fashion. The influence, whether good or bad, of the drug culture, opened people's minds and made them aware that war is not a lot of fun. It was a very experimental period. A lot of freedom was created. There was a lot of crossing over, combining different styles of music. Rock 'n' Roll became a melting pot of music."

"It definitely changed me, in that I left school to become involved in music as my mainstay in life. As a result of that, you leave home, where your roots are," he added wistfully.

"The Sixties made the world smaller. All over the world, there are people who love that music."

"Rock 'n' Roll became legitimate then. It was, 'Look, this guy's making millions! It really must be a job!' Actually, they didn't realize that it's still just a hobby that you get paid for."

"Summing it up, I'd say the Sixties music scene was a period of creative freedom where one was compelled to express their satisfaction or disappointment in the human race and the state of the world."

Steppenwolf continued with several personnel changes, albums and tours, until 1972. They officially disbanded on Valentine's Day, 1972, because they felt that it was better to put the group to rest with dignity than to drag it through the mud, as it were. Jerry formed a new band with keyboardist Goldy McJohn called Manbeast, a four piece, that was unable to secure a record deal. He and Goldy then started a seven piece group called Seven, a progressive rock project that never jelled. In 1974, it had become painfully apparent that none of Steppenwolf's former members were able to put together a workable alternative. Bowing to pressure from promoters, there came

JERRY EDMONTON

JERRY AT HOME BEHIND HIS SIMMONS SET, 1988.

about what Jerry described as, *The great, unexpected reunion of Steppenwolf*, with new guitarist, Bobby Cochran. Three albums were released from 1974 until 1976. *Slow Flux*, on Mums Records, a division of CBS Records, *Hour Of The Wolf* on CBS, which Jerry called a *sonically superior record*, and *Skullduggery*.

"Unfortunately, CBS didn't have a great deal of faith in Steppenwolf, so, due to a lack of support from them, the last two albums didn't take off to any degree. At that point, our three album deal with CBS had expired, so they put out a compilation that is really rare called, *The Best Of Steppenwolf: Reborn To Be Wild,* on Epic Records. It's a pretty nice collection of the best songs off the last three albums we did. The band was slowly deteriorating in terms of concert attendance. We felt that once again, it was best to put the band to rest for the second time and save ourselves the embarrassment of playing the lowest level of club in order to make a buck. So, the band ended for the second time around the end of '76."

After Steppenwolf expired, Jerry began writing with his brother Dennis. After putting together a solid list of material, the Edmonton's formed a new group called Tara, that featured a woman who played Celtic harp. Unfortunately, Tara couldn't get a record deal. In 1978, Dennis and Jerry formed another group, The Bland Band, that came very close to inking a deal with Elektra

Records, but it was not to be. Once again, the record execs passed.

1979 brought another new project for the Edmonton's, a four piece band called Green Wheels, that covered Melanie's old hit, *Brand New Key*, to capitalize on the roller skating craze that had hit California. Signed to Ariola American Records, *Brand New Key* got limited play in dance clubs, but unfortunately, the company went out of business just as the record began to catch on.

Jerry handled all the disappointment philosophically. "How many times can you get involved with something like Steppenwolf? The old records were still selling and I was collecting royalties, so there was no immediate burden to find financial resources. The last part of the Seventies was a period of experimentation as far as writing and co-writing with my brother, which was fun. I got more into production. It rekindled my fondness for the technical end of things. The late Seventies was a tough time to get any record execs to listen to you due to the glut of bands that were around. Every kid in the neighborhood was in a band back then. Even with our credentials as Steppenwolf, it was very hard to get anyone to pay attention. They said, 'that's dinosaur music!'

Jerry found that disco and punk rock definitely influenced his style. When punk was happening, Dennis Edmonton wrote a lot of new wave-oriented material, which Jerry thought was fun, as it brought back the spirit of early Rock' n' Roll in many ways.

"A lot of the bands that got major attention, I have to say, were pretty bad (laughs). There wasn't much regard for capabilities, especially in the vocal department. If it excites you, it excites you. If there's an audience for it, fine. I just hope all those bands were having a good time while they were doing it. It was fun doing some recording of things that were punkish. It really gets your right hand in shape playing eighth notes that fast! On the other hand, disco didn't do much for your kick drum technique, playing quarter notes that consistently and uncreatively, I must say. I think disco music was accomplished much better using a LinnDrum. Unfortunately, it put a lot of drummers out of work. Some of the less mechanical disco stuff that Rod Stewart got into with Carmine (Appice) playing drums was nice."

Dance music's prevalence made Jerry very conscious of rushing or dragging tempos. A drummer playing live in the studio had to set a tempo and keep it there.

"Later on in production, you would splice together different sections and if there was a variation in tempo, it just wouldn't work. The music demanded the use of a click track, which was kind of uncomfortable. Playing with a click without other musicians isn't much fun. You might as well use a machine. I had more fun programming a Linn than sitting down and actually playing the drum part for five or six minutes straight."

"The main thing I got out of punk was humor. I had a lot of laughs listening to the punk stuff from out here on the California coast. I don't think it changed anything. It probably reminded a lot of older people that they were young once and it's OK to be different and it's OK to do your own thing, and it's OK to have fun. For the younger people, it gave them the opportunity to blow off steam, just like the early Rock 'n' Roll did for us guys. Socially, it got people fired up and kicked them in the ass. It grabbed people by the throat and shook 'em up a little bit. It's OK to dress up crazy and enjoy life. Human beings are pretty fun-loving animals. Punk created a focal point for a lot of kids. It gave them a rallying point."

Today, Jerry keeps up with current drummers like Phil Collins, Omar Hakim, Manu Katche and Jon Farriss, the drummer with INXS. These four are his favorite contemporary players.

"Phil Collins...the guy is perfect! Beautiful feels, great vocalist, great producer, good songwriter. The guy is totally well-rounded. Omar Hakim has a great feel, as does Manu Katche. Jon Farriss is exciting, new, and still Rock 'n' Roll. He's definitely important to the band's total sound. It's hard for me to say why I like a drummer or a band. They're good! They sound good. They feel good. If I met them personally, I might hate them, but I've heard Phil Collins is a true human being. I also like Stewart Copeland...beautiful interpretations of reggae feels, but still Rock 'n' Roll and *fast*! He has a very good sounding drum kit and great timing. Jerry Marotta on Peter Gabriel's albums...wonderful playing. I love John Robinson's playing on the last Steve Winwood album. I have a lot of respect for a drummer who can drop into anyone's project and make it groove."

Unlike many of his Sixties contemporaries, Jerry has totally immersed himself in the world of electronic percussion. He claims that he never touches his acoustic drums anymore and now relies on Simmons and his Linn to get the sounds he needs. Using the Simmons is much more fun, he says.

"I don't have to deal with the inherent delays of working with acoustic drums...broken heads, tuning problems, unwanted rings, temperature changes, all the rattling noises that drive producers and engineers crazy. The hours of setup time in the studio is now a matter of minutes. I can also record incredible tracks at home using my own recording gear and take them into any studio and transfer them to multi-track and get excellent results, whereas, with my acoustic drums, I'd have to use a sound-proof room, because they'd be all miked and neighbors always hate the kid on the block who plays drums, if you know what I mean."

"Having all this new electronic equipment that generates MIDI information, opens up a whole new world for drummers that was only previously available to keyboard players. If you're doing a session and want a conga sound, now you can just throw a switch on your kit and get it. You can totally change your drum kit sound. It's endless. Electronic drums allow the new drummer an opportunity unheard of before to practice. You can live in an apartment with three roommates with walls that are paper-thin. When you come home from school or work, you can sit down behind your electronic drums and rehearse, practice or compose without bothering anybody. There are rubber practice pads and Remo pads, but hey, they don't sound like real drums. A pair of headphones, a set of electronic percussion, and you're in heaven."

"The first time I sat down behind the Simmons and kicked the kick drum and hit the snare, I said 'Right, this is it.'"

"The technology available today has been a boon to drummers, whether it's acoustic or electronic percussion, because the recorded sound of drums is hundreds of times better than what it used to be. Noise gates and limiters eliminate a lot of the annoying sounds and the move toward digital recording, sonically, is better than analog. I like being able to take a digital master and dupe it in different digital formats and still retain the original sound."

"New technology has never intimidated me at all. I think it's very exciting to see what lays around the corner."

The last band situation Jerry was involved in was a group called Steel Rose, that got together in the early 1980's and included former Steppenwolf bassist George Biondo and two women. One single was recorded on Dore' Records, but it didn't do too much sales-wise. They played a lot of local club gigs during the period of 1984-85 in the Los Angeles area, while shopping around their self-produced demo tape. When one of the women in the band left and the other decided to have a baby, Steel Rose split. At that point, Jerry decided he was fed up putting bands together that went nowhere. Today, he's still heavily involved as an equal partner in Steppenwolf, Inc. John Kay tours with a hand-picked backup hand billed as John Kay and Steppenwolf. The old Steppenwolf albums have been recently released on compact disc and the group continues to bring in handsome royalty checks for Jerry and John. *Born To Be Wild* is used often for TV commercial purposes and recently popped up in a segment of the show, *A Year In The Life*, during a high school reunion scene. Jerry keeps busy writing new material these days, while enjoying the good life in southern California.

"I'm having a lot of fun again with music. I'm not looking at it like 'Oh my God, I've got to put a band together!' I don't know what the future holds, but I've still got my drums, so I intend to keep playing when I feel like playing them, with whom I feel like playing with, for as long as I feel like doing that."

In his free time, Jerry enjoys photography and has a darkroom in his home. He's done some commercial sessions with former band associates and has racked up some credits as a photographer.

He was married during the 1970's, but divorced in 1981, living on his own until 1986, when he met a woman named Lisa Chapin, who had a young son named Ian. Today, the three live together as a family and Jerry, who came from a loving and stable family, is clearly delighted with this arrangement. Lisa is a very artistic woman who hand-tints black and white photographs and she and Jerry have been working closely in the photographic field.

"Maybe that will be a career for me in my old age, doing black and white photography and hand-tinting it with her."

"I guess you could say my personal life is pretty enjoyable. I get concerned living in California about earthquakes and I'm always thinking about the world situation. Steppenwolf product is still selling quite nicely and that's given the members who participated in songwriting something to fall back on.'

JERRY EDMONTON

Jerry's taste in music runs the gamut from the progressive New Age music of Tomita, Larry Fast and Kitaro, to Celtic harpist Ellen Stivell, to Tears For Fears, Depeche Mode, Wang Chung, and the FM radio rock of Bryan Adams, Phil Collins, Sting, Peter Gabriel and Steve Winwood. He also likes listening to the old Steppenwolf tracks on CD, as well as Eric Clapton, The Beatles, Stones and ZZ Top, when he's in the mood to rock.

"Drummers or any musicians for that matter, are like painting a picture. Each one of us is a color. Some bands have certain colors that stand out more than others. But that's fine, if that's the picture you're painting. So, be a true color. Paint with music. Paint pictures for people to hear, be them pretty, be them ugly, be them happy, be them sad. But do them to the best of your ability."

EQUIPMENT:

Jerry is one of the few drummers this author has known that never went through the *pots and pans* phase of drumming. He was fortunate to have parents who bought him drums as soon as he became interested in the instrument. His first kit was purchased in 1961 and was a Broadway set, most likely English-made, in gold sparkle, with a 5' x 14"snare, 8' x 12' rack tom, 14' x 14' floor tom and a 20" bass drum. Included also were 12" hi-hat cymbals and an 18" crash-ride, both of dubious origin. The hardware was the standard lightweight stuff of the day. The set came with calf heads. At the time, Jerry used very thin Ludwig sticks, which he described as pencil sticks.

In 1963, he traded in the Broadway kit for a white Marine Pearl Ludwig set, with a 20" bass, 14" snare, 13" rack tom and a I6" floor tom. The cymbals were replaced too, with 15" Zildjian hats, an 18" Zildjian crash and a 20" Zildjian ride in medium weight. The hardware was Ludwig, and the drumheads were plastic this time.

"The reason I chose Ludwig was because that was the name to have in my area. The two music stores in Oshawa carried a good array of Ludwig equipment. If you were a drummer, you used Ludwig drums. That kit was used to record the Jack London and The Sparrows album. I added a 16" Zildjian medium crash to the set and started using a thicker nylon-tipped stick, most likely Ludwig also."

Jerry took the Ludwig set to New York in 1965 to record the Sparrow tracks for Columbia, only to have them stolen from the group's station wagon in front of the Albert Hotel in Manhattan.

They were replaced by a four piece Rogers Set in black oyster pearl. The switch to Rogers drums came about after Jerry tried a Swiv-O-Matic Rogers bass drum pedal and found it very much to his liking, infinitely more comfortable to his foot. He also liked Rogers mounting hardware much more, as it was stronger and much more adjustable than other conventional drum hardware. The black oyster Rogers set again had a 20" bass, 14" chrome snare, 13" rack tom and a I6"floor tom. He used the same basic Zildjian cymbal setup as before.

In 1967, the black oyster pearl Rogers were also stolen "somewhere in Laurel Canyon." Jerry's replacement was another Rogers, a five piece kit, the one he used throughout Steppenwolf's days and right up to the time he began using electronic drums. This is his favorite set and he still has them.

The kit is a Rogers Holiday model in silver sparkle, consisting of a 20" bass, 12" and 13" rack toms, a 16" floor tom and a 5" x 14" chrome Powertone snare. During the Seventies, Jerry also used 5" x 14" and 6" x 14" Ludwig snares and 6" x 14" Pearl snares as well.

His cymbals at the time were all Zildjians again, including 15" hats, 20" heavy ride, 18" heavy crash, 18" medium crash and an 8" splash mounted between the rack toms. The splash was later replaced by a loosely fitted set of 14" hi-hat cymbals, also Zildjian, set up in a permanently closed position. He also used a cowbell attached to the hi-hat stand, resting between the cymbals and the first rack tom. All the hardware was Rogers Swiv-O-Matic. Jerry claims the Rogers hardware was very reliable for many years, although he eventually began using Tama hardware.

Remo Emperor or CS heads were Jerry's usual choice for the Rogers kit.

The Rogers Holiday set was finally retired to the recording studio in 1971. It was then that Jerry purchased a maple wood Ludwig set with a 22" bass, 16" floor tom, 14" and 15" rack toms and a 6" x 14" snare. This set included the same Zildjian cymbal configuration as Jerry previously used with the Rogers kit. He chose larger drum sizes due to Steppenwolf's increased stage amplification and used the Ludwig set until Steppenwolf's final dissolution in 1976. At one time, this set was recovered in a black and silver geometric design, but has since been stripped down and painted in what Jerry described as battleship grey. The set used all Rogers mounting hardware, allowing Jerry to mix and match drums in the studio at will.

During Steppenwolf's days on the road, Jerry primarily used either 2B or 5B model drumsticks and eventually switched to Regal Tip nylon Rock sticks. His choice of stick lately is the Hot Stix Rock model in red.

In the early 1980's, Jerry made the switch to using Simmons electronic drums almost exclusively. He bought two SDS-5 sets in red, both seven piece kits, with two brains ands Peavey amplification gear to power them. He's looking at more advanced electronic digital drums to replace the Simmons now, but still gets a kick out of the analog sounds he gets from the SDS-5's. Though he clams he never touches acoustic drums anymore, he did use his old Rogers kit live with Steel Rose, as late as 1985.

Jerry uses Pearl mounting hardware, Tama cymbal stands and his ever-trusty Rogers Swiv-O-Matic bass drum pedal on the Simmons. He's also very fond of using a Lindrum together with the Simmons to trigger additional sounds and for composing purposes. A Yamaha digital reverb and Ibanez digital delay are also employed.

Over the years, Jerry has always preferred not to use too much muffling on his acoustic drums, just the occasional wad of paper gaffered to the snare head or a pillow or blanket inside the bass drum to cut down on ring in the studio.

"Of course, with the Simmons, that's all unnecessary now," he added.

Today, Jerry has no real need for a drum technician or roadie, but when touring with Steppenwolf, Steve Palmer, a fine drummer in his own right, was Jerry's right-hand man, always ready with spare equipment and able, according to Jerry, of setting up the drumset within an inch of the way Jerry would set up himself.

"He could practically change a bass drum head while I was still playing!"

"I have no feelings either way about Japan's domination of the drum market. The stands and mounting hardware is great, but for a while I thought that that even though the hardware was big, a lot of it was garbage. Rivets would come out and the plating would peel off. It just didn't hold up. I think Tama's got that together pretty darn good now. That and the Pearl hardware is pretty rugged stuff. I'm out of touch with the quality of American acoustic drums. My Rogers set held up much longer than the Ludwig kit I got after that. I still like the sound and feel of older acoustic drums. The Rogers have incredibly thick shells, the silver sparkle is still silver and is still on there, and the hardware and lugs look fine. I don't know whether current drums will hold up any better. I guess time will tell."

Jerry also plays a bit of guitar and uses a Martin acoustic to write on. Back in his early days, he also played blues harmonica as well.

STYLE AND TECHNIQUE:

To describe Jerry Edmonton as a no-frills player is really not accurate, for his rhythmic explorations on cuts like "Renegade" and "For Ladies Only" proved that for a totally self-taught player with little background in technique and who, admittedly never "learned how to play drums properly," he was very capable of incorporating complicated jazzy figures, working closely with either the band's lead guitarist or keyboardist Goldie McJohn.

In his formative years, Jerry listened more closely to the overall sound of the music as opposed to singling out the drummer. He claims to have forged his playing while taking in the sound of great bluesmen like Jimmy Reed and Muddy Waters. The drummers on some of their records were a source of inspiration, as were several English players like Ringo Starr, Charlie Watts, Keith Moon, Jim Capaldi, and Mitch Mitchell.

"Ringo's sizzling hi-hat sounded like searing, white light to me. I'm sure I used that sound quite a bit. Charlie Watts had an attitude that you shouldn't take it all too seriously, it's still Rock 'n' Roll. Keith Moon? Say no more! He influenced me to begin hitting the drums hard. Beat 'em, smash 'em, hit 'em hard! That helped me later when we got very loud onstage. Jim Capaldi was a very tasteful, sensitive player and Mitch Mitchell reminded one of how free one could be and still rock. The older blues drummers just laid down incredible grooves, using quarter notes on the hi-hat and tricks like that."

Back to the jazz influence, Jerry admitted having a liking in his youth for Joe Morello, certainly one of the finest technically-oriented jazz players of the Fifties.

When Jerry decided to play drums, he simply sat down and played along with his favorite blues and R&B records, copying the figures he heard. His brother

Dennis was the only timekeeping device he used to tighten up his own time.

"He's a great rhythm guitar player. We used to call him *the machine*, because he has better time than a lot of drummers."

Jerry is, first and foremost, a solid, straightforward rock drummer, plain and simple. Humility prevents him from boasting about his talent and achievements. Real drummers, he contends are guys who have studied, who can spark anyone's music at a moment's notice. He never considered himself that type.

What he perhaps does not realize is that drum chops can be learned on the street, on the gig, where it counts. Experience was Jerry's teacher.

When I began listening to Edmonton in 1968, I was attracted to his almost constant use of the hi-hat in either a tight closed, or semi-closed position. I was one of those annoying drummers who flailed away on my ride cymbal, creating a wash of overtones, sometimes to the dismay of my bandmates. Jerry's hi-hat technique changed that and thankfully so. If you listen to the first two Steppenwolf albums in particular, you'll hear his hi-hat all over both records.

The beginning of "Born To Be Wild" contains the signature Edmonton hi-hat pattern: quarter note beats as opposed to eight notes, laying down a marvelous rock groove.

His fill-ins were usually very confident and supple and although they occasionally seemed as if they would not fit within the framework of the music due to their highly syncopated nature, they always did! Jerry most definitely used the snare drum as the center of his fill-ins and also used his kick drum within fills as well. Toms were primarily used for accents. His cymbal crashes were always well-timed. Many of the bass drum patterns Jerry used were the result of years of absorbing rhythm and blues styles. Again, syncopation was the word, with a very pronounced black feel (See Selected Cuts).

Edmonton's timekeeping ability as a whole was very relaxed and steady, but once in a great while, tempos had a tendency to pick up on a final chorus, or during a guitar solo. In those days, click tracks were not used as they are now. It's easy to become excited when the band is really kicking it out and the adrenaline is pumping.

Jerry was always loose enough and was given the freedom to change rhythmic patterns sometimes as many as three or four times within one piece of music.

He has no set routines to prepare for drumming, but if he hasn't played in a while, he simply plays a lot of eighth note hi-hat figures to loosen up the wrists and hands.

"That wrist gets stiff and cramps up if you don't keep it moving. Mentally, I prepare myself by being confident that I know the tune we're going to do. Because I don't read charts, I have to listen to a cassette of it or perform it in a rehearsal a few times to lock it into my brain. If I know I have it in my head, that's all the mental preparation I need to walk in and lay down a track. Live situations? I still get nervous a bit. You never know how it's going to go. It's the great unknown. You walk out

JERRY EDMONTON

onstage and that's the thrill of it...it's live! (laughs) There's no rewinding the tape and doing it over! I always get a little nervous, but I take a few deep breaths, make sure the equipment is all together, look out into the audience and see if they look happy, and hell, off you go."

Jerry has his own way of interpreting drumming.

"When I drum, I really like to listen to the band as a whole. That way I can keep the music moving forward and create spontaneous interactions between myself and the other players whenever possible."

"Most of the time, the drummer should be the one who sets the tempo, but he or she must be sympathetic, of course, towards the capabilities of the vocalist and their interpretation of the song, and of the other players manual dexterity. I have had problems at times when I've felt a tune should be a little uptempo and a less experienced guitarist may have had difficulty executing the song at that

tempo, but generally, the drummer should be in the driver's seat."

"Play with confidence and conviction. Nobody wants to hear an uncommitted, middle of the road performance. Try to understand the arrangements of the songs you are performing. I find it a great advantage to know the lyrics or melody in your head so you can compliment, yet stay out of the vocalists way."

"Learn to love machines. If you don't, you're missing out on a lot of creative help and you're missing out on a lot of fun too. The way vocalists, composers and producers are working today, you could also be missing out on a job if you can't program, operate or understand some of the various drum machines available. Experiment with sounds. Don't be satisfied with the same old drum kit that you feel comfortable with. There's a vast arsenal of traditional and exotic percussion, plus limitless electronic and

SELECTED CUTS:

Sookie Sookie (Dunhill LP #DS-50029, *Steppenwolf*) This is the first cut on the first Steppenwolf album, and it's a Don Covay tune, a funky, hard rocker at a medium tempo, that is one of Jerry's favorite drum tracks. His fills are mostly sixteenths on the snare with the first beat of every sixteenth grouping on the rack tom or between the snare and bass drum. The main rhythm pattern is quarter notes on a closed hi-hat and snare on two and four.

"Born To Be Wild" (Dunhill LP #DS-50029, *Steppenwolf*) This is the one...THE classic Steppenwolf track with Jerry's unforgettable drumming; the familiar quarter note hi-hat riff, the switch to four snare hits to the bar on the second half of the instrumental break, and of course, the famous two bar snare-bass-crash cymbal solo that has been copied by virtually every drummer who has ever played the song. It would be unthinkable to change it in any way, because it's perfect. I once tried playing something else besides the Edmonton break on this tune at a gig several years ago. The band looked at me like I was insane.

"Disappointment Number (Unknown), Lost And Found By Trial And Error, Hodge Podge Strained Through A Leslie, Resurrection, Reflections" (Dunhill LP # DS-50037, *The Second*) Despite the many titles, this is a complete piece of music, usually referred to as a musical trip through the history of the blues by Steppenwolf fans. Jerry appropriately starts the acoustic part of the piece off using brushes until hitting a tom tom riff that brings the tempo up to a shuffle, then into a more modern soul music groove. His timekeeping is very self-assured on the organ solo and on into the closing, where he kicks into a rousing double time chorus to the end, that brings the mood back to one of acoustic introspection.

"Move Over" (Dunhill LP #DS-50066, *Monster*) If there's one cut that exhibits the sheer speed of Jerry's wrists, this is it. He executes blinding single strokes on the snare that follow imaginative fill-ins of quarter notes and triplets. When you consider Jerry cut this track using matched grip, with the butt end of his left stick on the drum, the clean quality of his single strokes boggles the mind. Anyone who plays traditional and matched knows how difficult it is to make fast singles work with matched grip, and how difficult it is to fit them into a hard rock context.

"Renegade" (Dunhill LP #DSX-50090, *Steppenwolf 7*) "Renegade" gives Jerry a chance to flex his creative drumming muscles. The first two bars are highlighted by his sparse timekeeping on snare and bass drum alone and later, adding quarter note cowbell shots. He adds effective accents on the hesitations during the choruses with the snare. While the extended guitar solo overtakes the proceedings, Jerry pours on the rhythmic juices, bringing the music up to fever pitch, working very closely with Goldie McJohn's Hammond organ riffs this time, keeping the meter in check, and contributing some of the most unabashedly forceful playing of his career.

sampled sounds available for the modern drummer. These can create any mood you need to enhance a composition. Think like an orchestra. The rest of the band will probably thank you for it and think you are one heck of a smart guy."

"The drummers role in music has drastically changed since the introduction of drum machines. A drummer who has creative ideas, good timing, confidence and a positive attitude working with others, may not be enough today. One must embrace all the aspects of modern and future technology, so when the challenge arises, they are ready and capable to participate. That type of participation is determined by the type of drummer you are. There are the hired hands and equal participating group drummers. If you are an equal part of a band, your role is determined by yourself based on what the goal of the band is. As a hired drummer, your role is based more on your ability to express other people's ideas. so you must be able to accomplish this with all available equipment."

"As far as developing the proper attitude, if you're really young, just hope you have good parents! Don't take it all too seriously. Music is to be enjoyed, not belabored over."

"Learn to love. Learn to love again. If you're in a group, you'll sometimes really hate the people you're working with, but learn to love everyone. Be honest. Be compassionate about what you're doing, but be fair. Don't take drugs. Don't get drunk on the job."

"If drumming makes you happy, then drum with confidence and use all of the natural and manmade tools of your trade."

"Be a drummer. Drum. Send your message in your own special way. Play the music you know is right. The music your heart tells you is right."

"Jupiter Child" (Dunhill 45 #D-4182) This was the B-side of the "Rock Me" hit single, a record that featured Jerry's drums predominantly on both sides. "Jupiter Child", a science fiction story, was co-written by Jerry and sports a memorable funky rhythm pattern that took me a few weeks to learn properly when I was a teenager learning to play. This pattern starts the tune and is repeated right before the final instrumental riff. His fills throughout are excellent too.

"Tighten Up Your Wig" (Dunhill LP #Ds-50037) This is a great Chicago-style blues from Steppenwolf's second LP that John Kay admittedly lifted from Junior Wells. It harkens back to the days when Steppenwolf was The Sparrow, and it finds Jerry hitting snare shots on the and of two and four, with solid sixteenth note tom fills. It's one of the band's lesser known tracks, but a good one at that.

For Ladies Only (Dunhill Lp #DSX-5010 For Ladies Only) At over nine minutes, For Ladies Only is Steppenwolf's longest album track, and the LP on which it appeared was their last before they broke up in 1972. The cut showcases more of Jerry's quarter note hi-hat, and gives him a rare chance to show off his jazz-inspired chops behind Goldie's piano solo on the extended instrumental break. Featured is some sensitive ride cymbal and snare work. On the final chorus, Jerry forcefully pushes the band along, changing his patterns no less than four times on all four choruses to the fadeout, from eighth notes on the ride cymbal, to eights on the hi-hat, to a hot boogaloo soul beat on the ride and snare, and finally, to four beats on the snare with eights on the hi-hat. The third chorus with the soul beat picks up tempo noticeably, but who cared? It's very exciting drumming!

Monster (Dunhill LP #DS-50066, Monster) Monster is a highly political number co-written by Jerry, and it allowed him to stretch out a bit on drums. Particularly noteworthy is the bluesy middle section where he plays in three four with the band playing in four. The fill-ins are strong and confident, almost Keith Moon-inspired and the cymbal bell work is also good. The timekeeping is right on the money.

Straight Shootin' Woman (Mums LP #X-698, Slow Flux) Another Edmonton composition, Straight Shootin' Woman is like nothing else Steppenwolf ever recorded, with it's rolling triplet intro and boogie woogie bounce, complete with a funky horn section. Jerry's fills are almost jagged, but they work. It's very evident that the drums are given upfront treatment on this cut, but why not? The drummer wrote the song.

JERRY EDMONTON MEMORIAL

Over the years, this writer received many words of thanks for covering various Sixties rock drummers, but no one has been mentioned more than the late Jerry Edmonton, drummer with Steppenwolf. It seems the often-times quiet, diminutive Canadian influenced more drummers than even he could have imagined.

Jerry was killed in a car accident on November 28, 1993, the night before Thanksgiving, while running errands just minutes from his home. Steppenwolf fans, myself included, were stunned and shocked by the news. Jerry and I had become friendly after the first edition of *GRDOTS* was published and in gratitude, he sent me a Ludwig Supraphonic 400 snare he had used with the band. It occupies an honored place in my drum collection to this day.

At the time of his death, Jerry performed only occasionally in the Los Angeles area and was enjoying photography and other hobbies. He continued to play at home regularly on one of his two sets of Simmons drums.

Approximately one year after Jerry's passing, I got a call from his widow, Lisa McCrohan. Lisa and I had talked shortly after Jerry's death about her plans to dispose of his equipment. Lisa's son, a budding drummer, was to keep the cymbals, and the two Simmons sets were consigned to sale at a local music store. Steppenwolf singer/leader John Kay wanted Jerry's silver sparkle Rogers set. Lisa had decided to give me Jerry's Ludwig drum set, the kit previously covered in aluminum wrap with painted black chevrons. She was positive Jerry would have wanted me to have them. I was beside myself with a mix of emotions. About ten days later, I was the proud recipient of Jerry's vintage Ludwig kit, and it remains in my possession, awaiting restoration. Needless to say, receiving this gift was gratifying, exciting and yet upsetting, as I knew the original owner would never play them again.

Jerry Edmonton was a truly great rock drummer, a successful man of strong opinions and ideas, a man of talent, conviction and dedication to his craft, and a man of musical and personal integrity. He is sorely missed by many.

"Be a drummer. Drum. Send your message in your own special way. Play the music your heart tells you is right."

BOBBY AS HE APPEARS TODAY BEHIND
HIS MULTIPLE TOM LUDWIG MAPLE KIT

B·O·B·B·Y
ELLIOTT

You would think his name would be a household word in the domain of rock 'n' roll, but Bobby Elliott has never received his just credit.

COZY POWELL, who has drummed for the likes of Jeff Beck, Rainbow, and lately, Emerson, Lake and Powell, called Bobby Elliott his prime reason for taking up the drums. Phil Collins also cited him as one of his main influences.

Bobby was one of the first drummers to get away with integrating jazzy patterns in Top 10 chart material, and his work has been a constant source of inspiration to drummers all over Europe for nearly three decades. But for some unknown reason, Bobby Elliott, who for twenty-five years has been the rhythmic backbone of The Hollies, one of the few surviving bands of the original mid-Sixties British Invasion, has been all but ignored by the general drumming community on this side of the Atlantic. Mention his name to players like Dino Danelli, and the recognition and admiration is obvious. Mention his name to the average rock fan, however, and you're likely to get a "Who's he?"

Anyone who has played drums in the same rock band constantly for twenty-five years deserves at least some credit, wouldn't you agree? Especially if his work with that band had always been very creative and extremely tasteful. You would think his name would be a household word in the domain of Rock 'n' Roll, but Bobby Elliott has never received his just credit. Perhaps this is due to the highly professional but low profile he has kept all these years. He always disliked the screaming fans and autograph seekers of the Sixties, in fact, found it rather frightening. He never had a scrape with the police or was involved with any decadent goings-on, like some other rockers. He simply did his job with little fanfare and did it to the best of his abilities, nothing more, nothing less. Until now, there have been few in this country who have taken the time to say what a fine drummer and musician Bobby Elliott is, and that's a damn shame.

Bobby was born approximately thirty miles north of Manchester, England, in a small town called Burnley. His parents were named Bob and Edna Elliott. Mr. Elliott was a master cabinet maker, who owned his own business, one that was started in the late 1800's, by Bobby's grandfather, Hartley Elliott. Mrs. Elliott ran a grocery shop and the family lived upstairs. The sounds of big band, swing, small group jazz, and early Rock 'n' Roll captured young Bobby's imagination, and at the age of thirteen or fourteen, he became interested in playing drums. He quickly fashioned a pair of wire brushes and a miniature drum set, using cookie and biscuit tins taken from his mother's store. His first *cymbals* were the lids of cooking pots, to which Bobby added

BOBBY ELLIOTT

THIS PHOTO OF A VERY YOUNG, SHORT-HAIRED BOBBY WAS TAKEN IN NOVEMBER, 1961.

rivets. His snare drum was put together with elastic strips and parts from a construction kit, as was the hi-hat. With his first crude drum set together, he began to play along with jazz records by Gerry Mulligan, Stan Getz, Dave Brubeck, and other American musicians. He preferred American drummers for their learned, methodical approach to the instrument. He still does to this day. Bobby especially enjoyed the work of jazz drummers Joe Morello, Larry Bunker, and Mel Lewis, but never outrightly copied their styles. He decided instead to forge his own brand of drumming.

Although Bobby was never really formally trained, and admittedly, never practiced very much, he did take a few lessons on a casual basis from a local drummer who was studying at the time. He paid the fellow five shillings to teach him what he had just learned.

Bobby's first playing experience came about while sitting in at a local jazz venue, the Sefton Club. When the bands' drummer would take his turn fronting on lead vocals, usually on three blues numbers, Bobby would be called up to take over the drum chair. He also gained valuable experience working with a big band at the local dance hall. By this time, he had pieced together his first proper drum set, an old Premier snare, hi-hat, and a bass drum of unknown origin, that was twenty-two inches in diameter and comically, about six inches deep! By this time, Bobby had also been turned on to Rock 'n' Roll and rhythm and blues. England was heavily into its love affair with black, American music by this time.

"Well Robert, the drums are a pleasant hobby, but you'd be better off to put your time into school or a trade."

So spoke the senior Mr. Elliott, and undoubtedly millions of other fathers worldwide. (Strangely, I heard almost those exact words from my old man too). Nonetheless, young Bobby was determined to have a go at music as a career and decided to go professional, by joining a local three-piece rock band around 1961 called The Dolphins, who were doing quite well, occasionally backing singers who came up from London in need of a back-up band. The Dolphins' guitarist was Tony Hicks, who later joined The Hollies, who had just been formed in

Manchester, by Allan Clarke and Graham Nash. The Hollies manager was intent on recruiting Tony for the group, despite his tender age of sixteen. Hicks agreed to join on the condition that Bobby be brought in also. At that time, The Hollies weren't making enough money to afford the luxury of a road manager, and as their current drummer owned a van with which he carried the band's equipment, the group was not in a position to fire him. So, Bobby was not permitted to join The Hollies until several months later. In the interim, he auditioned for and got a job with Shane Fenton and The Fentones, a group styled along the lines of Cliff Richard and The Shadows, a very popular, pre-Invasion English group. Bobby remembers being driven down to London by his father, and queuing up in line, the last drummer to audition. He got the gig and stayed with Fenton until The Hollies made a place for him in the band.

Years later, Bobby found out that Keith Moon was also in that queue.

Shortly after joining the band, Bobby and The Hollies scored a recording deal with EMI. From the very beginning, Bobby was given the freedom to be creative in the studio. He also participated actively in arranging The Hollies material.

"There was no doubt I could play whatever I wanted," Bobby explained. "When you go into the studio as a youngster, you want to get everything in including the kitchen sink, but apart from being told by Ron Richards, our producer, to keep things simpler, I was given my head all the time."

Bobby found the attitudes of British recording engineers and technicians rather stiff at first.

"The recording people at Abbey Road used to walk around wearing starched, white coats. I remember having to bribe the engineer when we were recording *Stay*, one of our first singles, with a large whiskey at the pub. He wanted to use only one mic' on the drumkit, and I was pretty sure we'd get a better bass drum sound by close-miking the bass drum. I also remember draping my Grannie's curtains over the bass drum to get the sound right on that tune. The recording engineers and techni-

BOBBY IN AN EARLY BAND, CIRCA 1960. NOTE THE TWO GUITARISTS PLUGGED INTO ONE AMP AND LACK OF A HI-HAT.

cians were really set in their ways back then at EMI. They were used to recording symphony orchestras and things like that. I suppose we pioneered quite a few recording techniques there by suggesting things."

The Hollies recorded all their Sixties material at Abbey Road Studios, usually under the supervision of the above mentioned Ron Richards.

Bobby feels he never had any difficulty working within the confines of the studio, but does think The Hollies were never able to capture the excitement of their live sound properly on record. The Hollies did their best work onstage as opposed to the studio. Consequently, Bobby feels the drum sound he got in the Sixties in the studio was tinny and thin, mixed far too low in conjunction with the other instruments. When queried which Sixties Hollies drum tracks he liked, he replied there were none.

Bobby thoroughly enjoyed the grind of constant touring.

"That's all we understood. The Hollies were a live band. We were used to working onstage in clubs, dance halls, and theaters. As with The Beatles, our first album was the stage show. The American R&B numbers we did live constituted our first and even some of our second LP's. We were on the road, traveling in a van, working all over England, Scotland, Wales, and enjoying it enormously. As we got more successful, we'd do maybe two shows a day broadcast over the BBC at lunchtime, maybe *Ready Steady Go* at teatime (*RSG* was a famous English rock TV show). Then we'd do a gig in the evening around London. It was rather exhausting, but we didn't look at it that way. It was a way to escape from the north of England, from the run-of-the-mill jobs our friends had. It was five guys escaping in a van, doing a hobby and getting paid for it, which we thought was great!"

And succeed they did. The Hollies notched up over twenty consecutive chart hits, a feat unequalled even by The Beatles. Their record of smashes is phenomenal. The hits included "Just One Look," "Here I Go Again," "I'm Alive, "Look Through Any Window," "I Can't Let Go", "Pay You Back With Interest," "Bus Stop," and "Stop Stop Stop," the last two charting well in the USA. The Hollies came to America for their first U.S. gigs in 1965 at the Paramount Theatre in New York City. While in this country, Bobby spent a lot of his free time soaking in the American jazz scene. It was in New York that he met and listened to a drummer named Ray Lucas, who was then working in the King Curtis Big Band.

How does Bobby feel today, looking back at The Hollies Sixties recordings?

"I think our music was pretty good. There are a lot of our records I like. When you go back to 1963, when things had to be recorded almost all at once, you can feel the enthusiasm more on the earlier tracks because we were actually doing a performance live in the studio and not like today."

A lot of our Sixties stuff was done on first or second take. And the sessions back then were rushed. Ron Richards, as good as he was, didn't like too many takes, and wanted to get things done as quickly as possible. I guess you can't argue with success, but if you listen to some of our songs, there are quite a few mistakes. But there we are. The atmosphere made up for it."

BOBBY ELLIOTT

YOUNG MAN WITH DRUMS: NOTICE THE MATCHED GRIP THAT BOBBY HAS USED SINCE THE BEGINNING OF HIS CAREER.

During the late Sixties, The Hollies replaced the departed Graham Nash, and notched up their biggest worldwide hit, "He Ain't Heavy, He's My Brother." In 1972, the band scored their biggest chart hit in America with "Long Cool Woman In a Black Dress," which went to the top of the charts. According to Bobby, it was probably the most un-Hollie song ever, as it featured only a single lead vocal throughout, as opposed to the group's characteristic three-part harmony vocals. It was done on second or third take and was not intended as a single at all. In 1974, the band racked up another huge hit, "The Air That I Breathe," a tune that showed off the brilliant three-part harmonies mentioned.

The Hollies went through the Seventies, recording quite a few LP's and doing numerous tours. They finally gained the financial success that they deserved during this period.

The late Seventies brought Bobby the much-desired improvement in studio drum sounds he had longed for. Disco and punk were dominant in the late Seventies in England and in the USA as well, and Bobby felt the influence of both.

"Disco encouraged me to lay down (the beat) more. In the Sixties, maybe I was a little more lightweight and too eager to please myself. During the Seventies, I was laying it down and getting underneath things more. Some of the punk-type bands reminded me of early Sixties bands to some extent, like The Big Three, who came out slightly earlier than The Hollies and The Beatles. I think also cocking snoot at the big business establishment of the recording industry, which was getting glossy and super-hyped, was a good thing. So yes, I did enjoy the punk thing while it lasted. It's probably my sense of humor. I tend not to take things too seriously. The raw energy of punk in the Seventies was very much like the Sixties, with the sweat and casual attire. The Hollies, in the early Sixties, before we started wearing suits, were similar in a way to some of the punk bands. We were cleaned up a bit for recording."

Although Bobby admitted to liking quite a few contemporary American and English drummers, he could not recall any names.

What does he feel, are the basic differences between British and American drummers?

"America has a great high school education system that schools drummers and musicians much better than here. So therefore, I think that American drummers are better educated and more technically proficient. The American way of life is more conducive to attack and pace and crispness and hipness, that the British have, but not to the same extent as the Americans. British drum-

Bobby admitted being impressed by some of his English and American Sixties contemporaries.

"In the early Sixties there was a fellow called Bobby Graham who played with Joe Brown and The Bruvvers, who were a British band, but he also did some studio work with P.J. Proby and Brenda Lee and others. He was a very solid drummer and never got the recognition he deserved. I wouldn't say I was influenced by him, but I admired his playing. The American drummer Earl Palmer was an influence rock-wise, on the Little Richard records and other West Coast recordings. I looked up to Hal Blaine too, whom I met while at the Mamas and Papas sessions in California.

"I'd sum up the Sixties period as one of musical pioneering, of getting ripped off, of doing things the hard way. Although those things are still happening today. I don't know whether it changed me or not. It certainly changed some of my friends, one or two of whom aren't around now. I think I was quite fortunate. I never got involved with any of the then *fashionable* heavy scenes. It was just a different way of growing up, a very pleasant period in my life."

mers get away with things due to flair and daring. I think I've always been rather daring, sometimes hit and miss, but that has been part of the fun of it. An American drummer wouldn't do it that way. He would go more by the book. That's why British drummers created more individual styles, unorthodox, if you like."

How does he feel about recording technology today versus the Sixties?

"In the Sixties it was twin track and quarter inch tape. It was very effective and a nice atmosphere. Today, it's lovely and easy. You can record on twenty-four or forty-eight tracks, slice by slice, layer by layer, all very casual, but where's the atmosphere?"

"New technology doesn't intimidate me at all. It's a challenge. I do work with a click track."

Presently, The Hollies are still going strong, having recently re-signed another recording contract with EMI. Three original members remain; Allan Clarke, Tony Hicks, and of course, Bobby Elliott. They have added three other musicians to help out onstage and in the studio; bassist Steve Stroud, guitarist/vocalist Alan Coates, and keyboardist Denis Haines. The band had recently returned from a short Far East tour at this writing and spend a fair amount of time every year touring Europe, where they are still very popular. Their new single is due out in England in early 1988. Unfortunately, there are presently no plans to tour America, although hopefully, that will change.

Today, Bobby Elliott is a happy and fulfilled guy. He lives in Colne, Lancashire, in the north of England, in a large renovated farmhouse, on over four acres of land, with his longtime girlfriend, Maureen Hicks, sister of The Hollies guitarist, and their black cat, Smudger. Bobby keeps busy, when not working with The Hollies, by playing casual jazz gigs at local pubs with his friends. He enjoys helping local musicians in any way he can.

"It's good to try and put something back into the business, because the business has been pretty good to me."

He expects The Hollies to keep playing, "as long as the phone keeps ringing! Even if The Hollies wind up one day, I'll keep playing locally around the pubs, or maybe playing with other bands. Who knows?"

Bobby is also a partner in a company that installs telephone systems and markets satellite television equipment.

Attributing his physical fitness to heredity, Bobby stated that he doesn't have to exercise in any way to prepare for drumming. He watches his diet and although he enjoys a few glasses of wine or beer, when he is working with The Hollies, he curtails the alcohol. He prepares himself mentally for drumming by coordinating his mind and body subconsciously, in a way he could not explain.

He still doesn't practice as much as he should.

"If The Hollies have had a week or two off, I'll go into the barn before I go away and loosen up by playing the drums for a while."

When asked how he would like to be remembered, Bobby replied simply, "As a bloody good drummer and a decent human being."

No sweat, Bobby.

BOBBY'S PREMIER ENDORSEMENT AD. THE SET WAS GOLD SPARKLE. PREMIER ALSO GAVE HIM A BLUE PEARL SET THAT BOBBY DISLIKED.

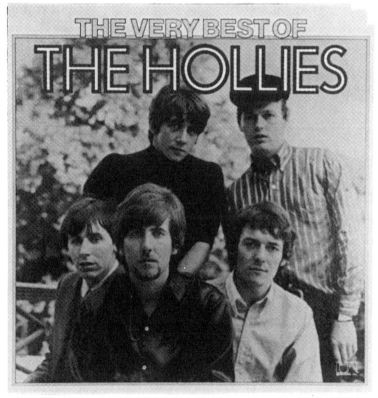

THE COVER OF THE UNITED ARTISTS' ALBUM, *THE VERY BEST OF THE HOLLIES*, NOW OUT OF PRINT.

k very clo...
...on into third place.

...n guitarist over Bruce Welch and
...recast last month, he and Paul
...ners of the songwriter section.
...s guitarist list with Animal Chas
...ve him and just behind the very
...Wyman. Donovan was obviously a
...arist award although Dylan and Baez
...s to count.
...drummers' roll of honour, but that's

what you a...
moving, smoothly-ope...
Finally, you have voted "Yesterda...
arrangement for 1965, so Paul McCartney scores a...
he would be the first to point out that George Martin d...
superb job of translating his ideas into beautiful music.
So there we have the proof of your liking and respect for the
musicians who are keeping Britain right at the top as one of the
world's leading popular music producers.

10. Russ Co...

BASS GUITARIST

1. **Bill Wyman**
2. **Chas Chandler**
3. **Paul McCartney**
4. Eric Heydock
5. John Rostill
6. Peter Quaife
7. Paul Samwell-Smith
8. John Entwistle
9. John Stax
10. Frank Allen

RHYTHM GUITARIST

1. **John Lennon**
2. **Bruce Welch**
3. **Brian Jones**
4. Graham Nash
5. John McNally
6. Chris Dreja
7. Ray Davies
8. Spencer Davis
9. Brian Pendleton
10. Alan Laud

LEAD GUITARIST

1. **Hank Marvin**
2. **Jeff Beck**
3. **George Harrison**
4. Keith Richard
5. Tony Hicks
6. Eric Clapton
7. Pete Townsend
8. Dave Davies
9. Hilton Valentine
10. Jimmy Page

ARRANGE-MENT

1. **Yesterday**
2. **Satisfaction**
3. **Still I'm Sad**
4. Help!
5. My Generation
6. Look through any window
7. House of the Rising Sun
8. I'm Alive
9. For Your Love
10. Stop

...od

Paul McCartney and John Lennon, best songwriters

The Hollies, best group on stage

Eric Burdon, best recor...

EQUIPMENT

The first drum Bobby every bought cost him two pounds. It was a very old Premier snare drum with calf-skin heads. It came with a pair of sticks and brushes. He later purchased the previously-mentioned six inch deep bass drum, a hi-hat and crude bass drum pedal.

A few months later, Bobby persuaded his father to lend him sixty pounds to buy a white pearl Premier drum kit, second-hand. The pearl, in Bobby's words, had turned to a "browny, tobacco-smokey color." The bass drum was 20" wide, the rack tom 8x12, and the snare was a 5x14. The set also came with some Super Zyn cymbals, a Premier bass drum pedal and other hardware. The floor tom was not what Bobby called "a proper floor tom," but was a 14x14 on a floor stand. He also bought a 20" Ajax cymbal and put rivets into, as that was what the jazz players supposedly had in those days.

He later traded the Premier kit in at a music store for a new Ruby red set of Trixon drums. The set came with calf heads and Bobby had a very hard time getting plastic heads to fit properly. Replacement parts were also difficult to come by with Trixon.

"The Trixon bass drum was actually quite good. That set went through the jazz groups, the big band, and right up to The Hollies first couple of records. It was the Trixon bass drum that we used on "Stay", which was one of the best bass drum sounds I got, especially for 1963."

Bobby had also purchased his first Avedis Zildjian cymbals by this time also.

He soon replaced the Trixon snare with a Ludwig Acrolite snare drum. The Acrolite is an inexpensive, aluminum alloy drum.

The sizes of the Trixon set were as follows. 14x22" bass drum, 9x13" rack tom, 16x16" floor tom. The set also included a Premier flush-base hi-hat, and a Fleetfoot bass pedal, superseded by a Ludwig Speed King.

After a short time with The Hollies, Bobby traded in the Trixon kit for a new silver sparkle set of Ludwig drums that consisted of a 22" bass drum, 400 chrome snare, 9x13" and 16x16" toms. He also bought a set of Paiste Formula 602 15" hi-hat cymbals that he still has to this day, and a Formula 602 18" crash cymbal with rivets that he used on many of The Hollies recordings.

BEST G...
ON STAGE

1. Hollies
2. **Rolling Stones**
3. **Animals**
4. Who
5. Shadows
6. Yardbirds
7. Beatles
8. Moody Blues
9. Kinks
10. Manfred Mann

MMER

Elliot
Bennett
Moon
Baker
Watts
tarr
Hugg
ince
Avory
lcCarty

Donovan, best folk guitarist

**CLIPPING FROM
BEAT INSTRUMENTAL'S
1965 AWARDS ISSUE.**

Mike Vickers, brass/woodwind player

Alan Price, best keyboard player

Bobby Elliot, best drummer

In 1965, Premier approached Bobby to endorse their drums. He agreed, but unfortunately, had to surrender his Ludwig kit to Premier as his part of the agreement. Premier gave him two sets. One was a gold sparkle kit, 22" bass drum, 8x14 rack tom, and a 16x16" floor tom. Although Premier gave him various snare drums, Bobby continued to use his chrome Ludwig 400 snare. The other Premier kit was a dark blue finish with a 20" bass, 8x12" and 16x16" toms.

According to Bobby, "It wasn't a very good kit."

"The nice thing about the Premier deal was that they gave me quite a bit of exposure in the musical press. There were half-pages saying, 'Bobby Elliott of The Hollies uses Premier Drums.' They were quite nice to me. While I was with them, I tried to get them to improve their range (of drum sizes). They didn't make a 9x13" tom and I tried to persuade them to make one. Of course, you got the old, 'We don't have any call for it. People don't want it.' Every other company made a 9x13 rack tom."

Bobby also designed and built a spur to prevent the Premier flush-base hi-hat from creeping, but the company seemingly was not interested, as they told Bobby it was lost at the factory.

"Obviously, they weren't interested in improving anything."

When Bobby's three year endorsement deal with Premier ran its course in 1968, he went back to Ludwig while on tour in America, and agreed to endorse their products. He has been with Ludwig ever since, but is currently negotiating a deal elsewhere.

The first Ludwig kit Bobby received was a blue sparkle set with a 22" bass, 9x13" and 16x16" toms, 400 snare and all Ludwig stands and pedals. The Speed King bass

drum pedal remains Bobby's pedal of choice. He has been using Speed Kings steadily since 1963.

He does, on occasion, use a Tama Camco bass drum pedal for jazz work.

In the early Seventies, Bobby replaced the blue sparkle Ludwig kit with a silver sparkle, double rack tom set, made up of 22" bass, 9x13", 10x14" and 16x16" toms. He still uses this set today for practice and for his local jazz gigs.

In the Sixties, Bobby became an endorsee of Paiste cymbals, which he swears by.

"Paiste are the best cymbals, because they are very consistent. Their service is excellent and they are very nice people to do business with."

At the time of his switch to Ludwig, Bobby's cymbal setup included the 15" Formula 602 hi-hats, with a Ching-Ring fixed above them. That Ching-Ring was used on many Hollies records. He also used an 18" Zildjian or Super Zyn crash, the 18" Formula 602 crash with rivets, and a 20" Avedis Zildjian ride.

Into the Seventies, Bobby used nothing but Paiste cymbals, starting with Formula 602's, but switching to the 2002 series later. He used Sound Edge hi-hats during this period.

Bobby's current Ludwig set is a natural maple kit with single-headed rack toms, 8", 10", 12", and 14," with a 16x18 floor tom, 6 1/2x14 Black Beauty snare, and 22" bass drum. The set came with 15" and 16" rack toms, but Bobby doesn't use them. His hi-hat pedal is made by Sonor, his bass drum pedal is the ever-present Speed King.

The current Elliott cymbal setup includes Paiste Sound Creation hi-hats, an 18" 3000 series crash, a 1000 series Rude Power Ride, a 3000 Power Ride, a Novo, which is a china-type cymbal, plus another 18" 3000 crash. All of them are fairly heavy cymbals.

BOBBY ELLIOTT

THE HOLLIES, CIRCA 1964, WITH ORIGINAL BASSIST ERIC HAYDOCK. BOBBY IS ON THE FAR RIGHT.

For jazz work, Bobby uses a 20" 2002 Paiste ride with rivets. He also uses a Sound Creation Dark Ride, which gives him a nice pingy sound.

As far as muffling the drums are concerned, Bobby tries to work with The Hollies sound engineer to achieve the best sound wherever the band is performing. He uses a cut-out ring from an old drum head on the snare, and finds this type of arrangement ideal for his damping needs. The single headed toms need virtually no muffling, but Bobby would prefer double-headed toms on his next kit. The 18" floor tom does need muffling, however, so chamois leather is used. The front head of the bass drum has an 18" cutout and the drum is muffled to obtain a tight sound.

The Hollies are using at this time, a sound company from the north of England called Wigwam Sound. Although Bobby didn't know what type of microphones were used on his set, he said he was very happy with the stage sound he had.

When queried as to the Japanese domination of the drum industry, Bobby replied, "They make very good drums. It's a shame about America falling by the wayside, because all my heroes played American drums, whether Ludwig, Gretsch, Slingerland, or whatever. The Western drum manufacturers have only got themselves to blame for the Japanese domination of the drum market. The Japs have kept to their regular formula of taking other people's ideas and improving on them, and it's up to American, British and European companies to get back on a level track with the Japanese."

"As far as contemporary stands and fittings, the quality is excellent. They're very well engineered and light years away from the Premier flush-base hi-hats and horrors like that from the early Sixties. I like the sound of my old Ludwig kit for jazz and small room music, but feel modern equipment is better suited for professional theater situations or large stadium work. New equipment is much more sturdy and will stand up better to the punishment equipment has to take nowadays."

"Craftsmanship wasn't any better in the Sixties. People look back at the era with nostalgia thinking things seemed better. Japanese drums today are made better than anything from the Sixties."

"Paiste Cymbals are very keen on getting drummer feedback. Maybe they've taken note of comments I've made over the years on sounds I require or just general comments on how a cymbal performs."

Bobby's choice of sticks are Tama oak 216-P, a straight-grained model that rarely breaks, according to him. Prior to the Tamas, Bobby used Pro-Mark oak 2-B's, which are slightly heavier than the Tamas. He uses Calato Saul Goodman Model felt mallets on a couple of songs for cymbal rolls and tympanic effects. His favorite drum heads are Remo Ambassadors, particularly for the snares. He uses Remo Pinstripes on heads on the toms and heads on the bass drum.

Bobby also uses a set of Paiste finger cymbals for *Soldiers Song*, one of The Hollies newer tunes.

Electronically speaking, Bobby uses the Linn and Oberheim drum machines in the studio, as well as the Yamaha RX-11, Roland TR-505, and Roland CR-78 drum machines. The CR-78 is used live to lay down Latin rhythms on a couple of songs. He simply plays along with the box.

Bobby tried Simmons drums in the studio in the early 1980's, but preferred the sound of acoustic drums and has never used the Simmons since. He does, however, trigger electronics in the studio off his acoustic drums.

He is currently experimenting with Roland PD-31 drum pads, that are linked to a Roland 626 drum machine and the Roland MIDI interface, the PM-16. If this setup works out, Bobby plans to begin use of sampled sounds.

STYLE AND TECHNIQUE

Like so many other well known, exceptional drummers of the Sixties, Bobby Elliott began his musical career with dreams of becoming a hot jazz player. Undoubtedly, he saw the chance to make a good living playing rock, as England was literally exploding with R&B-oriented bands in the early Sixties.

Other than a few casual lessons from an acquaintance, Bobby was completely self-taught. Music studies in school were not to his liking and he never participated in this area either. He did spend quite a bit of time playing along with records by American jazz greats, as has been mentioned.

From the very beginning, Bobby was determined not to copy any particular drummer. His goal was to create his own style based on his musical tastes and experiences.

"I've never been conscious of actually copying any particular person, or having anyone's influence come out in my playing. It's difficult for me to look out from the inside to see how the drummers I liked influenced me."

"I think basically, that my style is my style, and it's been created out of my upbringing, maybe my lack of

"It's all well and good being great on the practice pad and the practice kit, knowing all the sticking and the rudiments. But at the end of the day, if you can't deliver on the stage, there's no real point."

above: **ANOTHER CONTEMPORARY ACTION SHOT ON TOUR WITH THE HOLLIES.**

right: **A HANDBILL ADVERTISING THE HOLLIES 1988 TOUR. BOBBY IS PICTURED ON THE FAR LEFT.**

tuition and playing jazz and playing rock. It's a Bobby Elliott fusion and it's unique to me."

Bobby feels that relaxation is important for any drummer.

"Obviously, the ultimate aim is to get as relaxed as possible, because you play better if you're relaxed. That can be a frame of mind. I've found that being on the road for a long time can make you relaxed because you're so bloody tired. Sometimes I'll have a bath or a shower before a show and that's relaxing."

Bobby states the drummer's primary role in music is to keep good time. Did he ever have any timekeeping problems?

"It's never really been a problem, but in the early days, The Hollies were (and still are) a very exciting band. In the very early days, it was a case of rushing through things and creating such an excitement onstage, that the whole band would speed up. That was innocence and growing up, as well as sheer flamboyance."

"Obviously, there are a lot more things than just keeping time. A drummer must enhance whatever is happening around him, so therefore, you've got to be a bloody good listener. You've got to be able to hear everything

and then you've got to complement whatever is going on. The drums ought to be a springboard, a trampoline, to inspire fellow musicians to reach heights they have never reached before, to cajole or prod the band or soloist into reaching the ultimate. Also, light and shade is very important in a drummers playing. He should know when to take a backseat. And again, I can't be too emphatic on being a good listener."

"A good drummer should be thinking mentally ahead of the action, preparing the ground for the oncoming force, whatever it might be."

"It's all well and good being great on the practice pad and the practice kit, knowing all the sticking and the rudiments. But at the end of the day, if you can't deliver on the stage, there's no real point."

And deliver consistently onstage and in the studio is something Bobby Elliott has done for twenty-five years. Solid, steady and tasteful are three adjectives that best describe his drumming. There is the obvious jazz influence apparent, particularly when listening to older Hollies material. Listen to the ending of "Pay You Back With Interest" for a prime example of Bobby's jazzman sensibility.

BOBBY ELLIOTT

THE COVER OF THE *WHAT GOES AROUND...* LP, 1984.

Listening to the Hollies back catalog of recorded work, and it is a very large catalog as could be expected, one gets the feeling that Bobby could always be called upon to play what was right for each song. In that way, he could be perhaps compared in some ways to Jerry Allison, Buddy Holly's drummer in The Crickets. Both drummers did what was necessary to make any song work properly, whether it be a sensitive ballad like "The Air That I Breathe," a rocker like "Bus Stop," or something more exotic, like "Stop Stop Stop," with its effectively placed cymbal/snare hits on the chorus.

The Hollies latest records reveal that Bobby has indeed become more conscious of dance groove drumming. Much of 1983's What Goes Around, the reunion LP with Graham Nash contains tunes with a persistent four-on-the-floor dance groove, some done with electronics, some with acoustic drums. As always, Bobby Elliott delivers the goods consistently.

SELECTED CUTS

"Look Through Any Window" (United Artists LP #UA-LA 329-E, *The Very Best Of The Hollies*)
Bobby offers up some very inspired and imaginative fill-ins during the bridge and before the last chorus. He even kicks in a nice, short closed roll at the end.

"Stop Stop Stop" (UA LP #UA-LA 329-E)
If you listened to "Stop Stop Stop," you might wonder why it was picked to be in this section. The drums are almost inaudible throughout, except on the chorus, where Bobby hits two of the most perfectly placed snare/cymbal hits one could imagine, an absolutely essential part of the song. Without them, the tune just wouldn't work. Listen for yourself and see. The pattern he plays on the verses, by the way, is a very simple two-beat bass drum lick with steady quarter notes on the hi-hat and a two and four rimshot on the snare.

"Here I Go Again" (UA LP #UA-LA 329-E)
Bobby pushes this Merseybeat-style rocker along from the very beginning with incredible time, going from a two-to-the-bar snare pattern on the verse, to a four-to-the-bar riff on the chorus, one of his favorite tricks. The feeling is one of acceleration without any real increase in tempo.

"Long Cool Woman In A Black Dress" (EPIC 45 #5-10871)
This is solid groove rock drumming from beginning to end, so spare, straightforward and lacking in frills, that the drums create tension out of sheer simplicity. It leaves you practically begging for more. It's also a fine example of what an effective timekeeper Bobby Elliott is.

"Carrie-Anne" (Epic 45 #5-10180)
The calypso-like intro belies the fact that "Carrie-Ann" showcases some of Elliott's best recorded work. His sixteenth note fills every two bars on the verses are a vital and highly recognizable part of the song. As he so often does, Bobby breaks the action up, changing patterns on the chorus to a solid four beats on the snare, and adding more very strong fill-ins throughout.

"Dear Eloise" (Epic 45 #5-10251)
Recorded during The Hollies flirtation with psychedlia, "Dear Eloise" is one of the best examples of Bobby's harder style of drumming, particularly during the bridge and final chorus, where some of his fills are so strong and manically exciting, you might wonder if Mitch Mitchell was lurking nearby.

"Pay You Back With Interest" (UA LP #UA-LP 329-E)
With no less than three tempo changes, including one that is in three/four, "Pay You Back With Interest" is a perfect example of Bobby's fertile, jazz-inspired imagination. Listen to the floor tom lick on the bridge and the jazzy time on the ride cymbal all by itself at the end. Absolutely brilliant!

"I'm Alive" (UA LP #UA-LP 329-E)
Incredibly, the only Hollies tune that ever reached number one on the British charts in May, 1965, "I'm Alive" spots more forceful, confident timekeeping and fills from Bobby, including a double-time switch at the end, a very popular trick that was used extensively by many Sixties bands.

"If The Lights Go Out" (Atlantic LP 800 76, *What Goes Around*)
This is a good representation of where Bobby's drumming is at in a contemporary setting. Listen closely for the highly syncopated bass drum part that occurs within the song, as well as the thoroughly-modern-sounding fills, that feature the higher-pitched concert toms.

"Casualty" (Atlantic LP #800 76, *What Goes Around*)
"Casualty" was done with Elliott programming the Oberheim drum machine. Unafraid of technology, Bobby openly admits to liking machines, if they are used properly. While it's fairly obvious that a machine is doing the work here, the guy who programmed the tune used some imagination when it came to the breaks and fills. It also shows Bobby's current penchant for using a four-beats-to-the-bar bass drum dance groove.

*The author regrets that the original catalog numbers of the United Artists material described were not available. All the above UA selections were originally released on Imperial Records, now defunct.

BOBBY ELLIOTT TODAY

Bobby Elliott continues to play with The Hollies, who have been together for over forty years and remain a big attraction in Europe and Asia. Unlike other Sixties groups that rely exclusively on past glories, The Hollies are moving forward with new material and a record deal with EMI in Europe. Bobby expects a US release as well for this CD, and a 2006 tour stateside. The band is currently recording tunes by songwriter Rob Davis, who is a friend of their bass player, Ray Stiles. Other band members are writing as well for this project, which is set for tentative release around January 2006. When Bobby and I spoke, he was fresh off a recording session.

Last year, The Hollies' lead singer, Carl Wayne, passed away rather suddenly from throat cancer. You may remember him as the original lead singer of The Move, a pioneering British power pop/rock Sixties band.

"It was a great shock to all of us. We worked with him up until about four weeks before he died. The doctors operated, put his throat back together and they thought they had it all, but they didn't and he died within weeks of our last gig together," said Bobby. Pete Howarth has replaced Wayne with The Hollies and, according to Bobby, is doing an admirable job.

I asked Bobby what factors allowed The Hollies to go on for so long as an active band.

"We have a quite a large back catalog of songs that people still remember and like to hear. We spend a great deal of money on staging, lights and sound to give people a great show. It's a two-hour-and-fifteen-minute show, so people get their money's worth. We do about an hour, take a twenty-minute break, towel off or change and come back and do an hour and fifteen. That's always been the English tradition. It gives people a chance to go get a drink or whatever they want to do. The theatre or venue becomes our home for the day and the band and the crew enjoys that. We just came off a German tour and will start the British leg soon, with an appearance at the Royal Albert Hall."

Bobby recently switched to DW drums and Zildjian cymbals and is very happy with the change. He used to endorse Premier drums and Paiste cymbals.

A RECENT PHOTO OF BOBBY IN CONCERT BEFORE HE SWITCHED TO DW DRUMS.

"The DW birch drums I have are just great. I bought them last year from Scheerers Drum Shop in Leeds. I have the Broken Glass Glitter finish. It looks like aged silver sparkle, almost like champagne. I have 10", 12", 14" and 16" suspended toms, an 18"x22" bass drum, and am still using a Premier maple snare on my live kit that's a 6½" deep model, but I'd like to try the DW aluminum snare. The Premier is just the best-sounding snare for live purposes. I have a Yamaha hi-hat given to me by the late Cozy Powell that I use live and my bass-drum pedal is the DW 9000 series double pedal."

Bobby's cymbal setup is 14" K hi-hats, a 12" splash, 17" and 18" K crashes, a 19" K Dark crash/ride and a 20" ride without a stamp or model name. He still keeps a good supply of old Paiste cymbals on hand, and owns quite a few vintage Ludwig sets, including kits used with the Hollies over the years and one special blue pearl Ludwig set owned and well used by legendary British jazz drummer Kenny Clare.

"I have been quite pleased with Zildjian cymbals and have been with them for about eight to ten years. I'm always looking for the elusive 'perfect' ride cymbal like so many other drummers. Some days, I think I have found it; other days, not!"

When asked to comment on new music, Bobby stated, "I like any music that's quality, especially if there's a good rhythm section. Of course, I like jazz especially, but if it's a string quartet or whatever, as long as it's well played, that's fine. I picked up a lot of Latin music the last time I was in Miami, Florida, and I recently downloaded some tunes by Brooks & Dunn because I liked the bass drum sound on their records. Some of the newer country music is quite good."

Bobby finally broke down and bought a PC and is enjoying the Internet, after years of resisting technology.

"I feel like I've come out of the steam age!"

PUBLICITY SHOT OF KENNEY TAKEN TO ACCOMPANY *FACE DANCES* PROMO BOOKLET, 1979.

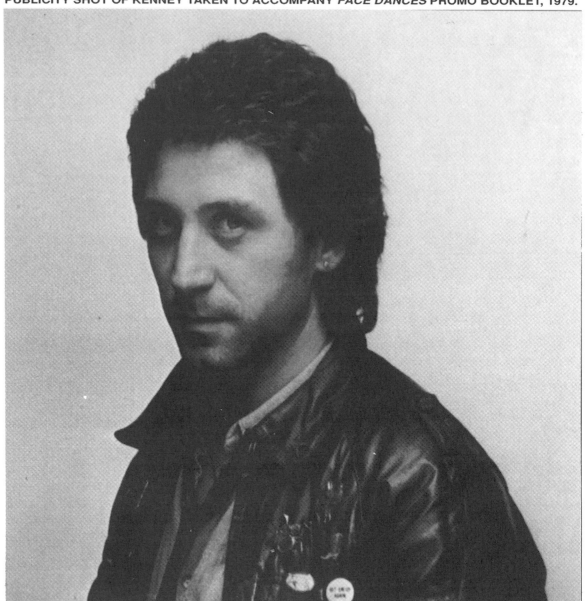

KENNEY

Kenney played obsessively.
He would get up at 6:30 in the morning
and play until he went to school,
waking the whole neighborhood.

LISTEN TO THE INCENDIARY DRUM BREAKS ON THE SMALL FACES TUNES "Understanding" and "All Or Nothing," the wild tom-tom solo seemingly inspired by Gene Krupa on Rod Stewart's "(I Know) I'm Losing You," the steady groove on Jerry Lee Lewis' version of "Drinking Wine Spo-Dee O'Dee," the effective simplicity of The Rolling Stones "It's Only Rock 'n' Roll," and the understated funk of The Who's "Eminence Front," and you'll have a pretty clear picture of what a marvelous drummer Kenney Jones is, and has been since the crazy days of mid-60's Mod England.

As a charter member of the Small Faces, Kenney experienced teen idol worship in England, and in the revamped Faces with Ron Wood and Rod Stewart, tasted U.S. stardom for the first time in the early to mid-70's. After The Faces burned themselves out in an alcoholic haze, Kenney retreated to the relative security of the London session scene, where he gained even more respect as an outstanding studio player, working with the abovementioned Jerry Lee Lewis, Joan Armatrading, Chuck Berry, The Stones, and The Who. And in November 1978, he was asked to join The Who after the death of his friend Keith Moon. The Who apparently never even considered anyone else for the job except Kenney. He accepted the gig, and worked as a full-fledged member until their end in 1983. Since then, The Who have gotten back together for special occasions, like the Live Aid concert and most recently, for the British Music Awards show, where they were given a special award celebrating their twenty-fifth anniversary.

Kenney, an only child, was born in Stepney, in the east end of London on September 16, 1948, the son of Sam and Violet Jones. Mr. Jones was a truck driver and Mrs. Jones was a housewife. The east end is the roughest, poorest area of London, and Kenney was a young hooligan who was not afraid to fight. At the age of twelve, he and a friend began washing cars for extra money and one day while cleaning a car, they decided to form a skiffle group. Kenney's instrument of choice was not drums, but the banjo. However, when he went to look at a banjo at a music store, the last one had been sold that day.

By then, Kenney had gone through the normal phase of banging on biscuit tins and other objects. One of his friends had an old drum at home that Kenney began playing with, and suddenly the realization hit him that drums were the right instrument.

JONES

KENNEY JONES

"I pride myself on playing an accoustic instrument and I think that to jump straight in on electric drums is wrong."

■

ON BRITISH TELEVISION WITH THE SMALL FACES, CIRCA 1965. KENNEY STILL HAS THAT BLACK LUDWIG KIT.

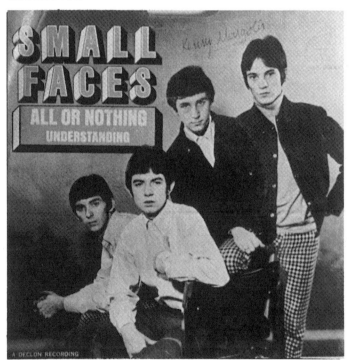

THE EXTREMLY RARE PICTURE SLEEVE FOR THE SMALL FACES' "ALL OR NOTHING", 1966. KENNEY IS THIRD FROM LEFT.

"I took to it like a duck to water," Kenney explained. "That was it!"

Now that he had decided to learn drums, acquisition of a kit was the next step. After trying out an inexpensive set at a music store and discussing price, Kenney rode the bus back home, "borrowed" ten pounds from his mother's purse, went back and put a deposit on the set, with an agreement that it would be paid for on a hire/purchase plan, the English equivalent of time payments. Upon returning home, he was severely reprimanded by his mother, who instructed him not to tell his father. That evening, the salesman brought the drums to the Jones household and set them up while Kenney's father stood by, dumbstruck. The salesman played a jazz beat on the snare with brushes, handed them to Kenney and said, "Now you do it." Nervous and fully aware that if he flubbed, his father would order the drums out of the house, he took a deep breath and repeated what the salesman had done well enough that Mr. and Mrs. Jones agreed to let him keep the kit, partially in hopes that it would help cure Kenney's gang land attitude.

Now that he had a drumset, Kenney played obsessively. He would get up at 6:30 in the morning and play until he went to school, waking the neighborhood. At lunch time, he would go home and play until it was time to return. After school, he'd play straight through, sometimes until 10:00 in the evening.

"My parents helped me out a lot. Playing drums in a house is very difficult in a built-up area, so all the neighbors used to complain. I drove them crazy, but my parents were very good about it and it's paid off."

Kenney is a completely self-taught drummer who learned by listening and watching other drummers. He was invited to take drum lessons at school, but turned down the offer, as it appeared boring at the time. Later, he regretted not having that formal musical education.

He spent much time playing along with records like "12th Street Rag" and other jazz and blues records. In Kenney's own words, he learned to play by listening to a lot of "fuddy-duddy" music. Along the way, he got turned on by Rock 'n' Roll as well.

The first time Kenney played in front of an audience, was with a jazz group at a local pub. Underage, he went in and watched the drummer for three or four weeks, until the man asked him to sit in. Petrified, he sat behind the drums and kept simple jazz time with no problem. It was his first time working with other musicians and he never forgot the incredible feeling of playing with a group of people. The bartender pulled him aside and told him his younger brother was a guitarist who wanted to form a group. The brother turned out to be Ronnie Lane and after the two chatted a bit, they decided to get a band together. Hooking up with two other fellows, they named themselves The Outcasts and got into the music of Chuck Berry, Duane Eddy, early Beatles, and of course, The Shadows, England's number one instrumental group. The Outcasts worked the circuit and eventually secured a residency at a local pub, where they earned about forty pounds for a weekend, money that helped Kenney pay for his hire/purchase drums.

The Outcasts soon changed personnel and took the name The Pirates. Ronnie Lane decided to forsake rhythm guitar for the bass, so he and Kenney went back to the music shop where Kenney had bought his drumkit and made the acquaintance of another salesman at the store.

"We went in there and this over-helpful little kid was helping us and he was a really powerful character. We hung around the shop all afternoon playing with him and he got the sack, so we invited him to come to the gig that night. That turned out to be Steve Marriott. We had him come up onstage and play and he broke the piano. We got thrown out of the pub and lost our residency. We had a great time though and Ronnie and I left the band that night. That was the beginning of The Small Faces. Once we formed the band, we toured without a name. A young lady gave us the name eventually and we laughed at it, but it stuck."

By then, Kenney had quit school and gotten a couple of jobs, first as a stevedore at the docks loading pickle barrels and then making guitar and bass amplifiers. When he was fired from the second job, he took an entirely different course of action.

"We decided to turn professional. We went up and down the country knocking on people's doors. Peter Stringfellow had a club called the MoJo in Sheffield and we played there and built up a following. That's where Don Arden, The Small Faces future manager, heard about us. He came to see us and offered us everything. Six weeks later we had a record in the charts and that was called 'Whatcha' Gonna' Do About It'."

Kenney was only sixteen when the record hit. Television appearances followed soon also. Although The Small Faces signed a percentage deal with Arden, in the end, they saw very little money. The group became synonymous with the Mod movement much in the same way The Who did, and it wasn't long before Kenney and all the group members, Marriott, Lane, and keyboardist Ian McLagan, had charge accounts at every smart boutique on Carnaby Street. They had an image to maintain and Don Arden apparently spared no expense in keeping that image intact.

In a matter of weeks, The Small Faces were instant pop stars. The hits kept coming: "Sha-La-La-La-Lee," "My Mind's Eye," "All Or Nothing," and "Itchycoo Park," which was their only US hit. Kenney found himself the recipient of the usual Sixties fan hysteria.

"At first it was very exciting and quite flattering, and like everyone, you end up with a small large head for a couple of months until the reality hits you and it becomes quite unnerving and you wind up not liking it at all. Now I've learned to deal with it in the best way I know how."

Although he was given much freedom (and has with all the groups he's been in), Kenney went through the normal jitters in the studio.

"I got the usual nervous twitches that everyone gets. Everyone runs through the song and learns it and it goes well, but as soon as the red light goes on, you tense up slightly. I've learned to overcome it somewhat, but it still seems to stay with you.'

The relentless touring of the Sixties was a tiring yet rewarding experience.

"It was very hard work back then. In those days, we'd sometimes play for twenty minutes or forty minutes. We'd play Manchester one evening, and a bit later would drive very fast to somewhere like Leeds and do another concert, but yes, it was a very exciting time."

KENNEY LOOKING MISCHIEVOUS IN THIS VINTAGE SMALL FACES PHOTO.

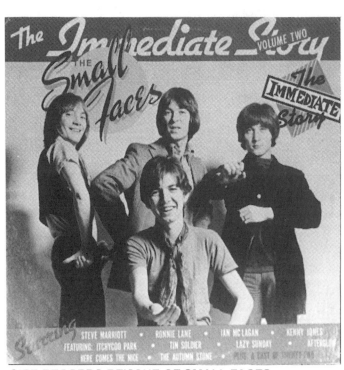

SIRE RECORDS REISSUE OF SMALL FACES MATERIAL. KENNEY APPEARS TO BE DIRECTING TRAFFIC.

KENNEY JONES

KENNEY IN THE DRIVER'S SEAT.

"I got the usual
nervous twitches that
everyone gets.
Everyone runs through
the song and learns it
and it goes well,
but as soon as the red
light goes on,
you tense up slightly."

■

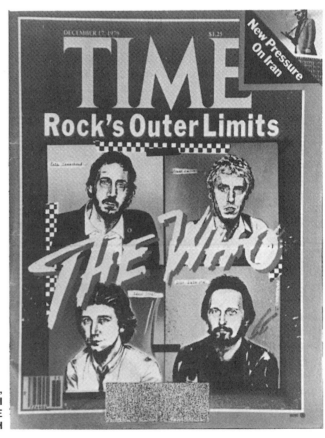

**KENNEY MAKES THE COVER OF *TIME* MAGAZINE,
DECEMBER 17, 1979, SHORTLY AFTER THE CINCINNATTI
TRAGEDY WHERE ELEVEN WHO FANS WERE
TRAMPLED TO DEATH**

"I think the music we made in the Sixties holds up quite well today. The creativity of The Small Faces was brilliant. I think the band was great. The Faces were different...a very partyish-type band. All the ingredients, the musicians, in those bands, were sensational. Steve Marriot had a great voice and his and Ronnie Lane's ability to write great songs was important. With The Faces, I also thought Rod's (Stewart) voice was sensational...Woody was a great musician. The Faces actually didn't play consistently that much because we were all drunk most of the time. The recording techniques are better today, but if you listen to an early record now, you'll find a simpler approach. Everyone plays those records to this day, so I guess they hold up well."

As The Small Faces grew more successful, they drastically cut their touring down to the point where they spent most of their time in the recording studio, eager to explore the many possibilities that environment offered. After the release of the *Ogdens Nut Gone Flake* LP, a concept record, the group, by now disillusioned with the many business hassles that sometimes go along with the music world, split up when Steve Marriott left to form Humble Pie. The remarks he made to the British music press about forming a new group with "better musicians" confused and hurt Kenney and the rest of the band. About six months later, Kenney, Ronnie, and Ian decided to reform, with Ron Wood, just out of The Jeff Beck Group (where he played bass) on guitar. Beck vocalist Rod Stewart used to come to rehearsals just to listen and at Kenney's insistence, Rod joined up and completed the new group. With new personnel came a name change and The Small Faces became The Faces.

This writer had the good luck to see The Faces at their musical prime in Charlottesville, Virginia, in the spring of 1971. To this day, I am hard-pressed to think of a more exciting live band! Rod Steward had two mic's, one on either side of the stage, and spent most of the concert running back and forth from one to the other, usually just in time to sing the next verse. The bottles of Jack Daniels bourbon and Mateus wine that each member brought out were drained dry by the end of the show and yes, the music was slightly ragged, but the energy level was incredible, especially when Ron Wood, cigarette dangling out of his mouth or from the headstock of his custom-made Zemaitis guitar, would launch into a jam that was most likely based around a chunky chord sequence, very often with distinct Chuck Berry leanings. And what was Mr. Jones doing while all this was going on? Kenney was laying down some of the loosest drums extant. He had to, for The Faces were the musical epitome of looseness. Some might say sloppy, but that was one of the attributes that made them what they were, an incredibly joyous, unpredictable Rock 'n' Roll band.

By 1973, The Faces were popular enough to easily sell out large venues like Madison Square Garden. Ronnie Lane left to go solo, and was replaced by Japanese bassist Tetsu Yamauchi. The live LP that came out at this time, *Coast To Coast/Overture And Beginners* is a pretty good example of The Faces live sound, although it was never quite the same after Ronnie left.

Rod Stewart had been releasing solo albums since his departure from Jeff Beck and had scored hits like "Maggie May," and "Every Picture Tells A Story." The plan was for Rod to record separately from The Faces, but the group would be backing him up on a few of his albums anyway, and it was inevitable that Rod would eventually go off on his own, which is what happened. In 1975, after Ron Wood agreed to go out in Mick Taylor's place with The Rolling Stones on a US tour, The Faces did one final farewell tour of the states, using Jesse Ed Davis as an added guitarist. The show I saw at Roosevelt Stadium in Jersey City that summer was good, but nothing compared to The Faces of four years prior. The magic was missing the sheer exuberance and craziness was gone. It was a band on its last legs and it showed. Woody went back and joined The Stones permanently, Rod launched his very lucrative solo career, and Kenney retreated to the saner environment of the recording studios. He had planned to stay with Rod and actually helped Stewart put his band together, but just before their first tour, Kenney decided he didn't want to be viewed as a member of a backup band, and left. This was when he began to make his name known as an in-demand session drummer.

After years of roadwork in two bands, Kenney took it easy for a while. A horse lover, he indulged his passion and rode and played polo quite a bit, doing session work whenever he felt like, for whomever he desired. When the opportunity to do both the Chuck Berry and Jerry Lee Lewis London session LP's availed itself, Kenney jumped at the chance to play with two of Rock 'n' Roll's founding fathers, although the Lewis sessions proved to be a bit unpredictable due to The Killer's irascible nature. And he also did some work with his old mates, The Who.

Kenney played on the first few Joan Armatrading albums and even did a session with a big band, led by his father-in-law at the time, band leader Tony Osbourne. For that session, Kenney was forced to read a chart, something he had never experienced before. With Osbourne's help, he pulled through the session with flying colors.

Although doing sessions was financially rewarding, Kenney realized he never intended to dedicate his life to it. Session work was just too much of a physical and mental strain. He wanted to be in a band again.

He was soon granted his wish.

On September 6, 1978, Kenney attended the British premier of *The Buddy Holly Story* and the party afterward, hosted by Paul and Linda McCartney. He chatted for a while with his friend, Keith Moon, mingled, had a couple of drinks and went home. The next day, the news was all over: Keith Moon had died of a drug overdose, a terrible accident. Although The Who were, of course, in a state of shock, within several weeks, they decided to offer the gig to Kenney, who, after some serious thought, accepted the job as Keith's replacement.

Immediately, Kenney became the object of much speculation among the world rock press. How did it feel to fill the shoes of the seemingly irreplaceable Moon? Would he copy Keith's style and licks? Did he think the sound of The Who would now change with him in the driver's seat?

Kenney simply told everyone that he would never, ever try and copy Keith in any way and he intended to be himself. That is exactly what the rest of The Who expected of him, no more, no less.

KENNEY JONES

With the press activity temporarily silenced, Kenney had one week over the Easter holiday to learn about thirty Who songs. Although he was friends with the band and had done sessions with them, he was hard pressed to learn their stage act. But the pressure was on, and as their first live show at The Rainbow in London proved, Kenney came through like a champion.

The Who's sound did change with Kenney. Keith Moon was such an unpredictable drummer, that Pete Townshend and John Entwhistle were constantly on guard, lest the songs fall apart on-stage due to Moon's excesses or timing inaccuracies. Kenney was completely opposite, a simple straight-on player, and though he was forced to begin using a larger drumkit and to duplicate some of Keith's parts, Kenney brought a stability to The Who's music live, that it had never known before. What came out of the studio, however, was a whole 'nother story.

Face Dances was the first Who album to feature Kenney, and the first for their new record label, Warner

As far as his personal life, Kenney recently moved to an old estate in Surrey, England. He lives with a woman named Jane Andrew, their six month old daughter, Casey, and Kenney's two sons from his previous marriage, Dillon, 16, and Jesse, 11. When he's not occupied with his horses, Kenney enjoys listening to a broad spectrum of music, from Eric Clapton to Willie Nelson.

"The only kind of music I don't like is punk."

Kenney is also very keen on financial investment.

"I've always been interested in financial things. In other words, business, the stock market, property. It's all very well earning money, but you've got to try and do something with it when you get it, so I quite enjoy dabbling in that area whenever I can. It's not my career, being a musician and playing in a band is."

A serious car accident in 1984 left Kenney with pulled ligaments, nerve endings, and numbness in two fingers and the thumb of his left hand.

"You don't overcome physical or mental problems until you go through them. It helps you to understand

Asked whether he had any advice for young drummers, Kenney jokingly replied, "Yeah, don't take up drums! (laughs)"

Brothers. To the band as a whole and many of their older fans, this writer included, it was an artistic failure. Pete Townshend, who for years, had given his best material to The Who, now kept it for his solo albums. The Who just didn't sound like The Who anymore. The songs were lightweight, with exception of John Entwhistle's, which were almost heavy metal. Kenney's drums were not well recorded or mixed, and his playing hardly seemed inspired. To be fair, he was going through a painful divorce at the time and was constantly being interrupted during the sessions. Naturally, this affected his musical output in an adverse way. Today, *Face Dances* is easily obtainable in the cut-out bins, as is its follow-up, *It's Hard*, which was a bit harder-edged, but in the end proved to be The Who's swan song. There certainly were moments on both albums when Kenney kicked the band in the der-riere, but they were few and far between.

In 1983, The Who completed one final go-round, a long American farewell tour, that ended on December 20th, in Toronto. No one in the band except Pete was giving the press any real answers. Perhaps they would reform to do an occasional short tour, or the odd one-nighter. John, Roger, and Kenney wanted The Who to continue, but Pete, tired and worn out after so many years of punishing tours, had had enough. Shortly after the Farewell Tour was over, Pete Townshend announced he was officially leaving The Who.

With The Who now history, Kenney once again was able to enjoy the fruits of his hard work. He built a studio in his barn and installed a twenty-four track recording facility with intentions of exploring the use of his voice. Several years earlier, he had done some singing on a couple of tunes he liked, Jackson Browne's "Ready Or Not," and Mentor Williams' "So High." Much to his delight and amazement, Kenney discovered that indeed, he *could* sing. Although these recordings have never been released (or completed for that matter), Kenney does intend to get them out on the market eventually.

your own instrument. But you must overcome them. The car crash has kept me off the road for nearly four years. A drunk driver smashed into us and I now bear the scars. It still hurts on rainy days and if I move quickly, I never know when the pain is going to come back. I've learned to cope with it and play, and it seems to be OK."

"When I've taken the odd little 'thing,' like booze or anything like that, it definitely inhibits one's playing, so I don't drink anymore. Any kind of drug or thing like that will affect your playing. You should not play with any drug, because the buzz of being straight has been forgotten about and it's fantastic. You do play much better."

Did Kenney ever think The Who would tour or perform again?

"No, I think The Who is finished. I know Roger, John, and I would do it, but Pete just can't handle it. I think Roger and Pete want to work together again, be it an album or whatever, but they won't call it The Who unless they get pressure from a record company."

And would The Faces get back together for a tour as has been rumored?

"We actually did that a couple of years ago when we did a show and raised money for Multiple Sclerosis and Ronnie Lane. Rod was there and it was fun, but there was no tour. I'd do it , because I love playing with those people."

At the moment, Kenney is putting a new band together with Paul Rodgers, former vocalist with Free, Bad Company, and most recently, The Firm. Kenney couldn't go into great detail about this new band when we talked, but he was very excited about their future.

"I would like to be remembered for being just me: A simple, honest approach to drumming. I have no selfish ambitions, but enjoy my instrument and play it to the best of my ability."

Asked whether he had any advice for young drummers, Kenney jokingly replied, "Yeah, don't take up drums!" (laughs)

EQUIPMENT

As is the case with almost all drummers, Kenney, as a child, was a "compulsive tapper" who amused himself by beating on biscuit tins, boxes or anything else that approximated the sound of a real drum. At twelve, as mentioned, he had the luck of having a friend who had an old drum that Kenney had access to. That was all it took. He knew what he wanted to do from then on.

His first kit, the one acquired on the hire/purchase agreement, was an Olympic set that consisted of snare, rack, and floor toms, and a bass drum in white marine pearl. According to Kenney, they were all standard sizes, and the set was second hand. (The reader should be aware that sizes of drums is a subject that Kenney wastes very little time thinking about, so please don't expect too many specifics in this area, although sizes will be provided when they are known. He cares more for the sound of the drum than the dimensions.)

The cymbals that came with the Olympic set were substandard.

"They were atrocious and were made out of tin." Kenney's next set turned out to be a disaster.

"That was quite a weird time actually. I was looking for different things, and at that time, Trixon had brought out a drumkit that was a funny shape. Me being young and wanting to experiment, figured, 'I'll go buy that,' because it was different. The bass drum was shaped like a tank wheel (flat on the bottom!). It wasn't all round. If I can remember correctly, the toms were larger on top than the bottom. The top skin was one size and the shell reduced smaller on the bottom. I got this kit and it sounded awful! I bought it on impulse and when I played a few rock beats on it, all the lungs on the snare drum snapped, one by one. Everything broke on it, so I threw it away."

Having learned his lesson, Kenney next bought what he described as a "sensible" drumkit, a Ludwig set in silver sparkle, again, in standard sizes, most likely 9x13," and 16x16" toms, 22" bass drum, and 5x14" snare. He also had progressed to a better set of cymbals by this time. Kenney feels that his drumming improved greatly when he got this LAround the time of The Small Faces formation, Kenney traded in the silver sparkle Ludwig for another Ludwig set, this time in black. This kit was purchased second hand from Brian Bennett, the drummer in The Shadows. The sizes were 9x13," 16x16", 22," and most likely 5x14."

"I've still got that black drumkit. It's my favorite."

Kenney hooked up at this time with Paiste cymbals, who had asked him to endorse their products. He stayed with them for quite a few years. The first cymbal Paiste sent him was a huge 26" ride that he still has. Unfortunately, Kenney had a real problem with the Paiste cymbals breaking. He did not secure a drum endorsement deal with any one company during the Sixties.

"Premier and Ludwig were after me, but I was too confused to go with either of them. I thought I should go with Premier because they were English and I felt more loyal, but the American drums, the Ludwigs, were far superior, so I thought the easy way out was to pay for them myself and not get into squabbles."

Other Ludwig kits followed. With The Faces, Kenney primarily used two sets, either a natural maple kit, with three toms, one rack and two on the floor, snare and bass, or a custom-painted kit, with the same number of drums, but in a pink/black/white stripe pattern. This is the set pictured on the inner sleeve of the *Coast To Coast/Overture And Beginners* live LP. For studio work, Kenney preferred the maple Ludwigs. This set appears on the sleeve of the Jerry Lee Lewis *London Sessions* album, with what appears to be a Rogers bass drum mount Swiv-O-Matic cymbal holder.

Kenney also used a Premier kit with The Faces.

"I finally succumbed to Premier," he admitted. That set was most likely the same one rack tom/two floor toms configuration.

When Kenney joined The Who in 1978, it became necessary to use a much larger kit than he had ever had previously, due to the nature of The Who's music. His choice was again Premier, in gloss white, this time with six rack toms and one floor tom, with what looks to be a 24" bass drum, and all Premier hardware.

On the Who's Farewell Tour in 1983, Kenney switched over to Yamaha, and for the first time, appeared onstage with two bass drums. Many were fooled into thinking Kenney actually used the second bass drum. They were wrong. Its purpose was merely as a stand to hold up two toms and to balance out the set from a visual standpoint. The truth is, Kenney has never approved of the use of two bass drums, feeling that it throws the drummer off too much and clutters up the sound.

The black Yamaha Recording Custom set used on that tour was sized as follows: 8x8," 8x10," 8x12," 10x14," 16x16," and, 16x8" toms, 14x24" and 14x22" bass drums, and either 5 1/2x14" or 7x14" chrome snare drums. His cymbal setup was, 14" Paiste 2001 hi-hats, 21" China, 16" Zildjian crash, 14" Sabian crash, 17" Sabian ride, 16" Sabian crash, 16" Zildjian crash, and an 18" Zildjian Pang. All the hardware was Yamaha 9000 series.

"At that time, I felt that Yamaha was the best. This was around '82, I think. I realized that though they're a great kit, really magic, I felt like experimenting more and changing, so it looks like, at this stage, I'm going to go with a young company that's very old, in other words, Remo Drums. Remo makes all the skins for every single drum in the world, even Yamaha. They've just come out with a new drumkit and I think they need all the support and help they can get. Also, one of my main reasons for using them is because it's probably one of the cheapest kits on the market, so it's not out of reach for young drummers who are just starting out who want a nice kit. Certain drumkits are getting so overpriced, it's beyond the average kid on the street to save up and go out and purchase a kit. Remo have new ideas like quick-release skins, and I believe they're going to get better, and better, and better, so eventually, they'll be up in the top five. I have no doubts."

Kenney prefers smaller cymbals.

"I don't like them when they ring on for too long. I like them to make their point and finish. Paiste were great in

KENNEY JONES

the Sixties and early Seventies, then I went into Zildjian, and in the Eighties, I switched to Sabian, which I currently endorse at the moment."

Today, Kenney uses drumsticks that are custom-made to his specifications, but it wasn't always like this.

"I was so confused about sticks in the early days, that I went through a stage where I used Ringo Starr sticks, because they were nice and fat and wouldn't break. I've never liked thin sticks, because they made the drums sound thin, especially rimshots. I use a fairly hefty stick. The ones I've been using for years are my own brand of drumsticks that I have made. They're not on the market. They're just for me."

Kenney used Evans heads in the Sixties, but switched to various Remo heads in the early Seventies and has been with them ever since.

He does not like to muffle his drums in any way, but sometimes is forced to do so when recording. British jazz drumming great, the late Kenny Clare, taught him to use a full pack of cigarettes on the snare, taped loose enough to lift off the head slightly when the drum was hit and quickly come down again to dampen the head. Kenney said this method works quite well.

He is not surprised by Japan's current domination of the drum market.

"In the early days, Ludwig made the finest drums in the world, in my opinion. I did hear that in the late Sixties, early Seventies, Japan bought out America's supply of weathered wood and that's why they have turned out great copies of guitars and drums. They had the supply of all the good wood. Ludwig, by this time, was getting into more and more mass production and so was everybody, but they were forced to use material that was available to them which was improperly-seasoned wood."

"The overall quality of drums today is excellent. There isn't really a dodgy drumkit on the market. They're all pretty good actually. I maintain that if a drum is round and it's got the right skin on it, it's going to sound just as good as any other bloody drum. All this business with 'It's thicker' and 'Big two inch ply' and 'This layer and that layer' is a lot of old bollocks.'

"I remember the sound of older drums being good and simple. Older drums were basically a smaller, more simple drumkit, which makes you play simpler. It's a far more honest approach to drumming. Now you've got massive drumkits in different sizes and it makes you want to play them all. I think the craftsmanship on the older drumsets was good. The old ones look like classic 50's cars, and I prefer their look to these modern ones. I still have some of those old kits."

IN CONCERT WITH THE WHO, 1979.

ADDENDUM:

August, 1988

It was reported in the current issue of *Rolling Stone* magazine this week, that Kenney Jones has officially left The Who, who are busy in the preliminary stages of recording their first album of new material in several years. The LP marks the band's twenty-fifth anniversary. There is no decision yet whether The Who will tour in support of the album.

Likewise, there was no mention made of a replacement, permanent or otherwise for Kenney, who is preoccupied in putting together a new band with vocalist Paul Rodgers.

No other information is available yet on this mysterious new band.

STYLE AND TECHNIQUE

The essence of Kenney Jones' drumming style is basic simplicity. This is not to imply that he's a retiring, shy player. Quite the contrary, he's one of the most muscular, energy-filled rock drummers in the business.

An admitted fan of Al Jackson, the great R&B drummer, Kenney also admires the playing of Gene Krupa, Buddy Rich, British jazzman Kenny Clare, Carmine Appice, Charlie Watts, Bobby Elliott, Ringo Starr, Steve Gadd, Andy Newmark, Simon Philips, Steve Ferrone, and Simon Kirke, former drummer with Free and Bad Company.

Kenney has an overall relaxed feel and is capable of making his fellow musicians groove without effort, one of the true signs of an outstanding drummer. Although straightforward is an oft-used adjective, it fits the Jones method of drumming, as do uncluttered, uncomplicated, and reliable. And he's a marvelous timekeeper, one of those fortunate individuals with nearly perfect natural time.

Kenney has used matched grip for years. To generalize that British drummers prefer this style of holding sticks is not inaccurate.

When queried about the drummer's role in music and his philosophy on drumming, Kenney replied, "A drummer should know where he sits in the band, in other words, his place in the band should be complimentary to the rest of the band, and not try to lead in any way, or put in fill-ins that don't fit just because he's excited. He should just know his place and be a drummer in a unit. Teamwork and simplicity are really important."

"Young players should have an alert mind and be sensitive to the other band members. Attitude affects performance severely. You've got to feel good to play good. We're all musicians and we play our emotions, so, you can't actually get behind the drumkit or any instrument if you've just had an argument with your wife or anybody, because it reflects on your performance and it comes across. The idea is to stay as calm as possible and don't let any bad vibes penetrate you before a performance. Or, just discipline yourself to shut these things out."

"I've always thought that American drummers had the slight edge over English drummers. Apart from America being a remarkable, huge country in comparison with England, we were always starved for music. There was a lot more happening in America, so people could be influenced more. For drummers, there was a lot more jazz going on. You've got New Orleans and that influence and you could see some of the all-time greats, while here, you have to wait years to see anybody. In technical ability. American drummers have the edge."

Kenney feels that exercise is very important for drummers.

"I do exercise and think it's essential if you've got a long tour coming up, or anything, really. I always work out in a gym or jog to get my lungs working. Breathing is very important if you're a drummer. I used to drink and play, but I don't anymore. I find that I'm more aware and my performance is better."

He also gave up smoking cigarettes years ago as well.

As far as mental preparation for drumming, Kenney had this to say. "It's a basic inward discipline, trying to get your concentration span up and trying to sharpen up. Playing drums is one thing, but remembering routines and bits and pieces like that are all very important. I only practice drums when I feel like playing. It's not really practice, it's more just me playing about behind the drums really. I try to play as often as I can just to keep sharp. I'm always on the lookout for new licks and fills. If I feel like playing, I'll play for five minutes or an hour, whenever I can."

"For young drummers, I'd recommend they broaden their horizons and outlooks and try to remember in this world of technical instruments and drum machines and electric drumkits what a bloody drumkit is! A real drumkit. An acoustic drumkit. I pride myself on playing an acoustic instrument and I think that to jump straight in on electric drums is wrong. You must understand the rudiments of natural drumming in order to eventually use drum machines and all kinds of electronic equipment. I don't see what's wrong with using the electronics with a real drumkit. One or two is OK, but not a whole kit. I get fed up listening to all this 'bing/boong' (imitates sound of electronic drums)."

Kenney personally uses no electronic drums or drum machines of any sort although he is used to working with a click track in the studio when it's needed.

He disdains the use of an oversize drumset (although he was professional enough to realize that he had to use one with The Who), feeling that a four or five piece kit makes a drummer play with more imagination and with greater precision. Too many drums sometimes make for busier playing, and that is something Kenney finds unnatural.

In his interview in *Modern Drummer* magazine several years ago, Kenney was quoted as saying to your players, "If you want to play drums, go out and buy yourself a standard drumkit—a bass drum, a top tom tom; a Charlie Watts kit, basically—and practice. Once you learn to play that, then you'll know what drums you want after that. You do not need anymore than that anyway."

KENNEY JONES

SELECTED CUTS

"All Or Nothing" (RCA Victor 45 #47-8949)-One of the greatest Small Faces tunes and a very rare picture sleeve single "All Or Nothing" is a real raver, and Kenney kicks the band effectively on the chorus, with very well-placed accents and splashy ride cymbal work. His fills are the personification of youthful abandon.

"Understanding" (Pride LP# PRD-0014, Small Faces, *History Of The Small Faces*)-Kenney opens this one up with a one bar intro and executes some very imaginative and aggressive one and two bar breaks that show a similarity in style to Keith Moon, which is not surprising, owing to the fact that The Small Faces basic approach early on was greatly inspired by The Who. The drums on "Understanding," as well as on many other older Small Faces tracks, were well-recorded and brought forward in the mix, a rare occurrence for the mid-Sixties.

"(I Know) I"m Losing You" (Mercury LP#SRM-1-606, Rod Stewart, *Every Picture Tells A Story*)-Rod Stewart usually used some or all of The Faces on his solo albums and this cut contains the whole band. Without a doubt, it's Kenney's finest moment on record and the closest he's ever come to taking an extended solo. His use of dynamics is masterful. The basic time pattern is eighth notes on the hi-hat and two and four on the snare, with a cymbal crash on the four of each measure leading up to the drum break. The break itself is mostly sixteenths, with frequent accents on the first beat of each sixteenth grouping. Guitarist Ron Wood adds chunky barre chords for the first section. The insistent tambourine is probably played by Rod, and it accompanies the entire break, which can only be described as rhythmically intense. With added echo, the drums sound positively huge. When Kenney pulls back into the chord structure, he switches to four beats on the snare and the tempo picks up noticeably. I dare you to listen to this incredible drumming performance and sit still.

"Maggie May" (Mercury LP#SRM-1-609, Rod Stewart, *Every Picture Tells A Story*)-Kenney's playing on "Maggie May" has been described as a "good example of barrel-house drumming," and that's true, but it's really a very loose, rolling drum track, with Kenney playing quarter notes on a partially open hi-hat, with fills that are equally loose and uncomplicated. It's beauty is in its lack of pretense.

"You're My Girl (I Don't Want To Discuss It)" (Bootleg LP, Rod Stewart And The Faces, *Plynth*)-A very energetic performance by Kenney makes this one of the best cuts on this long-unavailable bootleg album, released in the early Seventies. It's now a very rare collectible among Faces fans and sounds as if it was recorded very early on during the group's life. Listen to Kenney's fills, particularly the ones that interplay flams on the snare with the bass drum, if you're lucky enough to find a copy of this record.

"Too Bad" (Warner Brothers LP#BS-2574, The Faces, *A Nod Is As Good As A Wink To A Blind Horse*)-"Too Bad" is a rocking Chuck Berryish tune, the type of song The Faces played so well. Kenney boots the tempo along nicely, goes into a slower time pattern on the bridge, and races into high gear on the ride-out, with hesitation accents that ritard slightly. All around, a fine drum track.

"It's Only Rock 'n' Roll" (Rolling Stone LP#79101, The Rolling Stones, *It's Only Rock 'n' Roll*)-"It's Only Rock 'n' Rol"l is a fitting example of Kenney's honest simplicity. His admitted debt to Al Jackson is evident, and according to Kenney, who sat in on the session because Charlie Watts was unavailable, many people thought it was Charlie playing. Their styles *are* somewhat similar. It also proves another significant fact; Should Charlie Watts ever leave The Stones, Kenney would be a serious candidate to replace him.

"You" (Warner Brothers LP#HS-3516, The Who, *Face Dances*)-*Face Dances* was the first Who album with Kenney and it was largely a disappointment, not only to the group's fans, but to the band members themselves. *You* is a John Entwhistle composition, and one of the only times Kenney really let go on the record. His time-keeping is rock solid, the accents are perfectly slotted in, and his fills on the chorus work admirably. *Face Dances* might have been a better album had there been more tracks like this.

"Eminence Front" (Warner Brothers LP#23731-1, The Who, *It's Hard*)-It's a funky Kenney Jones on this tune, one of the better tracks from the final Who LP. "Eminence Front" remains a popular and highly-aired FM radio staple to this day. Kenney lays down a subtle, solid groove without being overbearing. He sticks to the hi-hat, snare, and bass. Strangely, some accused The Who of "going disco" when this was released.

"Cry If You Want" (Warner Brother LP#23731-1, The Who, *It's Hard*)-This is unlike anything Kenney played with The Who, with its very militaristic, rolling snare drum routine that is almost Bolero-like in its quiet intensity. "Cry If You Want," the last cut on *It's Hard*, ends The Who's long and distinguished career in a fitting way: with snarling feedback and slashing power chords. A perfect climax.

KENNEY JONES TODAY

Kenney Jones wrapped up his tenure with The Who in 1983 after the Live Aid concert under a cloud of suspicion. It was widely reported that The Who were less than happy with Jones's drumming, particularly on the band's two final albums, *Face Dances* and *It's Hard*. Singer Roger Daltrey, never one to keeps his opinions to himself, was publicly critical of Jones on several occasions. It was also rumored that Kenney was on the verge of "getting the sack" at the time of Townshend's defection from the band and their final tour.

Kenney commented, "The band split up actually. We went back and did Live Aid in '83 and by that time, I was working with Paul Rodgers in The Law.

"I did some work with Pete on his *Empty Glass* album and there was the track "Rough Boys" that should have been a Who song, but Pete was more concerned about saving good songs for his solo projects. He was really messed up with booze and drugs at the time too. When The Who needed good songs, he withheld his best stuff. Roger Daltrey missed Keith and wished he would just walk through the door and rejoin the band. Nobody will ever be right for The Who. Keith Moon couldn't be replaced. I didn't even want the fucking gig at first, but they talked me into it. Keith was a very good friend of mine and I was with him the night he died. Also at the time, I was going through a divorce and Roger was chummy with my ex-wife, which made things a little sticky.

"I had no problems with John Entwhistle or Pete, in fact I recorded a song with Pete called 'Hard To Hang On To' not long ago that he posted on his web site."

To sum it up, it is this author's opinion that Kenney Jones has always been and remains a hard-hitting, solid rock drummer, and there's no point dwelling on rumors and hearsay. Given The Who's penchant for chaos and airing their grievances publicly, life with the band must have been difficult.

Kenney does manage to get in a swipe at The Who in the song "Where Are You?" from The Jones Gang's new CD. "There will be more on The Jones Gang later. The song was written in jest, but it is poignant and tells the truth. I think this is what The Who should have been doing musically when I was with them. Who fans will like it."

What did Kenney think of *Face Dances* and *It's Hard*?

"They're awful. The band hired Bill Szymczyk to produce and he had worked with The Eagles and other California bands. My drums sounded like cardboard boxes. Just terrible. I was the new boy in the band and didn't want to make waves. I should have spoken up. I wound up with Eagles drum sounds on those records."

When his time with The Who ended, Kenney teamed up with singer Paul Rodgers, late of Free, Bad Company and The Firm, in a new band called The Law. One tune called "Breaking The Law" was a minor hit and the band had some MTV and radio success with it, but The Law never went further, remaining a one-shot studio project.

And what about a Faces reunion?

"We get together about every seven or eight years and do something. There's always a reunion gig going on. We did an appearance at the BPI awards show a while back. I did a club gig with Woody [guitarist Ron Wood] not long ago and Mick Jagger jumped up and sang a few. I see Rod occasionally. Mac [Faces keyboard player Ian McLagen] shows up too, so yes, there's always the possibility that we'll play together. Woody and Mac played on my new album. Woody has been very supportive and did the cover art. If The Faces want to do a tour someday, I'm all for it, but my new band is of more importance right now. As far as Rod's new crooning style, I give him credit for reinventing himself and singing standards. I like some of that music, but I think he needs to get a pair of jeans on and sing some rock 'n' roll again."

The Jones Gang was wrapping up a short promotional tour in the USA, doing TV appearances, radio, and in-store "unplugged" concerts, when Kenney and I spoke. The Jones Gang's music is mainstream rock with a modern edge and the band includes singer/songwriter Robert Hart, who was with a later version of Bad Company, and bassist Rick Wills, a longtime veteran of the British rock world. Their first CD, *Any Day Now*, had just been released when we talked. The disc, which carries a low list price of $9.98, appears on a new label, AAO Music's Reality Records, an arm of the TransWorld retail record chain in the US. TransWorld operates the FYE store group. Kenney is excited about his new band, the record and their business arrangement. He considers The Jones Gang to be the best musical project he's been involved with in a long time.

"By signing with Reality, what we've done is eliminate the middleman. Traditional record companies are folding left and right and don't have the money anymore to do proper promotion, plus it's so hard to get a record deal now. Reality is giving us promotional support, plus TV, radio spots and much more. We're getting everything we need from them. It's a brave new venture, a new paradigm you might say, and we are privileged to be part of it."

As far as equipment, Kenney is still using Yamaha drums, which he has endorsed for years. In the late Eighties, Kenney was interested in Remo drums, but found them to be of poor quality.

"We tried them out, but they fell apart really easily. They were very poorly made. The shells were of a composite material and the lugs weren't even lugs at all. They don't make them anymore."

KENNEY JONES'S CURRENT PROJECT, THE JONES GROUP.

His current Yamaha set was custom-made to his specs. Kenny is also a Sabian cymbal endorser and believes he was their very first signing.

Kenney has been working on his autobiography for about fifteen years and expects to have it on the market next year.

"It's not just about me as a drummer. Of course, all my musical activities are in there. It starts when I popped out into this world and takes in my early life and more. I did other things before I became a working drummer." Kenney would not divulge the title.

With his financial future secure, Kenney, always the avid horseman and polo player, opened Hurtwood Park Polo Country Club in Surrey, England. The facility started as a private enterprise, but went public after a short time, for polo enthusiasts and the country-club set. Hurtwood also offers catering and hosting for private parties and corporate affairs. Although Kenney is the owner, he spends literally no time whatsoever attending to club business.

"You might say it's a hobby gone out of control. I originally set it up for me, my son, who's a professional polo player, and for our friends, but we decided to go public. I've hired people to manage it for me. I don't spend any time overseeing things. The press has tried to make me out as being some kind of country squire, but I'm still a music squire!"

DON'T LET THE INNOCENT EXPRESSION FOOL YOU! KEITH IN 1967.

KEITH MOON

"MY GOD, WHO WAS THAT MADMAN IN THE TARGET SWEATSHIRT?"

IT IS SPRING, 1 9 6 5

•

An impressionably young fourteen year old drummer is watching *Shindig*, one of several rock shows of its type, created by television moguls to cash in on the lucrative teen market. The clean cut emcee introduces a new band from England called The Who. The Who? What kind of name is that for a band? Oh well. Might as well see what they're all about. The singer has blonde hair and looks exceedingly surly. The guitarist has a huge nose and whips his arm around the strings of his Rickenbacker guitar like an out of control windmill. The bassist stands there looking bored. But the drummer! He's attacking his Ludwig set with a wild, reckless abandon never seen before. How does he hit those things so hard and fast? All the while he's pummelling the drums, he sits there looking like a lost puppy, occasionally breaking into a fearful grimace. My God, who was that madman in the target sweatshirt?

The impressionable teenager's life is changed forever that night. His heart pounding, he practically falls over with excitement.

Next day, he tells all his friends at school about this new band called The Who. They all laugh at the group's silly name.

Spring turns to summer and the teenager learns the drummer's name is Keith Moon. This news is supplied by *Rave* magazine, a trendy British rock publication that has begun to filter into the states. The articles tell of equipment destruction, guitar feedback, uncompromising music, and the volatile nature of The Who's personalities. Two more appearances on *Shindig* follow, including a film of The Who at the Richmond Jazz Festival in England, in which Pete Townshend smashes his guitar. The kid can't believe his eyes. During the melee, Keith Moon continues to pound his drums with the power of a runaway train. What a show!

KEITH MOON

HIS EXPLOITS ARE THE STUFF OF LEGEND, AND UNFORTUNATLY, THE GENERAL PUBLIC PROBABLY REMEMBERS HIM MORE FOR HIS ANTICS THAN FOR HIS INCREDIBLE MUSICIANSHIP.

AN EARLY SHOT OF THE BEACHCOMBERS WITH A VERY YOUNG KEITH ON THE ROOF OF THE GROUP'S VAN. NOTE THE TRIXON FLOOR TOM.

ANGRY YOUNG MEN: THE WHO CIRCA 1964. KEITH IS ON THE LEFT.

The teenager, now a confirmed Who fanatic, goes down to the basement, puts his copy of *My Generation* on the stereo and plays along. At the end, he completely obliterates his beloved new set of champagne sparkle Slingerland drums, throwing them around the room, Zildjian cymbals and all. He joins a garage punk band and quickly gains a reputation for kicking over his drums and generally playing like a crazy man, something his schoolmates find amusing and just a little bit strange.

His once new drums begin to show the wear and tear of abuse. Cymbals are cracked, sticks and heads are broken constantly and hardware falls to pieces, much to the consternation of the teenager's father, who never understood his son's fascination with drums anyway.

Kindly permit me this indulgence, but the teen in question is this writer and no names, dates, or places have been changed to protect the guilty. What you have read is the truth. Keith Moon and The Who changed my life.

It is highly unlikely that any drummer, at any time, in any musical situation, ever attacked a set of drums with the blinding ferocity and no-holds-barred aggression of Keith Moon. During his long tenure with The Who until his tragic, accidental death in 1978, Keith distinguished himself not only for his drumming, but for his off-stage shenanigans as well. His exploits are the stuff of legend, and unfortunately, the general public probably remembers him more for his antics than for his incredible musicianship. People recall his uncontrollable humor, his penchant for smashing up drumsets, hotel rooms, TV sets, and cars. And they remember his personally destructive nature. Beneath all the lunacy was acute alcoholism, a serious problem with drugs, a failed marriage with a daughter he adored, extreme insecurity, and above all, the undeniable urge to make others laugh at him, a trait he exhibited since childhood.

It is impossible to write a straight piece on Keith from a drums-only point of view. The craziness of his life and everything that went with it are too much a part of the big picture, for Keith Moon seemed bigger than life to me and many others. At the end, as he was about to be replaced in The Who, after he had lost his musical edge, had gained weight, and then had valiantly tried to put his shattered life back together, he accidently took too many muscle relaxers called Heminevrin, and never woke up. It was a tragic loss.

Keith John Moon was born on August 23, 1947, to working class parents in the Wembley section of London, England. Reportedly a happy and active child, he delighted in boyhood pranks, much to the distress of some of his teachers.

At twelve, Keith joined the Sea Cadets, an organization not unlike the Boy Scouts. He took up the bugle and later switched to trumpet, which was abandoned once he sat behind a friend's drum set. Keith and the other boy would set up in a garage and play along with records. When the friend's parents decided to sell their son's drums, Keith's father bought them for about $50.00 and the young Moon was on his way. Although Alfred and Kitty Moon thought drums were a passing fad, Keith began to get gigs with local bands, playing weddings and some Rock 'n' Roll as well. He liked the American big band drummers with all their power and flash and also developed a passion for surf music. His first real band was a surf-styled group called The Beachcombers. At this juncture, he worked an endless series of day jobs, none of which worked out. It is safe to say that his parents, seeing his inability to cope with the workaday world, encouraged him to stick with the drums and further his musical. career.

Although The Beachcombers worked regularly, Keith grew tired of their material and outdated image. It was 1964 and groups like The Beatles and Rolling Stones were starting to make it, not only in England, but Stateside as well. Working on the same circuit of clubs, was a band from the working class Shepherd's Bush area of London, Known as The Detours, who were making a name for themselves with their rough interpretations of American R&B and blues. One of them was a skinny art student who played guitar without inhibition. The bassist was a schooled musician who just stood onstage looking detached, and the singer was a small, blonde tough guy, who kept the others in line with his fists. The drummer, who was older than the rest and didn't fit in, was fired, and stand-ins were being used until a permanent drummer could be found. All this sounded quite daring to the restless Moon. He knew they were a better band than The Beachcombers. so he decided, one way or another, to audition and get into The Detours. Keith followed them around for a while and convinced a friend to ask The Detours if he could sit in at a gig. After fortifying himself alcoholically, Keith, dressed like a gingerbread man in brown suit, shirt, tie, and shoes, took the stage and tore his way through the Junior Walker tune, "Roadrummer," and a couple of other songs. He broke the other drummer's bass drum pedal and hi-hat stand. Immediately, The Detours knew they'd found the right drummer. They invited Keith to play their next gig, never actually telling him he was to be a full-fledged member of the band. Years later, Keith would tell this story with the irony of a man who had just been "sitting in" for the last ten or twelve years. It was meant to be amusing, but it barely hid Moon's insecurity. He had joined The Detours first and foremost, as a fan of their music. He remained essentially that until his death.

With Keith on drums, The Detours *became* The Who.

The Mod phenomenon was exploding in England. It had started a couple of years earlier as a small movement among middle class kids who were obsessed with Ivy League clothes, short, neat hairstyles and hip, American music like Motown and Stax soul. Following some serious brawls between Mods and Rockers, the fad spread nationwide. Peter Meaden, at that time The Who's manager, decided his boys should be the musical standard-bearers of Mod. He convinced them to change their name to The High Numbers and secured them a one-shot deal with Fontana Records for one single. Two songs were written, "I'm The Face" b/w "Zoot Suit," both rip-offs of American blues tunes. One thousand copies were pressed, and despite Meaden's efforts to promote the record, it flopped. The band fired Meaden and changed their name back to The Who, picking up two new managers, Kit Lambert and Chris Stamp, who quickly got the boys a regular Tuesday night residency at London's Marquee Club. Using a clever marketing strategy to lure the Mods in, The Who began to pack the club on what

KEITH MOON

THE DRUMS WERE SMASHED, BASHED AND TRASHED ON A NIGHTLY BASIS, AND WERE OFTEN THROWN OFF THE STAGE.

left: KEITH IN ACTION, 1967

below: KEITH SHOWN HERE INSPECTING HIS EQUIPMENT.

was usually a dead night. The Who's stay lasted for six months and it was during this time at a gig at another club, the Railway Tavern, that their infamous destruction routine came about. The Railway had a low ceiling and Pete Townshend accidentally broke his guitar's headstock off after leaping into the air. So it wouldn't look contrived, Pete proceeded to destroy the guitar completely, amidst the enthusiastic cheers of the audience. People began coming around to see "the group who smashed their gear." Townshend was encouraged by The Who's management to continue the carnage and Keith, being a "great joiner-inner" in the words of Townshend, started kicking his drums over. The rowdy Mods, eager for violence, ate it up. The drums were smashed, bashed and trashed on a nightly basis, and were often thrown off the stage.

It's no wonder The Who ran up amazingly large debts that took them years to pay off. There were few corporate sugar daddies giving them free gear.

The Smash-'em-up routine ended in Europe in 1967, where The Who, now with several hit records under their belt, were established stars. But America still had to be conquered, for they only had a small (but loyal) following here. Was all the destruction just show, or was there more to it? According to Moonie, there was. He told *Melody Maker* the following.

"When Pete smashed his guitar it was because he was pissed off. When I smashed me drums, it was because I was pissed off. We were frustrated. You're working as hard as you can to get that song across, to get the audience by the balls, to make it an event. When you've done all that, when you've worked your balls off and given the audience all you can give and they don't give anything back, that's when the fucking instruments go."

The Who never hid their dirty laundry as most groups do. Their arguments were put on public display for all to see. Roger Daltrey fought with Pete for leadership of the group and seemingly, they all fought with Keith over his occasional erratic sense of tempo and his personal excesses. Even the usually taciturn John Entwistle raged at Moon over his timekeeping. As a bassist, he was in the unique position of having a lead guitarist who played like a rhythm guitarist and a drummer who played every song like a long drum solo from beginning to end. It's no wonder John developed his rock solid, lead bass style. In essence, John and Keith *were* the lead guitarists. Their records throughout their career reflected this fact, particularly on The Who's first few singles, which were among the best records they ever made. (See song descriptions and transactions later in this chapter)

In 1967, The Who set out for America, with the powerful Frank Barsalona Talent Agency booking them. They were given a space on a Murray the K show in New York and continued to destroy their instruments for American audiences, who were astounded by all the wreckage. Another tour opening for Hermans Hermits and The Blues Magoos followed and it was during this trip to the states that Keith pulled off one of his most famous acts of lunacy.

The occasion was Keith's twentieth birthday (although he told everyone it was his twenty-first), the place, the Flint, Michigan Holiday Inn. Decca Records, The Who's U.S. label, organized a party for him, complete with a five-tier cake. They rented the banquet room and naturally, there was a lot of drinking and loud noise. Eventually, other guests began to complain, so the manager came in and got nasty. Keith picked up what remained of the cake and shoved it right into the manager's puss. Not content with merely hitting the manager with the cake, Keith, well in the bottle, took off, with members of the band and road crew in hot pursuit. He grabbed a fire extinguisher, ran into the parking lot and began spraying cars with foam, inside and out. With everyone chasing him, Moonie dropped the fire extinguisher and dove into the pool. Unfortunately, there was no water in the pool and Keith landed flat on his face, breaking off a front tooth. Kit Lambert and Chris Stamp calmly paid for the damage and Keith was dragged off to a dentist, who was forced to operate on him without benefit of anesthetic, due to the high alcohol content in Keith's system.

And yes, Keith *did* drive a Rolls Royce into a swimming pool, and yes, he tried to ride a Hovercraft onstage at a Who concert, only to unceremoniously dump the craft and himself into a pond near the stage, a feat that required the police to extricate him from the muck. Let's not forget the time he blew the toilet off the wall of a fine hotel with an M-80 firecracker, or the numerous times he stripped naked in pubic, or his Hitler uniform, or the incidents of wearing women's clothes or bondage gear. The hotel rooms, the TV sets, the cars, were all paid for. The lunacy overshadowed the kindness Keith was capable of. He was fond of entering a pub and buying the house drinks for the entire evening. On another occasion, he picked up a homeless man off the street in London, bought him a fine dinner and booked a suite for the unfortunate man in a swank hotel. He paid cash for everything.

In 1969, The Who broke through to mass acceptance in America with success of the so-called rock opera, *Tommy*. Celebrated performances at Woodstock and the Metropolitan Opera in New York City, as well as regular tours in the states, cemented their reputation as the premier live rock band of their time. As Moon grew wealthy, his looning continued unabated. So did the booze and drugs.

A few times, he collapsed onstage. On one occasion, The Who were forced to bring a young man named Scott Halpin out of the audience to finish the concert on drums. Moon was unconscious backstage. Roger Daltrey and John Entwistle were adamant that Keith should be fired after the *Quadrophenia* tour in 1973, but they relented, mostly out of loyalty. Keith's drumming was marvelous on the classic *Who's Next* LP from 1971, but as the excesses continued, the quality of his work slid off. The *Quadrophenia* LP was the first evidence that Moon was beginning to slow down. The old urgency just wasn't there for the most part, although he did have a good go at "The Real Me." one of the best cuts from that LP.

Moon had married young, at nineteen, and his wife Kim had given birth to a daughter named Mandy, whom Keith doted on. The marriage went through many rocky times as could be expected, and the couple split up in the early 1970's. Moon never fully recovered from the divorce, although he planned to remarry at the time of his death. He decided to move to America around 1976 and

KEITH MOON

ALL THOSE YEARS OF CRAZINESS, OF LIVING ON THE EDGE, FINALLY CAUGHT UP WITH KEITH MOON.

THE COVER OF THE WHO'S FIRST U.S. DECCA LP, 1966. KEITH IS ON THE FAR RIGHT.

PROMO SHOT, TAKEN IN 1967 DURING THE WHO'S "DANDY" PERIOD.

settled in California to live out his fantasies of sun and surf, claiming himself a tax exile. He stayed but nine months and returned to England for good.

During the recording of the *Who Are You* LP, Keith tried to match his former glories, but it was not to be. He did a good job on the title track, but as Dave Marsh pointed out in his excellent book, *Before I Get Old, The Story Of The Who*, Moon had a very hard time keeping up. His responses were slowed considerably and he was not used on at least one cut, *Music Must Change*, as he could not handle the six/eight time signature. He did work with a click track and supposedly did well with it.

On the night of September 6, 1978, Keith, accompanied by his fiancee, the beautiful Annette Walter-Lax, attended the premier of *The Buddy Holly Story*, and an after-film party given by Paul and Linda McCartney, who own the rights to all Holly's material. Keith was in good spirits and was very pleasant company according to those present. He drank only white wine and had been making a serious effort to pull himself together, lose weight and regain his musical edge. Upon returning home, he gulped a handful of Heminevrin, prescribed to him to help his withdrawal from alcohol, and went to sleep. Around 7:30 AM, he woke up, cooked a steak, ate it, and washed it down with champagne. He took another handful of pills and went back to sleep. Annette discovered him dead later that afternoon.

His homeland and the rock world were stunned by the loss. The three remaining members of The Who were shattered. John Entwistle was conducting an interview with some Irish journalists at his home when he learned of Moon's death. When one of the journalists asked about the future of the group, Entwistle, who was trying to maintain his composure and keep the news about Keith quiet, burst into tears and told them what had happened. The thankless task of telling Keith's mother fell upon Pete Townshend.

All the years of craziness, of living on the edge, finally caught up with Keith Moon. He had become a celebrity in his homeland not only for his musicianship, but for his eccentric nature. He was loved and revered by the British press, who found his antics to be great copy.

The Who vowed to forge ahead. Moon's passing relieved them of a great weight, as they were now able to musically change the band. Faced with the nearly impossible task of replacing Keith, their initial plan called for the use of different drummers for different projects. The drum chair would not be filled on a permanent basis. But by October, the decision was made to replace Keith permanently and the job was offered to Kenney Jones, a good friend of the band, a former member of the Mod group The Small Faces, and later, The Faces, with Ronnie Wood and Rod Stewart. Kenney took the gig.

Above all else, Keith Moon must be remembered as a great musician, an innovator ,and a huge influence on the world of rock drumming. There had never been anyone like him before. There have been imitators, but there was but one Keith. There will never be another like him.

As Roger Daltrey put it, "He was a bloody institution, he should have been nationalized."

Hey, Keith. That fifteen year old kid from 1966 will never forget you either.

EQUIPMENT:

Keith Moon collected fine automobiles when he became successful. He treated them not as precious possession, but as tools to be used and abused at will.

He viewed his equipment likewise. His drums were meant to be played. Hard. And kicked over. And thrown into the audience. And sometimes splintered and blown up.

Obviously, he was not the type to wax poetic over a pre-war Radio King snare. The drums were simply objects to be used in a no-nonsense fashion, and they could always be replaced if they broke.

Keith's first drumkit was a cheap, nameless affair, that was eventually traded in when he joined The Beachcombers, for a Premier set.

The earliest photos of Moon with The Who show him playing a four piece Ludwig *Super Classic* oyster pearl set like Ringo Starr's, consisting of 22" bass drum, 13" rack tom. 16" floor tom and a 5 1/2x14" 400 snare, with a 20" ride, 18" crash and 14" hi-hats, all Zildjian. This set was replaced by another Ludwig *Super Classic* set, most likely in silver sparkle, but with the addition of another 16" floor tom to his right, in classic Buddy Rich style. This was the set he used on Shindig. When these drums bit the dust. Keith purchased a six piece Premier kit in red sparkle, made up of a 22" bass drum, two rack toms, probably 7x14"s, or 8x14"s, two 16" floor toms, and a chrome Ludwig 400 snare. A second bass drum, one additional rack tom, and another floor tom were added shortly thereafter, making Keith one of the first rock drummers anywhere to employ the double bass/multiple tom setup so common today. Moon felt the necessity for two bass drums, as The Who got progressively louder. Further discussion of his double bass style appears in the section regarding style and technique. His hi-hat was kept in a semi-closed position.

At *Monterey Pop*, Keith used a silver sparkle Slingerland double bass set, and not Ludwig, as has been erroneously reported. At this point, The Who were destroying so much equipment, that their management and road crew procured whatever they could get, either under supposed endorsement deals, or at the least expensive price possible. If a drum splintered, it had to be replaced quickly and cheaply.

From late 1967 until the end of his life, Keith proudly used Premier drums exclusively.

His best known Premier kit and certainly one of the most famous in rock history, was the *Pictures Of Lily* set, named after one of The Who's singles. It sported photos of The Who's logo, pictures of Keith, Victorian era nude photographs, and the apt statement: "Keith Moon. Patent British Exploding Drummer. This kit was used through the 1969 *Tommy* period and even though it was custom made, was treated no better than any other set Moon used, in fact, this was the kit Moon blew up on *The Smothers Brothers Show*. Obviously, Premier was able to supply replacement drums to match at will. The specifications on the *Pictures Of Lily* kit were: two 22" bass drums, fitted with Rogers tom holders. The bass drums were attached together with metal brackets to keep them from moving. There were three rack toms, either 8x14" or 7x14", depending upon what Keith could get, three 16" floor toms, two to the right, one to the left, and a 5 1/2" chrome snare. Keith helped design the set himself and also convinced the Premier engineers to fortify their hardware in order to withstand his all-out assault. It is safe to say that by the sheer force of his musical attack, Moon did much to strengthen drum hardware for all of us. Premier was always willing to do a lot of customizing to make Keith's drum more sturdy. They highly valued him as an endorsee and consultant.

Once the *Lily* set was replaced, retired, or destroyed (probably all three), Keith used for several years, the two bass-three rack-three floor tom setup, primarily in black, silver or gold finishes. In 1973, he again expanded his set, with the acquisition of 12", 13", 14", 15", and 16" single headed concert toms mounted on floor stands, used in addition to his six double headed toms. He even managed to squeeze in a set of timbales. His snare drums were usually Premier, Ludwig, or Gretsch.

It is interesting to note that used only a single bass drum in his kit while recording *Who Are You*, the last Who LP he appeared on.

Keith favored Zildjian cymbals, but liked Paiste also. He usually used a 22" ride and 18" and 20" crashes, with 14" hi-hats. Even though he broke them regularly, Keith reportedly loved 16" Paiste *Formula 602* crash cymbals. The *602* is a light, jazz cymbal. Need I say more? He also used a china-type cymbal during the sessions for Who Are You, as well as a gong for live and studio work.

Keith probably used at least one or two woodblocks live and in the studio for the cut "Magic Bus."

He occasionally used tympani in the studio, and Remo *Ambassador*, *Black Dot*, or Premier drumheads. They seldom lasted more than a show or two, because Keith often broke them all at the end of the night. This writer witnessed just such a trashing during the '71 tour at Forest Hills, Queens, New York.

His choice of sticks were usually Premier, in medium to medium-heavy weights.

Those who worked for The Who and Keith in particular, insist he was fussy about his setup and tuning. He seemingly cared a lot more for his drums than one would believe.

KEITH MOON

THE WHO, CIRCA 1968.

STYLE AND TECHNIQUE:

Keith Moon was a completely self-taught musician and never learned to read music or execute patterns "properly" from a drumming point of view. He simply did what so many rock players used to do and have done since; he listened to others and sat behind the kit and began to play. As is the case with all exceptional drummers, he had the raw talent to pull it off. One could wonder what Keith's playing would have been like had he taken the time to study properly, but then, he wouldn't have been the Keith Moon we knew. He simply chose to do it himself. In his article on Moon, written for *Modern Drummer* magazine, Bruce Wittet noted that Keith had "strong wrists and good hands, and he developed these early in his career; most of the waving of arms and legs was show. He had good, clean chops, much as he would often deny it." Wittet was correct in his observation.

Unquestionably, Keith preferred American drummers like Gene Krupa, Buddy Rich, and Jo Jones of the Count Basie band, over most British drummers. American drummers were more spontaneous and a lot flashier than their British counterparts. Moon's stick twirling came from Krupa, but he added his own flourishes as well. Keith used to bounce his sticks off the floor toms high into the air, usually during a break in whatever song he was playing. He would invariably catch them just in the nick of time. He threw sticks into the audience, and his well know practice of holding the sticks with the ends pointing downward was copied by many drummers, including Mike Hugg of Manfred Mann.

Other American drummers Keith admired were D. J. Fontana, Elvis Presley's first drummer, and modern jazz players like Elvin Jones, Tony Williams, and Joe Morello.

As for his fellow Britons, Moonie supposedly liked Ringo Starr, Charlie Watts, and later, John Bonham of Led Zeppelin, and Rob Henrit, formerly with Argent, now with The Kinks.

It would be easy to characterize Moon's style of drumming as busy, but the nature of The Who's music left many holes that Keith often plugged with a fill-in. He told *Melody Maker* in 1972; "My whole of style of drumming changed when I joined (The Who). Before, I'd just been copying straight from the records, but with The Who I had to develop a style of my own."

Moonie used two bass drums of course, but preferred playing the same pattern simultaneously on both drums, due to the sheer volume of The Who's live act. He did break bass patterns up from time to time though.

Regarding Keith's fill-ins, he usually used triplet or sixteenth note patterns utilizing his full compliment of two bass drums, snare and numerous toms. Every drum was used. There was nothing up there for show alone. He seemed just as comfortable going from low toms up to high toms, and very often started fills with a cymbal/snare combination. He punctuated Pete Townshend's material with lots of open cymbal rolls that achieved a wash effect. There is also evidence that Moonie was able to lead fill-ins off with his left hand. He was so active and animated behind the kit, that occasionally, drums would topple during a particularly wild fill.

A drummer's main function is to keep good time and make the music feel good. There's no question that Keith made The Who's music work, but the truth of the matter is that his timekeeping was at best, hit-or-miss. As previously mentioned, this caused many fights within the group over the years. By today's rigid standards, Keith's timekeeping would be considered appalling. And he made mistakes in concert that threw the rest of the band for a proverbial loop. The alcohol and drugs didn't help matters at all either. When he was good, he was phenomenal. When he was bad, he was horrific.

Keith did learn to play along with presequenced synthesizer tracks on stage for *Baba O'Reilly* and *Won't Get Fooled Again*, and he usually did pretty well.

At the beginning and during his best days with The Who, Moon was a top-of-the-beat player. As the effects of his excesses took over, he slowed up considerably. The in-concert segment at the end of the film *The Kids Are Alright*, is difficult to watch without sadness. The ravages of alcohol, drugs, and too many years of on-the-edge living were evident. He was overweight and barely able to execute simple fills. There was no anticipation, just resigned accompaniment. He looked old and tired. Incredibly, he was only thirty years old at the time.

There's little doubt that Moon would have been replaced in The Who even if he had lived. Prophetically, Keith picked Kenney Jones as his successor during a band meeting shortly before his death.

SELECTED CUTS AND DESCRIPTION:

"I Can't Explain" (Decca 45 #31725) - The first Who single and certainly one of Keith's finest performances. His playing is explosive, with some of the hottest snare drum fills extant. He is so dominant on this cut, he practically overshadows the rest of the band. The eighth and sixteenth triplets Moon hit right before the choruses are sheer genius. According to author Dave Marsh, "What Moon adds here is what he would always add; suspense. He was not only a drummer with amazing rhythmic ability and endless imagination, he understood each song The Who played and got inside it, peeling and prying until he cracked it open. Moon propels it into a new dimension and in the process invents an entirely new approach to rock drumming."

"Substitute" (Atco 45 #45-6409) - Keith's timekeeping and wild fills are nothing short of brilliant. Once again, he is the dominant member of the band on this cut. Listen for the two bar drum break complete with Keith's wrenching scream right before the last verse.

"My Generation" (Decca 45 #31877) - This is the chaotic side of Keith Moon personified. The fill-ins and timekeeping are so hot, it makes one wonder if Moon was possessed by supernatural demons during the recording session. The now-famous thrash-and-bash feedback section at the end is Moon's ticket to total drumming insanity, as he attacks the set in a completely unrestrained out-of-control manner.

"I Can See For Miles" (Decca 45 # 32206) - This is perhaps, the ultimate Who single and without a doubt, one of Keith Moon's greatest performances on record. Once again, Moon gets inside the song, with a complete understanding of what-beat-goes-where. His tom tom punctuations, cymbal washes, and galloping, sixteenth note snare pattern during the chorus are masterful, creating a mood of high tension.

"Pinball Wizard" (Decca LP #DXSW-7205, *Tommy*) - This cut is the tasteful side of Moon. The drums don't come in until the chorus, but Keith uses the spaces in between for effective cymbal crashes. The one bar break right before the bridge is an excellent combination usage of hi-hat cymbals, snare and toms.

"Young Man Blues" (Track LP # 2406 001, *Live At Leeds*) - Live Moon, and one of his finest. His tom tom flourishes show what a fast pair of hands Keith possessed. His timekeeping again, is good, but the track never loses its sense of elasticity.

"Bargain" (Decca LP #DL 79182, *Who's Next*) - *Who's Next* was recorded at The Who's zenith in 1971. Similarly, Keith was at his height also. His drums are all over this track and his performance is mind-boggling. The fills are tight and strong, the subtler sections of the song are treated tastefully on Moon's part, and the double bass drum roll through the synthesizer break is breath-taking.

"Behind Blues Eyes" (Decca LP #DL 79182, *Who's Next*) - Keith sits out the first three-quarters of this song and literally explodes into the last verse with some incredible pyrotechnics. Live, he used to use the quieter section of this tune to make faces and generally clown around. On record, it's no laughing matter. This is serious Moon at work.

"Won't Get Fooled Again" (Decca LP # DL 79182, *Who's Next*) - If "I Can See For Miles" is the ultimate Who Single, then this is their most immortal album cut. Keith shows his complete understanding of the tune, by supplying exactly what was needed to make the piece work. The fills are perfect, the timekeeping patterns are broken up somewhat by syncopated figures on the snare and toms and the drum break right before Roger Daltrey's ear-piercing scream is one of the hottest in rock history.

"The Real Me" (MCA/Track LP # MCA2-10004, *Quadrophenia*) - By the Time *Quadrophenia* was recorded, Keith had begun the slide into alcoholism and drug use. However, his playing, particularly on this cut, is as powerful and expressive as anything he had ever done. The tom tom fills placed between the vocal figures on the chorus, work wonderfully and the whole cut has a sense of urgency that would soon disappear from Moon's playing altogether.

(The Author acknowledges the article on Keith Moon written by Bruce Wittet for *Modern Drummer Magazine* as a reference source.)

KEITH MOON

KEITH LOOKING MENACING IN THE MID-
SEVENTIES.

"HAILED AS GENIUSES WHEN WE WERE A BUNCH OF SCUMBAGS."

KEITH MOON MEMORIAL

In the years since his death, "Moon the Loon" has finally been recognized more for his tremendous natural talent and contributions to rock drumming and less for his offstage insanity. Unfortunately, what has come to the surface since his death was Keith's numbing and ultimately deadly reliance on liquor and drugs to sustain him through his days of lunacy during The Who's glory years. Moon fans always knew of his abuses, but many never thought the problem was so extensive, until it was too late and Keith was gone.

Two books have been written on Moon, the better of which is *Moon: The Life And Death Of A Rock Legend* by Tony Fletcher. In the book, a fascinating, brutally honest and hard-hitting 608-page volume, Fletcher theorizes that Moon took the drugs, drank the booze and committed the acts of craziness and destruction to cover his own lack of confidence and unhappiness with his personal life. That theory seems right on target. The drummer made halfhearted attempts to sober up and get straight, but never really succeeded in getting his life in order. Of course, it was his eventual undoing. Fletcher states that Keith should have gone into counseling and reasons that if he had gotten his life together, Moon might have had a resurgence of his abilities that would have driven The Who to new musical heights. As it was, Keith was burned out physically, emotionally and spiritually by the time he was thirty.

Moon apparently believed too much in his own invincibility and learned the truth the hard way. It's entertaining but useless to think about what might have been had Keith lived. If he were still with us, his life would have surely made good viewing on VH1's *Behind The Music.*

On the up side, countless articles have been written since the drummer's death praising his work and abilities behind the drumset. Even the late jazz drummer Tony Williams said of Moon, "He was beautiful. Totally free." The tributes have continued for years. Well-known rock drummers like Neil Peart, Mike Portnoy and many others have credited Moon repeatedly. It's about time.

The Who were never the same after Moon's death; musicians with distinctive styles are never easy to replace and he was no exception. Kenney Jones tried and had his moments of brilliance on live shows. Simon Phillips provided a more aggressive style that suited the band somewhat, but ultimately, his fusion jazz/rock approach failed to fit the band properly. Ringo Starr's son, Zak Starkey, a friend and protégé of Keith's during his childhood and an excellent young drummer, probably did the best job of filling Moon's shoes most recently, but he has reportedly left The Who for the drum spot with Oasis. At this writing, it would appear that The Who, now down to Pete Townshend and Roger Daltrey, the surviving original members, are in need of a new drummer. Any takers?

When this author saw The Who with Phillips and a small army of studio musicians live in concert some years back, Pete Townshend said, "I'd like to introduce you to the twenty-six people we had to hire to replace Keith Moon."

I can think of no better way to end this chapter on one of rock's greatest drummers.

"I was a rust repairer . . . and a full-time survivor. I survived all the major earthquakes, and the Titanic, *and several air crashes."*

—*From the film* **The Kids Are Alright**

SANDY'S LUDWIG ENDORSEMENT PHOTO, 1961.

"If you give kids too much encouragement, it takes away their incentive of perseverence and curiosity."

sandy nelson

MY HAT IS OFF TO SANDY NELSON.

Any why is that, you ask?

Sandy Nelson helped do for rock drummers what Gene Krupa did for jazz drummers back in the 1930's and 40's: he made the public sit up and notice that drummers were more than just that hide beater in the back of the bandstand. Sandy helped make the Rock 'n' Roll drummer a member of the band that demanded and got respect and acknowledgement.

And how did he do this?

By creating his own identifiable sound using echo-chambered tom toms primarily, and for being the only rock drummer in history to sustain a very successful career by releasing all-instrumental drum solo records aimed at the exploding teenage audience of the late 1950's and early 1960's. For these accomplishments, Sandy Nelson deserves a very special place among rock drummers.

Although others like Cozy Powell have tried to emulate the Nelson approach with rock drum solo records, none have been able to achieve the degree of success attained by Sandy. He is the undisputed master of the genre.

Sandy's records usually featured primitive, twangy guitar a la Duane Eddy and sometimes a New Orleans, second line feel. Sandy was, and still is very fond of that particular style. And the drums were always mixed up-front, something that was just not done in 1959. No doubt about it, Sandy Nelson helped make Rock 'n' Roll just a little bit nastier back in those days of annoyingly saccharine teen idols like Fabian, Paul Anka, and Frankie Avalon.

Amazingly, Sandy released thirty-three albums, and while it's true that some of them were throwaways, that's still quite a feat for a drummer with an artificial foot.

• •

IN 1965, SANDY SWITCHED BACK TO GRETSCH DRUMS. THIS SET WAS RED SPARKLE.

Sandy Nelson was born December 1, 1938, in Santa Monica, California. His parents were named Lydia and Lloyd Nelson. Mr. Nelson was a film projectionist at Twentieth Century Fox film studios in the 1940's.

The Drum Bug bit Sandy early.

"At the age of four or five, my parents used to have these wild parties during World War II and they used to play all these records by Benny Goodman, Gene Krupa, Illinois Jacquet, Duke Ellington, and Lionel Hampton.

Some of those records were like dope to me when I was about five or six. I used to smuggle them out of the living room and take them up to my room and play them on my own little machine at three in the morning. It was like I *had* to hear them. One of them was called *Rose Room* (Benny Goodman) and another one was *Song Of India* (Tommy Dorsey). Something about that minor key was infectious, which maybe was the germination for 'Let There Be Drums'."

Sandy's parents bought him his first set of drums when he was seven. It was an old set even then, with a ship and palm trees painted on the front head of the bass drum, a small metal snare, red temple blocks and a Chinese cymbal that in Sandy's words, "didn't swing."

He played simple patterns on the snare drum, but grew tired of the set, because it just wasn't hip enough, as the smaller, bebop-style sets were just coming into vogue. Eventually, the old drum's heads broke and they were soon trashed.

From there, Sandy tried the piano and played a little boogie-woogie, but had trouble with the turnaround, as there was no one to teach him.

real fascinated with being a musician, hearing all their sarcasm and talk. Chuck Molinari and Remo Belli worked behind the counter, and once, they had a marathon where they had to keep the drums going for a certain amount of hours. I got to sit in for about ten minutes with Terry Gibbs (well known jazz vibraphone player) and that was my first jazz sit-in. I loved jazz and loved to listen to Shelley Manne, Barney Kessel, and Ray Brown on record. Around that time in 1956, there was a low, low budget television show on Channel 13, the *Zeke Manners Show*. He did a copy of Dick Clark's *American Bandstand*, with teenagers dancing, and he had a drummer with a cap with a feather in it and a big German nose, who came in and played along with the records. His name was Sammy Weiss, who was Jack Benny's drummer. I used to stand in back of the camera and watch him play to records by Ernie Freeman and others."

"I talked my mother into buying me a used set of drums, that was more of a bebop set, with a silver sparkle twenty inch bass drum, one tom tom, a snare, a small cymbal and no hi-hat. I used to have wet dreams over owning a hi-hat. During high school, I started a little band with two other guys, a sax player named Dave Shostac and a piano player whose name I can't remember. We had a job that paid $2.50 a piece and we were so bad, we got thrown off the gig."

Sandy and Dave decided to get a new piano player, who turned out to be Bruce Johnston, who later went on to fame as a member of The Beach Boys.

What got Sandy interested in Rock 'n' Roll were not the mushy records of the day, but those of Little Richard,

"I used to have wet dreams over owning a hi-hat."

Throwing stones into a nearby storm drain created a fascination within Sandy for an echo effect, a sound that he would use years later while recording.

His parents never encouraged him too much and looking back, it was the right thing to do.

"If you give kids too much encouragement, it takes away their incentive of perseverance and curiosity."

By 1950, Sandy had joined a small orchestra at school, playing snare, bass drum, and triangle.

"You couldn't play all three at the same time. I guess they had a strong union!"

At about the same time, television was just gaining acceptance and Sandy used to ride his bicycle up to Hollywood and sneak into KLAC studios, where he also became interested in radio. While hanging around the TV and radio studios in Hollywood, he couldn't help but see the recording studios too and the musicians in action. His love affair with drums was rekindled.

"I started going up to Drum City, a drum shop on Santa Monica Boulevard. It was owned by Roy Harte and his father. Roy was a studio drummer at NBC and all these drummers would hang out there and I started to get

Shirley and Lee, and Fats Domino. "I had heard that it was the same drummer on all those records and I wanted to meet him. I thought, 'How does he do it?' I used to listen to 'Slippin' And Slidin' over and over again and try to play along with it, thinking the drummer was doing something with the floor tom on that track."

In 1957, Sandy, Dave, and Bruce were playing off and on with a fellow named Barry Martin. "We did a few Bar Mitzvah's and small gigs and Barry landed a contract with Liberty Records, who informed him that he had to use studio men. We were invited to come up to watch them do the track and it made us feel a little bit bad, but this was my chance to meet the drummer that was on all my favorite Rock 'n' Roll records, and the drummer's name, of course, was Earl Palmer. That was it! Being impressionable and watching him play in the studio was really gangbusters! I even bought a Week-At-A-Glance date book just like he had. Same color. I've had them every year since 1957."

By this time, Sandy had quit high school and worked for a while as a laborer at Twentieth Century Fox studios. He continued to gig with Bruce Johnston and another sax

sandy nelson

SANDY, CIRCA 1964.

player named Bobby Raye, a Mexican. He also worked as a ticket taker at the Bruin Theater. While employed at the Bruin, Sandy began taking drum lessons from Bob Winslow, a former student of Murray Spivac. Winslow started him on an old drum book called *Short Rolls And Progressions*, an introduction to five and six stroke rolls. He also showed Sandy how to play even double strokes, that, according to Sandy was a forerunner to "Teen Beat" and "Let There Be Drums."

Bobby Raye managed to get Bruce and Sandy a $10.00 recording gig at American Recording Studios. It was his first paid session job.

Shortly after, Bruce and Sandy joined Kip Tyler's band. Kip led the band that backed up DJ Art Laboe's Rock 'n' Roll shows at El Monte Legion Stadium and other venues. Kip's current group were all leaving to join Duane Eddy. Sandy had met Art Laboe previously from his days hanging around the local radio stations.

"Working those shows was a rich experience. We backed up all the local groups like The Penguins, Rosie and The Originals, Ritchie Valens, and others. Laboe also featured the band on his weekly television show from KTLA and that was our first experience of fame. Girls were screaming for us and so forth."

At the end of that summer, Bruce, Dave Shostac, and Sandy began gigging at a hot springs ranch in Hemmett, California. Back in those days, guitarists were hard to find. Session ace Mike Deasy did some of the gigs, but the group got the phone number of a guy named Phil Spector, who played very loud guitar for the time. Phil joined up.

"Some people would complain that he played too loud. He played a lot of Buddy Holly stuff, and he'd just come back at them and say, 'Fuck you! Rock 'n' Roll is supposed to be loud!'"

Phil began hiring Sandy to do demo sessions and one

of the tunes he cut that turned out to be a master was "To Know Him Is To Love Him," by The Teddy Bears. Phil even cajoled Sandy into backing up The Teddy Bears live, much to the consternation of Kip Tyler, who was still Sandy's employer at the time.

Sandy's first recording session proved to be a turning point in his career. He met and became friendly with Richie Podolor, whose family owned American Recording Studios, as has been mentioned. Richie was a classical guitarist who also played Rock 'n' Roll and had done some session work with Connie Francis and others. Podolor liked Sandy's drumming and wanted to help him put out his own record.

"I was just starting to invent a beat that you could dance to that was a combinatin of Cozy Cole's 'Topsy, Part II' and Ralph Marterie's 'Caravan,' mixed with what I heard a strip drummer do at a club called The New Follies. Richie liked the way I played and wanted to collaborate with me."

That was the beginning of "Teen Beat," but back to that in a minute.

"At the end of '58 and into early '59, I was doing a few sessions here and there. Phil Spector started using Hal Blaine, who had just gotten off the road with Tommy Sands. Hal had gone out and bought a whole lot of tom toms and I was kind of hurt. I guess Phil liked Hal better than me, but by then, I was thinking about doing my own record anyway. Hal was very aggressive, and I wasn't. The funny thing is, I started doing fills on multiple toms from things I heard Earl Palmer do. Hal must have heard that and ran with it."

"I'm the type of person who doesn't like to be told what to do. I don't like regimentation or discipline, and even during recording sessions for other people, I found it too regimented. I wanted to do it my way and be the boss, so I made a demo, a rough idea of 'Teen Beat,' just a drum track with no guitar. I played it for Art Laboe, who liked the title and the idea. He said, 'Let's slow it down and add a guitar.' I wanted to use Richie Podolor on guitar, so we did the actual master that summer (1959) with Richie on guitar, Bruce Johnston on piano, and then overdubbed Guybo Smith on bass, plus another guitar, played by Barney Kessel, overdubbed."

"About a week later, I was over at my mother's apartment where I lived and two girls I knew from high school ran upstairs screaming, 'They're playing *Teen Beat* on Art Laboe's Show!' 'That's impossible,' I said. 'It's not even out yet.' I turned it on and sure enough, Art was playing an acetate of 'Teen Beat', just trying it out to see if he wanted to release it. He got a lot of calls, so he put it out on the Original Sound label and it broke in Miami, Omaha, Jacksonville, Minneapolis, and Chicago, so I had a hit."

"Teen Beat" sold about 750,000 copies on its initial release and eventually topped the million mark when it was re-recorded and re-released on Imperial Records. It rose to the Top Five on the *Billboard* charts.

"Teen Beat" launched Sandy's solo career and made the record-buying teenage public aware of the drums as they had never known them before. Suddenly, drums were a perfectly viable solo instrument in Rock 'n' Roll

Sandy was talked into touring to promote "Teen Beat," called the Harvest Moon Dance Party, with Johnny and The Hurricanes, Skip and Flip, and Freddy Cannon. Skip and Flip backed Sandy up on "Teen Beat." The tour was a success. Sandy continued to do session work, particularly for Bob Keene's Del-Fi label and several others. He backed Mel Carter, Ron Holden, Hollywood Argyles, Joel Hill, and Ritchie Valens on record as well as others. He also did an album with Gene Vincent.

Around this time, Sandy met The Ventures at American Studios. Their drummer had been injured and they needed someone to fill in for an upcoming tour, so Sandy took the gig.

"All that snow and those long jumps between towns made me think, 'Gee, if I could get one more hit and really make some money,' because I really didn't have an artist contract with 'Teen Beat,' just a songwriter's contract. I didn't make much from it. I had joined Imperial Records and had had a few flops. I wanted to get another hit and get paid for it this time, and sure enough, that was 'Let There Be Drums.' I borrowed some of Cozy Cole's swingy, open rolls for that."

"Let There Be Drums" was a logical extension of "Teen Beat". Released in the winter of 1961 on Imperial, it sold about a half a million copies and rose to number five on the charts. The LP that followed the single likewise sold about 500,000.

" 'Let There Be Drums' was just a bunch of wild tracks that I spliced together. 'Birth Of The Beat' came from the same bunch of tracks. Eddie Raye, the A&R man at Imperial, let me do whatever I wanted. I had total control."

"Here's a funny story about Eddie Raye and me. Included in a session in 1962, we did a version of 'Kansas City' that had some one bar breaks and I didn't want to do them. So when it came time to do the breaks, I did them as badly as I could, thinking 'surely they won't release this take!' We did 'Honky Tonk' just as bad too and they haunt me to this day. They were released in Europe a few years ago on a re-package. What you put in those grooves is going to come back at you."

"As far as recording in the early days, like I said, I could do what I wanted. There was no pressure...no engineer to say,

spend an hour getting EQ and a mix and to try and put duct tape all over my tom toms. I didn't have to contend with that in those days."

Sandy never enjoyed touring and roadwork.

"There were a few funny moments, but I never liked touring. In 1962, Elliot Ingber and a few other friends talked me into going on tour. We had a station wagon with a trailer and traveled all over the Midwest and it was really rough. The car's engine fizzled out around Minneapolis. We had it fixed twice. It wasn't much fun."

After the tour ended in April, 1963, Sandy, who had bought a motorcycle (among other things) with his royalty money, was riding down Mulholland Drive. Coming around a corner, he collided with a school bus. His right foot was caught in the bus's rear wheel. Rushed to the hospital, the foot was amputated.

The loss of a limb is traumatic for anyone, but to a drummer, it's positively disastrous. While in the hospital, Sandy went through hell, afraid he would never play drums again, that his career was through. He spent several months recovering, until he was fitted with an artificial limb. Once he was back on his feet, Sandy began playing the bass drum with his left foot, the hi-hat with his artificial right foot. He rigged up the hi-hat with a board to make it

SANDY MUGGING FOR THE CAMERA, CIRCA 1969

sandy nelson

A LATER SHOT OF SANDY BEHIND THE RED GRETSCH SET DOING THE STICK TOSS. THIS PHOTO WAS TAKEN IN THE 1970'S.

then...the *White Album* and *Sgt. Pepper*. One way or another, I really wasn't into the English groups. It probably was an unconscious jealousy because they helped knock me off the charts. Of course, I had a lot of responsibility for that happening."

How does he feel today about the music he recorded back then?

" 'Let There Be Drums' gets a lot of play on oldies stations and gets played in Europe a lot. It was almost the first disco record. Eddie Raye called me and said that they were playing 'Let There Be Drums' in a discotheque in France and I didn't know what the hell that was and didn't really care. The discotheque was a nightclub that played records and it started in France. 'Memphis,' by Johnny Rivers and 'Let There Be Drums,' were supposedly the first things that were played in discos that were popular."

Was Sandy influenced in any way by other Sixties drummers?

"No, I wasn't. I wasn't doing much playing then anyway. However, at the time, other Sixties drummers were influenced by me, although I didn't know it."

"I slept through those years, or passed out as the case might be. So, I can't say I could name any drummer who stood out. I always listened to Earl Palmer and liked him."

"The Sixties didn't change me at all, but I think I had a hand in changing the music of the Sixties. Possibly with '*Let There Be Drums*,' which was ahead of its time. It was almost metal rock for that day. Before that, Rock 'n' Roll was sort of *gingerbready* in a way. This has been brought to my attention by other people."

"I slept through most of the Seventies too. About the only thing I did then was a drum track I did in my garage that was used in a film short called *The American Time Capsule*, that was popular on college campuses and network shows. I did a few Japanese albums with Daryl Dragon (from Captain and Tennille) arranging and playing most of the instruments. I did a poor version of '*Dance With The Devil*' at the same time Cozy Powell's version was taking off in Europe. I didn't want to do someone else's drum record, but United Artists talked me into it and sure enough, mine was not a hit. It got a few plays in Europe and all it did was spoil it for Cozy, so I have apologies for that."

In the Seventies, during the time he kicked his drinking problem, Sandy began playing drums in a bar in Santa Monica, with a piano player named Dick Leslie, a fine jazz musician.

"It was a rich experience learning jazz tunes and standards. My old love of jazz and big bands started to come

easier to work with. Realizing that he could adapt to his handicap, he was determined to continue drumming. The power of positive thought worked and Sandy gained new confidence behind the kit. His problems, however, had seemingly just begun.

"In 1963, Imperial Records was sold to Liberty Records. I could have gone to Tower Records with my old friend, Eddie Raye, but I stayed with Imperial and that's when the fun began. There seemed like a dozen A&R men there, all telling me what to do and what to record. I had to do instrumental versions of the hits of the day and I hated it! I wanted to do my own sound. There was one fellow who kind of went along with me, so we did 'Teen Beat '65' ' and another thing called 'Boss Beat' that Jimmy Messina and I put together, so it wasn't all bad, but it got worse.

Sandy spent the remainder of the Sixties and a good part of the Seventies in alcoholic oblivion.

"The less creative control I had, the more drinking I did. The more drinking I did, the less creative I got anyway. It perpetuated itself, I guess."

When questioned as to whether or not he listened to any rock drummers, American or British during the Sixties, Sandy replied, "They didn't inspire me all that much. I was going through an unhappy marriage and was drinking a lot, so I kind of slept through the English groups, but later on, hanging around some of the local bars in Santa Monica, I did kind of get into The Beatles

back with that gig. It gave me good experience dealing with the public...they're three feet away from you."

The Seventies brought punk and disco to the fore. Sandy has his own opinions on these subjects.

"Very often, like a lot of older people, I would get annoyed with loud Rock 'n' Roll and the clothes they wore, but I can't hold it against them. When I see youngsters who want to play rock, I was doing the same kind of thing back in 1958 and '59. I used to go barefoot and hang out in coffeehouses and in Hollywood, so I really don't have any complaints. I wanted to do it my way. Punk musicians are just kids like I was who want to play. Disco drumming didn't move me all that much. I want music to breathe a little, to have color and dynamics and creativity."

"Young people today don't have much incentive. It's like there's no tomorrow and I can't much blame them. It sort of seems that way. The music reflects what's going on with young people, but maybe this is just a period of regrouping. Maybe some kind of hope will come back. I really don't follow today's rock music, in fact, for a while, I thought Pat Benatar was a brand of suntan lotion, but I understand there are groups now that have messages of peace and I think that's great. I can't see anything wrong with peace. No one wants a Big Brother, but if we don't behave ourselves as human beings, we'll have to have a Big Brother."

Sandy mentioned Anton Fig from the David Letterman Show as an outstanding rock drummer.

"He plays rock the way it ought to be played. Good rock drummer. Cozy Powell is a good drummer, but I think he should use smaller sticks...not bang everything so loud. That's the way it is with rock music. You play everything as loud as possible. My friend, Harry Ravain, is a very good New Orleans-style drummer. He's taught me a lot."

"Harry and I did some overdubbing on an album last year and we had to use a click track and I didn't like it. It was obscene! They tried to convince me that that's the way they do things nowadays, but I guess I'm just an old dog...can't learn new tricks."

"Another rock drummer I like is my friend, Don Bonebrake (from the band, X). Even though he does a lot of programming of drum machines, he really wants to be a good musician and is now studying with Murray Spivac, who I studied with about thirteen years ago."

Sandy also mentioned jazz drummers Shelly Manne, Jack DeJohnette, and Art Blakey as personal favorites.

When queried as to how he feels about recording technology today versus the Sixties, Sandy was adamant.

"I think it stinks! Everything has to be isolated and studios have to be dead. The best studio I ever recorded in was called The Annex of the old Radio Recorders Studios in Hollywood. The whole room was live with baffles to accentuate different frequencies. You could walk in and clap your hands or play a trumpet and the whole room would come to life. Lawrence Welk did his TV tracks there. James Brown, Frank Sinatra, Glenn Miller, Spike Jones, and Elvis Presley all recorded there. Whoever took over that studio made it dead, so there goes an old workhorse of the recording industry. The way they record drums these days sounds like they're playing

on Kotex boxes in a clothes closet. There's no resonance to them. I don't mean to sound like sour grapes...I'm happy with what I'm doing."

"Right now, I'm playing with a little jazz group called The Midnight Swingers. We're having a ball. We've got piano, trombone, sax, bass, and drums. After all this time, I'm finally doing what I wanted to do, just lay back and play jazz and be creative, although I'm always open to new ideas on the drums. I'm always practicing and studying.

Now divorced, Sandy lives alone. He has two children, a son and a daughter, who he sees regularly and doesn't spend much time hanging out in bars anymore when he's not working. He owns a home in Southern California, "with two toilets and a large fish pond."

"I'm staying sober and drug-free. I stopped doing all that in 1976. I like to drive out in the desert, go to truck stops and have chicken-fried steaks. When I'm home, I like to practice and B.S. around with other drummer friends like Harry Ravain or Don Bonebrake. I'd like to do some drum clinics sometime if it's feasible. I still draw royalties, mostly from Europe and Australia for 'Let There Be Drums'. They've been re-packaging a lot of my old stuff over there and they're selling. I've taught drums off and on, mostly for free, to people who really want to learn. I don't do session work. I was supposed to do a session with Josie Cotton, but they used a drum machine instead. I think I could have given her a good feel. I listen to a little jazz on the radio at home and love Mel Torme and any singer that does good old standards. I don't like to listen to the way out, free form stuff. It's too long-winded. I guess I'm just not hip.

When speaking with Sandy, one thing you immediately become aware of is his slightly crazy, offbeat sense of humor. Several times during the course of our conversation, he did impressions of people like Lawrence Welk, W.C. Fields, and Louis Armstrong. He even joked about the time he drank a bottle of rubbing alcohol, an incident that certainly wasn't funny at the time it happened.

"I'm going to play drums until I drop dead!"

EQUIPMENT:

Before getting his first drumset, Sandy banged on trash cans that he overturned. This arrangement gave him a conga drum effect that he liked.

As previously mentioned, he received his first real set as a gift from his parents at age seven. The set was Leedy, with a very large bass drum, probably a 26" or 28," with a ship painted on the front head. The snare was metal and Sandy did not recall the size. Included also was a Chinese cymbal and temple blocks.

The first set Sandy used professionally consisted of a 22" Gretsch silver sparkle bass drum and a small tom and snare that were of a different finish. He added a floor tom later. His choice of cymbals over the years has usually been A. or K. Zildjian.

Before "Let There Be Drums" hit the charts, Sandy bought a black Gretsch set in 1960, a four piece kit. After his chart success in 1961, he traded the black set in for a Ludwig kit that consisted of two 13" rack toms, a 16" floor tom and unspecified sizes on the bass and snare. The

sandy nelson

finish was silver sparkle all around. Sandy got an endorsement deal with Ludwig and told me a funny story.

"I remember creating quite a stir when Bob Yeager of the Pro Drum Shop told me that Ludwig wanted me to send them a picture of myself behind the Ludwig set. I was so drunk in those days, I sent them a picture of me behind a red sparkle Gretsch set instead. I understand that created quite an uproar up there at Ludwig, so my apologies..."

The above mentioned red sparkle Gretsch set was made up of a 20" bass, 13" and 16" toms, and a 5x14" snare. Sandy got that set around 1965.

"I liked that red Gretsch set. The snare had a nice wooden sound. I wish I still had it, as drummers always say." His current snare drum is a deep, Sixties vintage Ludwig.

Sandy still uses the bass drum from that set and it has now been refinished white marine pearl, with Pearl lugs and hardware. The rest of his current setup consists of 10" and 12" rack toms (the 10" is single-headed) and a 15" floor tom, all Pearl drums, in white marine pearl.

The hi-hat is still positioned to allow his artificial right foot to control it. Sandy uses a heavy 18" Zildjian Symphonic cymbal for a ride and a 16" Sabian crash with a rivet that he also uses to ride on occasionally.

"I'm a little suspicious of new drums. It seems that the older drums had better shells."

Sandy expressed a desire to one day work with a drum manufacturer to develop new products.

"I was at the PAS (Percussive Arts Society) convention a few years ago and wound up doing an inadvertent drum clinic with the rudiments for some people standing around the Drum Workshop booth and I really like their snare drums."

"For years I've been used to Japanese oak sticks. I can't get away from them. I use Pro-Mark 5A's."

STYLE AND TECHNIQUE:

"I'm very pleased with the reception people give my music," says the soft-spoken young percussionist who is destined, in the opinion of critics, to become the world's greatest drummer.'

So spake Sandy Nelson and the Imperial Records publicity machine, and while he never became the "world's greatest drummer," Sandy Nelson could really play those blankety-blank drums, to borrow one of his song titles. It is true he took a simple, very primitive formula and flogged it to death, release after release, but he was also a serious experimenter, who used drumming and sound effects in interesting ways and combinations. He attempted and usually succeeded in creating percussive moods (kinda' like those ridiculous old LP's you always see at garage sales and flea markets for 10 cents, only better), using exotic instruments, mixed with contemporary drumming, much of which came from years of listening to big band swing and jazz in general. As a child, it is also interesting to know that he harbored a great love for the wacky, novelty records of Spike Jones, where wild sound effects were the norm. Put all these factors together with Sandy's sense of humor and you'll have a pretty clear picture of where his sound came from.

On the technical end, Sandy knew his rudiments cold and spent much time later on studying and working out on the practice pad. Although the disposable nature of some of his hits might tend to lead the serious listener to dismiss him, Sandy is, in truth, a solid, inventive drummer with a high developed rhythmic sense. The man really can play!

And play he does, almost every day. At nearly fifty years of age, Sandy is undoubtedly a better drummer today than he ever was before, now that he has more or less left Rock 'n' Roll behind for jazz, his real musical love.

According to Don Bonebrake, "Sandy is always practicing, always learning. The first time I went over to his house, I sat behind his drums and played a lick he liked. He had me go back and play it again and teach it to him. I couldn't believe I was showing him something of my own! He's great at naming beats. He called that one the *Don Bonebrake Beat #One.*"

As far as his practice routine goes, Sandy had this to say.

"I have a whole set of practicing do's and don'ts. On a night that I'm playing, I shouldn't practice at all. Generally, the best kind of practice for me is drum charts played real slow and easy. I get a kind of spiritualism out of it. I like to be alone when I practice. Sometimes I'll sit in a quiet room and play one beat on a tom tom and listen to it ring and sit there for maybe thirty seconds and go from there."

"Playing jazz, I've noticed that time is very important. I've developed sort of a third eye...a time eye. It's almost like seeing spots in the middle of a highway, or a pulse. I really don't know how to describe it, but it's good, whatever it is."

"One day, I might decide to be real rudimental and strict and flawless. I'll practice the flam series, the first couple of pages of the *Stick Control* book, and get off on that spiritually and maybe to through the rudiments. Playing them sometimes inspires me to invent something on my own."

"Sometimes I just sit down and go crazy and be a nine year old child with his first set of drums. That's always fun. I remember an article years ago by Carl Palmer saying that when he sits down behind the drums to practice, he just plays his all instead of leading up to something or warming up slow. I can see merit in that."

"I've noticed that a lot of well-studied drummers, I wouldn't hire to play at a dogfight. They're fascinated with their technique, speed, and the licks they've learned. They have no intention of listening to the band or making the music sound good."

Sandy advised young drummers to, "Study and learn technique, but keep it in your pants. Don't let it interfere with your actual playing. If you study good technique, it will sneak up into your playing anyway. Don't be conscious of it. When you start to study, it will actually set your playing back at first, but it will jump ahead later, if you've got your head on right."

SELECTED CUTS:

(The quotes are Sandy's)

"Teen Beat" (Original Sound 45 #5)-Sandy's first hit and the cornerstone of the "Sandy Nelson Sound." Musically, "Teen Beat" is a "jungleized" 12 bar surf blues progression, with Sandy playing double strokes between the toms and snare, heavy on the echo, please. The instrumentation is so sparse, the guitars ands piano don't even come in full throttle until half way through and they have very little to do, as the drums and bass dominate the mix. Sandy said the idea for "Teen Beat" came from a mixture of licks borrowed from Cozy Cole, a record called "The Swag," and from a drummer he heard playing in a Los Angeles strip joint. "Nothing like a pretty, naked dancing girl to inspire music."

"Let There Be Drums" (Imperial 45 #5775)-The second hit and we're talking primitive stuff here. The liner notes to Rhino Records LP, *The History Of Instrumental Rock* sums it up; " "Let There Be Drums" sounds like a cross between "Wipeout" and Duane Eddy's *Rebel Rouser*, and is simplicity itself: a gruff-toned ascending guitar figure, and a primal beat." The *primal beat* consists of sixteenth note inter- action on the snare and rack tom, with explosive accents on the floor tom and a strip beat on the snare and cymbals toward the end. You begin to get the feeling that Sandy had discovered a formula.

"Drummin' Up A Storm" (Imperial LP #9189 *Drummin' Up A Storm*)-"If it ain't broke, don't fix it"…Sandy must have felt compelled to stick with the crude formula again on this one, a cut that sounds like "Son of Let There Be Drums." Of course, in those days of grade C horror movies, hamburger drive-ins, and tail fins, this fit right in.

"…And Then There Were Drums" (Imperial LP #9204…*And Then There Were Drums*)-This is a speed- ed-up "Son Of The Son Of Let There Be Drums," but this time, with a guitar riff that is so raw and primi- tive, any junk/punk band like The Cramps would be proud to call it their own. Sandy overdubbed the guitar himself, by the way. The tom tom riffs are descended from Gene Krupa's "Sing Sing Sing," and are pretty neat in their own right.

"Around The World With Drums" (Imperial Lp #9189 *Drummin' Up A Storm*)-At 11:15, this piece is a remarkable percussive tone poem of sorts, in which Sandy combined sound effects like a wind machine and an echo chamber, with exotic percussion instruments like the lujon, boobams, shakers, gongs, congas, and a slide whistle, plus an overdubbed snare drum, evoking images of Africa and the Orient, along with horns and crowd noise. After all this has taken place, it's back to the good old USA, with a strenuous workout on the drumset. This was recorded on two Ampex machines with no mixer and cheap, old Shure mics'. " "All Around The World With Drums" sounds like a demo record for a chain of cheap music stores."

"Freak Beat" (Imperial LP #9340 *Cheetah Beat*)-"Freak Beat" was recorded in Sandy's garage studio, using plastic bedpan urinals! I kid you not. Sandy would try anything on record at least once. " "Freak Beat" sounded like some kind of fake Elvis Presley swamp beat."

"Castle Rock" (Imperial LP #9189 *Drummin' Up A Storm*)-Proof positive that Sandy could really swing when he wanted to, "Castle Rock" is a jazzy jump blues with nice horn and guitar work. The guitarist was probably Barney Kessel. Sandy's twenty-four bar drum break is very hot and definitely Krupa/Rich-inspired.

"Civilization" (Imperial LP #9204…*And Then There Were Drums*)-Gives Sandy over eight minutes to fool around with percussive sounds and moods. What the listener hears in the beginning and through- out most of the proceedings is a tape loop of a real cricket and a garden hose adding water to a swim- ming pool. There's some eerily-chorded guitar work and the obligatory reverb-laden snare and toms. Some of the guitar playing sounds vaguely Middle Eastern or Greek. On top of all this, we're treated to inner city traffic noise, layered over modern jazz-like drumming, followed by rather odd, bluesy guitar licks and a gong crash, that brings about the return of the cricket and the garden hose. Strange, you say? "Buddy Holly was not the first guy to use a cricket on record, I was!"

"Tub Thumpin" (Imperial LP #9189 *Drummin' Up A Storm*)-Take a Bo Diddley beat, add a scratchy gui- tar, bass, some toms, and a bunch of two bar snare breaks that sound the same and what have you got? An instant sleaze-rock classic! It's amazing what one can do with so little. "I overdubbed the bass. We recorded this one in a storeroom."

"Back To The Beginning" (Imperial LP #9345 *The Beat Goes On*)-Yet another percussive mood piece, "Back To The Beginning" is the Nelson vision of Creation, with a wigged-out recitation (by Sandy, of course), wild animal and insect sound effects, a backwards tape or two, more wild tom-tomming, and a rudimental snare solo that's capped by a tropical rainstorm. This track was also done in Sandy's garage on a three track Ampex recorder.

SANDY NELSON TODAY

Sandy Nelson sold his house in the Los Angeles area in the early Nineties to escape the threat of earthquakes, and most likely to find a more positive environment in which to play music. He now lives in Nevada where he operates his own company, Veebletronics, Inc., and performs with the James Quill Smith Band. Veebletronics specializes in marketing MIDI tracks of Sandy's drumming for sampling purposes. The James Quill Smith Band operates out of the Las Vegas area and their music is of the rock jam band variety, with a sound reminiscent of The Grateful Dead, The Rolling Stones and The Band. According to their publicity, the band has a strong groove sensibility in large part due to Sandy's drumming. Their web site was under construction at the time of this writing and emails to the band's publicist came back as undeliverable. The group has one CD, available on the website www.mbus.com or from the band's management care of Johanna Nezhoda, Mp3 Sound Records, 2232 S. Nellis #169, Las Vegas, NV 89104. At age sixty-seven, Sandy Nelson is still playing rock drums and is apparently showing no signs of stopping anytime soon.

"Study and learn technique, but keep it in your pants."

MICHAEL STUART-WARE

Sometimes a drummer makes his mark and disappears, only to resurface again at some point down the road—either as an active, working musician or as a result of his notoriety as a member of a group with whom he played. The latter is the case with Michael Stuart-Ware, drummer with the legendary Los Angeles band Love. Michael's drumming on the classic *Forever Changes* album has cemented his name in the hearts and minds of Sixties rock fans worldwide, although he also played on Love's second album, the uneven, though occasionally brilliant, *Da Capo*. Released in the fall of 1967, *Forever Changes* was Love's masterpiece, an unforgettable, ambitious collection of low-key, introspective songs, replete with brass and strings, that has stood the test of time and regularly shows up on many "best album" lists of critics and rock publications, including *Rolling Stone*. Truthfully, *Forever Changes* was a flop at the time of its release. History and hindsight have fortunately treated it with the respect it deserves.

The members of Love almost didn't play on *Forever Changes*. The band, which gigged infrequently and hardly ever ventured outside Los Angeles, was in terrible shape at the time of the sessions, due to inactivity and their ravenous consumption of all manner of drugs. Session players were brought in, including drummer Jim Gordon.

Elektra Records, the band's label, had other ideas, but let's not get ahead of ourselves. Love returned to the studio well rehearsed several weeks later and successfully cut the tracks that produced *Forever Changes*. Michael's contributions to this unforgettable, complex record are many. His playing was highly appropriate, sensitive yet forceful, creative and precise. He also contributed percussion and background vocals. Although the drums were not well recorded, there's no denying Michael's percussive ability.

Michael Stuart-Ware, known back then simply as Michael Stuart, was born in Texas and spent his early life there until his father took a job that necessitated a move to southern California. Michael had already discovered his natural talent for drums, inspired by Earl Palmer and his playing on Little Richard's hits. A lackluster student by his own admission, Michael pursued drumming throughout high school. He and his friends primarily listened to jazz artists like Miles Davis, Cannonball Adderly, Gerry Mulligan, Art Pepper, John Coltrane and Bill Evans. Michael also drew major inspiration from Joe Morello and his work on the classic jazz album *Time Out* by the Dave Brubeck Quartet.

"It's no surprise that when it came time to purchase my first real set of drums, naturally, I ordered the Joe Morello sparkling silver Ludwigs I found pictured predominantly in my most prized Ludwig catalog. From the beginning, I discovered I had elasticity built into the ligaments of my shoulders, wrists and elbows that allowed me to put out a lot of

energy and control. It felt like I had built-in electronic jackhammers; the sticks felt like they belonged in my hands."

Michael turned his life around, worked hard to improve his poor schoolwork and drumming and received the Outstanding Musician of the Year award in his senior year of high school. He played in a few bands and worked local gigs at that time and scored a scholarship to Pepperdine University. After a short time, he found the school's strict, religion-based rules and regulations not to his liking. After transferring to UCLA, Michael dropped out of college, having joined a band called The Fender Four, whose members originally hailed from Baltimore. The group, with Michael onboard, played around Southern California, eventually landed a record deal with Decca and changed their name to The Sons of Adam. Several garage-rocking singles (including a cover of The Yardbirds' "You're A Better Man Than I"), endless gigs, a freak modeling assignment and a movie appearance followed, but the Sons of Adam stalled out without getting a hit record. Michael had meanwhile become acquainted with members of the band Love, and feeling frustrated at The Sons' lack of success, accepted an offer to join Love, who had already recorded an album for Elektra Records and seemed poised for bigger things. The band wanted to replace their drummer, Snoopy Pfisterer. Michael had some reservations.

"Love had a tendency to play out of tune and their reputation as drug users was well known. My drug usage at the time was limited to smoking a joint with friends while listening to music. That was about as close to the edge as I cared to be."

With Michael onboard, Love almost immediately went into the studio to record their second album, *Da Capo*. Gone was the snarling, Rolling Stones/Byrds–informed folk-rock of their first long-player. *Da Capo* was a quieter effort, dominated by Arthur Lee's melodic flights of fancy, including the jazzy "Stephanie Knows Who," with its 3/4 to 5/4 time changes, "Que Vida!," with its lilting Latin rhythm, the rocking "She Comes In Colors," and the regrettable eighteen-minute jam, "Revelation," which takes up all of side two and has been vilified soundly over the years by fans and critics. Michael's drum solo at the end of the jam is well structured, concise and effective.

"I used Snoopy's Ludwig drums on 'Revelation.' He had two mounted toms. Why did I use Snoop's drums? I was totally unaccustomed to taking drum solos and since it was so out of character anyway, I figured the extra tom might help me do something better that I wouldn't have been able to do as well with one tom. I was desperate, man!

"I've heard *Da Capo* referred to as one of the best A-sides in pop music. Side two was an attempt by Arthur to get the group released from its contract with Elektra. We had better material that we never recorded that would have made a much better side two. I was shocked when Arthur started running the *Da Capo* tunes by me. The transformation of the group from heavyweight material like 'My Flash On You' [from the first album], to little ditties like 'Que Vida!' was overwhelmingly disappointing, but I decided to hang in there anyway and see what happened."

What happened was Love's inability or lack of interest in playing outside of the Los Angeles area for reasons including their aforementioned dependence on drugs. The group did little to promote *Da Capo*, and Elektra's publicity efforts went only so far.

The band members lived in nice rented houses, drove Porsches (albeit used ones), hung out, lived the California lifestyle, got high and played infrequently, living on weekly salaries that allowed them the luxury of avoiding day jobs. Michael never saw a dime in royalties from either *Da Capo* or *Forever Changes* at the time, but sued in 1971 and won a modest settlement of $6,000.

When it came time to record *Forever Changes*, Love was in no shape to handle the stress of the recording studio.

"We had problems from the outset. First, the guitar players couldn't get in tune. Then, we realized we hadn't spent much time getting our parts right in rehearsals. Problem was, there was no urgency. We got high too much and figured we'd get it all right when we got to the studio, that it would all come together. We were wrong."

Arthur Lee and Elektra's management team hastily decided to bring in studio musicians to lay the basic instrumental tracks. This didn't go down well with the band, but there was little they could do. Michael resigned himself to percussion overdubs and the occasional background vocal.

Next day, session mainstays Jim Gordon, Carol Kaye and others were brought in to cut the tracks. All the band members were present and watched numbly as these consummate professionals effortlessly cut one song, "The Daily Planet." The results were deemed acceptable at the time.

The following day, a representative from Elektra called the band and told them a decision had been made to give Love as much time to rehearse and get their songs together as they needed. To their credit, Elektra Records rejected the idea of using studio musicians and opted to have Love record the rest of their album without help, save for the brass and string players. Several weeks later, after intense individual and group rehearsals, the band reconvened at Sunset Sound in Hollywood and laid down the tracks that comprised *Forever Changes*. This time, it all came together. Michael played drums on every cut except "The Daily Planet." The story of how *Forever Changes* was recorded has been a source of controversy for years among Love fans. Now, the mystery is resolved.

But from the start, Michael was unhappy with the recording mix. "From the first playback, I could tell the

drums weren't mixed right—and not just the drums. Other things were wrong with the sound as well. Things were muddy and out of balance. When I pointed this out later to Arthur, he threw up his hands and accused me of looking out for myself. Later, after the record was released, Arthur admitted without a shred of remorse that I was right."

At that point, Love made feeble attempts at touring, but missed gigs and blown opportunities became the rule rather than the exception. The band showed up hours late for a concert at a college in upstate New York, and when Arthur Lee discovered they were second-billed to Frank Zappa & The Mothers at the Miami Pop Festival, Love pulled a no-show, much to Michael's dismay. *Forever Changes* wasn't selling either. The members began to drift apart. Bassist Ken Forssi took a short-lived job with Hannah-Barbera Studios as a graphic artist, guitarist Bryan McLean tried to get his solo career started and Arthur Lee ultimately announced he was splitting the original Love line-up and hiring new members.

With Love on the rocks, Michael did some session work and pondered gigs with singer/songwriter Danny O'Keefe and Neil Diamond. He refused both because the music didn't appeal to him. In Michael's book, *Behind The Scenes On The Pegasus Carousel,* his description of a live Neil Diamond show circa 1968 is hilarious. We'll discuss this book later on.

With his musical prospects looking grim, Michael considered a job working in a recording studio, but let it slide, then enrolled in law school and dropped out after two semesters, unable to concentrate on his schoolwork. He wanted to get away from the music business and the debilitating world of drugs that had sapped the life right out of Love.

"Professional music was like Disneyland: a good place to visit, but you don't want to live there. I wanted to be normal. I crammed a lot of 'abnormal' into six years while I was a professional drummer and needed to get away from it. I was fed up with the music business. It took me years to get clean from all my drug habits. I had become absolutely addicted to the 'getting high' solution to any difficult problem, or to try and have a good time. I did them all. I loved the drugs…I hated the drugs…and I wanted to stop, but I couldn't break free, because they were everywhere, man. You couldn't avoid them. I began to reevaluate my decision to get into professional music in the first place, so I took a job doing offset printing in LA, worked as a product inspector on a loading dock and climbed telephone poles for a few years pulling cable. I enjoyed all my day jobs."

In 1975, Michael met and later married his wife, Susan, and they have two sons: Kyle, now grown and attending film school in Los Angeles, and Brent, himself a rock guitarist, enrolled in community college. The family settled in South Lake Tahoe, California, and lives there still.

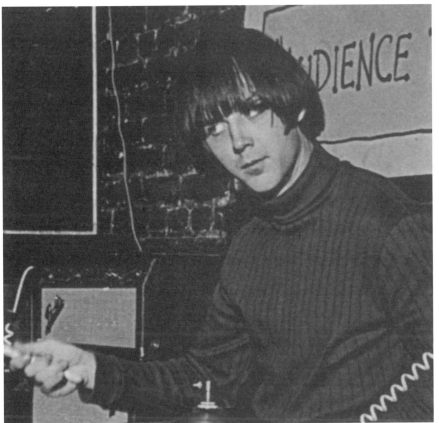

MICHAEL ONSTAGE WITH LOVE, CIRCA 1967.

EQUIPMENT

Michael played his silver Ludwig kit with The Sons of Adam and Love and later hocked and finally sold the set after leaving music. The set was a standard Ludwig Super Classic of its day: 14"x22" bass drum, 9"x13" and 16"x16" toms, and a chrome Supraphonic 400 snare, a duplicate of Joe Morello's set, as previously stated. His cymbals were A. Zildjians: 20" ride, 16" crash and 14" hi-hats. Today, Michael plays a set of black Tama Starclassic Performer birch drums: 16"x22" bass, 9"x12" and 11"x13" rack toms, a 16"x16" floor tom and a 5½"x14" wood snare with Remo Pinstripe heads all around. The cymbal setup is basically the same, but Michael sometimes uses an additional 16" Zildjian crash as a "quiet ride" cymbal that he says works well with brushes. Michael's hardware was Ludwig back then, and is now exclusively Tama. His sticks have always been Ludwig 5A or 5B models, usually with plastic tips.

SUGGESTED LISTENING

Michael's recorded output is small, but of high quality. The Sons of Adam's Decca recordings are well worth hearing, but exceedingly hard to find, and quite pricey as collectible garage rock 45s go these days. A small-indie label reissued them years ago, but this extended play 45-rpm is also tough to locate. On Love's *Da Capo*, Michael shines on "Stephanie Knows Who" and "She Comes In Colors," but his work on all the tracks is very good. *Forever Changes* should be listened to in its entirety as one would approach a piece of classical music.

After the realization that *Forever Changes* had become an acknowledged masterpiece of late Sixties rock, and after another writer tried and failed to publish a book on Love, Michael took the bull by the horns and wrote *Behind The Scenes On The Pegasus Carousel With The Legendary Rock Group Love*, a fascinating tell-all story of the band, the Los Angeles rock scene and the drugs that proliferated within the music community. Now in its second printing, *Pegasus Carousel* is published by Helter Skelter Publishing in the UK.

And after years of drumming inactivity, Michael is now the proud owner of a new set of black Tama Starclassic drums. Michael no longer plays with a band and has no plans to (although this author is trying to get him to do so), but enjoys playing along with jazz and blues on the radio at home.

Even if Michael Stuart-Ware never plays another gig, he can and should be proud of his contribution to rock music in the form of *Forever Changes*. In all, he played exactly what was necessary for each song and in doing so helped create a true Sixties rock masterpiece.

If you have never experienced this unforgettable album, I strongly urge you to do so. It is available as a CD reissue on Rhino Records at all better record stores. *Forever Changes* isn't get-down, feel-good party music. It demands attention. But trust me on this one: it's well worth the effort.

VERY SPECIAL MENTION

GINGER

*At forty eight years of age, He seems to have mellowed
quite a bit and has owned up to his early days
of rage and obstinance, appearing apologetic.*

Many writers, myself included, always thought Ginger Baker looked like some weird character out of a Charles Dickens novel.

With that fiery red hair, frightening, boney appearance, overblown ego, hot-headed attitude, and well known fondness for the ingestion of certain illegal and alcoholic substances, Baker seemed the ultimate stereotype of the nasty, I-used-to-be-great rock star burnout. His biting sarcasm and obvious contempt for some of the musicians he has worked with over the years, has lent considerable credence to the image.

Flash back to 1968.

Cream was very popular amongst those musically aware, especially with young musicians. Suddenly, all the older British Invasion rock went out the window, as local bands added tunes by Jimi Hendrix, Vanilla Fudge, The Doors, and Cream. At that time, Cream, Eric Clapton, Jack Bruce, and Ginger Baker, were rock demigods, the three finest, most

BAKER

GINGER BAKER

ONE OF CREAM'S EARLIEST PROMO SHOTS, 1966.

"...at the great age of sixteen I came home and told me mum that I was leaving the job next week, and I was leaving home as well."

—Musician Magazine

adventurous musicians, hence the rather egotistical name. Their stripped-down, three piece format was blues-rooted and sometimes experimental in the studio and highly improvisational live. They quickly got such mundane tasks as singing out of the way, in order to concentrate heavily on over-amplified jamming, that turned nearly every song into a wailing cacophony of sound, a musical free-for-all, with each member fighting the other two in a power struggle for victory. In their heyday, Cream could be electrifying at best. Toward the end, on their final tour of the States in the fall of '68, they were excessive, overbearing, sloppy, tasteless, and finally, boring beyond belief, a huge disappointment to their worshipping fans. They were also not on speaking terms with one another. Sometimes, as in the case of The Who, personal differences produce memorable music amidst the tension. In Cream's case, it produced a lot of unlistenable live trash.

From there, Baker went on to play with Blind Faith, Ginger Baker's Air Force, The Baker-Gurvitz Army, (he seems to like military names, eh?), worked with African musicians, drummed for Hawkwind, Atomic Rooster, and John Lydon's band, Public Image Ltd. Nothing that Baker has done since Cream has equalled his success with that band.

Perhaps you are now asking yourself just why Baker was included in this volume? Simple, he belongs here. I don't know the man personally, but his reputation has followed him for years. Firsthand accounts by journalist friends and acquaintances confirmed the rudeness with which Baker conducted himself. He was not a pleasant individual to deal with.

This author does, however, have a great deal of respect for Ginger Baker, the drummer. The man brought a real savageness to rock that has barely been equalled since. He was more than a mere timekeeper, he was very musical behind the kit. His African, jungle-inspired tom tom work guarantees a place in the Rock Drummers Hall Of Fame. Even his slashing patterns alone on "Sunshine Of Your Love," earned Peter "Ginger" Baker the right to stand with the very best. In his wilder days, Ginger undoubtedly would have been the first to tell you all this anyway.

Born August 19, 1939 in Lewisham, London, England, Ginger later moved with his family to New Eltham, a quieter suburb. He gained a reputation for eccentric behavior and supposedly found drumming to be a very natural, easy thing to do. His family was not musical at all and were all tradesmen-bricklayers, builders, and so forth. Ginger developed a strong interest in bicycling and for a while, planned a career as a cyclist.

As a teenager, Baker entertained his friends by drumming on his desk at school and one night at a party, they talked him into sitting behind a drumset. He took to it right away and discovered he could play the first time he tried.

In a recent interview in *Musician* magazine, Ginger commented.

"So I made my first kit out of biscuit tins–a toy kit. Then I'd only been playing for three months, but I got an audition with a trad band–quite a good one actually-and told 'em I'd been playing for three years. So I showed up at the audition with me tin drums–told 'em my regular drums were broken–and they were incredulous. But I got the gig, and straightaway I went home and told me mum, so she lent me fifty quid and I bought a good drumkit. All calf skins in those days. I knew within three months of having that kit that that's all I wanted to do. In fact, at the great age of sixteen I came home and told me mum I was leaving the job next week, and I was leaving home as well. And nobody could believe it, but I did it. Because one week, I actually earned twelve pounds playing the drums."

Baker's earliest influences were all American drummers–Baby Dodds, Art Blakey, Elvin Jones, Max Roach, and Philly Joe Jones. As with most of his British contemporaries, Baker came from a jazz background, but soon was lured by the intoxicating spell of rhythm and blues, which swept over England in the early Sixties. After a period working with various jazz groups, Ginger joined the Graham Bond Organization, a seminal R&B outfit, where he gained his first real taste of fame and adulation. It was also during this time that Baker began using heroin.

Although he claims to have never been seriously addicted to the drug, which used to carry a certain mystique for Fifties jazz players as a relaxant, Baker supposedly didn't kick smack until five or six years ago. Back in the Cream days, he was rumored to be a speed freak as well. It was the drug that allowed him to play so fast, some thought. Baker hotly denied ever being an amphetamine user, reiterating time and again that he is naturally a very "speedy" person, a ball of energy.

In any case, Ginger worked with Bond and Alexis Korner's Blues Incorporated and made friends with the likes of Paul McCartney and Charlie Watts, as well as Jackie Bruce and Eric Clapton;. In 1966, Baker, Clapton, and Bruce formed Cream. They scored hits in Europe and the States and their history and music has been already mentioned earlier and documented elsewhere. Baker has decidedly bitter memories over those days. He commented in the *Musician* interview.

"I gave up hassling and hassling with Cream and Blind Faith. The 60's was when everything sort of amalgamated into one movement and it was really nice. As for Cream...basically there was a time when I wanted to do it (again). There was a time when I really needed some money–everything had gone positively haywire. And I actually asked the other people if they'd like to do it and the reply I got from one of them–who will remain nameless–was 'I'm not doing it just to help you,' see. Now–so I've heard–they're both quite keen to do it...I'm afraid I'm not. I would have done it seven years ago for the bob, and I think perhaps it would have been a very bad thing to

have done. I wouldn't have learned the things I've learned over the last seven years. You see, I'm not rich anymore. I have found really good friends and they don't include the other members of Cream. The rich, successful bit, I'm not fucking interested in it. I want to play with only who I want to play with. And that does not include Jack or Eric at this moment, and I don't think it ever will–those days have gone."

"The only thing that kept Cream going as long as it did was the fact that it got successful. It was my idea–it was my band, in fact, originally. For me, it was a plan to make number one records and it did just that. The reason I stayed with it was because it would have been stupid not to; everything we did turned to gold."

One thing Cream did was to force those who looked askance at Rock 'n' Rollers and make them realize that there was some virtuosity going on. Ironically, Cream spawned thousands of bad imitators worldwide, players who didn't have one tenth the chops as Ginger, Jack, or Eric. Suddenly, every young drummer, who only months before had mastered "Wipeout", was now expected to play "Toad," Baker's fifteen minute drum solo opus with Cream. Ginger surely did turn a lot of heads around in the late Sixties.

Here's how veteran British music writer Chris Welch analyzed Baker's playing in a 1983 *Modern Drummer* article.

"A lot of Ginger's strength lay in his feet. Although wiry to the point of being skinny, he had tremendous reserves of energy in his legs, largely the result of frantic cycle racing. When he switched to two bass drums in 1966, his celebrated solo, "Toad," was given extra dimension, and he was able to create a torrent of sounds that he could control like an engineer in charge of power ducts. His use of cliff-hanging suspense, long tension-building phrases, bebop style accents, and cymbals rolls all helped open the eyes and ears of rock drummers to the potential of their kit."

The high point of "Toad" of course, was Baker's locomotive-like sixteenth note hammering on his twin bass drums.

Among the best cuts he recorded with Cream were "White Room," with its five/four intro, "Sunshine Of Your Love," "Traintime," spotlighting frantic brush work," N.S.U.," "Sweet Wine," and "I Feel Free," with its intricate hi-hat rhythms.

After Cream called it a day, Baker reportedly muscled his way into Blind Faith, one of the first so-called "supergroups," that included Clapton, Baker, Steve Winwood, and bassist Rick Grech, formerly from the group Family. They recorded and released an album on Atco, briefly toured the States and fell apart due to internal struggles.

The use of drugs intensified as Ginger formed his own group out of the ashes of Blind Faith. Steve Winwood came over on organ, Graham Bond played sax and his old friend, famed British jazz drummer and notorious junkie, Phil Seaman, played second drums. This was Ginger Baker's Airforce. They toured in Europe and America and recorded two LP's that sold primarily to Cream fans. It was a very loose amalgam of musicians and the music was best described as African-inspired jazz/blues. Like Blind Faith, Airforce didn't last long.

GINGER BAKER

From there, Ginger purchased a recording studio in Africa and moved to the so-called "Dark Continent" to play and record African musicians like Fela Ransome-Kuti, with whom Baker collaborated.

When his fascination with African music waned, Baker moved back to England in the mid-Seventies and formed The Baker-Gurvitz Army with brothers Adrian and Paul Gurvitz, later adding vocalist Snips, formerly of The Sharks. The music was the most commercial hard rock Baker had ever played, a calculated money-making venture that produced two decent albums that promptly went nowhere. They broke up shortly after.

At this time, Baker quit music altogether and took up the game of polo, with the intention of pursuing it full time.

bought an old farm, rebuilt the dilapidated house on the property and began tending some two hundred olives trees in his fields. Suddenly, the wild man found himself a farmer with a prospering business in southern Italy. This is the life he lives to this day. Although he occasionally plays a few gigs for some extra money, Baker now considers himself a farmer first, a drummer second.

As far as equipment, Ginger has used Ludwig drums since the early Sixties and swears by them. The silver sparkle set he used with Cream consisted of two bass drums, a 22" and a 24," 8x12" and 9x13" rack toms, mounted with Rogers fittings, and most likely two 16x16" floor toms. He has owned and used a very old wood Leedy 5" snare for years. He still uses it almost exclusively. His cym-

His biting sarcasm and obvious contempt for some of the musicians he has played with over the years, has lent considerable creedence to the image.

GINGER WITH JACK BRUCE AND ERIC CLAPTON, CIRCA 1968

He bought a stable full of polo ponies (or is that polo-ponies, *Honeymooners* fans?) from an Argentinian horse dealer and was unmercifully ripped off, as the horses proved unsuitable for polo.

He spent four years away from the drums in a futile attempt at establishing himself as a top polo player. He briefly formed another band called Energy, and developed an interest in rally driving.

In 1980, it was reported in *Melody Maker* that Ginger was to join Atomic Rooster. He worked with them for six months and left to temporarily join Hawkwind, where he stayed for another six months only to leave in disgust at their lack of musicality.

In 1983, Baker found himself broke with no work in sight. On top of all that, the British government said he owed sixty thousand pounds in back taxes. With no way of paying his debt, Ginger had two options; stay in England and face the music, or skip the country fast. He chose the latter, packed all his possessions and his girlfriend into an old Land Rover and drove across Europe, where he settled in southern Italy. He got a deal with the Italian label, CGD Records, and formed a new trio, Bakernband, with New Jerseyite Doug Brockie on guitar, and Chicagoan Carl Hill on bass. This band fell apart quickly too. (Brockie immediately returned to the Jersey club scene, where he unsuccessfully tried to capitalize on his association with Baker).

Since 1983, Ginger has released a couple of solo albums that received only limited distribution in America. He

bals have always been Avedis Zildjians, that include a 20" *Earth* ride, a 20" ride, 16," 18" crashes, a 22" riveted crash, a 13" flat crash, 8" splash and 15" hi-hats. Ginger now also uses a China type cymbal, Evans Hydraulic heads and Ludwig sticks. He currently owns two Ludwig sets, one at home in Italy and one in storage here in the States. Both are mahogany finished and are most likely smaller sets than what he used in the Sixties.

Since his flight from England, Baker has toned down the drumming histrionics to concentrate more on playing straight time with more solidity than ever before. He was profoundly affected by the dance music craze and his playing today shows it.

And there appears to be evidence that Ginger The Bad Boy has drastically toned down his attitudes as well. At forty-eight years of age, he seems to have mellowed quite a bit and has owned up to his early days of rage and obstinacy, appearing apologetic. The drug and alcohol abuse are apparently over and he seems happy and settled on his farm. There is no reason to believe he will ever return to music as a full time pursuit, but who knows?

No one approached the drums the way Ginger Baker did in the Sixties. He was a total original, one of the most distinctive drum stylists in the history of rock.

Let's remember him for that alone.

His biting sarcasm and obvious contempt for some of the musicians he has played with over the years, has lent considerable credence to the image.

GINGER BAKER TODAY

The famous red hair is gray now and arthritis has invaded his joints, but Ginger Baker will have celebrated his sixty-sixth birthday by the time this book lands in readers' hands. Baker made history in May 2005 when he reunited successfully with his old Cream band mates/adversaries Eric Clapton and Jack Bruce for a four-night stand at the Royal Albert Hall in London. The shows sold out in record time and scalpers were charging unheard-of amounts of money for seats. The shows went off without a hitch—no fighting, no arguments, no instruments thrown. The band has plans for only three more gigs at Madison Square Garden in New York City, but as we've seen over and over, things change quickly in the world of rock music.

Over the years, Ginger Baker has stayed musically active, usually playing music that's just a little left of center, and certainly not made for mass public consumption. In 1990, he released a solo album of third-world music called *Middle Passage*, produced by Bill Laswell, his frequent collaborator over the years. It featured bassist Jonas Hellborg and singer Jens Johansson. Baker has done other albums with these musicians. Also in 1990, Baker joined the hard-rock trio Master Of Reality and appeared on their CD *Sunrise On The Sufferbus*, which was recently rereleased. A new Masters Of Reality disc appeared in 2004 that contains Baker on drums. Another Baker solo album, *Going Back Home*, appeared in 1994, and yet another, *Coward Of The County*, in 1999.

In 1994, Jack Bruce and Baker put together a band called BBM that featured blues guitarist Gary Moore and reprised the Cream sound in many ways. Critics savaged the band's debut disc and they broke up. Baker played on Moore's solo disc during the same year. In 1995, he recorded with ex-Police guitarist Andy Summers and released jazz trio discs in '94 and '96 with Charlie Haden and Bill Frisell. In 1999, Baker released a disc with DJQ 20 and helped his son, Kofi, on an album with his band, Riddlehouse.

As always, Baker lived like a gypsy during the Nineties. He sold his olive farm in Italy and moved to California, but no longer lives there either. He is most likely back in England now, but that's not certain.

In terms of equipment, Baker now uses and endorses DW drums after years with Ludwig, and remains loyal to Zildjian. His Cream reunion set was in a green satin finish.

Baker appeared at the Modern Drummer Festival several years ago and performed an extended solo that earned him a standing ovation. This author later saw him walking through the lobby with a few staff members from *MD*. Based on Baker's reputation for surliness, a decision was made to refrain from questions.

GINGER BAKER WAS STILL PLAYING LUDWIG DRUMS WHEN THIS RECENT PHOTO WAS TAKEN.

HAL AND TOMMY SANDS, CIRCA 1959 IN WHAT
APPEARS TO BE AN ENDORSEMENT SHOT FOR
ROGERS DRUMS. NOTE THE BONG0 MOUNTED
UNDER SAND'S LEFT HAND.

STUDIO PLAYERS HAVE ALWAYS BEEN THE REAL UNSUNG HEROES OF ROCK 'N' ROLL. The guys behind the scenes who make the records miss out on most of the adulation, glamor, and groupies, but the good musicians, the busy ones, do partake of the financial rewards. Let's face another fact; A musician with a wife and family will usually reach a time when he no longer wants to continue running around the world on tour anymore. The studios, once you're lucky enough to become entrenched, can be just like a steady job, provided you get the call often enough. If you get to the point where you're cutting four or five sessions per day, you've got it made, at least until the next young, fast gun comes around to challenge you.

Studio musicians will always be with us, but for drummers, the gigs have dwindled considerably due to the proliferation of drum machines. Players who were once in-demand studio drummers like Andy Newmark, Jim Keltner, and Jeff Porcaro, have been forced to become computer programmers or face possible unemployment or extinction.

Of all the studio drummers who come to mind, The Dean, The Big Daddy of them all, is the incomparable Hal Blaine, who reigned supreme in the studios of California in the 1960's. He was *Numero Uno*, the guy who graced more hits than any other drummer alive. To paraphrase another writer or two, it would be much easier to put together a list of artists Blaine has *not* worked with, than it would be to compile such a list for those whom he has worked. In short, Hal Blaine, a six-time Grammy Award winner and the possessor of over three hundred gold records, quietly influenced more drummers than you or I would care to count, and along the way, graciously helped many young drummers get their first break. Ask John Barbata or Jim Keltner how Hal helped them.

He was
Numero Uno,
the guy who
graced more hits
than any other
drummer alive.

BLAINE

HAL BLAINE

HAL BACKING JAN & DEAN IN CONCERT AROUND 1964. THE BASS DRUM HEADS HAVE CARICATURES OF J & D.

HAL ON TAMBORINE WITH MEL TAYLOR OF THE VENTURES ON THE SILVER SPARKLE GRETSCH SET.

"I was the only white kid in these all-black clubs and I was accepted as a young white drummer who played good."

Do you remember, "Mr. Tambourine Man," "I Got You Babe," "Just Like Me," "Da Doo Ron Ron," "Good Vibrations," "Walking In The Rain," "California Dreamin'," "Stoned Soul Picnic," "Up Up And Away," "Bridge Over Troubled Water," "A Taste Of Honey," and "Kicks?" They were all huge hits and every one featured the drums of Hal Blaine. Although it's by no means complete, a list of artists Blaine has worked for reads something like this; Tommy Sands, Elvis Presley, Pattie Page, Sam Cooke, Frankie Avalon, Bobby Darin, Sonny and Cher, practically every act on Phil Spector's Philles Records label, The Grass Roots, The Byrds, The Monkees, The Mamas and Papas, The Fifth Dimension, Jan & Dean, Chad and Jeremy, Paul Revere and The Raiders, Martin Mull, The Carpenters, Simon and Garfunkel, Steely Dan, Seals and Crofts, Paul McCartney and Wings, George Harrison, John Lennon, and John Denver. He's also done literally thousands of television shows, jingles, commercial and film scores.

No wonder the license plate on his car used to read "Top Ten!"

Hal was born the son of Russian immigrant parents in Massachusetts, but lived his early childhood in Hartford, Connecticut. He spent many Saturday afternoons at the State Theater listening intently to the big name swing bands of the day.

"I spent so much time there when I was a kid. I saw every big band and every famous vocalist of the day. It was an amazing education that really opened my eyes to music."

When Hal was nine, he took apart one of his parent's kitchen chairs and used the pieces to beat out rhythms on pots and pans. Sensing his budding talent, his older sister bought him a drumset for his thirteenth birthday.

The Blaine family moved to California when Hal was fourteen and it wasn't long before he was working casuals and local dances. He lived in the projects and consequently made friends with black kids, who turned him on to rhythm & blues. Hal also enjoyed singing, comedy, and dancing and won the jitterbug contest in high school with a black girl he was friendly with.

He briefly tried his hand at standup comedy, singing and acting, but when these didn't pan out, Hal, who up to that point has been totally self-taught, decided to go back to square one and learn drums from the ground up. After a stint in the Army, Hal moved to Chicago and with the G. I. Bill and help from his family, enrolled in the Roy Knapp School Of Music. He studied there for three years, majoring in drums and minoring in piano, while also studying theory and harmony. He helped support himself by working nightclub gigs with local jazz groups, including one led by former Benny Goodman sax player, Vido Musso.

Hal eventually returned to California and began playing around the San Bernardino area.

"I was the only white kid in these all-black clubs and I was accepted as a young white drummer who played good. I listened to drummers like Sharkey Hall, Jesse Sailes and or course, Earl Palmer. They were the main black drummers who did blues, R&B, and Rock 'n' Roll. The people who went to these clubs were blue collar workers and once Friday night came, they just wanted to party. They used to go into a frenzy over a slow blues. I used to sit in at JD's Rose Room, Jack's Basket, and the Oasis Club, over on Central Avenue in Los Angeles. All those clubs are gone now. I used to sit there and soak it all up, learning all the time. I loved what I heard."

Hal got his first real break when he joined Tommy Sands' backup band. From there, he hooked up with pop singer Patti Page and this helped him get gigs doing the scores for some of Elvis Presley's throwaway movies. Hal even got to appear in some of them.

As a result of his work with Presley, Page, and Sands, the word began to spread that Hal Blaine was the man to call when a solid, reliable drummer was needed. The session work started coming in and the guy who called Hal the most was the enigmatic genius, Phil Spector. Sandy Nelson had done a couple of sessions for Spector, but it was Blaine who became the house drummer for Philles Records.

From his interview several years ago in *Modern Drummer* magazine, Hal commented on his days with Spector.

"Phil Spector, God bless him, used to let me just go nuts on records. It was really from Phil and the Crystals and the Ronettes and all those wonderful records we were doing and I would go totally bananas on the endings of those songs. None of that has ever been duplicated. People have hired the same musicians, the same studio, the same engineer to get the same thing, but it could never be duplicated. To this day, only Phil Spector can get that sound."

I asked Hal what it was it about those Spector records that made them so successful?

"It was a totally new sound–a 'wall of sound.' No one had ever used three or four or five guitars, two bass players, and six or seven percussionists before. There was a great camaraderie going on at those sessions. Phil used to hold me back like a race horse–'Hold it.' 'Hold it.' 'Hold it.' 'Ok, Go!' The sessions were intense, but they were real loose at the same time. The Spector sound was literally forming before my eyes. It was great fun, absolutely memorable. The only problem was that Phil never wanted to take a break. You practically had to beg him to let you go to the john! Phil let me do whatever I wanted, so I did some outrageous stuff."

"The Spector band, 'The Wrecking Crew,' became the most wanted group of musicians in the world. The Beach Boys hired the whole group later and we did all their records too."

How would Hal describe a typical working day back in the Sixties?

"Well, I'd get up around 6 AM, at least two hours before my first session. That would be around eight or nine in the morning. Maybe I'd do a score at the Disney Studios from nine to twelve. Then I'd do a rock session from one to four at United or Western Three Studios.

HAL BLAINE

From there, I'd maybe do a TV show from five until eight in the evening. I'd take a break, then do say, a Beach Boys session from midnight until all hours of the morning. Sometimes we'd fall asleep in the studios next to our instruments and they'd have to wake us up to start over the next morning."

"That Western Three studio became the mecca for so many sessions back then. The Mamas and Papas and The Beach Boys did a lot of things there."

"It wasn't all solid work. Sometimes I'd go to do a Brian Wilson session and only play for about twenty minutes, then leave. I'd get paid for the whole thing."

One of Hal's most memorable drum parts was the beat he inadvertently created for The Ronettes "Be My Baby." Hal commented about how it came about.

"I really did that by accident. So many things are created accidentally it seems. Phil wanted to hear the fourth beat in every measure go CRACK! Somehow, I just did the rest of it—boom—ba—boom-CRACK. Another thing I did spur of the moment on that record were the quarter note triplets on the fade. Phil loved those. He made me do them all the time from then on! That lick became associated with me and a lot of drummers have told me that when producers or engineers want that, they just say "Hal Blaine!" Max Weinberg told me Bruce Springsteen did that to him once when they were recording. I guess I became famous for having my own sound."

Another part of the Blaine sound was the way he tuned him drums and the volume at which he played in the studio in the beginning.

HAL SEEMS INTENSELY INVOLVED DURING THIS SESSION. THE FLOOR TOM APPEARS TO BE A TIMBALE!

"When I first started in the studios, the producers used to say,'Why are you hitting those things so goddamned loud?! You're pushing the needles way into the red.' H. B. Barnum, the well known producer, who I must mention, stuck up for me and told them, 'You better listen and accept what this guy's doing and saying, because this is the coming sound of drums in the studio.' Another thing I caught a lot of flak for was the way I tuned my drums. Most studio drummers at that time tuned real high. The drums sounded so damned tinny to me. I tuned them down to their proper pitch in relation to the size of each drum. Now everyone does it and that's how it should be."

Hal's method of tuning gave him the idea for a multiple tom setup.

"In 1962, I got this idea to build a drumset with a lot of tom toms. I talked to my friend, Howard Oliver, and he built them for me. The set had 6," 8," 10," 12," 13," 14," and 16" toms, with my Ludwig chrome snare and a 22" bass drum. We showed the drawings to Ludwig and they copied it and called it the *Octaplus*. I was the guy who designed that concept and I had the first set like that."

I mentioned that another very well known rock drummer I had interviewed recently claimed he had had the first *Octaplus* outfit, to which Hal sputtered, "Bullshit! He probably wasn't even born when I invented that drumset!"

Did Ludwig ever compensate him financially for the design? With a touch of bitterness in his voice, Hal remarked, "They gave me drums whenever I wanted them, but that's all. There wasn't any money. I guess you can't patent a drum."

Hal's choice of cymbals over the years has always been Zildjian. He uses either 12" or 14" hi-hats, a 22" medium ride, 17" sizzle, 16" crash and a 9" splash, as well as a China-type on occasion. He's used the same cymbals nearly all his career. Was he given the freedom to create his own drum parts on sessions?

"Sure. People hired me because they knew who I was and that I would play something that fit the music. In the case of movie or TV scores, you played what was written out for you, but on rock or pop sessions, I was usually given *carte blanche* to create whatever I thought was best. Paul Simon and Art Garfunkel always gave me *carte blanche*–totally."

What types of sessions were his favorites?

"You know, the sessions I liked best were the ones where we recorded nice ballads, like The Carpenters 'We've Only Just Begun.' Things like that. I have a knack for interpreting lyrics musically and those sessions were great. I also want to mention a real sweet guy I worked for named Don Piestrup, who is the number one jingle guy on the West Coast. He's an absolutely brilliant arranger and we did jingles and commercials for just about every commercial product you can think of–McDonald's was just one of many."

In the late Seventies, with studio work beginning to dry up, Hal agreed to join John Denver's road and studio band. Hal stayed with Denver until 1984, when he retired. One gets the impression that his exit from the Denver band was not a happy situation.

On the road with Denver, Hal used a four piece set of Ludwig drums.

"Ludwig gave me a raw (unfinished) maple set and I had them painted with American Indian symbols. I still use that set around here for casual gigs."

"Around here" is Scottsdale, Arizona, where Hal now calls home. The wild life of Hollywood finally got to be too much and he got out.

"I just didn't feel like getting on that freeway and driving ninety miles per hour anymore."

Several years ago, Hal wrote an advice column for *Modern Drummer* magazine. "I did that for over two years They asked me to do a column and I told them I didn't want to do one about learning drums, but I would do an advice column. You wouldn't believe some of the letters I got. Kids who wanted to be drummers and were going to commit suicide—kids whose parents didn't understand them. Some of those letters were really depressing, but I tried to give them good advice. I still get letters from kids like that."

How does he feel about the changes that have taken place in recording technology lately?

"These young engineers who are coming up now want everything one level—LOUD! Everything has to be played at maximum volume all the time. A lot of it is theatrics. Let's face it, if an engineer comes over to your bass drum and moves the mic' a sixteenth of an inch, you know that's theatrics."

Besides his gigging, Hal is involved in fund-raising work locally and enjoys that very much. He has also completed his autobiography and although there is no set working title, Hal expects it to be released this winter. He will do a promotional tour to support it.

What advice could he impart to young drummers?

"Know your craft so you can be the best you can be. Be happy with the music you play. Study, learn to read. Learn about music-theory, harmony. Drummers who know how to read are much more confident. Learn every aspect

A CLOSE-UP OF THE OCTAPLUS RACK TOMS. HOWARD OLIVER. MADE THE DRUMS AND USED LUDWIG HARDWARE AND FITTINGS.

How much is he still working?

"I consider myself semi-retired now. I really don't want to work much. I'm glad I took a pension out years ago, because I don't have six-figure years anymore. I work around here locally. Sometimes I do country western gigs or jazz, or even rock gigs. I'll put on a cowboy outfit one night and a tux the next. The overall quality of musicianship around Scottsdale is pretty piss-poor, but I've found some good people. They're delighted to have me playing with them."

"I've done a few sessions in this area, but there really isn't much of a scene. I still go out on the road. I just did the Telluride Jazz Festival and have worked lately with Mason Williams David Grisman, and Mose Allison."

What are his feelings on the electronic revolution in the drum world?

"It's all evolution. *The Octaplus* set revolutionized the business and now drum machines are doing the same thing. They're quick and easy to use, they keep perfect time and have great sounds. One thing drum machines don't have is a heart. They can't respond to other musicians. Only a live musician can do that."

you can. Music and medicine are strange bedfellows. but they're both the same in that there are new breakthroughs all the time. Work with bass players and learn why they do certain things."

"I'm an accompanist. I've never been a soloist. I love comedy and that's all timing. You have to know when to inject a little comedy now and then. The key word that is important for drummers is—LISTEN."

"For someone who had such a great career, I've had a shitty personal life. I'm not trying to give you a sob story, but my first wife died. She was a real sick lady. The two kids we adopted—my daughter turned out fine, but my son is doing time behind bars and will probably spend the rest of his life there. He got involved with bad people. I've been married five more times to women who fell in love with me because I was a semi-name musician. Later. I found out that all most of them were interested in were my credit cards. I'm a sucker for tall blondes. I lost my house in Hollywood, my boat. I owned a vintage Rolls Royce and had to sell that. I took a beating on my boat. My sixth wife and I have just quietly separated and it really wasn't bad. We're still friendly."

HAL BLAINE

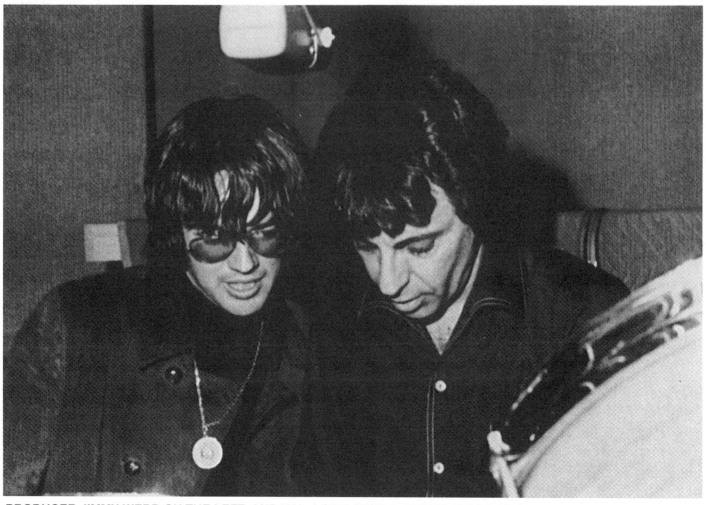

PRODUCER JIMMY WEBB ON THE LEFT, AND HAL, LOOK OVER A CHART, CIRCA 1966.

> ## "The key word that is important for drummers is— LISTEN."

"Through all the bullshit I went through, my drums were my best buddy. If I hadn't been working, I would have gone nuts."

"At this point, I don't have a lot to look forward to in life. All I ever wanted was the little house with the white picket fence. Every time I get the union newspaper from Los Angeles, a couple more of my old friends have died."

Hal isn't as depressed as he sounds. He has a nice home, investments, a pension and friends that care about him and his welfare. He plays only with whom, where, and when he desires.

Maybe he was just blowing off a little steam.

"You know, I'm going to be sixty years old this February. Sometimes it seems like I'm still fifteen playing my drums and trying to make something of myself. Looking back over my life, I ask myself, 'Where did it all go?' "

CIGARETTE IN HAND, HAL SWINGS INTO ACTION BEHIND HIS CUSTOM MADE OCTAPLUS KIT.

"There are a lot of great young drummers out there . . . but I wish they wouldn't get so many tattoos!"

HAL BLAINE TODAY

Session master Hal Blaine has been living in Palm Desert, California, for several years now and has formally retired from the music business. He appeared on the *Spiderman II* movie soundtrack last year and played on three albums: one by Jim Beloff, a jazz ukelele player from Los Angeles; one by a new Mexican artist named Alberto Galaz, whom Hal described as a "Ricky Martin–type" singer; and one by Mason Williams titled *Music For The Epicurean Harkener*, with whom Hal has had a close working relationship for nearly forty years. The Mason Williams disc was nominated for a Grammy.

Rob Cook's Rebeats Publishing recently rereleased Hal's book, *Hal Blaine And The Wrecking Crew*, in a revised and expanded format.

On his decision to retire, Hal said, "I just don't have the interest anymore. So many of my friends have passed away, retired or moved out of the area. I had lunch today with Tony Orlando's manager and was asked if I'd consider working with Tony. I turned them down. People call me all the time to do live dates. I get calls from jazz groups, but the thought of doing live work doesn't appeal to me anymore.

"The whole record business has changed so drastically from when I was working the studios. The record companies are repackaging all the old stuff and this entire Internet downloading of music has been very damaging. Let's face it, we're in a different era. Drummers growing up with hip-hop and metal are experiencing a very different world than I did. There are a lot of great young drummers out there doing some amazing playing though, but I wish they wouldn't get so many tattoos!

"I've been interviewed a lot lately for cable TV music documentary shows from A&E and others. I have one right here that I haven't watched yet. Some of these people want me to relate the entire history of The Beach Boys from start to finish. I can't get into that. I don't remember everything that happened!"

Hal has been endorsing and using Taye drums for the last couple of years and is very happy with them. He still uses the same Zildjian cymbals from his glory days in the studios.

"The people at Taye treat me so well and the drums are excellent. I didn't even want any drums and they insisted on sending me two sets. I used them last year on sessions and they sounded great. The Chinese take a lot of pride in their workmanship. Besides, I think the factory supervisors cut off their fingers if they make a little dent in a shell or screw something up!

"Lately, I've been sitting here watching the checks come in. Yesterday, I got a big one: a six-dollar SAG [Screen Actors Guild] check for a part I played in a Steve McQueen movie called *Baby, The Rain Must Fall*. Glen Campbell and I played members of Steve's band in the movie. Six bucks. Can you believe that?

"I would say to young drummers out there to learn about the pioneer drummers and read books like yours to learn. When I was a kid in Chicago, I had a big library of books about Gene Krupa and other swing drummers. That's how I learned. It's time for me to rest now and enjoy my retirement."

Hal Blaine's web site is www.halblaine.com.

HAL NOW PLAYS TAYE DRUMS.

AT PHILHARMONIC HALL, NEW YORK, NOVEMBER 1968.

MITCH MITCHELL

Mitch was one of a handful of totally distinctive drummers from the Sixties whose influence can be felt today among current, younger players.

J erry Edmonton commented in his interview that Mitch Mitchell was a perfect
example of how totally free a rock drummer could be and I agree with that
statement completely, for Mitch was one of a handful of totally distinctive
drummers from the Sixties whose influence can be felt today among many current, younger players. Carmine Appice considers Mitch one of the best and
most influential drummers from the decade, and he's not the only one who said
that.

Mitch is best remembered, of course, for his work with the Jimi Hendrix
Experience, a gig that lasted only a couple of years. In that short time, Mitch
carved his own niche as an unrestrained diamond-in-the-rough technician, a
fleet-footed, lightning-wristed player, whose modern jazz-rooted, improvisational
style well suited the soaring, highly emotional, exploratory, and sometimes
chaotic, wildly destructive guitar playing of Jimi Hendrix. After Hendrix's death in
1970, Mitch worked with Larry Coryell and Jack Bruce for a while and later
formed an ill-fated band called Ramatam. One LP was released on Atlantic
Records amidst a large publicity campaign, but Mitchell left soon after and has
scarcely been heard from since. Is he burned out? Has he lost the will to play
and his interest in drums? Only Mitch Mitchell knows the answers to these
questions and he doesn't like to do interviews.

Mitch was born in 1947 in England and attended a school for theatrically talented children. At a young age, he developed a strong interest in rhythm and
tap dancing. He also trained as a boy soprano while in school and began doing
jingle work. He was around a lot of drummers and had the opportunity to try his
hand behind the drumkit. Seeing Fred Astaire playing drums in a movie also
inspired Mitch to pursue the instrument. In actuality, he found very few drummers to emulate, preferring to listen to bass players for influence. Two drummers who did have a profound effect on Mitch were American jazz players Elvin
Jones and Tony Williams. It is Jones whom Mitch is most often compared to
from a stylistic viewpoint. From him, he gained the freedom of expression and
savage attack that appeared many years later with Hendrix.

MITCH MITCHELL

"I worked with the band for eighteen months and no one ever told me I had the gig."

SWEDEN, SPRING 1967.

As a teenager, Mitch worked in Jim Marshall's music store. Marshall is the man who makes the famed amplifiers so many hard rockers prefer. Mitch labored in the guitar section of the store and one day, took a casual lesson from a drum student at the school, who, according to Mitch, could cut a lot of Joe Morello's routines, note for note. So essentially, Mitch is totally self taught. He fully admits that his music reading is not good and that his knowledge of the basic rudiments is poor.

Through his job at Marshall's, Mitch started his drumming career as a substitute for Screaming Lord Sutch, Johnny Kidd and The Pirates, and others. He also worked with a few semi-pro bands including one that included Jim Marshall's son, a tenor sax player. Mitch did a stint playing in Hamburg, Germany, as many other English musicians did at the time. At the Flamingo Club in London, Mitch saw Georgie Fame, a British R&B singer/keyboard player and realized he would like to work with him, but that would not happen for a while.

Mitch then lucked into session work and soon after, joined his first all-professional band, The Riot Squad. When that turned sour, he went back to free-lance work with The Pretty Things and others. His friendship with producer Denny Cordell eventually won him the gig with Georgie Fame and The Blue Flames. From a 1982 interview in *Modern Drummer*, Mitch commented on his experience with Fame.

"I never really joined. I mean, I was doing the session with Denny Cordell and Clive (Georgie Fame's real name) said, 'Hey, do you fancy coming down to Brighton tomorrow?' So I say, 'Right,' and get down there and Bill Eyden is playing with them. So he did the first half of the set, I did the second half of the set, and they said, 'We'll be at the Manor House tomorrow, so bring you drums, alright?' So I had a session in the afternoon and then I go to the Manor House, and there's no one there. I mean, the roadies have set up the equipment, so I put up my drums and I leave a space because there's no one else's drums there. It gets to be ten-to-eight, and suddenly the band appears. I say, 'What's going on here?,' and it's sort of 'OK, well here we go, son. One, two, three, four...,' and I'm playing the drums. I worked with the band for eighteen months and no one ever told me I had the gig."

Eighteen months later, on a Monday afternoon,Fame fired the entire band. On Tuesday, Mitch got a call from Chas Chandler, ex-Animals bassist and manager of Jimi Hendrix. The next day, Mitchell played with Jimi and bassist Noel Redding and the gig was offered. Originally, it was supposed to be for only a ;week's worth of work, but as you must know, Mitch joined Hendrix permanently. He and Redding adopted Hendrix's wild look, complete with Afro hair and velvet and satin clothing. The original plan was to expand the band beyond the three-piece format, but after playing awhile as a trio, the decision was made to keep it as it was. Hendrix eventually tried to get Steve Winwood to join, but that never came about.

The Jimi Hendrix Experience, with personnel set, made their name first in England, with a series of club and concert appearances that attracted rock's elite, who were all curious as to what this uninhibited, black American guitar player was all about. It didn't take long for the word to spread; Jimi Hendrix and his band were destined for superstardom. When they came to America in the spring of 1967, they played at the Monterey Pop Festival, did some time at the Fillmore West, and were somehow booked as an opening act on The Monkees tour. When a few people complained about Hendrix's erotic showmanship, Jimi and the boys quit the tour in what now can be viewed as a great publicity move.

Along with Cream, The Jimi Hendrix Experience set the tone for what was to become the virtuoso era of rock music, the late Sixties. To put it mildly, Hendrix and his group gained a first-rate reputation in a very short period of time. In that brief period, Hendrix and his band mates were darlings of the music industry who could seemingly do no wrong. It wasn't long before it began to fall apart. Hendrix, a free-spirited individual, was beset by business problems and rapidly grew tired of the image he had created. He parted company with bassist Noel Redding and recruited an old Army buddy, Billy Cox, in his place. Mitchell continued to work with them for a while, but left in 1969. Hendrix formed a new group, The Band Of Gypsies, with Buddy Miles on drums, but they didn't make it, despite a live album recorded at the Fillmore East on New Years Eve, ushering in a new decade.

Mitchell, rested and renewed, came back on drums and worked with Hendrix and Cox until Jimi's death in September, 1970, the victim of a drug overdose. Hendrix, a musician who never stopped playing, recorded many bits and pieces during this time that were later finished after his death, often with studio musicians covering the uncompleted tracks. Once again, Mitch Mitchell dropped out of the picture, but not for long. He resurfaced in late 1970, as one-fourth of a jazz/rock quartet that included, as mentioned, Larry Coryell, Jack Bruce, and blind keyboardist Mike Mandel. The sound was fusion at its earliest, with several old Cream tunes like "Politician" thrown in to keep the audience happy. I was fortunate to have seen this band at the Fillmore and was naturally impressed with Mitch's playing. He still had the same magic hands and even used a double bass drumkit onstage.

Mitchell's brief tenure with Hendrix has been, to this date, the zenith of his career. There are many outstanding drum tracks he recorded with Hendrix, but some of the best are "Foxy Lady," with it's heated, yet controlled bashing, "Hey Joe," "If Six Was Nine," "I Don't Live Today," with it's explosive freak-out drumming at the end, and the lovely, "Little Wing," in which Mitchell proved that a drummer can play a ballad with imagination and still show off some chops.

As far as equipment, Mitchell used a five piece Premier kit with Hendrix on their first US tour that included Monterey Pop. From there, it was all Ludwig, first, a five piece set in black pearl, and later a kit in silver sparkle. Mitch's preferred drum set-up was snare, bass, one rack tom, and two floor toms, in classic Buddy Rich style. He used at least three crash cymbals, all A. Zildjians. Over the years, Mitch became an enthusiastic collector of old drums and cymbals, scouring pawn shops and out of the way music stores for hidden treasures. By the time he joined Jack Bruce, Mitch expanded his kit to include double bass drums and another rack tom. He kept this arrangement through his final days with Jimi as well, and

MITCH MITCHELL

SOUNDCHECK, HOLLYWOOD BOWL, SEPTEMBER 14,1968.

*Perhaps there was something in his personality
or maybe it was the reult of the experiences he lived in the Sixties
that caused Mitch Mitchell to withdraw from the rock scene.*

BACK IN ACTION, SPRING, 1987.

used the same chrome covered set at the Randal Island Pop Festival in New York City, in the summer of 1970.

The next project was Ramatam, a short lived band comprised of extroverted, but silly guitarist Mike Pinera, a founder of The Blues Image and also a member of the reformed Iron Butterfly, and April Lawton, another guitarist, whose name reportedly used to be Freddie until he/ she got a sex change operation … or so it has been said Their lone album with Mitch was passably good but hardly an earthshaker.

Ramatam played on my college campus in 1972 and live, they weren't too spectacular either. As the music columnist of the school paper, I drove over to the local Holiday Inn where the group was staying. As I was poking around trying to find the band Mitch drove up in a rented station wagon. Excitement gripped me as I ran over to meet him and ask a few questions. Clearly, he didn't want to speak to a punk college kid reporter and answered my inquiries as curtly and briefly as possible, refusing to talk about Hendrix in any way. I later found out from one of the roadies that it was Mitch's last gig with the band. He just didn't want to be bothered, and looking back, I can't blame him.

After exiting Ramatam for whatever reasons. Mitch Mitchell essentially disappeared from the limelight as a name drummer. He returned home and worked for a short time with a loose aggregation of players called Hinckley's Heroes. He bought a house in England and kept a place in New York City, spending quite a bit of time in this country frequenting jazz clubs and doing occasional gigs He became heavily involved once again in the studio scene, doing jingles. of all things, hardly stimulating work for a drummer of his stature and talent.

A very reliable source recently reported Mitch living in the Los Angeles area.

Maybe there was something in his personality or perhaps it was the result of the experiences he lived in the Sixties that caused Mitch Mitchell to withdraw from the rock scene. Regardless, one gets the feeling that he never lived up to his real potential. There was so much more he could have done and could still do, if he would only give it another chance.

ADDENDUM:

August, 1988:

It was just reported to me that Mitch Mitchell and Noel Redding toured with pickup musicians around the United States last year. Performing some Hendrix material and anything they could throw together with little, if any rehearsal. Mitchell and Redding simply did what Chuck Berry does all the time—they recruited guitarists and vocalists wherever they went, went onstage and played the gig. They did not perform in the New York metropolitan area to this writer's knowledge.

MITCH MITCHELL TODAY

Of all the drummers featured in this book, Mitch Mitchell is certainly the most mysterious. He seems to keep an extremely tight lid on his personal and professional activities and has done so since the 1970's. After participating in a few forgettable musical projects (like Ramatam) following Jimi Hendrix's death, Mitchell has remained largely out of the public eye, but we do have some interesting facts to share.

In the 1980's, Sky Saxon, former lead singer with The Seeds, claimed to be working with Mitchell in a band called 555 Dragonslayer, although to this author's knowledge, there are no recordings available. Most likely, this story is false.

Mitch was interviewed in the late 1980's by *Drum!* magazine, and although he spoke candidly about his years before and with Hendrix, he did not touch on his current activities. In the Nineties, Mitch became a DW drum endorser and appeared in an ad for the drums that ran in all the major drum magazines. A smiling, healthy-looking Mitchell was pictured sitting on a zebra-striped couch next to zebra-striped drum set.

In 1990, Mitch wrote a book called *Inside The Experience* about his days with Jimi Hendrix, but once again, there was no information about his current activities. The book is now out of print. At around the same time, he auctioned off a white Fender Stratocaster, reportedly the famous one used by Hendrix at Woodstock, for nearly $250,000, the highest price ever paid for a guitar at the time.

Mitch did a little session work and appeared on two cuts on Junior Brown's *Long Walk Back*. He also played on four cuts with blues guitarist Scott Holt on his *Dead Of The Night* disc. One of them was a new version of "Voodoo Chile."

Over the years, Mitch has been rumored to live in Atlanta, France or Nashville, the third being the logical choice. He occasionally turns up playing at the Exit/In club in Music City and performed there for music professionals during the NAMM show in 1999. He has also been seen frequently in Nashville-area music stores.

Most recently, Mitch has been working with a band called The Gypsy Sun Experience that includes former Hendrix sideman bassist Billy Cox, guitarist Gary Serkin and three female singers. No commercial recordings are available and not much else is known as of this writing.

Mitch supposedly jammed at the Exit/In in 2000 with jazz/rock fusion guitarist Larry Coryell and bassist Tony Berlin, but again, we don't if this is fact or fiction.

Finally, a reliable source in Canada who works in the percussion industry informed me that Mitchell is working a day job.

Whatever the reasons for his mysterious existence, we can only hope that Mitch Mitchell, the only surviving member of The Jimi Hendrix Experience, is healthy, happy and playing drums.

A RECENT PHOTO OF MITCH TAKEN SOMEWHERE AT A LIVE GIG.

RINGO

RINGO, CIRCA 1964

STARR

HE MUST HAVE DONE SOMETHING RIGHT. PEOPLE TO THIS DAY STILL LOOK FOR DRUMMERS "WHO PLAY LIKE RINGO"

Few of us who grew up in the 1960's will ever forget that special Sunday evening, February 9, 1964, the night Ed Sullivan, via his weekly television variety show, introduced the United States to The Beatles. Not since Elvis Presley, had there been such an explosive groundswell of excitement over Rock 'n' Roll. From that night on, the face of rock music was changed forever.
Thank you, Ed, wherever you are.

Seated on a riser behind a four piece Black Oyster pearl Ludwig set, was a slightly doleful-looking gentleman named Richard Starkey, better known to the world as Ringo Starr. His timekeeping was straightforward and painfully elementary, his fills achingly spare, economical, and sometimes awkward. Over the next several years, as others surpassed him in technical flash and impressive displays of chops, Ringo was criticized as being, well, less than talented. Time, however, has vindicated Richard Starkey. During his tenure with The Beatles until the group's demise, he did his job admirably, adding only what was deemed necessary to compliment The Beatles material. Ringo succeeded, simply because what he played was perfect for the music. He must have done something right. People to this day still look for drummers "who play like Ringo." If you don't believe me, just check the musical want ads. On top of all this, he certainly inspired countless millions of teenagers worldwide to learn drums.

There's no doubt about it. Ringo Starr was a very, very important rock drummer.

Born in the Dingle, a rough section of Liverpool, on July 7, 1940, Richard Starkey was an only child, whose father walked out when Richie was three. A sickly child, young Rich spent a total of three years in the hospital due to peritonitis and pleurisy. While hospitalized, he began banging on toy drums to pass the time and after regaining his health, bought a large, used bass drum and fashioned a pair of sticks out of scrap wood. His stepfather, a kind man who treated the boy as if he was his own, bought him an old drumset and Richie joined an amateur skiffle band in February, 1958, The Eddie Clayton Skiffle Group. No one in the band was proficient, but they played shows around Liverpool, usually for free. Unable to transport the set due to lack of a car, Ringo was forced to use just a snare, hi-hat, and cymbal, but it was enough to get by at the time.

RINGO STARR

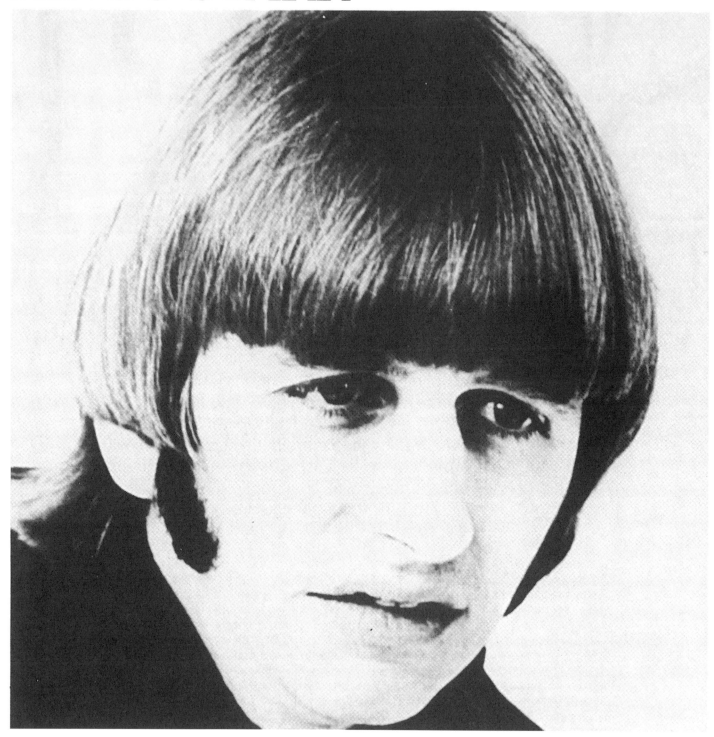

A CLASSIC MID SIXTIES PORTRAIT OF RINGO.

NOT SINCE ELVIS PRESLEY, HAD THERE BEEN SUCH A GROUNDSWELL OF EXCITEMENT OVER ROCK 'N' ROLL.

The only time Ringo ever tried to sit behind his drums and practice, it caused such a ruckus among his neighbors, that he never practiced again. Ever. He preferred to practice, make mistakes, and learn on the bandstand instead.

In 1959, Richie joined Rory Storme and The Hurricanes, a popular Liverpool beat band. The following year, the entire group gave up their day gigs and went pro. It was at this time they changed their names and Richard Starkey became Ringo Starr, due to the rings he wore even then in pre-Beatles days.

Rock 'n' Roll had caught on in a big way in England by 1959 and skiffle died out. Ringo immediately fell into rock and also developed a disdain for jazz, feeling the music lacked emotion.

PROMO SHOT FOR THE FIRST SINGLE, 1963. RINGO STILL LOOKS VAGUELY GREASY AS HIS HAIR GROWS INTO THE BEATLE CUT.

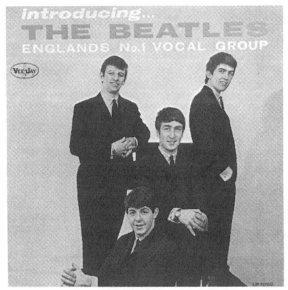

THE FIRST U.S. BEATLES LP, ON VEE JAY RECORDS.

U.S. ALBUM JACKET, BEATLES VI.

He grew a beard and worked the club circuit with Storme for over two years. Ringo even had his own section of their shows called "Starr Time," where he did about twenty minutes on lead vocals from behind the kit.

Playing the same clubs as Storme were The Beatles. Ringo met them and they became friends, so much so that The Beatles manager, Brian Epstein, asked Ringo to sit in one day as their current drummer, Pete Best, was ill. Ringo did the gig and liked playing with The Beatles. The feeling was apparently mutual, as Pete Best was eventually sacked and Ringo was asked to join.

In his 1982 interview in *Modern Drummer*, Ringo commented on his feelings about joining The Beatles.

"I felt The Beatles were a better band and I thought I had done everything our band could do at the time. We were just repeating ourselves. So it was time to move on again, and that's why. And I liked the boys as well as the music."

The firing of Pete Best created an uproar in Liverpool. Handsome and sullen in a classic James Dean way, Best had a following and there were shouting matches at Ringo's first few gigs with The Beatles of "Ringo never, Pete forever" and vice versa. It didn't last long, as Ringo was quickly accepted as The Beatles new drummer.

It wasn't all roses for the Fab Four right away. There were plenty more long nights in filthy clubs in Liverpool and Hamburg, Germany, for very little money, but everyone connected with The Beatles knew it was just a matter of time until the world discovered them. They were right.

The Beatles, through the tireless efforts of Brian Epstein, finally got a record deal in 1963. The engineer at the session was George Martin, the man who would play a very integral part in The Beatles music until their demise in 1970. George didn't care for Ringo's drumming and called in a session drummer, Andy White, to cut "Love Me Do" and the flip, "Please Please Me." Ringo played tambourine reluctantly. Ringo later dubbed his drumming on the album

RINGO STARR

"HELLO UP THERE" —RINGO LOOKS UP LAUGHING.

version of "Love Me Do" and it's virtually impossible to tell the difference in the two.

From then on, Ringo supposedly cut all The Beatles sessions, except the one that produced "Back In The USSR" and "Ballad Of John And Yoko," both of which featured Paul on drums.

This brings us to a couple of controversial points; First, how much of what was played on The Beatles records were Ringo's ideas? It has been reported to this writer by a few reliable sources that the other three Beatles dictated in exacting terms what Ringo played on record. Another musician, who toured with the group on their last US tour in 1966, related that in conversations with The Beatles, it was revealed to him that very often, each member of the band would record a different part of the drumkit. In other words, Ringo would play snare, John would play bass drum, George would play hi-hat, Paul would handle cymbals, etc. Indeed, there are pic-

tures taken around the "Sgt. Pepper" period of this actually taking place.

Second, New York session drummer Bernard Purdie made the claim several years ago that he "fixed up" at least twenty-one early Beatles tracks in 1964. Purdie is hardly a modest individual, so there's reason to doubt his words. Purdie's statement has always been hotly denied not only by Ringo, but everyone in the Beatles camp. At this late date, no one seems to know for sure anyway. If it makes Beatle fans feel any better, Purdie received several threats on his life after making this remark.

Ringo did take direction from John, Paul, George, and George Martin to a certain degree. All drummers have to deal with this sometimes unfortunate fact, particularly on original material.

Harkening back to the Ed Sullivan Shows, it was these few appearances onstage that set off Beatlemania in America, where we were still recovering from the

WHAT RINGO DOES,
IN THE MOST BASIC
OF TERMS,
IS MAKE THE MUSIC
FEEL GOOD.

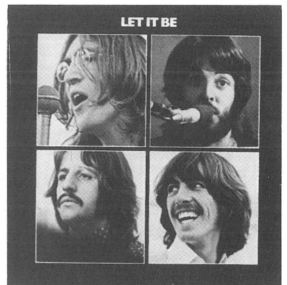

RINGO AT WORK.

THE END OF AN ERA.

assassination of President John Kennedy. The free world, weary of Cold War nuclear nightmare, needed four moptops from Liverpool, England. The Beatles became gods and their profound influence on sociological and musical events was enormous. Their success caused permanent changes in the lives of millions of people worldwide.

In the minds of some "serious" musicians, The Beatles and all the other long-haired bands they paved the way for, were a communist plot, a veritable scourge of musically inept hoodlums. It became fashionable among jazz players and purists to knock a Ringo Starr or a Charlie Watts. Of course, most of this criticism was borne from jealousy and it continues in some circles to this day. The Beatles treasury of music speaks for itself. Its place in history is sealed and the loudest "critics" eventually came over to their side, or were never heard from again.

For over two and a half years, The Beatles reigned

supreme on the charts and in the hearts of rock fans worldwide. There were other challengers, but none surpassed The Fab Four's extreme popularity. This is not meant to be a history of Beatlemania, but any discussion of Ringo must include some further mention of the group's total dominance of the popular music scene in those years. Needless to say, The Beatles received unmitigated amounts of praise, adoration, attention, and most of all, phenomenal sums of money. It was a whirlwind existence and it changed each member of the band in different ways.

They continued to release hit after hit, album after album, almost always of superlative musical quality. As The Beatles grew, their stature in the serious musical community grew to messiah-like proportions. The world seemingly waited for each Beatle record with fevered anticipation.

RINGO STARR

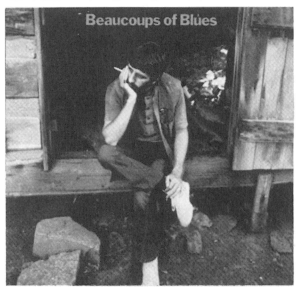

**above and opposite page:
A COLLECTION OF COVER SLEEVES FROM
THE STARR MAN'S SOLO CAREER.**

Ringo consistently supplied what was needed in every case. Respect was finally accorded his talents and deservedly so.

His personal life was also satisfying. Ringo married Maureen Cox, a hairdresser, in 1965. They had two children, both sons, Zak and Jason. Today, Zak Starkey is an up-and-coming drummer.

By the spring of 1966, it was becoming increasingly apparent that The Beatles were beginning to slip. The *Yesterday and Today* album was released with a cover photo of the boys dressed in white butcher gowns with raw meat and decapitated baby dolls. It was deemed offensive by so many record retailers, that Capitol pulled the LP within days and slapped a new cover, a completely innocuous photo, over the other. Those "Butcher Covers" are today highly prized collector's items that fetch big dollars among Beatle fans.

While on tour in the Philippines at that time, the group mistakenly ignored the invitation of Imelda Marcos, wife of President Ferdinand Marcos, and failed to make an appearance at a state dinner held in their honor. The next day, while boarding a plane to take them from the airport in Manila, The Beatles were booed, kicked, and roughed up by locals insulted at the gaff.

Right before they were to begin their US summer tour of 1966, John Lennon, who had become increasingly more withdrawn and tired of dealing with the pressures of being a member of The Beatles, unleashed a furious controversy when he remarked that The Beatles were more popular than Jesus Christ. What was meant to be a comment on the lack of religious convictions amongst the youth of the world, was turned around by the media and misinterpreted as an attack against Christianity. The ruckus that resulted caused Beatle record-burning rallies in the southern Bible Belt states and a general denouncing of the group. It was not a positive way to commence a tour, one that would prove to be their last.

Vern Miller, Jr., bassist for The Remains, the opening act on that tour, remembered Ringo in the following way.

"As a person, Ringo was very humorous and humble, friendly yet reserved. You couldn't really hear the drums too well, there was so much screaming. I recall he used to shake his hair a lot. When he'd hit his snare drum, it looked as if his stick hit the drum and stayed there. It's funny, because Albert Goldman mentioned the same thing in his new book about John Lennon. I didn't detect any boredom or disenchantment with Ringo. However, I did see that in Lennon."

It was announced upon completion of the 1966 tour that The Beatles would concentrate strictly on records.

Again, the Fab Four produced trend-setting and often exploratory works of music. 1967's *Sergeant Pepper's Lonely Hearts Club Band* turned millions of heads for its eclecticism and daring.

As The Beatles grew as individuals, schisms developed between the four. Paul McCartney attempted to take control and get them back onstage. He supposedly developed an overbearing authoritative attitude in the studio.

At one point, during the recording of the *White Album*, Ringo walked out and did not return for two weeks, and only after repeated calls and gestures from the other three.

Finally, in 1970 amidst a deluge of personal conflicts, business hassles, lawsuits, and intense acrimony, The Beatles split up. Although they worked together in different combinations again and continue to do so today, the dream was indeed over.

Ringo, slightly unsure of what to do with his life, recorded two schmaltzy solo albums, *Sentimental Journey* and *Beaucoups Of*

Blues, neither of which were big sellers. He also accepted acting roles in a few films, including *Candy*, *The Magic Christian*, and *Blind Man*. He soon returned with a vengeance to the recording industry with hits like "Oh My My," "You're Sixteen," "Photograph," "Backoff Boogaloo" and "It Don't Come Easy." On all of these, he continued to play as simply and uniquely as he had always done with The Beatles.

As the Seventies moved into the Eighties, Ringo continued to release solo LP's and singles, none of which registered with the public. He recorded with George Harrison and Paul McCartney, starred in a prehistoric movie comedy called *Caveman*, where he met and fell in love with his second wife, actress Barbara Bach, did a series of wine cooler commercials and generally lived the good life, enjoying his money. He has not released any solo recordings since the early 1980's. Incredibly, Ringo has been unable to get a record deal lucrative enough to make him return.

When analyzing Ringo's style of drumming, one must keep in mind that he is not a well-schooled player. From a purely academic perspective, Ringo Starr is a very limited drummer. By his own admission, he cannot execute a proper roll or a complete pattern of any sort around the snare and toms. What Ringo does, in the most basic of terms, is make the music feel good. He refers to his playing as being fraught with "silly fills," due to his self-admitted lack of technique, but he says it proudly. Often asked to comment on his drumming, Ringo has stated emphatically that he considers himself the best rock drummer. Maybe it's egotistical, but he has been and continues to remain in-demand as a session player.

Sometimes chops do not a real drummer make.

As far as equipment, Ringo's first set was an ancient kit that his stepfather bought him. He went from that to a better, more modern set of Ajax drums in the early Sixties, but was also photographed playing Premier drums. The famous Ludwig kit he used with The Beatles was, as mentioned, a Black Oyster Pearl outfit that consisted of a 22" bass drum, 9x13" and 16x16" toms, and a wooden Ludwig 5" snare. The snare stand was Ludwig, the cymbal stands Premier.

For a short period, Ringo used a white marine pearl set that he dubbed the "mini-kit." The sizes appear to be the same as his Black Oyster set, with the exception of the bass drum, which looks like a 20."

Around 1968, Ringo got the maple wood, double rack tom set that he used during the filming of *Let It Be*, the movie. On that set, he used nothing but calfskin heads and ultimately still prefers the warmer sound of these on the toms in particular. Ringo's playing has always featured an abundant amount of tom tom work. His main timekeeping tools are the snare, bass drum, and hi-hat.

Speaking of cymbals, Ringo's choice has always been Avedis Zildjian, usually a 22" ride, 20" crash, and 14" hi-hats.

Ringo summed it up in this quote from Max Weinberg's book, *The Big Beat*. "My soul is that of a drummer. It was luck that I happened to play in the biggest band on earth. We did make some real good music. But playing was all it was. If it hadn't happened, we could just still be playing in Liverpool. At one time I was an engineer in a factory and played drums part-time. But it came to where I had to make a decision—I was going to be a drummer. Everything else goes now. *I* play drums. It was a conscious moment in my life when I said the rest of the things are getting in the way. I didn't do it to become rich and famous. I did it because it was the love of my life."

RINGO STARR

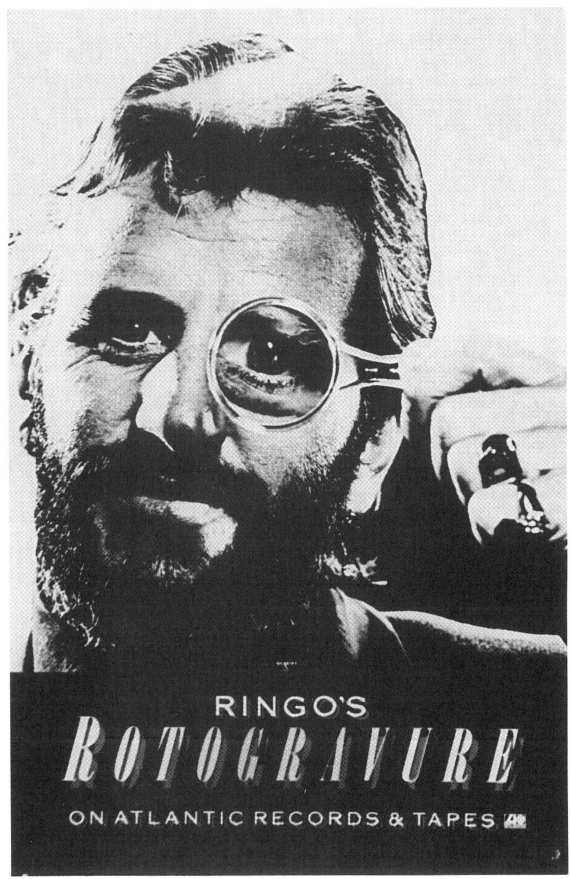

PROMO PIECE FOR THE *ROTOGRAVURE* ALBUM.

RINGO STARR TODAY

In 1988, when I attempted to set up an interview with Ringo Starr, it became apparent The Beatles' basher was in no condition to do much of anything, let alone talk to a music journalist for a book on Sixties rock drummers. By September of that year, Ringo and his wife, Barbara Bach, were beginning alcohol and drug detoxification at a clinic in Tucson, Arizona. They became involved in a twelve-step program called the Minnesota Method and it worked for the couple. Ringo hasn't had a drink or drug in more than fifteen years and, at age sixty-five, is healthy and productive. Ringo still practices transcendental meditation, which he learned from Maharishi Mahesh Yogi during his Beatle days. Ironically, Ringo was the most skeptical of the Maharishi at the time.

In a recent article in *Saga* magazine, Ringo said, "Even if I've not meditated for months, I can do it. It's something I do a lot more now than I have been over the last fifteen years. For me, meditation is a break from thinking. The benefits to me are quieting my mind and soul down."

Throughout the years, Ringo has toured regularly in the US and Europe with his All-Starr Band and, lately, The Roundheads—which have included Ringo's son, Zak Starkey, Peter Frampton, Jack Bruce, Dave Edmunds, Sheila E., Eric Carmen, Simon Kirke, Gary Brooker, Todd Rundgren, Colin Hay, Nils Lofgren, Mark Farner, Felix Cavaliere, John Waite, John Entwhistle, Joe Walsh, Rick Danko, Levon Helm, Randy Bachman, Billy Preston, Burton Cummings, Mark Rivera, Timothy Schmidt, Jim Keltner, Clarence Clemmons, Dr. John, Joe Walsh and others. The tours almost always sell out and draw critical praise. Each member gets a moment in the spotlight to perform his or her own signature songs. Ringo sees to it that his musicians are comfortable on tour and they respond in kind with praise for the boss. This writer saw The All-Starr Band a few years ago and can attest to the spirit of the band's camaraderie. Ringo was very generous in sharing the limelight. It was definitely interesting and entertaining to hear Ringo drumming to songs by Cream, Bad Company and even The Raspberries! Of course, he did a great job.

Burton Cummings said this in an interview for *In Concert in 1992*: "You realize now how much personality this guy has. He's charming to work for. He disarms any arrogance or condescension. There is no arrogance with this guy."

Nils Lofgren had this to say from a *Philadelphia Inquirer* story in 1995: "He's very laid-back and very generous. His idea is that you're not backup musicians playing Ringo songs, but a band that plays everyone's music as well as we can."

Over the years, Ringo has been in demand as a session drummer. A number of years ago, I was watching VH1 when the new Tom Petty video came on. Seated behind the drums was a clean-shaven Ringo playing great time and looking every bit like one of the boys in the band.

Glancing over the local music papers recently, it was evident that people are still looking for a drummer who plays "like Ringo." Since the first pressing of this book, Ringo has finally been accorded long-overdue respect and admiration from pro and amateur drummers and the music community in general. Public praise for the drummer's abilities and influence has been constant over the last several years. *Modern Drummer* magazine awarded him a lifetime achievement award not long ago. It's about time that happened. A gratifying tribute to Ringo occurred when famed jazz/rock fusion drummer Steve Smith admitted several years ago that he finally "got" what Ringo was all about after years of thinking him less than talented. And Steve was not the only one to experience such a revelation. But still, not everyone understands.

Occasionally, some misguided soul will post a thread on an Internet drum forum putting Ringo down. He is immediately assailed by hordes of drummers who do understand what Ringo does behind a drum set. Clearly, the man has more fans than detractors these days. To those of you who don't comprehend what Ringo is about, just listen for his rock-solid timekeeping, the way he colors arrangements with perfectly appropriate fills and the wonderful feel he has for the music at all times. If you don't get it after all that, you're hopeless.

Ringo has kept busy recording over the years as well. His latest is *Choose Love* and, as of this writing, Ringo is making the rounds doing television and radio shows for promotion. There is no Roundheads tour scheduled anytime soon, unfortunately. His previous release, *Ringo Rama*, sold weakly, but drew critical praise.

Ringo's other recent project is the book *Postcards From The Boys*, a collection of postcards the other Beatles sent to him while they were on holiday around the world. The cards were found recently, stashed in a shoebox; they brought back a flood of memories and a good idea.

In his *Saga* interview, Ringo commented, "I put the cards on the shelf and kept thinking, 'I should really do something with these.'"

Many of the cards had drawings on them and witty sayings, and together, they formed an interesting glimpse of what the other Beatles were up to at that point in time. Ringo decided to publish them in book form with all proceeds going to charity. Sales of the book have been brisk since its release in 2004.

On a personal note, Ringo maintains his chief residence in the Los Angeles area, but he and Barbara also spend time in Monte Carlo and their second home in Cranleigh, Surrey, England. Ringo likes the California sunshine and laid-back lifestyle.

To correct an error in *GRDOT*'s first pressing, Ringo has three children from his first marriage: two sons, Jason and Zak, and a daughter, Lee. As mentioned earlier in this book, Zak Starkey played drums with The Who for several years, but now occupies the drum chair with Oasis, and has fathered Ringo and Barbara's two grandchildren.

Ringo is perhaps one of the few drummers anywhere who has stuck with the same brand of drums and cymbals for more than forty years. He still uses and endorses Ludwig drums and Zildjian cymbals. Ludwig markets a drum set called the Fab Four Piece, a not-too-accurate recreation of Ringo's well-known Sixties kit, available, of course, in oyster black and other vintage-style finishes. Ringo appeared recently on television playing a blue sparkle Ludwig set, and this author saw him playing a champagne sparkle set in New York City a few years back. Ringo still owns all his old drum kits from the Beatle days: four oyster black sets, a silver sparkle set, and the famed blonde-wood five-piece kit used during The Beatles' last public performance on the roof of the Apple building. Photos of these sets appear in the book *Beatles Gear* by Andy Babiuk.

When Ringo turned sixty-four last year, many reporters asked him the inevitable question: How did it feel to reach the age of a beloved Beatles tune? In the *Saga* interview, Ringo commented, "Oh yeah…when I was twenty, sixty-four seemed ancient. Now my body's there, but in my head I'm still twenty-four. I guess that's how it works. When it happens to Paul, he's going to have to go to Fiji and hide from it. It's going to be hell for him."

A RECENT PHOTO OF RINGO ON TOUR, STILL PLAYING HIS BELOVED LUDWIG DRUMS.

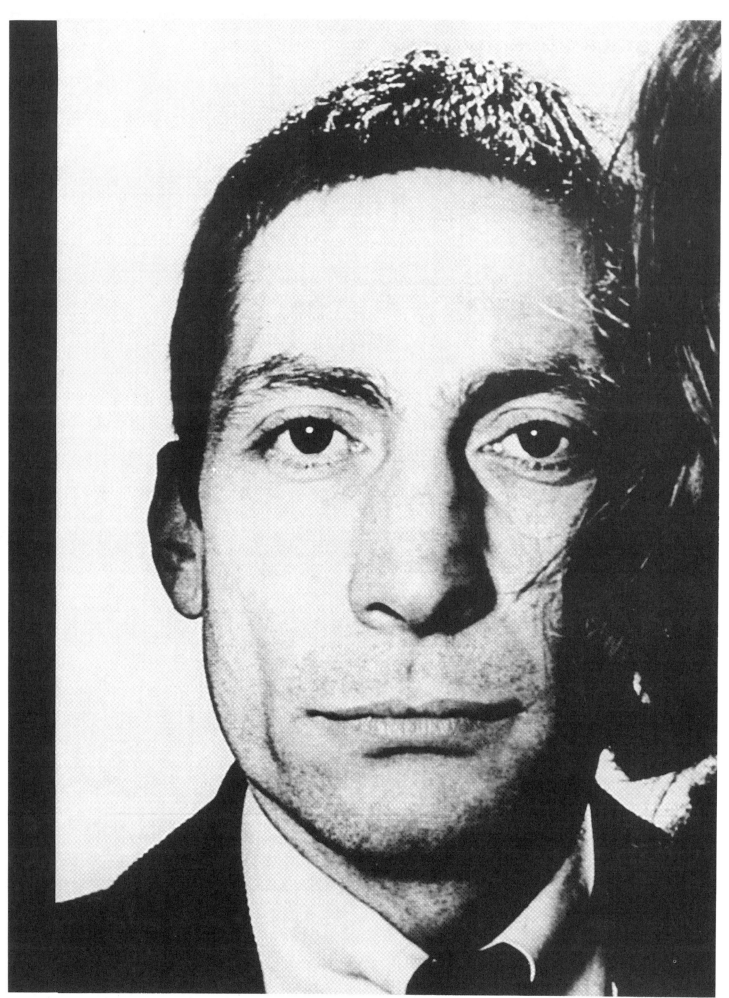

A CREW CUT CHARLIE AS HE APPEARED ON THE COVER OF *BLACK AND BLUE*.

CHARLIE WATTS

**In all the world of rock 'n' roll, can you honestly conceive of
The Stones with *someone else* in the drum chair?**

E HAS BEEN SITTING BACK THERE SINCE 1963, playing drums for the World's Greatest Rock 'n' Roll Band, just feeling lucky to be a part of it.

He still feels that way, but never expected it all to last for two months, much less twenty-five years.

They are a rock institution.

He is actually happier playing jazz.

Their image and lifestyle is a lot more exciting than his, the stuff that makes gossip columnists happy.

No matter where he is, he'd rather be home with his wife, daughter, and his collections of antique silver, American Civil War uniforms and weapons, and toy soldiers. Besides, he hated the hordes of screaming girls that followed the group around in the Sixties. The loss of privacy was maddening to him.

They are The Rolling Stones.

He is Charlie Watts, longtime drummer of The Rolling Stones, and in the late 1980's, he is one standard against which many, many rock drummers are judged, whether he likes it or not. You see, Charlie is a very self-effacing man. He always credits Keith Richards for inspiration. Keith turns it around and credits Charlie, who just does not like to talk about himself.

Think about this for a minute; In all the world of Rock 'n' Roll, can you honestly conceive of The Stones with someone else in the drum chair? Technically, any musician is indispensable. Players who are strong and stylized as Charlie is, indelibly stamp their musical imprint on whatever situation they're involved in. Drummers like this are the ones who make the music feel good, stimulate their fellow players, and create a highly individualistic role based upon years working with the same people. And if the band is wildly successful, the rewards aren't hard to take either. Charlie Watts has done all this and more. He is such an integral part of The Rolling Stones, that if he were to leave, it is questionable whether the band could continue. The vibe, the feel, would never be the same without Charlie's contribution. Without him back there, that wonderfully nasty feel would be gone. That nasty feel, is the key to the Watts style.

If you were to speak with Charlie, he'd tell you that he was a minimally talented Englishman who happened to get lucky. He's been quoted as saying that any drummer could play with The Stones, but he's wrong, of course, and thankfully so.

Should you question almost any mature rock drummer, professional or amateur, as to his or her opinion of Watts, you'd likely hear superlatives like, "solid," "great time," and perhaps the phrase, "everything a rock drummer should be." But in the early days with The Stones, Charlie was not recorded particularly well and was definitely not taken too seriously. On some of the groups' early records, he tended to push and pull tempos, and on occasion, his fill-ins were odd and barely fit right. Once in a while, he was even guilty of starting a song on an upbeat instead of a downbeat (check out "Little Queenie" on *Get Your Ya-Ya's Out*, or the beginning of the more recent single, "Start Me Up").

Charlie was one of those who, along with Ringo Starr, Dave Clark, and other Sixties rock drummers, were commonly criticized by jealous, holier-than-thou jazz musicians as being less than talented,"just a rock drummer." Little did they know.

Charles Robert Watts was born June 2, 1941 in London, England. Mr. Watts drove a truck for the railroad and Mrs. Watts was a housewife. Neither were musical, in fact, Charlie once commented that his family were lucky they were able to play the record player, much less a musical instrument. The family was comfortably working class and settled in Wembley, outside of London. Charlie showed an early aptitude for sports and art. His parents greatly encouraged his participation in both activities, but at the age of fourteen, his father bought him his first drumset, a pieced-together conglomeration that

THE WORN ALBUM JACKET TELLS THE STORY. CHARLIE IS SECOND FROM RIGHT ON THIS VERY EARLY ALBUM COVER.

STONES MANAGER AT THE TIME, ANDREW LOOG OLDHAM, ENCOURAGED THEM TO LOOK MOODY. THEY WERE AND THEY DID.

THE STONES FIRST GREATEST HITS PACKAGE, *BIG HITS (HIGH TIDE AND GREEN GRASS).*

Charlie, "Took to straightaway," according to Mrs. Watts. He had, by then, developed a strong interest in American jazz and as most young drummers do, would play along with his favorite records.

He especially enjoyed big band swing and small group Fifties jazz and singled out drummers Max Roach and Tony Williams as strong influences early on. He also developed a reputation as a sharp dresser, a trait he supposedly inherited from his Dad. His father accompanied him on clothes-buying sprees until he was seventeen and Charlie, to this day, has always favored conservative, Ivy League clothing, only occasionally succumbing to the usual rock star get-up of jeans, T-shirts, and so forth.

Keen on pursuing his artwork, Charlie enrolled in Harrow Art College upon completion of his basic education. At this time, the lure of American rhythm and blues caught up with him and after finishing art school, he joined up with a couple of different R&B outfits while working a day job at a London advertising agency. One of those groups was Alexis Korner's Blues Incorporated, where he met Mick Jagger and also worked with many other seminal British bluesmen like Dick Heckstall-Smith, Jack Bruce, Cyril Davis, and Graham Bond. When the gig began to interfere with his work at the ad agency, Charlie gave it up, and for a while, he appeared to be heading for a promising career away from music. Charlie knew what his destiny was, however, and was soon back in the musical swing of things, temporarily playing with a group called Blues By Six, when Mick, Keith Richards, and Ian "Stew" Stewart, then The Stones full-time piano player, approached him to join the fledgling group, who had just begun to call themselves The Rolling Stones. The Stones had used a few drummers before Charlie, including Tony Chapman and Mick Avory, who later joined The Kinks. Apparently, it was a very difficult decision for Watts. Keith Richards has often commented that asking Charlie to join was a decided step up for the group, that Charlie was doing fine without them already. Why should he join this ragtag bunch of bohemian layabouts? He had a prestigious job that paid him well, was playing drums as a profitable sideline, and really wanted to play more jazz, his first love. Charlie saw little potential with The Stones and carefully considered the decision. He asked Alexis Korner for advice, and he thought the group could do very well and that Charlie should join. With some reluctance and misgivings, Watts climbed aboard The Stones bandwagon in January, 1963.

Charlie was somehow attracted to the seamier side of what he saw in Brian Jones, Mick, and Keith. Something about their very tattiness stirred him in some way, undeniably a minor revolt against his very proper upbringing. Charlie was fascinated by his musical cohorts, and the rest of the band liked Charlie on a personal level as well. The relationship and good feelings have endured twenty-five years.

Now that The Rolling Stones were at last a complete band, they builtup their reputation by working the R&B club circuit and within a short period of time, secured a recording agreement with British Decca Records and London Records in America. Their first few releases didn't do much, but eventually, The Stones took off toward rock superstardom, as we all know. Their remarkable career has survived, despite many obstacles, a story that has already been well documented.

At first, The Stones horrified many older and more conservative types with their unkempt appearance, penchant for substances illegal, and irreverent interpretation of American black music. The Stones certainly ruffled a lot of feathers in their early days. It always seemed that Charlie was never really a part of all the wild goings-on that pervaded the group's existence. He was there, but not there at the same time. Charlie married his wife, Shirley, in the mid-Sixties, and always preferred his sedate home life to the more public lives of Jagger, Richards, Jones, and later, Ron Wood. Bassist Bill Wyman, whose real surname is Perks, by the way, rarely seemed to get into trouble either.

It didn't take long for Charlie to come to the conclusion that The Rolling Stones were an outstanding if not spectacular Rock 'n' Roll band. He has for years, been quoted commenting what a great band he's with and how fortunate he is to be part of such a tremendously successful project.

The Stones earliest records were little more than cover versions of their favorite blues and R&B tunes done in their own style. Charlie's drums were, in most cases, relegated to the rear of the mix, as they say. The practice of burying the drums was very common in the early to mid-Sixties. Consequently, it's rather difficult to always hear what Charlie was doing on those seminal Stones tracks. My earliest impression of Watts was hardly one of enthusiasm. He sounded just ordinary, no more or less talented than the average beat group drummer of the period. As mentioned, the drumming on the first few Stones albums is characterized by fluctuating tempos, as it was long before click tracks were used, as they are today. It presented a clear picture of a drummer with a good, basic feel for bluesy Rock 'n' Roll, who was rough around the edges, and was gaining an education in the art of recording, a learning process. The studio, with all its pressures to turn out commercial, polished records in a short period of time, is an intimidating experience for any inexperienced musician, no matter how hot his live chops are.

It wasn't until the release of *Get Your Ya-Ya's Out*, the second live Stones LP, that Charlie sounded relaxed, comfortable and confident. That was the recording that finally made this writer sit up and take notice that there might be something to this Watts guy at that. His work during the period that Mick Taylor played guitar with the group was at least better recorded, and there were selected moments of greatness, like the jazzy turnaround on "Can't You Hear Me Knocking," his appropriate, yet assertive accompaniment on "Wild Horses," from *Sticky Fingers*, the kick-it-out raunch of "Rocks Off," and the sensitive country shuffle rhythm of "Sweet Virginia," from *Exile on Main Street*.

The Rolling Stones have always been a band that experimented, being fans of many different types of roots music, be it reggae, soul, blues, country, or Chuck Berry-like Rock 'n' Roll. Charlie could always be counted on to provide the right sort of drumming to compliment each tune in question. Even when the band tried their hand at disco on "Miss You," Charlie was right there sounding contemporary, playing the obligatory four beats on the bass drum with the steadily open/shut hi-hat that was utilized on almost all disco records of the time. And on the 12" dance mix, the drums were mixed way up front for a change!

When ex-Face Ron Wood joined The Stones in 1975, it ushered in a whole new era for the group. Woody played more like Keith than had Mick Taylor, who was a more polished lead guitarist. With Taylor, the distinctions between him and Keith Richards were very noticeable. With Ron Wood, it became hard to tell who was playing what, as their styles were so similar. Also, Woody brought a new burst of creative energy to a band that had begun, at least on vinyl, to get stagnant. Undoubtedly, Charlie felt the effect of Woody's presence, and on 1978's *Some Girls* album, he is absolutely the dominant force throughout the record. His drums sound very live and are literally all over the LP. One critic and at least one local radio jock commented that *Some Girls* was "Charlie's Album" from start to finish. I have to agree. It contains Charlie's hottest drumming to date on cuts like "When The Whip Comes Down," "Shattered," "Lies,"and the incredible "Respectable," that highlights his favored four-on-the-floor bass

It didnt take long for Charlie to come to the conclusion that The Rolling Stones were an outstanding if not spectacular Rock 'n' Roll band.

THE BRITISH PICTURE SLEEVE FOR "SATISFACTION". CHARLIE'S DRUMS WERE BLUE PEARL LUDWIGS.

I HAVE NO IDEA HOW CHARLIE WAS PERSUADED TO POSE LIKE THIS FOR *GET YER YA-YA'S OUT*. IT'S SO UNLIKE HIM.

ONE OF THE EARLIEST ROLLING STONES PUBLICITY SHOTS. IT APPEARS TO HAVE BEEN RETOUCHED.

It always seemed that Charlie was never really a part of all the wild goings-on that pervaded the group's existence.

drum pattern. Gone was the nondescript drummer of the mid-Sixties. In his place was a man possessed, a drummer with what I earlier referred to as the nastiest feel for Rock 'n' Roll in the world. He hit the drums hard...the way they should be hit, and he wasn't afraid to make a stand and take over the proceedings when the time was right. It proved once and for all time that Charles Robert Watts is indeed, one of the very few real giants of the rock drumming world...although he'd never agree with you. Keith Richards has always been very vocal in his admiration for Charlie's talent and has consistently commented on Watts' contribution to The Stones music. From David Daltn's book, *The Rolling Stones, The First Twenty Years,* Richards commented.

"Everybody thinks Mick and Keith are The Rolling Stones. If Charlie wasn't doing what he's doing on drums, that wouldn't be true at all. You'd find out that Charlie Watts is The Rolling Stones.

The Watts style is first and foremost jazz-based, but he keeps those chops pretty much in the background with The Stones. Charlie is probably the loosest yet tightest drummer in rock today. If you don't understand that, listen to his drumming throughout the entire *Love You Live* double LP and pay close attention to cuts like "It's Only Rock 'n' Roll" and "Brown Sugar," where he constantly breaks up the beat, but not in an unobtrusive or disruptive manner. Listen to the part in "Brown Sugar" where Charlie plays time not on the hi-hat as he usually does, but on the floor tom and snare. Talk about hot and nasty!

Charlie has experimented with larger drumsets in the studio, but has always favored a very simple four piece set with a few cymbals. His reasoning is that he's just not good or imaginative enough to use a lot of drums. He claims to rarely use the tom toms at all, but of course, that's not entirely true.

The real key to the style of Charlie Watts is his inconsistencies. He makes mistakes...sloppy endings and lapses in tempo, plus occasionally blowing an intro, to hit the snare on one and three, as previously noted earlier. All these faults add to the total picture of the man and his talent. Hey, he's a human being right? One thing for sure, with Charlie, what you see (or hear) is what you get. Dino Danelli commented in his interview in this book, that what he likes most about Charlie is that he falls down in all the right places, much like the great drummers of New Orleans. (See Dino Danelli)

There are also moments of drumming excellence on all The Stones albums that followed *Some Girls.* On *Emotional Rescue,* listen to "Summer Romance,"and "She's So Cold." From *Tattoo You,* there's "Start Me Up,"and "Long Black Limousine," with it's bluesy brush work. *Undercover* has great drum tracks like the title cut and "She Was Hot." "Under My Thumb" and "Going To A Go Go" from *Still Life* are standout Watts cuts, and "Harlem Shuffle" and "Fight" from *Dirty Work* are also great drumming.

The Stones have been relatively inactive in the 1980's as far as touring, so Charlie has had time on his hands to indulge his love of jazz. His first outside project was an on-again-off-again boogie woogie big band called Rocket 88, that included Jack Bruce and the late Ian Stewart. With a complete brass section, they recorded one LP on Atlantic that sold primarily to Stones fans. In 1986,

Charlie organized his own band, The Charlie Watts Orchestra, and released an LP on Columbia Records, *Live At Fulham Town Hall.* With thirty-one members, it was a big band that included on the LP such jazz chestnuts as "Stomping At The Savoy," "Lester Leaps In," and "Flying Home." In typical Watts fashion, there were three drummers so the listener couldn't tell who was playing what on drums. And Charlie didn't even take a solo!

Besides his interest in jazzmen like Tony Williams, Max Roach, Jo Jones, and Buddy Rich, Charlie always idolized the music and life of legendary alto saxophonist Charlie Parker, a true modern jazz pioneer and tragic individual who died at a young age from the effects of personal problems, mixed with a lingering heroin addiction. In the mid-Sixties, Watts wrote a children's book, now long out of print, called *Ode To A High Flying Bird*, a tribute to Parker. It has now become a bit of a collectors item among Stones fans, and is reportedly a sensitive, moving paean to a fallen hero. Watts did all the illustrations as well.

As The Rolling Stones slide into their fourth decade, Charlie Watts enjoys a quiet, settled life in England with his music, art, horses, and various hobbies. He plays the occasional benefit, like the ARMS concerts, with old friends like Kenney Jones, Ronnie Lane, Steve Winwood, Eric Clapton, Jeff Beck, Jimmy Page, Bill Wyman, and Andy Fairweather-Low.

He has always and still sadly, shuns most interviews, preferring to retain his privacy.

Regarding equipment. Charlie used a white pearl Premier kit and a blue pearl Ludwig set in the band's early days consisting of a 22" bass drum, 9x13" and 16x16" toms, and a 5 1/2x14" snare. He was also photographed playing Rogers drums, a red sparkle set, but they may not have belonged to him.

By the late Sixties, it was Gretsch all the way and that is not surprising, as most of Charlie's drumming heroes played Gretsch in the Fifties. For the most part, the sizes were the same as his Ludwig kit, although he used very large rack and floor toms for a short while. The Gretsch sets have been either solid black, black pearl, or natural maple. With The Stones, Charlie has kept to Gretsch, but with his big band, he used a mix-and-match set, a Cal bass drum, probably a 22," 8x12" and 16x16" Gretsch maple finish toms, and a chrome Ludwig 400 snare.

His cymbals have always been Zildjian and Charlie has lately used a combination of a ride/two crashes and a China type cymbal.

The Rolling Stones are presently on the back burner. Mick Jagger released a solo album in 1988 that sold disappointingly. Keith Richards is wrapping up his first solo album, and Ron Wood toured with Bo Diddley last year playing large clubs. Bill Wyman is enjoying the good life with his own recording and writing projects and photography. There are no plans for a second Charlie Watts Orchestra LP or tour. It appears that after two years of public acrimony and rumors, The Stones will regroup in the near future, but that's still unsure.

Whatever Charlie Watts chooses to do with the rest of his career, his place in the annals of Sixties rock drumming history is assured.

Whether he likes it or not.

He hit the drums hard ... the way they should be hit, and he wasn't afraid to make a stand and take over the proceedings.

He hit the drums hard...
the way they should be hit,
and he wasn't afraid
to make a stand
and take over
the proceedings.

ANOTHER PHOTO TAKEN DURING THE SESSIONS FOR THE *HIGH TIDES* HITS PACKAGE.

CHARLIE IS AN ARDENT COLLECTOR OF CIVIL WAR WEAPONS AND MEMORABILIA.

"WHO, ME?"

The real key to
the style of Charlie Watts
is his inconsistencies.

THE STONES, 1986, BEFORE THEY TEMPORARILY
SPLIT UP IN ORDER FOR MICK JAGGER AND KEITH
RICHARDS TO COMPLETE THEIR SOLO ALBUMS.

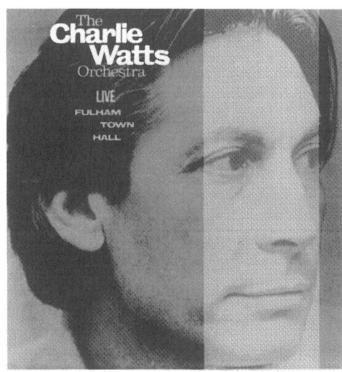

THE COVER FOR THE CHARLIE WATTS ORCHESTRA'S
ONLY LP TO DATE.

CHARLIE WATTS TODAY

Today, Charlie Watts is on tour once again with the Rolling Stones behind a great new CD, *A Bigger Bang*. At age sixty-four, Charlie shows few signs of "senioritis," other than the cans of *Ensure* he was seen drinking during the band's last foray around the world. Whatever it takes, I guess.

In June 2004, it was reported that Charlie had discovered a lump on the side of his neck and after tests, cancer of the throat was discovered, even though he had quit smoking in the Sixties. Charlie immediately entered into a six-week treatment program of radiation and chemotherapy together with a minor surgical procedure. Upon completion, doctors pronounced him cancer-free and cured, much to the relief of his fans and band mates alike. The treatments left him weak and a lengthy recovery period was necessary. Thankfully, Charlie bounced back in fine form.

When not making a living playing rock music, Charlie continues to pursue his lifelong interest in jazz, working now with The Charlie Watts Tentet, whose latest disc is titled *Watts At Scott's*, released on Sanctuary Classics Records in 2004. Charlie's first foray into leadership occurred in 1985 when he formed a big band that boasted more than thirty members (that's a *really* big band!) and featured many of England's best horn players. Columbia Records released their album *Live At Fulham Town Hall*. Charlie then formed a quintet of handpicked English jazz stars that largely paid tribute to legendary alto saxophonist Charlie Parker on the albums *From One Charlie* and *Tribute To Charlie Parker* and two other discs of non-Parker material called *Warm And Tender* and *Long Ago And Far Away*.

In 1997, Charlie also recorded a disc with his friend drummer Jim Keltner called the *Charlie Watts/Jim Keltner Project*, which featured Keltner's electronic samples and prepared sequences along with Charlie's acoustic drums. The resultant music was described as "techno, world beat, exotica," but once again, it was Charlie paying tribute, this time to his jazz-drumming heroes.

When Charlie is not playing music, he still collects antique drums, firearms, militaria of all types (with a specialty in the American Civil War) and much more, and helps his wife of more than forty years, Shirley, with her Arabian horses, which she breeds on the couple's farm. The farm can be reached via email at info@halsdonarabians.com, and its web site is www.halsdonarabians.com. Any horse lover would find the site entertaining and interesting.

Through my friend Rich King, vintage drum expert and Watts confidante, I was introduced to Charlie in 1991 at the Blue Note jazz club in New York City, where he was appearing with his quintet playing the Charlie Parker catalog. When I presented Charlie with a copy of *GRDOTS* before the show, the second thing he said to me (the first was "How do you do?") was, "Did you sign it?" I had signed it earlier in the day. We chatted for a minute, Charlie agreed to pose for a picture of the two of us, and I stayed and caught the group's first set. Charlie played straight jazz time and never even took a four-bar break. As expected, his time and feel were impeccable. Later that night driving home, I said to myself, "Charlie Watts asked for *my* autograph? There's definitely something wrong with this picture. How cool is that!"

For further reading on Charlie, go to www.charliewattsfanclub.net. There are many more web sites out there with information on the Rolling Stones' "drummer for life."

PHOTO COURTESY OF RETNA

CHARLIE PERFORMING RECENTLY WITH HIS JAZZ GROUP.

HONORABLE MENTIONS

The Good, the Bad, and the Missing in Action.

THE FOLLOWING SECTION IS AN UPDATED AND EXPANDED LISTING OF SIXTIES ROCK AND SOUL DRUMMERS WHO DESERVE MENTION, BUT DID NOT GET THEIR OWN CHAPTERS.

The choice was based primarily on the author's knowledge of Sixties rock, suggestions from others since the first publishing of this book, and various opinions, either positive or negative. Some of these opinions are based on a drummer's recorded work, keeping in mind that studio musicians were often used on recording sessions. In cases where we don't know for sure, we could only assume that a group's drummer appeared on the record.

Not every drummer included here was a member of a wildly successful band. Some were good players in also-ran groups. Others were merely passable drummers in multi-platinum situations. Some lingered around the scene for years, while others burned out quickly and left the business. Some have passed away.

The reader will notice that John Bonham, Dave Mattacks, Carl Palmer, Danny Seraphine, John Hiseman and a few others receive a token mention. Each got his start in the mid- to late Sixties, but achieved his greatest fame in the next decade.

Please keep in mind that it would have been impossible to include every single notable Sixties rock drummer, although the Internet has made it easier to locate names and information. There were good rock bands all over the world in the Sixties whose members will never be known outside of their own locales. To those drummers omitted and to fans of drummers who didn't make it here, my humblest apologies. We'll get you next time around.

SKIP ALAN (ALAN SKIPPER)

Skip Alan has been the on-again-off-again drummer with The Pretty Things since 1966. He replaced the band's original drummer Viv Prince. Skip's playing has always been straightforward and uncluttered and his work on the albums *Parachute* and *Freeway Madness* is especially noteworthy. The Pretty Things, never a big-selling band in the United States, nevertheless has a strong worldwide cult following and regroups every now and then for short tours and recording. During the band's frequent downtime, Skip has taken over his family business and has reputedly become a wealthy man as a result. He was diagnosed with high cholesterol and hypertension in the late Nineties and supposedly no longer plays drums. Given Skip's history with The Pretty Things, that could change at any time.

BILL ALBAUGH

Bill's lone moment of glory came on The Lemon Pipers' "Green Tambourine," the group's only hit, a forgettable piece of pseudo-psychedelic pop, notable only for Bill's jungle-like floor-tom break at the end.

JOHN "TWINK" ALDER

Twink Alder played with an obscure British R&B band called The Fairies in the mid-Sixties that released three very rare and now highly collectible 45's. He later joined The Pretty Things, played on *S.F. Sorrow*, one of the first rock concept albums, and reportedly subbed one night for an ailing Keith Moon in The Who. From there, John joined The Pink Fairies, a group that had nothing whatsoever to do with The Fairies, and eventually disappeared from view.

CHARLIE ALLEN

Charlie Allen was the drummer of the West Coast blues/rock outfit Pacific Gas & Electric, who later changed their name to PG&E at the request of the utility company of the same name. The band got together in 1966 and eventually had a hit with the song "Are You Ready."

CHRIS ALLEN

Chris Allen played with The Syn, a British psych/rock band that propelled bassist Chris Squire and guitarist Peter Banks into Yes.

FRANK ALLEN

Frank was the big, bearish, hard-hitting drummer with Johnny Kidd & The Pirates, a popular pre-Invasion British band that scored a sizeable hit with "Shakin' All Over," later recorded by The Who and many others. After Kidd was killed in a car crash in 1966, The Pirates broke up and later reformed amidst the excitement of late Seventies punk rock. The Pirates signed a recording deal with Warner Brothers and recorded at least two albums, both of which were released here in the States. A recent British CD proved the group was still together, but Frank Allen no longer occupied the drummer's chair.

HOWARD RICHARD "PISTOL" ALLEN

Pistol Allen was one of the great drummers of Motown and his playing graced innumerable hits by artists like Martha Reeves & the Vandellas, The Temptations, The Four Tops, Smokey Robinson and many more. Born in 1932, Pistol learned to play drums in school, participated in marching band and orchestra and moved to Detroit, where he worked in jazz and soul groups, eventually joining the Motown "Funk Brothers" studio band in the early Sixties. After Motown moved their operations to the West Coast, Pistol continued to play in the Detroit area and passed away in 2002.

RICK ANDRIDGE

Sixties punk fans will surely remember bespectacled Rick Andridge as the drummer with The Seeds, who scored a sizeable hit with "Pushin' Too Hard," and then proceeded to release two or three more singles with the same melody line and chord progression in a blatant attempt at repeating their success. The Seeds were hardly accomplished musicians and eventually disbanded after renaming themselves the Sky Saxon Blues Band, a move that did nothing for their careers. Interestingly, their albums remained in print for many years. The group still does the occasional gig.

GARY ANDRIJASEVICH

Gary was the drummer with the legendary Chocolate Watchband that emerged from San Francisco in 1965. Gary was a capable drummer, but it is now known that studio musicians were occasionally used on the band's recordings. The Watchband's recorded output was inconsistent, partly due to its members' fondness for all manner of illegal substances. They broke up and re-formed many times and produced three incredibly rare LPs on Tower Records, all of which now fetch high prices among record collectors. The Chocolate Watchband's music had a strong influence on many nouveau Eighties and Nineties punk bands, and a few years ago they reformed with four of the original five members, including Gary, for shows at *Cavestomp*, the now-famous annual NYC festival of old and new garage-rock groups. The Watchband appeared recently at a garage-rock festival presented by Steve Van Zandt and are currently touring as of this writing.

DESI ARNAZ JR.

If your father was a Cuban bandleader who sang "Babalu" with a conga drum, and your mother was a much-beloved, nutty comedienne, you'd naturally want to pursue a show-biz career too, right? And if your father's friend just happened to own a controlling share in a major record label, you'd take advantage of the situation and cut a few records with your teenage band, right? That's just what Desi Arnaz Jr. did with his group, Dino, Desi & Billy, all sons of Hollywood celebrities or high-powered businessmen. Needless to say, these three well-scrubbed teen boys took a lot of flak for it. DD&B had a minor hit with "I'm A Fool," and released LPs mostly of cover material. They faded into the sunset in the late Sixties like so many others, and Desi tried his hand at acting, finally overcoming a serious cocaine addiction in the 1980's. Today, Desi spends his time working with drug-addicted young people and making the occasional personal or TV appearance, often with his sister, Lucy Arnaz.

SCOTT ASHETON

Scott Asheton, original drummer with The Stooges, supplied the crude backbeats and renegade Bo Diddley rhythms on the group's debut album in 1969. The Stooges, all primitive musicians at best, introduced Iggy Pop to the masses. Rock n' roll was never meant to be brain surgery, after all. Scott was onboard when The Stooges re-formed for some shows in 2003.

CRAIG "BUTCH" ATKINSON

In 1966, The Count Five, from San Jose, California, notched a freak hit with "Psychotic Reaction," a Yardbirds rip-off. Their drummer was Butch Atkinson, and The Count Five never scored again, despite a few valiant attempts. When their musical careers dried up, the boys heeded the call of academia and returned to college.

CHRIS AUGUSTINE

The well-scrubbed, boy-next-door approach of Every Mother's Son got them one hit in 1967, "Come On Down To My Boat." While the rest of the band members waved flags and drank milk on the rear cover of their first and only album, drummer Chris Augustine was pictured reading *Playboy* magazine. Every Mother's Son didn't last long. It wasn't hip to be wholesome in 1967.

JOHHNY "BEE" OR "B" BADANJEKE

In the history of rock and soul music, Johnny Badanjeke must be hailed as one of the most ferocious drummers to ever lay sticks on a drum set. He rose to prominence as drummer with Mitch Ryder & The Detroit Wheels at the tender age of sixteen. His playing on hits like "Jenny Take A Ride," "Devil With The Blue Dress/Good Golly Miss Molly," "Sock It To Me, Baby" and "Little Latin Lupe Lu" shows a highly explosive, emotional drummer at work. We're talking real high energy. Listen to Johnny's eighth-note pattern on the floor tom and snare on the "Sheba" bridge section of "Good Golly Miss Molly" and you'll hear what I mean. Johnny cut his musical teeth on soul music and always named James Brown's drummers as influences. After The Wheels split up, Johnny rejoined Ryder in a band called Detroit that had one hit with a remake of Lou Reed's "Rock 'n' Roll." He later put together a band called The Rockets with former Wheels and Cactus guitarist Jim McCarty, and their lone hit was a version of Fleetwood Mac's "Oh Well." Johnny B continues to play drums today, but his activities are pretty far out of the public eye. For a while, he endorsed Flat Jacks drums, shell-less drums that made their brief appearance in the late Sixties, but eventually went back to a conventional Ludwig red sparkle drum kit.

RICKY BAKER

Ricky played with the Ohio-based Outsiders and you can hear his drumming to this day on their biggest hit, "Time Won't Let Me," a staple of oldies radio. When The Outsiders folded, Ricky's days of fame were over. The Outsiders recently re-formed for some live dates.

HONORABLE MENTIONS

Joe Bauer of The Youngbloods, second from right.

JOHN BANKS

John played with The Merseybeats from Liverpool. The band generated a lot of female fan worship for their good looks. They eventually changed their name to The Merseys and had a hit with "Sorrow."

JOE BAUER

A jazz player at heart, Joe Bauer was the talented drummer with The Youngbloods, who had their biggest hit with the Dino Valenti tune "Get Together," a battle cry for the hippie movement. Joe's playing was always tasteful and appropriate for the band's music, which ranged from psychedelic rock to good-time country and wistful ballads. After The Youngbloods broke up in 1972, Joe helped form Banana & The Bunch and eventually died of cancer.

FRANK BEARD

Although Frank Beard went on to great success and financial security with ZZ Top in the Seventies and beyond, he got his first taste of fame with The American Blues, a Texas-based power trio that cut a couple of now-rare albums for UNI Records. At one point, the band collectively dyed their hair blue to capitalize on their name. Frank, curiously the only member of ZZ Top who doesn't sport a long beard, continues to play with that little ol' band from Texas.

"BENNY" BENJAMIN

Stevie Wonder and his friends called him "Papa Zita," and his playing graced more Motown hits than any other drummer's. He and bassist James Jamerson were a deadly rhythm team, one that laid down some of the supplest grooves in the history of R&B. We're talking about Benny Benjamin, drummer extraordinaire and one of the true architects of the classic Sixties Motown sound. Benny's drumming career went back to the Forties, and he was well versed in swing, jazz and rhythm & blues by the time he came to Berry Gordy's attention. Benny was known for his thunderous tom fills and the distinctive, "slapped" snare/tom intro he used on many Motown hits. Later in his career, Benny regrettably became involved with drugs and eventually died of an overdose. His story and that of all the Motown session musicians was told in a recent film called *Standing in the Shadows of Motown*.

BOB BENNETT

The liner notes on one of the Sonics albums calls Bob Bennett's drumming "explosive," and that's an accurate word to describe this aggressive player from the Pacific Northwest. The Sonics were one of the first seminal Sixties garage bands and their records have been rereleased many times over the years, earning them legendary status and a large cult following. Listen to Bob's drum breaks on the song "Psycho" to hear how explosive he was.

BRIAN BENNETT

Brian was the drumming mainstay of The Shadows, the most popular British instrumental band in the Sixties, much like the Ventures in the USA. The Shadows scored over *twenty-seven* top ten hits before The Beatles even released their first single, survived the advent of younger, hipper bands, and continued to release records until their breakup in 1969. Brian was a fine player and although he wasn't The Shadows' first drummer, he was their best known. Brian eventually moved into studio work with relative ease.

RON BERG

Ron Berg played drums with Blodwyn Pig, a band formed by guitarist Mick Abrahams after he left Jethro Tull in 1968. Berg eventually joined a later version of Juicy Lucy.

MANNY BERTEMATTI

Manny Bertematti was a consummate professional and a talented drummer who never got much recognition during his time in the spotlight with The Blues Image. The band scored one large hit, "Ride Captain Ride," and were by far the most popular rock band in the Miami area. After The Blues Image broke up, Manny's high-profile drumming career seemingly came to an end.

PETE BEST

For the rest of his life, Pete Best is doomed to carry the stigma of being "the drummer The Beatles fired." He joined The Silver Beatles in 1960 and played the circuit of Liverpool and Hamburg clubs with them as the band paid their dues and honed their stage act. The story goes that Pete was fired after producer George Martin commented unfavorably on his drumming. The other school of thought says the other Beatles were jealous of Pete's good looks and popularity with female fans. In any event, Pete quickly formed the Pete Best All-Stars, but the group never went much farther than Liverpool. Needless to say, Pete missed out on the fame, money and adulation. He took a steady job with the government, married, raised a family, and makes appearances as a paid speaker at Beatles conventions around the world. He recently wrote a well-received book about his life with the Fab Four. Although Pete seems philosophical about his fate, his tone of voice and facial expressions can't hide the bitterness he must feel inside when discussing his relationship with the Fab Four.

BEV BEVAN

Bev Bevan of The Move, bottom center.

His approach was very heavy, perhaps a bit bombastic at times, but Bev Bevan carved his own niche in the annals of British rock history. He started out playing with Mike Sheridan & The Night Riders and, in 1966, joined The Move, a band that included guitarist/singer/songwriter Roy Wood. The Move barely made a dent in the U.S. charts, but scored several huge British hits and influenced other bands on both sides of the Atlantic, including Cheap Trick and The Shazam. The Move was always a highly controversial, incendiary band. Not content to smash up their instruments like The Who, they burned effigies, destroyed television sets, old cars and pianos onstage and insulted Prime Minister Harold Wilson with a lewd postcard, which they used to promote one of their singles, "Flowers In The Rain." The Move's management fostered their image as bad boys by dressing them in gangster suits. Later, they went "flower power" and tried valiantly to crack the U.S. market with the *Shazam* album on A&M Records, a classic power pop/hard rock LP. The Move morphed into Electric Light Orchestra around 1970, and Bev finally reaped the rewards of commercial success in the U.S. After ELO disbanded, Bevan joined the Ozzy-less edition of Black Sabbath. It's worth mentioning that Bev had one of the most unusual grips this writer has ever seen; he held his left stick in the traditional manner, but turned his hand upside down to play. Strange, for sure, and certainly indicative of a lack of proper training, but it worked for him. Bev's main choice of drums was usually Slingerland. Lately, he's been making his living as a disc jockey in England.

DAVE BIDWELL

In the Sixties, Dave was a member of Chicken Shack, an English blues band fronted by hawk-nosed guitarist Stan Webb. After the group fizzled out, Dave accepted an invitation to join Savoy Brown after Roger Earl left. Dave did a fine job drumming for Savoy Brown and stayed around for several albums, including *Street Corner Talking*, *Hellbound Train* and *Lion's Share*, some of the group's best work. Dave passed away in 1977, a victim of drug abuse.

JIMMY CARL BLACK

Jimmy was the original drummer with Frank Zappa's Mothers of Invention, whose first LP, *Freakout*, was unlike anything ever heard before. Conceived as a concept album and loaded with biting social, political and musical satire, *Freakout* upset quite a few people upon its release. Jimmy was a veteran rock drummer who joined The Mothers because he was tired of playing cover tunes and welcomed the opportunity to align himself with Zappa's band of merry musical pranksters. Of Native American ancestry, Jimmy was accomplished enough to cut Zappa's difficult arrangements and later went on to join a group of ex-Mothers called The Grandmothers.

DAVID "BIRD" BLACKLEY

David played with Kenny & The Kasuals, a very popular local attraction and a seminal garage-rock band from the Dallas–Fort Worth area.

CHARLES BLACKWELL

Charles played drums on Taj Mahal's earliest recordings, along with guitarists Ry Cooder and Jesse Ed Davis.

STEPHEN JO BLADD

Stephen Jo Bladd experienced rock stardom in the Seventies and Eighties with the J. Geils Band, but he started out playing in a group called the Hallucinations with Geils' singer Peter Wolf in the Boston area in the mid-Sixties. Stephen's playing has always been solid, energetic and imaginative. His good looks fit in well on MTV, and the J. Geils Band found a new audience on television. The group split up in the early Nineties, but regrouped for a short tour later on, with all its original members.

HONORABLE MENTIONS

THE BLUES PROJECT / PROJECTIONS

Roy Blumenfeld of The Blues Project, far right.

John Bonham of Led Zeppelin.

PAUL BLAKELY

Paul was the original drummer with Captain Beefheart & His Magic Band. He played on their early version of "Diddy Wah Diddy."

TED BLEUCHEL JR.

Although they were known as an outstanding vocal act, The Association could hold their own on their instruments too (they did have some help from studio musicians in the early days) and handsome drummer Ted Bleuchel Jr., proved himself a fine ballad player, whose shining moment we assume came on "Requiem For The Masses," where a military drumming influence was evident. The Association broke up for a while but re-formed in the Eighties with Ted on drums. When I caught them live in 1990, Ted was no longer with the band, so he has undoubtedly gone on to another career.

ROY BLUMENFELD

The drummer with the legendary New York band The Blues Project (dubbed "The Jewish Beatles"), Roy is a good player with a comfortably loose feel. He is also very versatile, an attribute that suited the Project's eclectic range of styles, encompassing rock, blues, folk-rock, psychedelia and jazzy instrumentals like "Flute Thing." When the band splintered, Roy helped put together Sea Train with bassist Andy Kulberg, and then formed a short-lived, updated version of The Blues Project with guitarist Danny Kalb. The original Blues Project occasionally gets together for shows in the NYC area. In the early days, Roy used a set of black Gretsch drums, but he later switched to red sparkle Ludwigs.

ROBIN BOERS

The Toronto-based Ugly Ducklings may have been the best Canadian garage band in the Sixties. Original pressings of their records fetch huge prices and Robin Boers was their drummer from start to finish. An animated player, Robin drove the group's music with taste and control. Like so many other Sixties bands, The Ugly Ducklings re-formed for occasional shows in the 1980's.

RONNIE BOND

"Primitive": that's the best word to describe the drumming of Ronnie Bond, who worked for years with The Troggs and supplied the Bo Diddley–like rhythm that propelled "Wild Thing" to the top of the charts. The raw sexual innuendo of "Wild Thing" made it a worldwide hit for the band from Andover, Hampshire, England. There were other hits like "I Can't Control Myself" and "Love Is All Around," and Ronnie could always be counted upon to provide something simple and effective. As of this date, The Troggs are still going strong, but Ronnie is no longer with them.

TERRY BOND

Terry played with England's Rockin' Berries from Birmingham. The group had a couple of U.K. chart success and eventually moved into the cabaret circuit mixing music and comedy.

JIM BONFANTI

Jim played drums with The Choir, the number-one band in Cleveland in the mid-Sixties, and they scored a regional hit with "It's Cold Outside," a great power pop-rock tune that should have gone further on the charts. Jim played for a short time with The Outsiders, and gained his greatest notoriety as a member of The Raspberries in the early Seventies. Keith Moon and other British drummers of the day influenced him.

JOHN BONHAM

In the first edition of this book, this writer declared that Led Zeppelin's John Bonham deserved a book of his own. That came to pass recently, with the publishing of *John Bonham: A Thunder Of Drums*, by Chris Welch and Geoff Nicholls, noted British music journalists. Nearly every rock drummer in the world owes a debt of gratitude to Bonzo. He practically wrote the book, along with Carmine Appice, Ian Paice, Keith Moon and a few others, on the way a hard-rock drummer should approach the instrument. Bonham used a simple, four- or five-piece drum kit and had one of the heaviest right feet in the business, with which he executed complicated hand/foot triplet patterns with relative ease, sending aspiring drummers into fits of rapture with his solo on "Moby Dick." Bonham got his start playing in semi-pro bands in the mid-Sixties and eventually landed a gig backing singer-guitarist Tim Rose. In 1968, he came to the attention of Jimmy Page, who was putting together a new band out of the ashes of The Yardbirds. That band was Led Zeppelin, and their story has been told and retold many times elsewhere. Bonzo remained the band's drummer until his untimely death from alcohol poisoning in September 1980. For the full story on John Bonham, pick up a copy of *John Bonham: A Thunder Of Drums*.

CRAIG BOYD

Craig Boyd played drums for The Hook, a band that featured guitarist Bobby Arlin after he quit The Leaves. Their approach was standard psych/rock fare of the day and they never cracked the charts.

DON BREWER

Don Brewer was a member of Grand Funk Railroad, but got his start with Terry Knight & The Pack in Michigan, in the mid-Sixties. Their lone LP on Cameo-Parkway Records is now a collector's item, and they had a minor hit with "I (Who Have Nothing)." Don later put together Grand Funk with guitarist Mark Farner, another member of The Pack, and their success in the Seventies is well documented elsewhere. When Grand Funk broke up, Don hung out, enjoyed his financial success, and hooked up with Bob Seger's Silver Bullet Band. He eventually rejoined a new version of Grand Funk and he's still in the drummer's chair today. A proud endorser of Peavey Radial drums (which are now out of production), Don was and still is an outstanding and influential rock drummer and quite a good singer as well, despite the negative press that has always dogged Grand Funk.

ALAN BUCK

Alan worked with The Four Pennies from Blackburn Lancashire. The group's singles never hit, they changed their name to The Pennies and sputtered to an end in the mid-1970s.

CLIVE BUNKER

Clive was the original drummer with Jethro Tull. He was a talented double-bass drum player and brought a sense of drama to the band's varied repertoire. Some of Clive's most memorable cuts were "Cat's Squirrel," "With You There To Help Me," "Aqualung," "Cross-Eyed Mary" and "Locomotive Breath." He left Tull shortly before they recorded *Thick As A Brick* and was replaced by Barriemore Barlowe, himself a very fine drummer.

JOHN BURDETT

John Burdett must have had a strong marching background, for that's the kind of rhythm he played on The Royal Guardmen's hits "Snoopy Versus The Red Baron" and "Return Of The Red Baron." You might say they found a formula and milked it to death. The Royal Guardsmen's LP's were loaded with inane originals and covers of current hits. One could surmise that the music world is a better place without them.

MIKE BURNS

Mike drummed for the band Stone Circus, whose only LP appeared on Mainstream Records, the label that launched the Amboy Dukes and Big Brother & the Holding Company.

RON BUSHY

If Ron Bushy had played nothing else but "In-A-Gadda-Da-Vida," he'd still belong in this book. Drummers over the age of forty or fifty either love or loathe his drum solo; the song itself is considered a classic by some and a meaningless piece of trash by others. No matter where your feelings lie, the fact remains that Ron Bushy was and still is a very intense drummer, with an acute sense of drama and attack. He was an army brat who fashioned his own drum pad and sticks out of scrap wood at a young age and was one of the first rock drummers to popularize the use of quarter-note time on the cymbals as opposed to eighth notes. His playing exhibited a military influence, and when Iron Butterfly changed personnel and direction in 1970, Ron proved he had a flair for R&B as well. With his devilish appearance and goatee, a mix-and-match set of dubious manufacture (which he later replaced with a set of clear acrylic Zickos drums) and some of the most tortured faces ever seen on a drummer (he always looked like he was in great pain), Ron stayed with Iron Butterfly through good times and bad, breakups and re-formations, and today, continues to play with a revitalized version of the Butterfly that includes bassist Lee Dorman. Ron uses DW drums these days.

JOE BUTLER

For a short while in 1965 and '66, the Lovin' Spoonful had the world by the tail with their good-time rock 'n' roll. Joe Butler was the group's drummer, and brought valuable experience, playing in twist bands on his native Long Island, New York. Joe was a limited, workman-like drummer, but he played exactly what the band's music called for, and it's no secret today that Gary Chester covered Butler's parts in the studio on their earliest hits. But Joe had a good way with shuffle rhythms, played Ludwig drums and Zildjian cymbals, and also handled himself admirably in the vocal department. He went on to try his hand at acting and was elected to the Rock and Roll Hall of Fame in 2000 with the rest of The Lovin' Spoonful. He continues to work in an updated, John Sebastian-less version of the band with original bassist Steve Boone and maintains an apartment in Greenwich Village in New York City.

HONORABLE MENTIONS

TONY CAHILL

Tony Cahill replaced Snowy Fleet in The Easybeats in 1967, after their long string of hits ended. His drumming on the tune "St. Louis" is strong and imaginative. Tony's current whereabouts are unknown.

GEORGE CAMERON

New York drummer George Cameron's drumming is pretty well buried in The Left Banke's recordings of "Walk Away Renee" and "Pretty Ballerina." The Left Banke was in a constant state of personnel disarray, although they have a loyal fan following to this day.

JIM CAPALDI

Jim Capaldi later established himself as a first-rate singer/songwriter, but he came to prominence as the drummer with Traffic, the band Steve Winwood put together after leaving The Spencer Davis Group in 1967. Their first three albums were musically varied collections, and Jim was competent enough to handle it all. After the release of Traffic's album *John Barleycorn*, he relinquished drum duties to session musicians like Jim Gordon or Roger Hawkins, remaining with the band as vocalist/percussionist. His solo videos eventually made it into rotation on MTV in the 1980's. Jim passed away from stomach cancer in March 2005. Traffic was recently inducted into the Rock and Roll Hall of Fame.

BUN E. CARLOS

Bun E. has smacked the skins for Cheap Trick from their inception, but in the Sixties, he played extensively with many bands, including one called Dalek & The Blackstones that recorded a few obscure garage-punk singles on a local Illinois label. Bun E. has always been a Ludwig player and has amassed a fantastic collection of vintage Ludwig, WFL and Leedy & Ludwig drums. He is considering building a museum to house and display them and remains as busy as ever with Cheap Trick.

ED "CASS" CASSIDY

The first thing you noticed was the bald head, back in the day when long hair was de rigueur. Then, you realized he was quite a bit older than the rest of the members of Spirit. And finally, once you listened closely, you would certainly notice that Cass was a very special rock drummer, a man with serious jazz credentials, one who approached the drums with a light touch. Back in a time when drummers sometimes bludgeoned their instrument into submission, Ed was an exception. His drumming was like rhythmic ballet and his fleeting sense of drama, airy timekeeping and no-frills approach propelled the eclectic California band Spirit in the late Sixties as they melded rock, jazz and folk elements into one of the most compelling sounds to emerge from that period. Ed was born in 1923 and began playing drums in the Thirties. He played with swing bands and grew fond of the new, modern style of small-group jazz that emerged after World War II. Ed eventually moved into the area of avant-garde and R&B-inspired jazz, country-western and classical music and worked with recognized giants like Dexter Gordon, Roy Ayers, Roland Kirk, Les McCann, Zoot Sims and Gerry Mulligan. He made first foray into rock while working with The Rising Sons, a Los Angeles group with blues leanings that included Taj Mahal and Ry Cooder. Good things were predicted for the band, but their records stiffed and they split up in 1966. Cassidy then formed another band, The Red Roosters, with his stepson, guitarist Randy "California" Wolfe. That band reformed as Spirit in 1967. For more than fifteen albums, Ed consistently displayed tasty chops and supreme good taste behind the drum set, and despite numerous personnel changes, Spirit continued as a working band for thirty years with California and Cassidy, the ever-present members. In 1997, Randy California drowned while swimming in Hawaii. Shortly afterward, Ed reformed Spirit with another guitarist and continued as Spirit Revisited until legal action prevented him from using the name. Along the way, Ed wrote a very useful book, *A Musician's Career Guide*, a practical how-to for aspiring musicians, and he's currently completing his autobiography. At over eighty years of age, Ed Cassidy continues to play drums in a group called the Fankhauser-Cassidy Blues Band. He must be the oldest performing drummer in rock music. In Spirit's early days, he played a vintage four-piece set of black diamond pearl Slingerland Radio Kings, then moved up to a psychedelic red Ludwig set with multiple toms and two gigantic concert bass drums on either side. This radical setup remains today, although Ed now uses a late-model Rogers set in the same configuration.

CLEM CATTINI

Clem played with The Tornadoes, a British instrumental band that had a hit in the U.S. with "Telstar" in 1962. They were the first English group to crack the American charts, but were never as popular at home as they were in the States. The group split in 1966, seriously out of step with the times and unable to compete with newer bands. Most of the members went on to become studio musicians and Clem Cattini, a well-schooled, all-around player, became one of England's best-known session drummers.

Ed Cassidy of Spirit, top middle.

GARY CHESTER

Gary Chester was not only one of the busiest East Coast studio drummers of the Fifties and Sixties, but he also worked numerous live dates and soundtrack sessions for major production companies. His list of hits includes "My Boyfriend's Back," "He's So Fine," "I'm A Believer," "Downtown," "Bad, Bad Leroy Brown," "Up On The Roof," "Under The Boardwalk," "In The Still Of The Night," "It's My Party," "Come A Little Bit Closer," "Stand By Me," "The Boxer," "Will You Still Love Me Tomorrow," "Save The Last Dance For Me," "Do You Believe In Magic," "Brown-Eyed Girl," and the list goes on and on. In the Seventies, Gary gave up the studio grind and concentrated on teaching at his farm in New City, New York. A marvelous technician, he proved to be as much in demand as a teacher as he had been as a session musician. An extremely opinionated man, he demanded much from his students and quickly gained a reputation as a hard taskmaster. But every drummer I ever met who studied with Gary thought very highly of him and his methods. In 1985, he wrote a book entitled *The New Breed*, which helped drummers develop left- and right-hand coordination on a large symmetrically arranged drum setup. He also released a cassette course to accompany the book. This writer had the pleasure of meeting Gary in March 1987 at the first *Modern Drummer* Festival at Montclair State University in New Jersey. At the time, I was considering the purchase of a drum machine in order to keep pace with the electronic revolution in drumming and to help tighten up my timekeeping. Gary seemed to take an immediate interest in me and encouraged me to make the financial investment and buy a Roland TR-505. Practicing with it, he said, would do wonders for my playing time. He was right. I was genuinely touched by Gary's advice and followed his suggestion. In August of that year, many of us were deeply saddened to learn of Gary's passing from a heart attack. A heavy smoker, he left a wife and five children, as well as hundreds of current and former students, whom he considered his "kids" as well. Gary is still sadly missed within the drumming community and was the recent subject of a feature piece in *Modern Drummer*.

DAVE CLARK

Drummers familiar with Sixties rock either love the drumming on The Dave Clark Five's records or they hate it. There seems to be no middle ground. The entire approach was based around the snare drum, with some of the hottest triplet fills anywhere. This writer has always been very fond of Clark's playing, or at least what I thought was Clark's. It has come to light recently that session drummer Bobby Graham played drums on the band's records, which isn't surprising. Watching Dave could cause one discomfort, even though he was a handsome guy. He sat high upon his throne, as if perched on sharp nails, and never seemed comfortable behind his various sets of Rogers drums. The DC Five was a carefully concocted commercial venture that succeeded beautifully from 1964 until Dave broke the band up in 1970. Their success came primarily in the U.S. Now a very wealthy man, Dave Clark has done better than ever as a producer of stage and television shows in Great Britain, and has no plans whatsoever to return to music. He even owns the rights to the entire catalog of old *Ready, Steady, Go!* TV shows, a treasure trove of British Sixties rock performances.

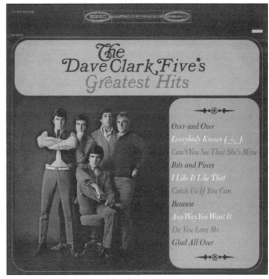

Dave Clark, seated in front.

MICHAEL CLARKE

The Byrds' original drummer, Michael Clarke could barely play when he joined the band. He was spotted walking down the street in Los Angeles and was asked to join based upon his hip good looks and Brian Jones–like appearance. His only experience up to that point had been a stint fooling around with bongos, but Mike worked hard on his drumming and although he didn't play on "Mr. Tambourine Man" (Hal Blaine cut the session), he improved and stayed with the band up until their country-rock period. After leaving The Byrds, Mike joined The Flying Burrito Brothers and later reaped his share of financial rewards with Firefall. He developed into a strong, groove-oriented drummer and settled in Hawaii, where he passed away in the early 1990's. Somewhere along the way, Clarke acquired the rights to The Byrds name, preventing any of the surviving members from using it, including Roger McGuinn. Clarke's estate has since "rented" the name to a group of unknown musicians, none of whom has direct ties to The Byrds. Roger McGuinn has since told this writer that it would take a costly court battle to get the name back and that he, David Crosby and Chris Hillman don't have the desire to pursue it.

E. G. CLAWSON

SRC was a band from Ann Arbor, Michigan, and E. G. Clawson played drums for them through all three of their albums on Capitol Records. The group never broke through nationally. Their music, gritty psych/rock, sounds dated today.

CREEDENCE CLEARWATER REVIVAL
·THE ROYAL ALBERT HALL CONCERT·

Doug Clifford with Creedence Clearwater Revival, playing Camco drums.

DOUG "COSMO" CLIFFORD

Doug was the well-known drummer in Creedence Clearwater Revival throughout their phenomenally fruitful existence as one of America's first genuine roots-rock bands. Before Creedence hit it big in 1968, they were known as The Golliwogs and wore furry hats onstage. Nothing happened until they changed their name and hit upon the rockabilly/swamp pop/roots rock sound that sold millions of records for the band into the early Seventies. If you thought Creedence's discs were memorable, their live shows were incandescent, and although the action revolved mainly around the vocals and guitar of John Fogerty, the other three members, Tom Fogerty, Stu Cook and Cosmo Clifford, could more than hold their own. Doug's drumming style wasn't based on technique, but he had a great feel for the music and did what was necessary to make the songs work. Watching Doug play could be a tad unsettling though. He held his left-hand stick in an unorthodox grip and sometimes looked stiff. He never played stiffly, however, and seemed to be one of the only major rock drummers (along with Beach Boy Dennis Wilson) who used and endorsed Camco drums. After Creedence broke up, Doug and Stu joined The Don Harrison Band and later re-formed Creedence without John Fogerty, renaming the band Creedence Clearwater Revisited. They are still going strong as of this writing, playing the old hits and gaining new fans. Doug uses and endorses DW drums these days.

BOBBY COLOMBY

Bobby is a very tasty jazz-rock drummer, an original member of Blood, Sweat & Tears, who stayed with them through their glory days of hit singles. Although Colomby never considered himself much of a technician, Buddy Rich repeatedly named him as his favorite rock drummer, a fact that probably astounds Colomby to this day. Bobby eventually left the music business and took a gig as musical correspondent for the television show *Entertainment Tonight*. He is also involved in record production.

DON CONKA

Don Conka was the first drummer with the Los Angeles band Love, but left before they recorded their first album, primarily due to a serious problem with hard drugs that dogged him throughout the remainder of his life. Snoopy Pfisterer replaced him.

JOHN CONRAD

The Mojos were another in a long line of Liverpool groups who tried to emulate The Beatles' success and missed the mark. John Conrad was their original drummer. The Mojos' old singles and one EP are extremely rare collector's items now. Conrad left the band and was replaced by Aynsley Dunbar.

DENNIS CONROY

No, Dennis was *not* the one with the hook. That was tambourine player "J.C. Hooke." The Cryan' Shames from Chicago notched a big hit in 1966 with "Sugar and Spice." They didn't come that close to the charts again, despite their best efforts and some experiments with commercial psychedelia and orchestration. Dennis's music career faded into oblivion when The Shames did.

RICK COONCE

Redheaded Rick Coonce played drums with The Grass Roots from right after the release of their first album until the beginning of the Seventies. Few people realize there was no real Grass Roots band on their debut Dunhill album. The songs that made up that recording were demo sessions by songwriters P. F. Sloane and Steve Barri. It wasn't until "Where Were You When I Needed You" became a hit that Sloane and Barri were forced to form a band of Hollywood folk-rockers into The Grass Roots. It's also common knowledge now that studio musicians were frequently used on Grass Roots sessions, so there's no way of knowing what tracks Rick played on. Having seen the band live at the Fillmore East however, this writer can attest to Rick Coonce's drumming abilities. My favorite Grass Roots track was always "Things I Should Have Said," with its Latin flavor, but did Rick play drums? Or was it Hal Blaine or Earl Palmer? We don't know for sure. After many chart hits, three original members of The Grass Roots left, with the exception of bassist Rob Grill, who still leads a version of the band on the oldies circuit.

JOE CORRERO JR.

When Paul Revere reorganized The Raiders in the late Sixties, he retained vocalist Mark Lindsay and dismissed everyone else. It was the age of virtuosity in rock, and Revere decided to get the best musicians he could find. The old Raiders had rarely played on the group's records, but that changed this time around. He brought in ace guitarist Freddy Weller, bassist Charlie Coe and the talented Joe Correro Jr. on drums. Joe's style was reminiscent of Dino Danelli's, and it's probably no coincidence that The Raiders' music took a turn toward rhythm & blues after Joe joined. Joe played on all the albums that followed, stayed with Revere through the Seventies and eventually fell from sight. Hopefully he's playing drums somewhere today.

TIM CORWIN

Tim played with The Ohio Express and should be mentioned for his good work on their first hit, "Beg, Borrow & Steal." From there, it was downhill, as the band became part of the egregious Kasenetz-Katz stable of bubblegum bands, along with The 1910 Fruitgum Company and others. Nothing more need be said about that.

PAUL COSENZA

Paul played with Michael & The Messengers on their regional hit "(Just Like) Romeo & Juliet."

JOHN COUGHLIN

John was the energetic headbanger with England's Status Quo, from their beginnings in the mid-Sixties and their hit "Pictures Of Matchstick Men" through their boogie days in the Seventies and into the Eighties, when he left the band for other pursuits.

JOHN COWSILL

John Cowsill could really play drums, and not badly. Of course, the stick-sweet pop-glop The Cowsill family passed off as rock was forgettable at best. The group's earliest singles were actually pretty good garage rock, but once The Cowsills signed with MGM Records, they began to project a gaggingly cute image that made most self-respecting rock fans hurl. It got them hits, so who's to argue? To paraphrase another writer, would you want to be in a band with your mom?

TERRY COX

Terry played with the British folk-rock group Pentangle and his light touch was well suited to the band's acoustic music. He also played mallet instruments with them.

DENNY "LUDWIG" CRASWELL

They originally got together to amuse and entertain their fraternity brothers, but in the summer of 1965, The Castaways, from Minneapolis, found themselves with a national hit on their hands, the rocker "Liar Liar," which rose to number twelve on the charts. Classic one-hit wonders, the Castaways were promptly never heard from again and Denny, who, despite his nickname, played Rogers drums, undoubtedly went on to another career.

CHRIS CURTIS

The original drummer with the Searchers, Christopher Curtis (né Crummy) recorded hits like "Love Potion #9," "When You Walk In The Room," "Needles And Pins" and "Sweets For My Sweet." In 1969, Chris left the band and was replaced by Billy Adamson. Chris died in early 2005.

GEOFF DAKING

Geoff played drums with The Blues Magoos, a New York City band that caught the coattails of commercial psychedelia with two hits, "(We Ain't Got) Nothin' Yet," and "There's A Chance We Can Make It." The Magoos eventually changed personnel and adopted a more jazz-like approach, but they never scored another hit. Geoff had a fast pair of wrists and was versatile and talented. The Blues Magoos reform for an occasional concert to this day, with Geoff on drums. Today, Geoff owns a company that makes high quality recording equipment.

RUDOLPH "CHIP" DAMIANI

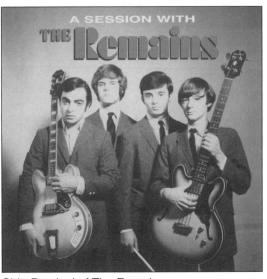

Chip was the primal pounder for The Remains from 1964 until spring 1966. A self-taught drummer from Waterbury, Connecticut, he relentlessly drove The Remains to stardom in New England and notoriety worldwide. In the summer of 1966, The Remains were the opening act on the final Beatles tour, but Chip had split by then, burned out by the grind and suffering from an ulcer. N. D. Smart II replaced him. For a good example of Chip's playing, listen to the live-in-the-studio version of The Yardbirds' "I'm A Man," released on Sundazed Records' *A Session With The Remains*. Chip is a roofing contractor today and still performs with The Remains, who have found a new audience both here and abroad. The band released a new album in November 2002 and play about six to eight concerts a year, mostly in Europe.

Chip Damiani of The Remains, second from right.

DARIUS DAVENPORT

Darius played drums with Autosalvage, a NYC band that recorded one psych-rock album on RCA Records in 1968. When the record failed to sell, they disbanded. Darius now lives in Napa, California.

TIM DAVIS

Tim Davis played drums with The Steve Miller Band on their earliest albums and was eventually replaced by Gary Mallaber, who helped revitalize Miller's career with hits like "Take The Money And Run" and "Jet Airliner."

BRIAN DAVISON

"Blinky" Davison gained his small measure of fame with The Nice, one of the earliest British art rock/classically inspired bands. Keyboardist Keith Emerson fronted the band. Brian had a nice, loose feel to his drumming, that's well illustrated on their version of Dave Brubeck's "Rondo," from the *Ars Longa Vita Brevis* LP. Emerson usually ended his performances by stabbing the keyboard of his Hammond B3 organ and knocking it over. After The Nice folded, Brian formed an acoustic/electric jazz/rock band called Every Which Way, whose first album of the same name was excellent, but did little to keep the group afloat. Brian then joined Gong and reunited with Nice bassist Lee Jackson in 1973 in a band called Refugee that released only one album. Broke and discouraged, Brian Davison did a little session work, then left the music business and was reportedly later seen panhandling in a London park. His whereabouts are unknown today.

BOBBY DAY

The Blue Things, a now-legendary Kansas folk-rock band, chose Bobby Day as their replacement drummer right before recording their lone RCA Victor album in 1966. Bobby was a good drummer, but his kit was mixed too low for this writer's taste on said LP (now an impossibly rare collector's item) and the group's follow-up singles afterwards. When The Blue Things dissolved in 1968, Bobby's "days" in the limelight were over too.

ROGER DEATHERAGE

Roger played with Chicago's Del-Vetts, whose "Last Time Around" is one of the great Sixties punk discs of all time.

JACK DECKER

The first drummer with The Critters, a New Jersey band that had hit singles like "Younger Girl" and "Mr. Dieingly Sad," Jack hailed from Newark and left the band after the hits ceased. Jeff Pelosi, another Jersey resident, replaced him.

ADOLPHO "FITO" DE LA PARRA

Perhaps the only Mexican drummer to gain some measure of fame during the Sixties was Fito de la Parra, the main boogie man in Canned Heat, a West Coast blues band that specialized in stretching the primal blues of John Lee Hooker into lengthy, freewheeling jams and solo vehicles for all the band's members. Fito emigrated to L.A. in the early Sixties and played with a number of local bands including The Sot Weed Factor, whose 45's are now collectible. Fito's style was simple and powerful: he was a left-handed drummer who used double kick drums. Most of Canned Heat's original members are now deceased, but Fito still leads a version of the band that tours and records.

JOHN DENSMORE

John Densmore refused to be interviewed for the first addition of this book despite several inquiries. As a drummer, he could be solid and steady or loose and disjointed, perhaps depending upon the song or the state of consciousness he happened to be in at the time. The Doors were not known for abstinence in those days. Before joining The Doors in 1966, John played in a band called The Psychedelic Rangers and had prior experience playing jazz. His drumming was very recognizable, and he had a style and approach that were his own. Thirty-two years after the death of Jim Morrison, The Doors regrouped with Scott Stapp of Creed replacing the Lizard King. John Densmore, financially able to do whatever he pleases these days, is also involved in modern dance and acting. It is interesting to note that as of this writing, The Doors of The 21st Century, as they now call themselves, have been touring without Densmore. Stewart Copeland, formerly of The Police, took his place briefly, only to be replaced by another drummer after a short tour. Densmore, who suffers from tinnitus, is reportedly on bad terms with Robbie Krieger and Ray Manzarek.

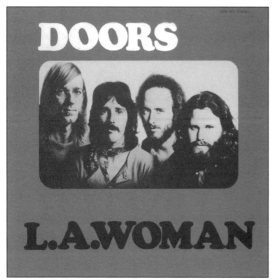

John Densmore of The Doors, second from left.

ERIC DILLON

Eric was a self-assured, steady drummer who played with Noel Redding's splinter group, Fat Mattress. Redding played bass with Hendrix, but played lead guitar with Fat Mattress, and his tastes were more laid-back and folk-rock oriented. Check out Eric's muscular drumming on the first Fat Mattress LP, if you can find a copy.

PETE DOBSON

The drummer with Juicy Lucy, a late Sixties British blues band, Pete was a basic, uncluttered groove player. Juicy Lucy's claim to fame was Glenn Ross Campbell, a pedal steel guitarist who played raunchy blues, and not one lick of country music.

DICK DODD

An ex-Mouseketeer, Dick replaced Gary Leeds with The Standells in time to record their hits "Dirty Water," "Sometimes Good Guys Don't Wear White," "Why Pick On Me" and the great "Try It," the best thing they ever did, a song that should have been a monster hit record but was banned on just about every radio station in the country. Seems the lyrics were a little too risqué for 1966. Dick used Slingerland drums back then and rejoined The Standells for occasional shows in the late Eighties and recently at Cavestomp in New York City.

MICKEY DOLENZ

Mickey Dolenz starred in an old television show called *Circus Boy*. So what if Mickey couldn't really play drums? It didn't matter at first—he was the Monkees' principal lead singer. Just about everybody knows the Monkees story by now: manufactured-for-TV rock band of itinerant folkies and actors living in a fantasy world of misadventures, created by a shrewd businessman and equipped with great songs by Boyce and Hart, Neil Diamond, Goffin and King, and others and backed in the studio by the cream of Hollywood session musicians. All the Monkees had to do was act cute and clever, but they took a critical slagging, and once it became clear they'd have to perform their hits live in front of hordes of screaming teenagers, Mickey worked hard on his drumming. Eventually, he became good enough to cut the group's studio sessions as well, as The Monkees set out to prove they were "real" musicians after all. As their brief time in the limelight spun down, Dolenz returned to a behind-the-scenes career in show business, producing and directing television shows in England. In 1986, three of the four Monkees teamed up again for a tour and discovered they were still popular enough to sell out stadiums. With guitarist Mike Nesmith back in the fold, they did a one-off TV special in the late Nineties and released a CD of new material. Mickey used Gretsch, Rogers and Slingerland drums back in the Sixties, and recently hosted a radio show on WCBS-FM in New York City until station bosses abruptly changed formats and fired him, along with veteran DJ Cousin Bruce Morrow, in June 2005.

BOBBY DONAHO

Bobby Donaho played in a legendary "lost" L.A. band called The Penny Arkade, which recorded almost two albums' worth of eclectic and high-quality country and folk-tinged rock, only to have the recordings remain unreleased until late 2004, when Sundazed Records acquired the rights and released a Penny Arkade CD called *Not The Freeze*. Bobby Donaho was a very capable drummer, quite able to handle a wide variety of styles and grooves. After The Penny Arkade split in 1968, Bobby continued to play and currently works with a Corpus Christi, Texas band called Third Coast Rhythm Section.

SPENCER DRYDEN

Spencer was the slightly offbeat, mysterious drummer with Jefferson Airplane during the hippie days of peace, love, dope, light shows and revolution. Spencer had a strong jazz approach to his playing that suited the loose, kinetic, drug-inspired jams that characterized the Airplane's music. Spencer's *Bolero*-like pattern on "White Rabbit" and his steady, insistent beat on "Somebody To Love" may be his best-remembered work, but he also experimented with free-associated, improvised percussion music and later played drums with The New Riders Of The Purple Sage. Spencer eventually reduced his role in The New Riders to percussionist and left altogether in the early Seventies. He later turned up in The Dinosaurs, a group that also featured fellow San Francisco rock veterans Barry Melton and the late guitarist John Cipollina, formerly of Quicksilver Messenger Service. Spencer suffered from poor health in his autumn years and passed away in March 2005 at the age of sixty-six.

Spencer Dryden of Jefferson Airplane, far right.

JOHN DUCKWORTH

John was the drummer with The Syndicate of Sound, his recognizable, Keith Moon–like triplet fills were one of the highlights of their only hit, "Little Girl," a tune that still gets occasional radio airplay. The SOS re-formed a few years ago for an appearance at Cavestomp in New York City.

HONORABLE MENTIONS

ROGER EARL.

Photo by Marko Shark

AYNSLEY DUNBAR

Aynsley Dunbar has always ranked in the upper echelon of English rock drummers. He's a marvelous technician, a real meat-and-potatoes basher, whose playing is always straight to the point, with no unnecessary baggage. Aynsley first came to public attention as a member of John Mayall's Bluesbreakers in 1967. A well-schooled, experienced player, he left to form The Retaliation, a fine blues/rock band I saw live at the Fillmore East. He then formed another band called Blue Whale, which didn't last long. Dunbar (perhaps foolishly) turned down the drum chairs with Led Zeppelin and The Jimi Hendrix Experience, and then joined Frank Zappa's Mothers, with whom he recorded eight LP's. He also worked with Flo & Eddie, David Bowie and Lou Reed, and joined Journey in 1973. He took John Barbata's place in Jefferson Starship in 1978 and spent most of his time as a high-priced session musician. He toured with Eric Burdon and The New Animals a few years ago, but was supposedly plagued with immigration problems and left the band. Journey was recently given a star on Hollywood Boulevard and Aynsley was there to help accept the award.

BERNIE DWYER

Bernie played with England's Freddie & The Dreamers, who scored hits with "Do The Freddie." The music was juvenile at best and Bernie, with his receding hairline, was older than most of the teen idols of the day. The band gets together for oldies tours, but Bernie's not part of the picture. He died in December 2002.

ROGER EARL

A fishing enthusiast with an interesting sense of humor, Roger Earl played drums for years with Savoy Brown during their early days as England's number-one boogie blues band. He left in the early Seventies with two other members to form Foghat, a band that achieved extensive success here in the States with their high-energy bluesy/roots rock n' roll. Roger sparked both bands in a very effective and simple way with a steady, driving beat, somewhat belying his use of a large, double bass drum kit. Foghat is still together with Roger, now a resident of Long Island, New York, behind the drums, despite having gone through extensive personnel changes over the years. The band's latest disc, *Family Joules*, is available on Foghat's web site, www.foghat.net.

LYNN EASTON

Lynn was the drummer behind some of the trashiest drum fills ever, those of The Kingmen's original version of "Louie Louie." Somehow, it seems impossible to listen to this classic piece of American rock sleaze without thinking of John Belushi gyrating in a drunken haze in *Animal House*.

RON EDGAR

Ron contributed the monster drum fills and stop time rhythms to The Music Machine's "Talk Talk," 1:56 of pure garage-punk aggression released in 1966. It was a challenge for young drummers to duplicate these fills in those days. Ron's playing throughout the Music Machine's first album was uniformly excellent and tight, but he left the band around the time their second album was released. In keeping with The Music Machine's sinister image, Ron wore one black glove and used a hip-looking set of solid black Rogers drums, in the days when pearl and sparkle finishes were the norm.

GRAEME EDGE

Graeme's entire career has been spent as drummer with The Moody Blues, who retain a very strong fan base throughout the world. He's a reliable team player, not a grandstander by any means, and is also known for his spoken recitations on the Moodies' recordings. When the group took an extended break in the Seventies, Graeme recorded and released two solo albums. He openly admits to enjoying working with electronic percussion and sees the Moody Blues as a productive band that will go on for many years to come.

GREG ELMORE

Greg worked with Quicksilver Messenger Service for years, through all their breakups, re-formations and personnel changes. In this writer's opinion, he was a stiff, technically limited player who never looked comfortable behind a drum set. A California native, Greg got his start in a garage band called The Brogues. In Quicksilver's early days, he played a large set of Rogers red onyx pearl drums that always sounded like cardboard boxes. Apparently, Mr. Elmore either never mastered drum tuning or used large amounts of gaffer's tape to deaden the sound of his kit.

GREG ERRICO

Greg Errico was the funky white drummer with Sly & the Family Stone, and his famous grooves, many of which have been sampled by modern hip-hop artists, have been extremely influential on drummers worldwide. The group's zenith was their appearance in 1969 at Woodstock, which was well documented in the film of the same name. Greg is still musically active on the West Coast.

JAN ERRICO

Jan played with San Francisco's Mojo Men and appeared on their only semi-hit, a version of Buffalo Springfield's "Sit Down, I Think I Love You." Sly Stone supposedly played with the group and co-produced the single. A woman in a band called the Mojo Men? I guess Jan didn't mind. Women's lib was a few years away.

JIMMY FADDEN

For more than thirty years, Jimmy Fadden has not only played drums with the Nitty Gritty Dirt Band, but has played guitar, mandolin and keyboards, as well as providing lead vocals. The Dirt Band remains a very popular concert attraction.

LEE FERGUSON

Lee was the drummer with We The People, a Florida band that recorded some of the era's greatest garage-rock, on Challenge Records.

BILL FIGG

Bill played with the Rationals from Ann Arbor, Michigan, a band from which big things were expected. None of their records really broke nationally, and the band split up in 1970.

BRUCE FINLAY

Bruce Finlay and his band, The Sorrows, were from Coventry, England, and formed in 1963. Their single "Take A Heart" reached #21 on the British charts, and the group had some success in Germany and Italy as well, before splitting in 1967.

SNOWY FLEET

Snowy was a Liverpudlian who played with The Mojos, but gained his share of notoriety as the drummer with The Easybeats, the most famous Australian band of the Sixties, whose lone American hit was the frantic and unforgettable "Friday On My Mind." The group's popularity Down Under caused riots and they are still regarded as musical gods on their home turf. Snowy left the band in 1967 and was replaced by Tony Cahill. The Easybeats regrouped for a couple of concerts in 1986 and Snowy was present on drums.

MICK FLEETWOOD

Although best known as leader of the hugely successful Fleetwood Mac, the lanky drummer got his start in the early to mid-Sixties working with R&B bands like The Cheynes and John Mayall's Bluesbreakers. Mick Fleetwood should be remembered as a simple yet effective drummer, a relentlessly steady timekeeper whose style was influenced by African rhythms and American blues. Like many other well-known drummers, Mick plays DW drums today.

HUGHIE FLINT

Hughie Flint played what might be the most god-awful drum solo in the history of recorded music on John Mayall's *Blues Breakers*, the record that launched Eric Clapton's stardom. The tune was Ray Charles's "What'd I Say?" If you think I'm being a little harsh on old Hughie, just listen. Flint sounds like he fell down a long flight of stairs with the drums close behind. Hughie later organized a band called McGuinness-Flint and enjoyed some success after leaving Mayall.

TOM FLYE

Tom was a member of one of the Sixties' stranger aggregations, Lothar & The Hand People. Lothar was a theremin, an electronic instrument widely used in horror movies. Their two LP's on Capitol Records are collectible and Tom went on to become a well-known record producer after Lothar & The Hand People bit the dust.

DAVID "FUZZY" FORE

David played drums with the Texas band Bubble Puppy until the early Seventies, but was the first drummer with Zakary Thaks.

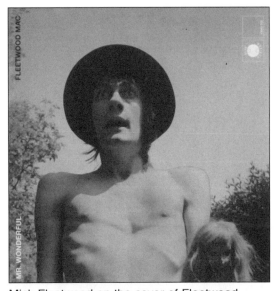

Mick Fleetwood on the cover of Fleetwood Mac's *Mr. Wonderful* LP, which was never released in the U.S.

JOEY FORGIONE

Joey was an R&B drummer from New Jersey who played with The Soul Survivors, who had one big hit in 1967 called "Expressway To Your Heart." His drumming on this track and their debut album was quite good and it seems apparent that Joey may have been a disciple of Dino Danelli. But back then, who wasn't, especially if you were from the New York metropolitan area. Joey died in 2003.

JIM FOX

Jim Fox, the bespectacled drummer with The James Gang, was one of the most rock-solid timekeepers of his day, a veritable living, breathing metronome, who colored the band's arrangements in a very simple and effective way. His greatest fame came in the early Seventies, however. Just about every rock drummer older than forty has copied his licks on "Funk #49" and "Walk Away" at one time or another. Today, Jim is involved in record production.

JOHN "DRUMBO" FRENCH

John drummed in the earliest version of Captain Beefheart's Magic Band, whose music could best be described as "outer-space atonal blues with odd time signatures." That's my quote, spoken from the standpoint of a longtime Beefheart fan. John was capable of handling whatever quirky time changes Beefheart threw at him with apparent ease. His style had its own oddball nature, probably learned after hours listening to avant-garde jazz. In 2003, some of the original Magic Band, including Drumbo, regrouped to perform Beefheart's material both live and on disc.

GERRY FREEMAN

The Applejacks were Brit one-hit wonders with "Tell Me When" in 1965 and Gerry Freeman was their drummer with the silver sparkle Ludwigs. The band never scored another sizeable hit and Gerry eventually married the group's bass player, Megan Davis.

MARTY FRIED

A clean-cut drummer with a light touch, Marty played with The Cyrkle, the only American band managed by Beatles manager Brian Epstein. The Cyrkle had two hits, "Red Rubber Ball" and "Turn Down Day," tried psychedelia, and eventually threw in the towel.

FROSTY (BARTHOLOMEW SMITH-FROST)

This rotund drummer became famous for his work with organist Lee Michaels. The two formed a very effective duo: Michaels also played bass pedals, providing a full sound. Hits like "Heighty Hi" and "Do You Know What I Mean" solidified their reputation. Frosty was a very passionate player who left Michaels in the early Seventies and formed a group called Sweathog that recorded two LP's on Columbia Records and split soon after. This writer bumped into Frosty in a local rock club in the mid-Seventies. He was trying to put together another band and was very forthcoming about past glories and substance-abuse problems. For the last ten years or so, Frosty has made a good name for himself as a busy session musician in Austin, Texas, and as a member of a band called Soulhat. He recently experienced some heart problems that temporarily sidelined his musical activities, but as of this writing, Frosty is playing again and hopefully in good health.

MARTIN FULTERMAN

Perhaps the only person in this book trained as a classical oboist, Marty Fulterman wasn't a bad rock drummer either. He was a member of The New York Rock Ensemble, a band that combined classical music with rock. Three of the band's members attended Julliard School of Music and their albums on Atco and Columbia sold pretty well. Although the classical routine was a novelty at first, The Rock Ensemble later attempted to shed the image, but by then it was too late.

DAVID GETZ

David drummed with Big Brother & The Holding Company during their days with Janis Joplin and beyond. David was a competent drummer and he's still playing with three other original members of Big Brother.

MIKE GIBBINS

Mike was the drummer with Badfinger, perhaps unfairly remembered as Beatles clones because they were discovered by the Fabs and recorded on Apple Records. The group was previously called The Ivies and got together in 1966. Badfinger's power-pop rock was hugely influential, but the band split up primarily due to bad business decisions and internal strife. Two of the members, Pete Ham and Tom Evans, eventually committed suicide. Mike Gibbins released a CD that was available on his web site, www.mikegibbins.com, but he died in September 2005.

Mike Gibbins of Badfinger, far right.

MICHAEL GILES

An original member of King Crimson, Michael's fine drumming on the group's early recordings was very influential on the current generation of progressive-rock drummers. Giles recently formed a group called Twenty-First Century Schizoid Men with other former members of Crimson.

KEN GIRVAN

Ken played with the English Mod band The Eyes whose sound was heavily influenced by the pop-art experimentation of The Who. They started life in West London as The Renegades, but changed their name in late 1964. Their first single, "When The Night Falls," is a haunting piece with Townshend-like guitar feedback, string scratching and mournful blues harp. Although it wasn't a big hit, it was enough for the band to turn pro. Three singles and an EP followed, but none hit the charts despite the band's active gig schedule. They split in 1967.

WHITEY GLAN

Whitey Glan is best known as a member of Lou Reed's *Rock 'n' Roll Animal* band, but he got his first taste of fame as a member of a Canadian group called Mandala, who were hyped as rock preachers. As could be expected, the public didn't buy it and Mandala broke up. Listen to the abovementioned Reed album if you want to hear Whitey really play the drums. Whitey also worked with Alice Cooper for a while and recently survived a bad car accident that has at least temporarily put a halt to his drumming career.

ALAN GORDON

You might know Alan Gordon as one-half of the songwriting team of Bonner & Gordon, who wrote "Happy Together" and "She'd Rather Be With Me," both huge hits for The Turtles. Alan Gordon started out in music as drummer for a New York City band called The Magicians that released a few good singles for Columbia Records in the mid-Sixties and were the subject of a television show called *Eye On New York*. Despite this, The Magicians never made it and split up in 1967. In 1999, Sundazed Records released all the group's singles plus unreleased tracks on a CD called *The Magicians: Invitation To Cry*. Alan was a decent drummer who obviously had more success as a songwriter. The Magicians reportedly still get together and play for fun.

JIM GORDON

Jim Gordon's story is perhaps one of the saddest and most perplexing tales from the rock underworld. Born in California in the mid-Forties, Gordon was attracted to drums early on and acquired his first set at age twelve. He participated in school music programs, gigged with a surf-rock group called Frankie & The Jesters, and gradually worked his way into the Los Angeles studios with the help of Hal Blaine. Jim toured with The Everly Brothers in 1963–1964 and, soon after, gained a sure foothold in the West Coast studios, quickly gaining a reputation as a "human metronome," a solid timekeeper, a much-in-demand drummer who could inject even the dullest song with excitement. He did sessions for Bobby Darin, Gary Puckett & The Union Gap, Glen Campbell, Gordon Lightfoot, Joan Baez and countless others, charging double union scale for his services. His future seemed assured. Or so everyone thought. In 1970, tired of the studio grind, Gordon joined Delaney & Bonnie & Friends for a tour that included Eric Clapton, George Harrison, Dave Mason and other rock notables. A critical and financial success, that tour opened other doors for Gordon, and he agreed to go out with Joe Cocker on the Mad Dogs & Englishmen tour in 1971, amidst an atmosphere of rampant hard-drug use, alcohol, groupies and general depravity. It was during that tour that Gordon began experiencing violent bursts of anger, so badly that he reportedly beat up his then-girlfriend, singer Rita Coolidge. Jim helped form Derek & The Dominoes with Eric Clapton and not only continued abusing heroin, cocaine and marijuana, but alcohol as well. After The Dominoes split, Gordon cut John Lennon's album *Imagine* and did some studio and live work with Traffic. He then joined the short-lived Souther-Hillman-Furay Band and the substance abuse continued unabated, as did Gordon's frequent trips to hospitals and institutions, where he complained of hearing voices in his head. Other musicians began noticing the changes in Gordon's personality. He became unruly, argumentative and unreliable. The high-paying studio sessions began to dry up and he was forced to turn to jingle work to survive. Gordon turned down a tour with Bob Dylan, stopped shaving, bathing and eating and tried to commit suicide. On the night of June 3, 1983, he entered his mother's house, bludgeoned her with a hammer and stabbed her three times with an eight-inch kitchen knife. He was arrested the next morning, drew sixteen years to life and was diagnosed as an acute paranoid schizophrenic. Gordon was incarcerated in San Luis Obispo, California, and remains behind bars to this day. He hasn't played drums in years and will most likely end his life in prison.

HONORABLE MENTIONS

George Grantham of Poco, top, second from right.

BOBBY GRAHAM

Bobby Graham enjoyed a very successful career as a session drummer in England that paralleled that of Hal Blaine in many ways. Both men worked night and day during the Sixties, cutting all types of sessions from TV and movie soundtracks to pop schlock with large orchestras, to rock, jazz and R&B, playing just about every style of music imaginable. Both recorded solo singles and albums, and both faced the hideous prospect of their careers disappearing as work for session players dried up in the Eighties. Bobby played on well over fifteen thousand sessions by his own estimate and worked with artists like The Kinks (he took the sticks away from Mick Avory in the early days), Them, The Animals, Dave Berry, The Pretty Things, P. J. Proby, The Walker Brothers, Dusty Springfield, Herman's Hermits, The Fortunes, Petula Clark, Brenda Lee, The Nashville Teens, Gene Pitney and the list goes on seemingly forever. Discouraged, Bobby eventually quit music for a career in photography, but soon put together a jazz group with which he works to this day. He recently completed his autobiography, which is available on his web site, www.bobbygraham.com.

GEORGE GRANTHAM

George was the drummer in Poco, pioneering country-rock band, formed by Jim Messina and Richie Furay after the demise of Buffalo Springfield. George was a very talented drummer who came to Poco's attention as a member of a Colorado band called Boenzye Creque. George stayed with Poco through the Seventies, left to work in Nashville with country/bluegrass star Ricky Skaggs and returned to the original lineup of Poco in the late Eighties. Besides being a fine drummer and vocalist, George is also a friendly fellow who once freely explained some of his licks to this curious journalist. As of this writing, George is recovering from a stroke that hit him in 2004, but let's hope he will again be firmly ensconced in Poco's drum chair soon.

LEE GRAZIANO

No relation to Rocky Graziano, the former heavyweight champion of the world, Lee was the drummer with The American Breed, who scored the huge hit "Bend Me, Shape Me." Lee sometimes appeared on TV sitting behind the drums, whacking his snare drum with his left hand while pretending to play a trumpet with his right, as the band lip-synched the song. Ridiculous? Of course it was. The American Breed later regrouped under the name Rufus with Chaka Khan as lead singer, but Lee had left the fold.

MARK "THE TWIG" GREENBERG

"The Twig," as he was called, hailed from Livingston, New Jersey, and played with Richard & The Young Lions, a Jersey band that scored a major hit with "Open Up Your Door" in Midwest markets in 1966. The record failed to break nationally, and after a couple more tries, the group split, only to re-form in 2000 with most of the original members, including Twig. Their first CD is ready for release at this writing, although vocalist Richard Tepp passed away in 2004.

HUGH GRUNDY

The rhythmic patterns on The Zombies' hits "She's Not There," "Tell Her No" and "Time Of The Season" were remarkable for their complexity and imagination, reflecting a jazz sensibility that set Hugh Grundy apart from the average British rock drummer. One listen to the group's first album proved that Hugh could kick butt, too, when called upon to do so. Listen to their version of "Got My Mojo Working." After The Zombies split, Hugh took a job in the record business and did quite well in that career. The Zombies got together for a one-off reunion concert several years ago.

JOHN GUERIN

John Guerin, who died January 5, 2004, at the age of sixty-four, was a drummer's drummer, a prolific musician, composer, producer and arranger, an excellent all-around player who could fit in with almost anyone in any musical style. Based on the West Coast, Guerin played with The Byrds, Them, Linda Ronstadt, Frank Sinatra, Joni Mitchell, Thelonious Monk, Dave Grusin, Frank Zappa, Peggy Lee, Ella Fitzgerald, Lou Rawls, Nelson Riddle and countless others, including many jazz luminaries in his later years. John was also a first-call session musician and played on many movie and television soundtracks. For years, John co-led the band L.A. Express with Tom Scott, enjoying success playing fusion jazz/rock. He remained active until his death of complications from pneumonia.

KEVIN GODLEY

Kevin played drums with The Mockingbirds along with bassist/songwriter Graham Gouldman. The band never found the elusive hit, but re-formed later as the wildly successful 10cc with guitarist Eric Stewart of The Mindbenders.

KEITH GUSTER

Keith Guster played with the British band Les Fleur De Lys. The band's records were adventurous and well produced, but they went nowhere and they broke up in 1969.

JOHN HALSEY

Although John Halsey is best remembered as Barry Wom of The Rutles, he got started as a pro drummer with Timebox from Southport, England. The band's recorded output was respectable and influenced by American soul music, but they missed the charts repeatedly. The band folded in 1969 and reemerged in 1970 as Patto.

RONNIE HARKAI

Ronnie played with The Outsiders at some point, but the extent of his involvement with the band is unclear.

BOBBY HARRISON

Bobby Harrison was the original drummer in Procol Harum, but did not play on their debut hit single "Whiter Shade Of Pale" as previously reported in the first edition of this book. The late, great B. J. Wilson was the drummer who cut the tune, as Harrison had been sacked prior to the band's first studio date. Bobby later turned up as lead singer in an English band called Snafu that had mild success in the mid-Seventies. He now lives in Scandinavia.

MICKEY HART

Mickey was the on-again-off-again drummer with The Grateful Dead and still performs with the revitalized version of the band, known as The Dead. He joined in 1968 and left to work on film scores and solo projects, only to return in the early Seventies. When The Dead became hugely popular, Mickey remained until Jerry Garcia's death. Frankly, he would have been crazy to quit. Hart became a millionaire as a result of his work with the band. He also wrote two books about drumming and spirituality and formed percussion ensembles, as well as amassing a museum-quality collection of percussion instruments. Today, besides his work with The Dead, Mickey is a tireless promoter of drumming in all its forms, and an endorser of Istanbul Agop Turkish cymbals.

DAVID HARVEY

A very basic yet creative drummer, David played in a later version of Them that did not include Van Morrison. With Morrison gone, the hits were finished and after a couple of good albums loaded with trippy West Coast psychedelia and raga/rock on Tower and Happy Tiger Records, Them sputtered to an end. By that time, John Guerin had taken Dave's place.

ROGER HAWKINS

Another guy who made his mark and has spent almost his entire career in the recording studio, Roger was the house drummer at Muscle Shoals Studios in Alabama. He played on countless R&B and rock sessions, backing up Aretha Franklin, Wilson Pickett and many others. Roger even toured and recorded with Traffic for a while, but eventually returned to session duties. A Southerner by birth, Roger lays down a rock-steady groove at all times, and that's why he was consistently in demand.

RICHIE HAYWARD

Richie Hayward has been Little Feat's drummer throughout the group's history and he's a master of the funky, greasy, laid-back New Orleans R&B drumming style. Richie was a member of a band called Factory in the Sixties that also included slide guitarist Lowell George. (Factory recorded one flawed album that was finally released a few years ago and is best left to remain in the bargain bins of the world.) These two would start Little Feat in 1969 with keyboardist Bill Payne and bassist Roy Estrada, and Richie has been with them ever since, despite a serious motorcycle accident in the mid-Seventies. He has also done extensive session work with Buddy Guy, Joan Armatrading and many others.

LEVON HELM

The Band's Levon Helm was the best singing drummer this writer ever heard, until throat cancer robbed him of his voice several years ago. Levon is an extremely personable, warm, easygoing, humorous man who never let sickness get him down. When cancer, brought on by years of smoking, deprived him of his singing talents, Levon dove back into the drums with the energy of a twenty-something, and within a short time began turning up as a session drummer, on many blues recordings in particular. When The Band finally came to an end for good with the death of bassist Rick Danko, Levon formed a group called The Crowmatix and then another called The Barn Burners, a band that continues to this day with his daughter Amy on occasional vocals. Levon still lives in Woodstock, New York, has for decades, and by all accounts, is getting his vocal chops back.

Little Feat's Richie Hayward, the author, and Jim Keltner, California, 2006.

Levon Helm of The Band, second from left.

RICK HENN

Well, we have a Chicken here (see below), so how about a Henn? Rick Henn played with The Sunrays, a California band managed by Murry Wilson, father of The Beach Boys' Wilson brothers, and the similarities—right down to The Sunrays' red-and-white-striped shirts—were no coincidence. The band scored with a couple minor semi-surf hits, "Andrea" and "I Live For The Sun," but their time had passed almost before it started, and after one album, The Sunrays disappeared. Surf music was pretty well finished by 1966.

BOB HENRIT

Bob has been a talented, steady and reliable drummer since the mid-Sixties, playing with The Roulettes, The Unit 4+2, Argent (he's on their hit "Hold Your Head Up"), and finally, The Kinks, where he replaced original drummer Mick Avory. Bob has also done extensive session work. He still plays today, does some writing for a drum magazine and owns a drum shop in England.

CHICKEN HIRSCH

Yes, they called him Chicken… He was the drummer for Country Joe & The Fish in their early days, but left the band before their appearance at Woodstock.

DAN HICKS

Better known as a singer-songwriter, Dan Hicks drummed with The Charlatans, harbingers of San Francisco underground rock.

JON HISEMAN

Jon has always been a distinguished and talented British jazz/rock drummer. He played the R&B circuit in the Sixties with a series of bands, including John Mayall's Bluesbreakers, Georgie Fame and the Graham Bond Organization, and achieved his greatest success with Coliseum in the Seventies. John also organized a rock band called Tempest in the Seventies and has done big band and jazz work since then.

EDDIE HOH

Eddie's biggest brush with fame came as a result of his association with Michael Bloomfield and Al Kooper on the *Super Session* album, but he also played with The Mamas & The Papas, Tim Buckley, Harry Nilsson and at least one version of The Flying Burrito Brothers. Eddie later became involved with session work, cut movie and television soundtracks and reportedly has been out of the music business for some time, down on his luck.

DAVE HOLLAND

Dave Holland was the leather-clad hard-rock drummer with Judas Priest from 1979 until 1988, but got his start as a member of Pinkerton's Assorted Colours, one-hit folk-rock wonders that charted in the U.K. with a tune called "Mirror Mirror," in December 1965. Dave went on to hone his chops with Trapeze, a late Sixties/Seventies hard rock/funk band that included bassist Glenn Hughes, a future member of Deep Purple. After leaving Priest, Dave worked with Hughes and Black Sabbath guitarist Tony Iommi on their solo projects and worked with Al Atkins, original lead singer of Judas Priest. Dave recently ran afoul of the law, and was convicted of sexual abuse of a minor. He is currently serving eight years in a British prison.

PAUL HOLM

Paul Holm played with The Syndicats, one of the wildest Brit R&B bands of the mid-Sixties. Their single "Crawdaddy Simone" was one of the toughest, nastiest records of the day even though it wasn't a hit. The group split up after bassist Kevin Driscoll destroyed a piano onstage with an axe. The mobsters who owned the ballroom threatened the band's "health and well-being" and they split up right then.

PETER HOORELBEKE (RIVERA)

Pete Hoorelbeke, aka Peter Rivera, was the outstanding lead-singing drummer with Rare Earth, one of the only white bands signed to Motown Records' subsidiary, Rare Earth Records. The group specialized in blue-eyed soul versions of Motown hits and reportedly sold twenty-five million records in their lifetime. Peter is still musically active.

KEN HORDICHUK

The Jury from Winnipeg, Manitoba, with Ken Hordichuk on drums, scored a Canadian hit with "Who Dat?" The record was released in the USA, but failed to chart. "Who Dat?" has become a modern-day garage-band staple.

MIKE HUGG

A talented drummer of South African birth who also played vibes and wrote songs, Mike Hugg played with fellow South African Manfred Mann from 1963 until 1972. He drummed on the classic hit "Doo Wah Diddy" and all the group's British Invasion hits. After the original line-up split, Hugg and Mann put together Chapter III to further pursue their jazz ambitions, but the band stumbled and never broke through to mass acceptance. Hugg left to try a solo career, but got nowhere. His song, "You're A Better Man Than I" was a hit for The Yardbirds, and we can assume that Mike did better over the years as a songwriter than he did as a drummer.

JOHN WILLIAM HUNTER

John played drums for The Hombres, one-hit wonders who had a freak smash in 1968 with the Dylanish "Let It Out (Let It All Hang Out). The band hailed from Memphis, Tennessee.

AL JACKSON JR.

Al Jackson was the Memphis Godfather Of Time, The Baddest Of The Bad, the drummer on almost every significant record released on the Stax label and its affiliates in the Sixties. As a member of Booker T. & The MG's, he backed Otis Redding, Rufus Thomas, Sam & Dave, Albert King, Johnny Taylor, Isaac Hayes, Wilson Pickett, Al Green, Aretha Franklin, Bill Withers and even Rod Stewart…and the list goes on and on. Al's drumming philosophy was to groove, plain and simple, and he never cluttered up the sound with unnecessary fills or tricks. When another drummer might add a fill to the end of a given song section, Al would purposely leave it out and time and again; the tension created was undeniable. The son of a prominent orchestra leader, Al had a strong jazz background and was reportedly a very stubborn timekeeper, so much so that he never admitted to rushing or dragging tempos. If there's one thing about Jackson's drumming that people remember, it was his uncanny sense of timing and groove. He has been described as a human drum machine in the days before click tracks were customarily used on pop sessions. Band mates Duck Dunn and Steve Cropper both agree that their time became much better after they worked with him. Jackson also influenced thousands of younger drummers like Kenney Jones and John Barbata, who called him the most dynamic drummer he ever heard. Although Al was purposely restrained in the studio (he preferred not to use crash cymbals on sessions because he felt that the sound offended women's ears), he really opened up onstage. Check out his work with Otis Redding on the *Monterey Pop* disc. He tears it up with some electrifying drumming. By 1975, Stax Records was floundering and Al Jackson, who had become an executive producer for the company, was owed a great deal of money. Lawyers were hired and a lawsuit had been prepared. The night before he was to appear at a hearing concerning the failure of Stax, Al Jackson was murdered, shot six times in his home in Memphis. Maybe it was a cruel coincidence, a botched robbery perhaps, or maybe not, but the reason for this tragedy has never been revealed. At this late date, no one is talking.

Al Jackson Jr. of Booker T. & The M.G.s, far left.

CHIC JAMES

Chic played with Chicago's New Colony Six and was with them from their inception until their demise.

BARRY JENKINS

Barry Jenkins is another in a long line of Sixties drummers who never garnered the respect and attention they deserved at the height of their careers and are all but forgotten today. Barry, who hailed from Weybridge, Surrey, played with The Nashville Teens, who had one sizeable hit with "Tobacco Road," which became a bar-band staple and has been covered by many other artists, including David Lee Roth. Barry left the Teens in February 1966 to assume the drum chair in The Animals, taking the place of John Steele. He quickly established his musicianship on tracks like "Inside Looking Out," "Don't Bring Me Down," and what proved to be one his shining moments, The Animals' version of Donovan's "Hey Gyp." If you were a young drummer in the mid-Sixties, you couldn't help but like Barry's playing on that cut. Pick up a copy and hear it for yourself. Eric Burdon split up the old Animals shortly thereafter and retained Barry in a new lineup that featured a young Andy Summers on guitar. Despite hits like "Sky Pilot" and "San Franciscan Nights," this version of The Animals fell apart in late 1968. With the end of the group, the end of came Barry Jenkins' days in the spotlight, although he was also a member of a band called Heavy Jelly, which he joined in 1970. Barry now owns and manages a vintage guitar shop in England.

ROGER JOHNSTON

Roger played with The Monks, famous for their monk's tonsure hairstyles and dark, loud, doom-laden, heavy music. The Monks retain a strong cult following to this day and still play together occasionally.

HONORABLE MENTIONS

BOB "CONGOS" JONES

"Congos" Jones was the first drummer in Dave Edmunds' band Love Sculpture and played on their first two LPs, both released on Rare Earth Records in the U.S. Terry Williams later replaced him right before the band split. Of course, Terry and Dave played together for years in Rockpile, along with Nick Lowe and Billy Bremner.

JACK JONES

Jack was the sometimes drummer with The Creation, a controversial and innovative British mod band that hit it big in Germany and never made as much as a dent in the U.S. charts. The Creation was a classic example of a "band gone wrong." They broke up and re-formed many times, mostly due to personal issues and disagreements over musical direction. Their guitarist, Eddie Phillips, who took a job driving a bus after the band folded, was the inventor of the violin-bowed technique, which Jimmy Page later stole. The Creation was fond of pop-art experimentation, much like the early Who, and burned self-created paintings onstage, among other visual gimmicks. Jack was a hard-hitting basher who probably never came across as well on record as he did live. His playing on "Painter Man" is strong and powerful. In 1984, The Creation regrouped once again, this time with Mick Avory, fresh out of The Kinks, on drums. Old grudges die hard: The Creation broke up again not long afterward, but re-formed for an appearance at Cavestomp two years ago.

MICKEY JONES

Mickey Jones worked with Trini Lopez, Johnny Rivers and Kenny Rogers & The First Edition, but is perhaps best remembered as the drummer who toured with Bob Dylan on the singer's infamous first electric tour in 1966. Everywhere the band played on that world tour they were met with boos and hostility; folk-music purists were aghast at Dylan's new electric folk-rock style. Mickey braved the bad vibes, filmed much of the backstage hijinks (which he later turned into a commercially available DVD) and eventually parlayed his acting talent into roles in feature films and television shows. He was a regular on *Home Improvement* and had a juicy part in Billy Bob Thornton's film *Sling Blade*, among others. A native of Texas, Mickey has lived on the West Coast for decades and plays drums as the spirit moves him these days.

URIEL JONES

When one thinks of those classic Motown hits of the Sixties, three drummers' names come to mind: Benny Benjamin, Pistol Allen and Uriel Jones. There were others: Marvin Gaye, Earl Palmer, Larry Londin and Stevie Wonder played drums on some Motown tracks, but the abovementioned three gentlemen cut the bulk of Hitsville USA's hits during their glory days. Uriel is featured prominently in the documentary *Standing In The Shadows of Motown* and he's still playing drums actively.

BRIAN KEENAN

Here's a guy who should have gone on to much fame as a drummer, but for some reason, it didn't happen. Brian Keenan had it all going for him—talent, good looks, a great band of four ex-gospel singers and strong material—but for some reason, he never ascended the stairs of rock stardom. The Chambers Brothers, four African-Americans who successfully made the transition from gospel to funk-rock and psychedelia, featured Brian, the only white member, prominently on their biggest hit, "Time Has Come Today," but that song proved to be their only big seller and the group eventually faded away. Brian's playing on the extended version of "Time" is nothing short of spectacular. He was a rock drummer who could swing, and he executed rudimental rhythmic patterns, including open and closed rolls and military-style licks. Any drummer as hot as Brian should have gone further, but it didn't happen. He dropped out of the public eye and passed away in 1986, his death reported in *Rolling Stone* magazine.

JON KELIEHOR

Jazz-trained drummer Jon Keliehor and The Daily Flash from Seattle, Washington, played rough psych-rock and eventually wound up in the Los Angeles area, where guitarist Doug Hastings joined Buffalo Springfield for a while.

MIKE KELLIE

A no-nonsense, straight-ahead rock player, Mike Kellie was the drummer in Spooky Tooth, a great but underappreciated band whose second LP release, *Spooky Two*, is one of the best hard-rock albums to appear in the late Sixties. Mike's playing on that landmark release was excellent, particularly on "Waiting For The Wind" and the epic "Evil Woman." Mike also did session work and appeared on Jerry Lee Lewis's *The Session Recorded In London* LP. In the late Seventies, Mike joined The Only Ones, a new wave band, and eventually returned to Spooky Tooth in their Seventies incarnation and again in 1999 for their *Cross Purpose* CD release. It was obvious from the first listen that advancing age had done nothing to diminish Mike's talent.

Spooky Tooth's reunion CD, *Cross Purpose*. Mike Kellie is on the far right.

SIMON KIRKE

Simon Kirke played drums with Free from 1968 until 1973 and went on to great success with Bad Company. His latest projects have included a long stint working with Ringo Starr & His All-Star Band, as well as reunion recordings and tours with Bad Company. Financially comfortable, Simon now lives in New York City with his family and only works when he wishes to do so.

SANFORD KONIKOFF

Sandy Konikoff played drums on Taj Mahal's early albums and did session work on the West Coast.

JIM KELTNER

This session ace and all-around great drummer made his debut with Gary Lewis & The Playboys and worked with Delaney & Bonnie, Gabor Szabo and Henry Gross in the late Sixties, both live and on record. His career really revved up from 1971 on, after he worked with George Harrison, Leon Russell, Ringo Starr and Bob Dylan among many others. Jim's list of session credits is so extensive, it fills pages, and while session work has become harder and harder to find these days, Jim stays busy and productive. What's his secret? Jim has a great feel for all types of music, has solid and unflinching time, good taste, and he's positive and easy to work with, not to mention clever and inventive. What's not to like?

BILL KREUTZMANN

"Bill the Drummer," as he was known in the Sixties, played with The Grateful Dead as far back as 1965, when they were known as The Warlocks. He was one half of the Dead's percussion team, the other being Mickey Hart. Bill adapted his style to suit all phases of Dead music, from blues, all types of rock, country, to spacey jams, ballads and even pseudo-disco. He stayed with the band right up until Jerry Garcia's death, reaped all the financial rewards and, in 2002, participated in the Other Ones concert, effectively the first official Grateful Dead reunion. He toured with surviving members of the band, including Mickey Hart, as The Dead in 2003 and 2004.

Bill Kreutzman, left, with Jerry Garcia, both members of The Grateful Dead.

NORM KUHLKE

Norm Kuhlke is a name many of you may not be familiar with. He was the enthusiastic, upbeat drummer with The Swinging Blue Jeans, a four-piece English band that hit the charts with "Hippy Hippy Shakes." The Blue Jeans, who wore Levis onstage, were one of a multitude of bands around Liverpool playing the same circuit as The Beatles. They broke up after the initial hysteria over the British Invasion waned in 1966. "Hippy Hippy Shakes" is now a bar-band staple.

RICHARD KUMER

Richard worked with The Fallen Angels (there were dozens of Sixties bands with that name), who during the height of psychedelia, cut two hard-to-find albums for Roulette Records that were festooned with paisley and pretentious liner notes guaranteed to warp the windmills and cavernous recesses of your subconscious mind. Neither disc sold very well and Richard hasn't been heard from since.

JERRY LA BREQUE

Jerry was the drummer with Teddy & The Pandas, at one time a hot garage-rock band that turned sweet and sugary when they recorded their first and only album on Tower Records.

MARTIN LAMBLE

Martin was the often-subtle drummer with the first version of Fairport Convention, a groundbreaking Sixties English folk-rock group. Fairport has had a long and checkered history with more personnel changes than one can count. Martin was killed in a car accident and replaced by Dave Mattacks.

JOEL LARSON

Joel was the talented drummer with Emmitt Rhodes' band The Merry-Go-Round. Their regional hit "Live" showed promise, but the group never topped it and split up in 1969.

RIC LEE

The brother of guitar hero Alvin Lee and not coincidentally the drummer with Ten Years After, Ric had a strong swing and jazz slant to his playing, but he could rock as hard as any of his contemporaries as well. He had a fast pair of wrists and has remained with Ten Years After from beginning to the present day, including a reunion tour in 1990 and a new CD recently released. This writer was frankly amazed at Ric's drum solo at a concert at Waterloo Village in Stanhope, New Jersey in 1990. It was one of the best I ever heard.

GARY LEEDS (WALKER)

Gary Walker got his start playing with The Standells for a few months and together with John Maus and Scott Engel formed The Walker Brothers. After moving to England to find their fortune, the group hit on a formula of highly orchestrated ballads in the style of The Righteous Brothers. The British hits mounted up: "Make It Easy On Yourself" and "The Sun Ain't Gonna Shine Anymore" were huge hits in the U.K. and respectable chart successes in the U.S. The group almost never played on their records, though, and after a short time, their music fell into disfavor. Leeds quit the group and put together a new band called Gary Walker & The Rain, but their time together was also brief.

PHIL LENOIR

Phil played good drums for a few British blues bands, most notably Black Cat Bones, who released one extremely rare album on Pickwick Records entitled *Barbed Wire Sandwich*. Future Foghat guitarist Rod Price was also a member.

GARY LEWIS

The son of comedian Jerry Lewis, Gary had several hits with his group, The Playboys, all of them sugarcoated rockers like "This Diamond Ring," "Everybody Loves A Clown" and "She's Just My Style." Gary played adequate drums, but rarely, if ever, played on the group's records. Earl Palmer or Hal Blaine cut the sessions and Gary handled live gigs. At the height of The Playboys' popularity, Gary was drafted, and after finishing his two years in the service, failed to reestablish his musical career, despite a few valiant tries. By this time, he was playing guitar and fronting a new band, featuring drummer Jim Keltner. Today, Gary Lewis still tours with a group of young Playboys, playing the old hits for aging baby boomers.

CARLO LITTLE

Carlo Little played with Screaming Lord Sutch, an outrageous and minimally talented English early Sixties rock 'n roll singer and noted eccentric, but is best known for giving a young Keith Moon several informal drum lessons soon after the future Who drummer began following Little around on his gigs. Little was a self-taught player who reluctantly agreed to help Keith after Keith offered to pay him. He simply taught Keith "what he knew" and nothing more, but it was enough to get the youngster started on the way to rock immortality.

MIKE LOVE

Mike Love played with The Uniques from Louisiana, a band that included future country music star Joe Stampley and his brother Bobby.

BOB MACVITTIE

Bob played with Sugarloaf on the band's one and only hit, "Green-Eyed Lady," a song still frequently heard on classic rock and oldies radio. Bob got his start playing with The Moonrakers, one of the better garage bands from Colorado. They recorded a few singles for Tower Records and one LP for Shamley Records that is extremely hard to find.

ROGER MANSOUR

If you were a teenager in the New York metro area in the mid-Sixties, you probably remember The Vagrants, from Forest Hills, Queens. Their gigs are the stuff of which legends are made. Leslie West (née Weinstein) came to prominence as the group's lead guitarist, and Roger Mansour, the guy with the long hair hanging over his horn-rimmed glasses, was the drummer. Roger was a capable player who used a multicolored sparkle set of Ludwig drums and one could definitely draw comparisons with Dino Danelli in terms of style and approach. The Vagrants, whose wild stage act included smashing instruments, were touted for the big time, but despite several great singles, including a killer version of "Respect," they never made it and broke up in frustration. Roger was reported managing a hotel in Florida at one point and now does Christian youth missionary work in the Caribbean.

FRED MARSDEN

Fred Marsden was the older brother of Gerry Marsden of Gerry & The Pacemakers. When the group broke up, Fred, older than your average rock musician, disappeared from the scene and never resurfaced. His drumming was adequate but hardly distinguishable from that of any other British Beat drummer of the period.

DEWEY MARTIN

"Good Old Dew" handled drum duties for Buffalo Springfield and brought with him a long career backing country/western performers in Nashville and Las Vegas prior to joining that band. Dewey was actually the most experienced musician in the Springfield. A Canadian by birth, Dewey, whose last name was actually Midkiff, was a reliable team player who did his job without flash and fanfare. He also relished his role as the Springfield's soul singer (check out his vocal on "Good Time Boy") and befriended Otis Redding right before his career took off. Dewey even wanted Otis to sing "Mr. Soul" with the band on a TV appearance after Neil Young quit (Neil quit Springfield *three* times altogether). After Springfield disintegrated for the last time in 1968, Dewey formed a band called Medicine Ball that lasted only one album. Dew and Springfield bassist Bruce Palmer eventually put together a band called Buffalo Springfield Revisited and toured for several years in the 1980's. Buffalo Springfield was eventually elected to the Rock and Roll Hall of Fame and finally got the widespread recognition they always deserved. Dewey generally divides his time between auto-repair work and music these days.

Dewey Martin of Buffalo Springfield, second from right.

LEE MASON

Lee Mason played with a Boston garage band called The Lost that recorded on Capitol Records. Although The Lost was a good band and their records deserved attention, they failed to break out of the New England area and split up by 1967.

NICK MASON

Nick Mason has been the drummer with Pink Floyd since their inception in the mid-Sixties. The Floyd was one of the first bands to experiment with spacey, psychedelic music and Nick's playing complemented their sonic explorations nicely on most occasions. Sometimes his drumming was serene and flowing, and sometimes it was brutal, jarring and primitive. The Floyd's greatest accomplishment was *Dark Side Of The Moon*, a record that stayed on the charts longer than any other in history. It turned the group into superstars. Today, Pink Floyd records and tours only occasionally and Nick enjoys the good life in England.

DAVE MATTACKS

Dave came to the public eye as drummer with Fairport Convention, perhaps the best and most popular of England's folk-rock groups of the Sixties. He replaced original drummer Martin Lamble and went on to work with the band sporadically for many years. Dave, who now lives in Massachusetts, makes his living primarily as a successful session drummer, and also plays live gigs around the Boston area as well as touring with Mary Chapin Carpenter and others.

JOHN MACAULEY

John was the drummer with Van Morrison's band, Them, who exploded out of Belfast in 1965 with hits like "Mystic Eyes," "Here Comes The Night" and "Gloria." Session musicians were used extensively on Them's discs, so we don't know if John appeared on record or not. He later joined up with other former members of Them in a band called Belfast Gypsies.

JIMMY MAY

Jimmy May played with a band called The Liverpool Five…from Spokane, Washington! I suppose they were trying to capitalize on The Beatles' hometown "Britishness." The Liverpool Five went the way of most Sixties bands—gone forever.

JIM McCARTY

Jim drummed for the legendary Yardbirds, Rock and Roll Hall of Fame inductees, from their inception in 1963 as the Metropolitan Blues Quintet to their demise in 1968 and rebirth in 1995. Jim was and still is a very reliable team player that can handle anything from Gregorian chants to down-home blues, hard rock and wild rave-ups with ease. Not a schooled drummer, Jim was loose and creative enough to complement The Yardbirds' improvisatory onstage explorations and has always been ready, willing and able to get the job done. After The Yardbirds split, Jim formed Renaissance with vocalist Keith Relf, took a futile stab at a solo career and resurfaced in 1984 with two other ex-Yardbirds in a band called Box Of Frogs that had a hit with "Back Where I Started." Jim put together his own band afterward, recorded two albums with a group called The British Invasion All-Stars, began composing and playing new age music, and reformed The Yardbirds with guitarist Chris Dreja in 1995. On September 1, 1997, The Yardbirds played Tramps in New York City and this writer was present for the event. Later on, musicians from the audience were invited onstage for a blues jam. After a few songs on tambourine, I switched places with Jim McCarty and played Yardbird favorites like "Five Long Years" and "Smokestack Lightning" with Jim to my right on tambourine. At one point, I looked around and realized, "I'm playing with The Yardbirds!" It was a once-in-a-lifetime experience I'll never forget. Jim still works with The Yardbirds, who toured the USA in 2003, 2004 and 2005, plays with the Jim McCarty Blues Band, continues to record and release new age music and remains a first-class rock 'n' roll survivor.

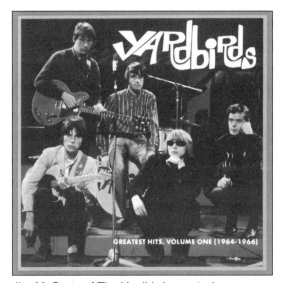

Jim McCarty of The Yardbirds, seated, third from left.

PETE McDANIELS

Another name from the dusty annals of English rock history is Pete McDaniels of The Birds (no, not The Byrds), a great blues/rock band that had a few minor hits in England in the mid-Sixties and never scored in the U.S. Future Face/Rolling Stone Ron Wood was The Birds' lead guitarist, whose material ranged from R&B and blues to Motown covers. It's a shame The Birds never went any further; they were an excellent band whose records crackled with excitement. Pete's playing was consistently strong and authoritative and his drums were always prominently featured and well recorded. The British Birds were as good as finished when the American Byrds broke through big on the charts first. Pick up a vinyl copy of *These Birds Are Dangerous* on Edsel Records, if you can find one.

DANNY MIHM

Danny played with The Flamin' Groovies, who burst out of San Francisco in 1968 with a sound that was fueled more by roots rock 'n' roll than by psychedelia. The Groovies never attained much more than cult stardom, despite several fine albums. Danny Mihm was and probably still is a very exciting, uninhibited player. He eventually worked for a while with former Groovies vocalist Roy Loney in a band called Hot Knives.

BUDDY MILES

Big, bad Buddy Miles rose to prominence as a member of Electric Flag, guitarist Mike Bloomfield's "American music" band. Buddy brought a lot of experience to the table from working the R&B circuit, doing stints with Wilson Pickett, Ruby & The Romantics and The Ink Spots, among others. A native of Omaha, Nebraska, Buddy was not only an aggressive drummer, but also possessed a very soulful voice and handled many lead vocals with The Flag, a band that lasted only one album in their original incarnation. After Bloomfield left, Buddy more or less took over as front man and then put The Buddy Miles Express together. Although the personnel were never stable, The Express released several moderately successful albums on Mercury Records. Buddy penned the rock classic "Them Changes" and then joined up with Jimi Hendrix in the short-lived Band Of Gypsies. He played on a few early jazz-fusion sessions that included guitarist John McLaughlin, but his career took a downturn in the Seventies. Buddy was arrested twice on drug charges and also caused trouble at the San Francisco offices of *Rolling Stone* magazine, where he went on a violent rampage, accusing the magazine of treating him badly. After serving time behind bars, Buddy resurfaced for a short stint as lead singer with Santana and got the gig as lead vocalist for the "California Raisin" commercials. This work, plus the album sales that resulted from the popularity of the Raisins, got him back on his feet financially. Buddy stays busy these days, touring, and playing drums and guitar, which for years, has been his second instrument. He recently recorded a good album with former Stevie Ray Vaughan sidemen Tommy Shannon and Chris Layton called *The Bluesberries*.

DON MITCHELL

The Moving Sidewalks may or may not ring a bell with you, but to Sixties garage-rock fans, they were one of the best bands from that time. They also served as the launching pad for the spectacular career of Billy Gibbons of ZZ Top. Don Mitchell was the agile and quick-wristed drummer with The Moving Sidewalks and his work should not be forgotten, particularly on tracks like the memorable "99th Floor," "Need Me" and "Every Night A New Surprise." The complete Moving Sidewalks catalog was released back in the Eighties on Eva Records.

RICK MOE

Rick Moe played with The Misunderstood, an apt name for this American band that relocated to England in 1966. Their ace in the hole was pedal steel guitarist Glenn Ross Campbell, who played some of the most mind-blowing, psychedelic, fuzz-drenched leads this side of Jeff Beck. Rick Moe was a solid if non-flashy drummer. The group's records failed to chart, they struggled constantly, and eventually they fell apart when their lead singer was forced to return home to answer the draft call of Uncle Sam.

RALPH MOLINA

Ralph has been playing with Neil Young's backing band, Crazy Horse, for more than thirty years. Before that, he worked with The Rockets, who recorded one album on White Whale Records around 1966. Ralph's approach to the drums is fundamentally simple and uncomplicated. You might say he's a classic behind-the-beat player. No criticism is implied, for Ralph does his job very well.

BILL MOONEY

No relation to Thom Mooney of The Nazz, Bill played with The Little Boy Blues, a Chicago garage band, who were a big draw on their home turf and cut a few excellent punky singles on small Illinois labels and later signed with Fontana Records. Their one album, *In The Woodland Of Weir*, is a pretentious conceptual experiment in pseudo-jazz that promptly went nowhere. The Little Boy Blues were never heard from again.

THOM MOONEY

Thom Mooney was a drummer we were unable to locate for the purpose of a detailed interview the first time around. I always liked his forceful, emotional playing and was distressed when a phone call to Todd Rundgren failed to reveal his whereabouts. On the night of August 28, 1988, I was reviewing a Marshall Tucker Band/Rita Coolidge concert and noticed that the drummer with Rita's band looked familiar. It was Thom Mooney, right before my eyes. With the original book's manuscript ready to go to press, it was too late to write an interview chapter, but I was able, through Thom's cooperation and the courtesy of Rita's manager, to go backstage and conduct an impromptu interview with this unsung and worthy rock drummer. Thom, a native of Altoona, Pennsylvania, occupied the drum chair for The Nazz, one of the first true power-pop rock bands and the springboard for singer-songwriter-guitarist Todd Rundgren. Keith Moon, Kenney Jones and Mike Kellie from Spooky Tooth heavily influenced Thom, and his best work with The Nazz included tracks like "Under The Ice" and "Wildwood Blues," his drum-solo number. After The Nazz disbanded, Thom hung out for a while in Los Angeles and had a hard time finding work, so he accepted a gig with an Illinois band called Fuse, which later became Cheap Trick. He worked in a rock cover band in Hawaii, returned to L.A., put together a band called Paris with Bob Welch and Glenn Cornick, and left that group to join another outfit called Tattoo that boasted guitarist Wally Bryson, just out of The Raspberries. When Tattoo folded after just one album, Thom grew tired of joining and quitting bands and set his sights on becoming a sideman, a hired gun. After cutting an obscure LP with The Curtis Brothers, Thom hooked up with Danny O'Keefe and also worked with vocalists Ronee Blakely, Cindy Bullens and Tanya Tucker ("Those tours with Tanya were horrible," Thom said). He also played drums on the last tour Roger McGuinn and Chris Hillman did together. Through them, he met Rita Coolidge, who had just split with husband Kris Kristofferson and was putting together a new road band. Thom landed the gig backing her, and by the end of the tour, he and Rita had become a romantic item as well. Thom eventually took over leadership of Rita's band and after a while, left the group to resume a steady schedule of session work with the likes of Jimmy Buffett, John Hiatt, Ken O'Malley, Scottish rocker Tom Maclear, Californians Bob & Wendy, Chris Spedding and John Andrew Parks, among many others. Thom has also become adept at the bodhran, a frame drum used widely in Celtic music.

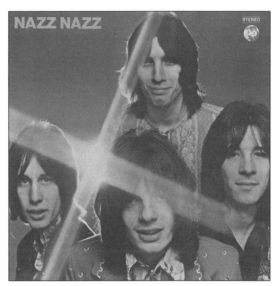

Thom Mooney of the Nazz, bottom center.

STAN MOORE

Stan played with legendary Texas garage rockers Zakary Thaks. David Fore of Bubble Puppy was the band's first drummer.

JOE MORRIS

Joe played with The Swingin' Medallions, whose frat-rock classic "Double Shot (Of My Baby's Love)" scaled the charts to number 17 in March 1966.

VICTOR "MOULTY" MOULTON

Moulty overcame the tragedy of losing a hand as a youngster to become a professional drummer. The rumor goes that he lost it while making a pipe bomb to blow up his school. Using an artificial limb, the Provincetown, Massachusetts-bred musician led a garage-punk band called The Barbarians that had a couple of regional hits like "Are You A Boy Or A Girl?" and "Moulty" in 1966. The group was no great shakes live or in the studio and Moulty was hardly an accomplished technician, bet should still be commended for having the courage to overcome a debilitating injury. Today he still lives in Massachusetts and is pursuing a career teaching self-defense. The Barbarians' biggest claim to fame was their appearance in the film *The T.A.M.I. Show*, which also featured The Rolling Stones, Chuck Berry and James Brown. Like some Sixties garage-band veterans, The Barbarians still get together for the occasional concert or club appearance.

DAVE MUNDEN

That's M-u-n-d-e-n…not Mundane, OK? For years, Dave played with The Tremeloes, who started their career backing English singer Brian Poole, an Elvis knockoff. During the British Invasion of the mid-Sixties, The Trems, realizing Poole was a has-been, chucked him and updated their sound, scoring a couple of U.S. hits like "Here Comes My Baby," which featured Dave's deft use of his ride cymbal bell.

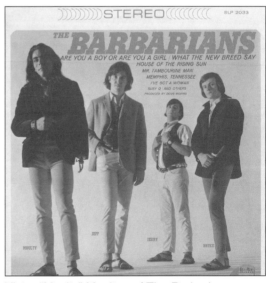

Victor "Moulty" Moulton of The Barbarians, far left.

BILLY MUNDI

Billy was an early member of The Mothers of Invention and left that band to join Rhinceros, one of the first manufactured supergroups. They had one semi-hit, "Apricot Brandy," recorded two albums of blue-eyed soul and rock on Elektra Records and split due to internal problems. Billy, an R&B player at heart, went on to other projects, but none with as high a profile.

DON MURRAY

Don played drums with The Turtles and The Crossfires, an earlier surf-music edition of the band. Don's soul beat was the main hook on their hit "You Baby." A solid drummer with a Brian Jones haircut, Don left The Turtles before "Happy Together" and got a job working in graphic arts. He returned to music in the Eighties and joined The Surfaris, with whom he played for fifteen years until his death on March 22, 1996, from complications following surgery.

KEN MURRAY

Ken played with Mouse & The Traps, a Texas band that scored a near-national hit with "A Public Execution," a blatant ripoff of Bob Dylan's "Like A Rolling Stone" and a garage-band classic it its own right.

TOM MURRAY

Tom Murray played drums with The Litter, perhaps one of the most legendary Sixties garage-rock bands. The band recorded two albums. Record collectors revere their ultra-rare single "Action Woman." The Litter has re-formed with at least a couple of original members.

TONY NEWMAN

An aggressive hard-hitting drummer, Richard Anthony Newman played on the Jeff Beck Group's second album, *Beck-Ola*, but got his first taste of success playing with Sounds Inc., an instrumental band that did quite well in England and was considered the second most popular instrumental aggregation after The Shadows. Following his stint with the mercurial Mr. Beck, Tony formed a short-lived power trio called May Blitz, whose two albums are now collectible. He later went on to play with David Bowie and landed lucrative session gigs.

MICHAEL NEY

Michael shared drumming duties with Dallas Taylor in the band Clear Light.

JIMMY NICHOL

Jimmy Nichol, the only part-time Beatle in history, subbed for Ringo on a 1964 European tour after The Beatles' drummer came down with tonsillitis and required surgery. Once the tour ended, Jimmy slipped back into obscurity. He will undoubtedly always remember his brief stint with the Fab Four, even if it was just for one tour. Jimmy was paid five hundred pounds and given a gold watch.

BOB NIX

Bob was the beefy drummer with the Georgia-based Candymen, who excelled at Beatles covers and recorded two albums for ABC Records in the late Sixties. They later evolved into The Atlanta Rhythm Section after a few personnel changes.

TONY O'REILLY

Tony O'Reilly played with The Koobas from Liverpool and their final single, Cat Stevens's "First Cut Is The Deepest," was a minor hit. Despite some good records, the band failed to score again and broke up after one album in 1969.

IAN PAICE

Ian is the longtime drummer for England's Deep Purple, one of the earliest heavy-metal bands, and a major influence on today's headbangers. Left-handed Ian, who has always been a very underrated player, achieved his greatest fame in the Seventies, is still active today with Deep Purple and is as well regarded within the drumming community as ever.

CARL PALMER

Carl was the well-known drummer with Emerson, Lake & Palmer, but he started out in the Sixties, working with Chris Farlowe & The Thunderbirds and Arthur Brown, among others. His greatest acclaim came during the Seventies.

DAVE PALMER

Dave Palmer was the original drummer with The Amboy Dukes, the band that launched guitarist Ted Nugent's career. The Dukes were a Detroit band and Dave's drumming on their hit "Journey To The Center Of The Mind" was exciting.

EARL PALMER

We're breaking out of our self-imposed Sixties time limits a bit here, but must include Earl Palmer, as he is perhaps the most recorded drummer in history. Earl got started playing professionally after World War II in New Orleans, his hometown. In the Fifties, he was the busiest drummer in the Crescent City and cut practically all the Little Richard and Fats Domino hits, plus many, many others. In the Sixties, he played on Motown hits by Diana Ross & The Supremes, The Four Tops, Smokey Robinson & The Miracles and The Temptations. Earl also cut sessions with Neil Young, The Everly Brothers, The Righteous Brothers, Ray Charles, Sonny & Cher, Joni Mitchell, Gary Lewis and even Tiny Tim. And this is just a very small list of the musical notables who have required Earl Palmer's services during his long and fruitful drumming career. Born to a vaudeville family, Earl played drums as far back as he can remember. His grandfather bought him his first set at age six. He studied formally at ten and soaked in the rich New Orleans musical heritage. After getting out of the service following World War II, Earl went back to school, studied piano and greatly improved his reading chops. While working with a local jazz band, he landed the studio gigs that resulted in those classic Little Richard, Fats Domino and Shirley & Lee records that have become rock 'n roll standards. When studio work began to dry up in the Seventies, Earl freelanced live with Percy Faith and Henry Mancini, among many others. Earl always considered his favorite recording to be the album he cut with Neal Hefti and Frank Sinatra, and takes pride in his versatility and ability to play all types of music. For a while, he worked for the Musician's Union in Los Angeles, holding down the job of secretary or treasurer. Earl campaigned hard for the rights of minorities and women in the music business and eventually returned to playing full time. Although not as active as he used to be and now in his eighties, Earl still plays occasionally and looks forward to playing drums for as long as his health will allow.

GENE PARSONS

Gene replaced Kevin Kelly in The Byrds in 1968. A multi-instrumentalist who also plays banjo and guitar and sings, he co-invented the famous Parsons-White String Bender for use on Fender Telecaster–type guitars and has released solo discs that are dominated by country and bluegrass. It is worth mentioning that, while a member of The Byrds, some within the music business disliked Gene's drumming style, including John Phillips of The Mamas & The Papas, who was quoted as saying that Parsons "couldn't play rock." Listen to The Byrds old recordings like *Dr. Byrds & Mr. Hyde* and decide for yourself.

JERRY PATTERSON

Jerry Patterson supplied the rocking backbeat on Sam The Sham & The Pharoahs' trash-rock classic "Wooly Bully." Stan Kesler, who produced the session, instructed Jerry to play a "Mersey beat," whatever that was. Perhaps Kesler was thinking about The Beatles at the time. Like many drummers in this book, Jerry disappeared from the scene; maybe he just got tired of dressing like an Egyptian.

JEFF PELOSI

Jeff replaced Jack Decker in The Critters and, in my opinion, was a much better drummer, displaying a strong R&B influence. Jeff's cousin, Paul Pelosi, graduated high school with me. Maybe that explains why The Critters played our senior prom!

JOHN PEREZ

John played drums with The Sir Douglas Quintet and cut their hit "She's About A Mover."

PEP PERRINE

Drummers who prefer the elongated "power" shells so prevalent in the drum world today may owe it all to Bob Seger's original drummer, Pep Perrine, who may have been the first drummer to install long extenders on his bass drums.

COLIN PETERSON

Colin played with The Bee Gees from their early days in Australia through their first few albums and singles. After leaving The Brothers Gibb, Colin dropped from sight.

GARRY PETERSON

The son of a drummer, Garry started playing at a very young age and has played with The Guess Who from the early Sixties to the present day. He played on all their hits, and consistently did so with good taste, showing an innate ability to handle many styles with authority. This writer has seen the re-formed Guess Who twice in concert and can attest to Garry's talent. Garry was last seen playing DW drums and Sabian cymbals.

Garry Peterson with The Guess Who, far left.

JOHN PETERSON

The drummer with The Beau Brummels and Harper's Bizarre, John enjoyed hit-single success with both bands. A competent rock drummer, he later left the performing end of the music business and took a job behind the scenes.

ALBAN "SNOOPY" PFISTERER

Snoopy played with Arthur Lee's group, Love, on their first Elektra album while still a teenager. He was a baby-faced kid with short hair, and his drumming was merely adequate for the group's folk-rock material. Snoopy, a classically trained keyboard player, gave up the drum chair to Michael Stuart right before the group recorded their second album, and switched to harpsichord and piano. He still corresponds with Love fans via the Internet, but is reportedly bitter about his days in the band.

DALTON POWELL

When Dwayne Quirico left The Bobby Fuller Four, Johny Barbata replaced him for a short time, but Dalton Powell was the band's permanent replacement and stayed with the group until Fuller was found dead in his car under very mysterious circumstances in 1966. That crime has never been solved.

ROGER POWELL

Roger Powell played drums for the legendary English mod soul band The Action and was part of their reformation in the 1990's. Phil Collins and Paul Weller are big fans of the group.

VIV PRINCE

Viv Prince, a notorious drinker and legendary party hound, was the dour-looking drummer with The Pretty Things. An undisciplined, loose player and showman, Prince contributed well to the Pretties' early material, especially tracks like "Roadrunner" and "Pretty Thing." He left the group shortly after being beaten up on a train during a German tour in 1967. Viv later played with The Honeycombs and Denny Laine, subbed a few times for an ill Keith Moon in The Who, and eventually left England for Portugal where he lives today, growing oranges and breeding pedigreed dogs. In 1999, The Pretty Things recorded a song dedicated to their former drummer entitled simply "Vivian Prince."

SKIP PROKOP

A Canadian with a lot of talent and promise and a very large set of drums, Skip played with The Paupers, who recorded two albums on Verve Records and broke up shortly afterward. Skip then played live gigs with the Super Session band with Al Kooper and Mike Bloomfield. From there, he put together the horn band Lighthouse and scored a few hits that still get airplay today. Over the years, Skip has done a lot of session work and composed music for films, and has been working a nine-to-five job in the communications industry for years.

BERNARD PURDIE

Bernard Purdie, studio drumming legend, used to hang a sign behind him in the studio that said something to the effect of, "If you want hits, call Bernard Purdie." Call it egotistical, but it smacks of the truth. For years, fellow musicians called him "Pretty," or more appropriately "Father Time," for the dynamic, relentless grooves he played on so many rock and soul records from the Sixties to present. He is the undisputed master of fatback drums and the originator of the "hi-hat bark." Purdie claimed to have played on records by The Rolling Stones, Dave Clark Five, The Animals and The Who, and has even said he "fixed up" some twenty-one early Beatles tracks, a claim that has been hotly denied by Ringo Starr and others associated with the Fab Four. Purdie received death threats from angry Beatle fans as a result of that remark. Truth is, he played drums on the soundtrack for the *Sergeant Pepper* movie. Over the years, Bernard has recorded or toured with Ray Charles, Aretha Franklin, Steely Dan, King Curtis, Jeff Beck, Erroll Garner, James Brown, Gato Barbieri, Hall & Oates, Paul Simon, Herbie Hancock, Jeff Beck and so many others. Well-known artists have cancelled or postponed tours if he was not available. Bernard Purdie is hardly a modest man, but given his record of achievements, he has a right to boast. Today, studio work is not as abundant as it was in the Sixties, but Bernard still cuts sessions (he's on the recent Jimmy McGriff compact disc), plays live gigs with several New York City–based bands, including The Hudson River Rats, and teaches and conducts drum clinics. So many well-known drummers have named Purdie as a major influence, there's no denying he's earned his place in the annals of rock and soul history.

CHUCK PURRO

A Boston native, Chuck worked with The Colwell-Winfield Blues Band in the Sixties and later joined The James Montgomery Band in the mid-Seventies. A skillful drummer, Chuck has labored for years in the shadow of others and has seemingly never gotten the break he deserves.

DWAYNE QUIRICO

Dwayne gained his small measure of fame with The Bobby Fuller Four. His drums are heard prominently on the rock classic "I Fought The Law," this writer's favorite song. Dwayne eventually left the band and was replaced briefly by Johny Barbata and eventually Dalton Powell.

HANK RANSOIME

Hank played with a band called Elizabeth that recorded on Vanguard Records. The group's sound was influenced by classical music.

TOM "AMBROSE" RAY

Most likely a self-taught drummer, Tom occupied the drum throne for The Leaves, a Los Angeles band that had a minor hit with the garage-rock chestnut "Hey Joe" in 1966. Tom's playing lacked pretense and was always straightforward and simple, a prime example being the track "Dr. Stone" from the band's first LP. His insistent bass-drum pattern and tom fills push the tune along forcefully. Tom, who seemed to be one of the few rock drummers who used Gretsch drums at that time, supposedly left the music business in the late Sixties and opened a talent agency.

EMMITT RHODES

Better known as a singer/songwriter, Emmitt played drums with The Palace Guard.

BOB RIGG

Bob Riggs was the drummer with The Frost, guitarist Dick Wagner's Michigan-based rock band. Their albums on Vanguard Records showed promise, but the band never broke through.

PRESTON RITTER

Preston was the original drummer with The Electric Prunes and his playing on their two hits "I Had Too Much To Dream (Last Night)" and "Get Me To The World On Time" is energetic and exciting. On the latter, Preston played one of the hottest Bo Diddley beats ever committed to vinyl. He left the Prunes not long after due to business and personality problems within the band, played with Linda Ronstadt and many others, and went on to various careers, including police and private investigation, missionary work and much more. Today, Preston still treasures the white marine pearl Rogers double bass set given to him by jazz great Louie Bellson. He did not participate on the Prunes' recent comeback album. He currently lives in California and writes for *Classic Drummer* magazine.

CRAIG ROBB (KRAMPF)

Craig was a member of The Robbs, a family rock group who were regulars on Dick Clark's afternoon TV show *Where The Action Is*. The Robbs had a couple of regional hits with "Race With The Wind" and "Rapid Transit," but failed to click nationally and eventually broke up. A very talented and tasteful player, Craig took his real last name back, married and started a family. He worked a series of day jobs, but never left the music business, and when the opportunity to go on the road with Little Richard presented itself, Craig never looked back. He became one of the most in-demand live and session drummers in Los Angeles, enthusiastically endorsed Rogers drums for years, and was prominently featured in their catalogs and magazine ads. Craig played with the Kim Carnes band for a while and produced her hit "Betty Davis Eyes." When work began to dry up in L.A. and the threat of earthquakes became too much to bear, Craig and his family relocated to Nashville, Tennessee. After a couple of lean years, Craig reestablished himself as a successful drummer and producer in Music City, and has worked with Melissa Etheridge and many others. Although Craig lost his beloved wife, Susie, not long ago, he continues to tour and produce records and is thankful for the great career he has enjoyed for so many years.

Craig Robb (a.k.a. Krampf).

TIM ROCKSON

Tim's drumming on The Lollipop Shoppe's "You Must Be A Witch" is savage and tense, with extremely high energy. Despite this great slice of teen-angst garage-rock, the band failed to score on the charts.

DAVE ROLAND

Dave played with The Wailers from Tacoma, Washington, the band that practically invented the Northwest rock sound.

RUTH ROMONOFF

Ruth drummed with The Hamilton Face Band, which recorded on Phillips Records. The group featured some striking horn charts, but never caught on.

MIKE ROSA (née ROZA)

Mike was a member of The Myddle Class, a New Jersey band that recorded under the auspices of Carole King and her then-husband Jerry Goffin on the couple's Tomorrow label. From the Berkeley Heights/Warren area, Mike was a decent musician who supposedly suffered so acutely from stage fright that gigs were sometimes cancelled or cut short due to his problem. The Myddle Class released three singles, none of which charted to any great extent, and they split in 1966. I own a never-released tape of the group's performance at a New Jersey high school gig and it shows The Myddle Class to be an exciting live act. Mike went on to help form and play with The Quinaimes Band. Their only album appeared on Elektra Records in the early Seventies.

RIC ROTHWELL

Ric Rothwell is a name perhaps known only to the most vociferous of Sixties rock historians. He played with Wayne Fontana & The Mindbenders and appeared on their U.S. hit "The Game Of Love." After Fontana left the group for a stab at a solo career, The Mindbenders had another smash with the ballad "Groovy Kind Of Love," which remains a staple of oldies radio today. Ric's drumming on this tune, with his military-style flams and drags, was appropriate and inventive. He used and endorsed British-made Beverley drums.

TOM RUGER

Tom played with the Florida-based Nightcrawlers and cut the session that yielded their one and only hit, "Little Black Egg."

JOHNNY SANDLIN

Johnny Sandlin made his mark as a record producer at Capricorn Records in the Seventies and also played bass with Cowboy. He got his start in the business as the drummer with The Hour Glass, Duane and Gregg Allman's early band. Fans and critics have vilified their two albums on Liberty Records for years. It's no wonder. They're atrocious.

JUAN-PABLO SANLLEHI

Los Bravos are remembered for their lone hit, "Black Is Black," and Juan-Pablo was the tall, dark and handsome drummer. The record's success was supposed to open the floodgates for more Spanish rock groups, but it never happened.

JOE SCALFARI

Joe played with The Jelly Bean Bandits who recorded one obscure and collectible album for Mainstream Records in 1968. The group broke up and re-formed in 2002, playing some gigs in upstate New York. They recorded their second disc that same year and have an active web site, www.jellybeanbandits.com.

DAVE SCHERSTROM

Dave Scherstrom played with Circus Maximus, a folk/rock/psych band best known for bringing Jerry Jeff Walker to the public spotlight. Dave brought a subtle jazz touch to the group's most famous track, "The Wind," a true Sixties rock masterpiece that still gets airplay on occasion. It's been a favorite of New York rock DJ Pete Fornatale for years.

TOM SCHIFFOUR

Tom's name may not be a household word, but you've surely heard his drumming on The Shadows of Knight's smash "Gloria," a cleaned-up version of Van Morrison and Them's song. Looking perpetually sad-faced, Tom was an able player with a good pair of hands, which he used effectively on cuts like "Oh Yeah" and "I Just Want To Make Love To You." Keith Moon may have been an influence, as Tom's playing shows evidence of that style. Tom used and endorsed Slingerland drums in the Sixties, and is pictured in ads from that time. He is reportedly still musically active and plays with born-again Christian bands exclusively.

JOHN SEITER

John played with New York's Spanky & Our Gang, a pop group that had hits like "Sunday Will Never Be The Same," "Lazy Day" and "Making Every Minute Count." Studio musicians were most likely used on the group's recording sessions.

RANDY SEOL

Randy played with The Strawberry Alarm Clock, whose biggest hit, "Incense and Peppermints," was commercial psychedelia. Their debut album featured the band decked out in beads and colorful kaftan-style clothing, sitting amidst paisley rugs and hippie trappings. When The SAC re-formed in the late Eighties, Randy was present.

DANNY SERAPHINE

Danny was the phenomenal jazz-rock drummer with Chicago for years until a mysterious and never-explained incident forced him from the band in 1990. Danny has been a great source of inspiration for drummers worldwide, but as his fame occurred primarily in the Seventies, his full story will be told at another time. Danny endorsed Slingerland drums during his days with Chicago and now produces Broadway plays and hosts drum clinics, among other things. He enthusiastically endorses DW drums today and is looking to get back into drumming as a profession as of this writing.

EDDIE SERRATO

At nineteen, Eddie Serrato was one of the older members of Question Mark & The Mysterians, a Michigan-based band of Chicanos who hit it big with "96 Tears" and "I Need Somebody." Eddie rejoined them during the Nineties for a series of personal appearances and recordings.

REGGIE SHAFFER

Reggie played drums with The "E" Types from Salinas, California. Bonner & Gordon wrote their best-known record, "Put The Clock Back On The Wall," but it wasn't a hit.

JERRY SHIRLEY

Jerry became came to the public eye with Steve Marriott and Peter Frampton in Humble Pie in 1968, but the group's real fame came in the Seventies. Jerry also played with a band called Natural Gas, participated in various reformations of Humble Pie, led a Marriott-less version of the band in the late Nineties, and made his living for a short time as an FM radio DJ in Ohio. He eventually moved back to England and was employed as a carpenter after a serious car accident. Jerry still plays the pub circuit, works with John Bonham's sister in a band and does session work.

MICHAEL SHRIEVE

Remember Santana's performance in the classic Sixties flick *Woodstock*? If so, there's no way you could forget Michael Shrieve's electrifying drum solo on "Soul Sacrifice." Using a four-piece set of champagne sparkle Ludwig drums and a couple of cymbals, Michael displayed some incredible chops for a drummer in his late teens. When his time with Santana ended in the early Seventies, Michael worked with a few bands, as well as Japanese percussionist Stomu Yamashta, and was one of the first drummers to embrace electronic percussion. Michael has moved in the direction of jazz-fusion music and we will undoubtedly be hearing more from him in the years ahead.

Michael Shrieve.

JERRY SLICK

Grace Slick's first husband played drums for The Great Society, one of the earliest San Francisco hippie bands. Columbia Records released two albums of their material *after* they broke up and *after* Grace joined Jefferson Airplane, where she went on to fame.

N. D. SMART II

The N. D. stands for Norman Dow. An Ohio native, N. D. got his first break when he replaced Chip Damiani in The Remains, just in time for that group's inclusion as the opening act on The Beatles' final tour in 1966. A talented gymnast, N. D. usually did a back flip off the stage as a climax to The Remains' sets. N. D. laid down the drum track to "Don't Look Back," The Remains' best-known recording. After The Remains split, N. D. joined Kangaroo, a band that included John Hall on bass, and eventually played with Leslie West and The Flying Burrito Brothers.

DONALD SMITH

Do you recall when bands had names like The Chromium Underwear and The Electric Toilet Seat? Donald Smith played with a Massachusetts group Tangerine Zoo, a band with two albums on Mainstream Records that did little to further their popularity. Donald's music career basically ended when the Zoo parted company, but the band has played together a couple of times since the late Eighties.

HONORABLE MENTIONS

"Smitty" Smith of Paul Revere & The Raiders, far right.

"LEGS" LARRY SMITH

"Legs" Larry Smith was the crazed drummer with The Bonzo Dog Band. He wore fake breasts and little-girl outfits and blew kisses to the audience, while dancing like a madman around the stage. The Bonzos were an indescribable band of English zanies, whose music included send-ups of Fifties rock, British music hall, jazz and just about everything else. One member, Roger Ruskin-Spear, did nothing but set off explosions and operate home-built stage props, including a motorized mannequin soldier that flapped his jaw and saluted. Larry and the rest of the Bonzos were better musicians than one might have thought, given their proclivity for comedy.

MICHAEL "SMITTY" SMITH

Smitty was the crazy drummer with Paul Revere & The Raiders during their halcyon days in the mid-Sixties. The Raiders were regulars on Dick Clark's afternoon TV show *Where The Action Is*, and viewers could usually depend on Smitty to do something wacky while the group lip-synched hits like "Just Like Me," "Hungry," "Him Or Me" and "Good Thing." What we didn't know at the time was that Smitty didn't play on the group's hits. Hal Blaine (who else?) cut the sessions. After leaving The Raiders, Smitty formed a band called The Brotherhood with ex-Raiders Phil "Fang" Volk and Drake Levin, an aggregation that recorded two albums on RCA and sank without a trace. Smitty passed away in 2001 and was laid to rest in his adopted state of Hawaii.

DANNY SMYTHE

Danny was a member of The Box Tops, Alex Chilton's band, and you've undoubtedly heard their biggest hit, "The Letter." That and their follow-up singles, "Cry Like A Baby" and "Neon Rainbow," were solid performances, but their LPs were uneven, and The Box Tops grew restless when the hits stopped. Chilton reorganized the group when most of the members returned to college, but that incarnation didn't last long either.

FLOYD SNEED

Floyd barely snuck into the late Sixties as drummer with Three Dog Night, who scored their hits primarily in the Seventies. The only black member of the band, Floyd was an animated, impassioned drummer with a super fat backbeat who learned from listening to R&B drummers like Al Jackson and Bernard Purdie. Floyd continues to communicate with drummers via the Internet who still name him as an influence.

ROGER SPENCER

Roger played with The Idle Race from Birmingham, England, the band that launched the career of guitarist/vocalist Jeff Lynne.

SKIP SPENCE

You may know him better as the wigged-out rhythm guitarist with Moby Grape, but before landing that gig, Skip Spence was the original drummer in Jefferson Airplane. He had never played drums before, but was recruited by Paul Kantner and Marty Balin at least partially for his looks. For someone who was essentially a non-drummer, Skip played pretty well on that first LP, particularly on the cut "Let Me In." Listen for his syncopated hi-hat work on that track. Skip's life ended in 1999; he was a victim of lung cancer and the mental illness that had dogged him since the late Sixties. Skip had been homeless and was a ward of the state of California at the time of his death.

TOM STALEY

Ah, a man with a sense of humor. Tom was the slightly offbeat drummer with NRBQ (New Rhythm & Blues Quintet), probably the only band that gave The Blues Image serious competition in Florida in the late Sixties. Although Tom is no longer with NRBQ, the band still retains a certain eccentric nature.

JABO STARKS

Jabo Starks is the one half of the team that practically invented funk drumming. Along with his best friend Clyde Stubblefield, Jabo worked with James Brown for years and their drumming had a profound effect on music in general. He and Clyde never received any royalties for their groundbreaking work with Brown, but over the years, the pair's contributions have earned them great respect within the music community (see Clyde Stubblefield below). There is much information on the web about Jabo and Clyde.

JOHN STEELE

John was the first drummer with The Animals and may have played on their earliest hits, "House Of The Rising Sun," "We Gotta Get Outta This Place," "It's My Life," "Boom Boom," "I'm Crying" and others, although session players were most likely used. John came from the same musical school of thought that bred other simple, uncomplicated players like Charlie Watts, Ringo Starr and Kenney Jones. His style was economical and right to the point. He left The Animals in 1966 and supposedly took a day job in the men's haberdashery business. After marrying and starting a family, John was offered a management job in a plastics factory and he worked there until The Animals re-formed and toured with all original personnel intact in 1983. John used a five-piece Ludwig set with a basic cymbal setup and the band sounded excellent live. Despite the years out of the music business, John played quite well. He and guitarist Hilton Valentine organized a band called Animals II and toured again in 1997 with The Yardbirds. Once again, John Steele proved himself fully capable behind the kit.

RICHARD STEVENS

Richard played with Frijid Pink, who scored a hit in the late Sixties with "House Of The Rising Sun."

DON STEVENSON

Throughout his musical career, Don Stevenson has been associated with Moby Grape. He was the one who flashed the infamous middle finger on the cover of the Grape's first Columbia album. In their infinite wisdom, the record company had the photo airbrushed over. This incident seems to be what Don is best remembered for, but I think it might be better to recall what a good drummer he was instead. The word that springs to mind about Don's drumming is *tight*. His Ludwig drums were very crisply recorded and his fills and timekeeping were equally so. Don handled sudden tempo changes and ballads easily, and excelled at shuffle rhythms. When the band's sound moved closer to country, Don adjusted his approach and did remarkably well. Moby Grape was a classic case of a band earmarked for stardom that did everything wrong: bad management, drug busts, failed promotional campaigns, drug and alcohol abuse, mental illness, inconsistent live gigs, etc. Don drifted in and out of the band for years and finally ended up a very successful realtor in northern California. He has no plans to return to music anytime soon.

CLYDE STUBBLEFIELD

Clyde, along with his best friend, drummer Jabo Starks, powered the funk and R&B of James Brown for years and, in doing so, left an indelible mark on rock drummers and drumming. He and Jabo are probably the two most sampled drummers in the world. Clyde's playing was generally subtler than that of Jabo, and over the years, he has also worked with Otis Redding, Phil Upchurch, Clayton Filyau, Bootsy Collins, John Scofield and many more. Jabo and Clyde recorded an instructional video several years ago called *Soul Of The Funky Drummers*. Unfortunately, Clyde was recently diagnosed with bladder cancer and a fund has been set up to help defray his medical bills: The Clyde Stubblefield Medical Fund, First Federal Savings, PO Box 1868, 605 State Street, LaCrosse, WI 54602-9962. Donations are much appreciated and welcomed.

GEORGE SURANOVICH

Mistakenly omitted from the first version of this book, George Suranovich played with a later version of Love, starting with the album *Four Sail*. He had a long history in drumming before and after that, as a musician with the U.S. Army, and a member of The Blues Image, where he replaced Manny Bertematti, and on stints with The Eric Burdon Band, Jimmy Witherspoon, his own group Tovarich, and later with Glen Campbell's backup band. George hooked up again with Love for a live album in 1981 and settled back in his hometown of Pittsburgh, where he played and taught drums. Years of overindulgence contributed to the heart attack that claimed his life in early 1990. George Suranovich had jazz and rock chops to spare and freely shared his knowledge with students and fans.

JOHN SUTTON

The Downliners Sect was an odd English R&B band with a strange sense of humor. Their records mirrored their attitude and their drummer John Sutton was with them in their best days. The Sect supposedly gets together to this day for the occasional concert or club appearance.

GEOFF SWETTENHAM

Geoff worked with Grapefruit, a British pop/rock outfit that included some involvement with the Vanda/Young writing team from The Easybeats. After a few LPs that received only lukewarm notices and sales, Grapefruit turned sour.

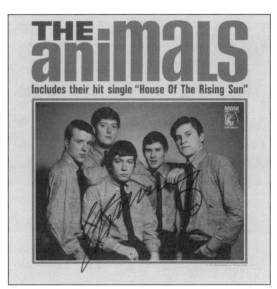

John Steele of The Animals, far left (autograph by Eric Burdon).

HONORABLE MENTIONS

RICHARD "DICKEY" TARRACH

"Dickey" Tarrach drummed for The Rattles, perhaps the best known Sixties band to emerge from Germany. The group was hugely popular in their homeland. They scored several Top 20 hits in Germany, made a film similar to *A Hard Day's Night* and established themselves in England as well. Their sound was rough R&B at first, but they rode with the times and changed, eventually scoring a worldwide hit in 1970 with "The Witch."

MIKE TATMAN

Mike played with The Human Beinz from Youngstown, Ohio, and their hit "Nobody But Me" is still a staple of classic-rock radio and is frequently used on television commercials and movie soundtracks. The band survived into the 1970's.

DALLAS TAYLOR

Dallas is best remembered as the drummer with Crosby, Stills, Nash & Young. Dallas always knew when to lay back in order to complement the band's acoustic music. Before joining CSN&Y, Taylor worked with a band called Clear Light, a group with two drummers that recorded one long-out-of-print and collectible LP on Elektra Records, that included the chilling cut "Mr. Blue," which was a bit of an FM radio hit. Taylor was fired from CSN&Y, but worked again with Stephen Stills in the band Manassas. Eventually, Taylor sank into the horror of heroin addiction, finally kicked the habit, and survived a liver transplant. He still lives in California with his wife, herself a recovering substance abuser. Taylor wrote a book several years ago called *Prisoner Of Woodstock*, and works today counseling drug addicts and playing drums occasionally.

DAN TAYLOR

Here's another name from the annals of Sixties rock obscurity. Dan Taylor played a large drum set with The Silver Apples, a NYC duo that recorded two LPs of futuristic synth rock. The group's records didn't sell much and have since become collectible rarities.

Photo courtesy of Photofest

Mel Taylor, far right, of The Ventures.

MEL TAYLOR

Since the early Sixties, Mel Taylor was the driving force behind The Ventures, the world's number-one instrumental band. His drum solos on The Ventures' version of "Wipeout" blew away those on The Surfaris' hit by a mile. Mel also did a lot of session work in the Hollywood studios. Despite senior citizen status, The Ventures are still together and remain a very popular attraction in Japan, where they tour regularly, Unfortunately, Mel Taylor passed away in 1997 and his son Leon has taken his place in The Ventures.

MICHAEL TEGZA

Michael worked with the band H.P. Lovecraft, a Chicago group that played some of the most eerie psych/folk/rock this author has ever experienced. Inspired by the horror fiction of author H.P. Lovecraft, the band certainly had an original sound, but split up after two albums. Michael joined Bangor Flying Circus, which recorded one album for Dunhill Records. In 1970, Michael reorganized the band as Lovecraft, with new members, but their two LPs went nowhere. Michael later played in a band called Aorta that released one album.

CLIVE THACKER

Clive drummed with The Brian Auger Trinity when the band's lineup included singer Julie "Jools" Driscoll, whose lithe appearance belied her powerful jazz- and soul-inflected vocals. They made the rounds of the American concert circuit and played the Fillmore East in New York City but never broke through big in the U.S. Clive was a very able drummer with a strong jazz background, a trait not uncommon in British drummers of the day.

DRACHEN THEAKER

This mystery man was reportedly the drummer on "Fire," Arthur Brown's biggest hit, but over the years, it has become known that Carl Palmer cut the track instead. The elusive Mr. Theaker worked with Arthur Brown, missed out on a chance to audition for The Jimi Hendrix Experience, was replaced in the Brown band by Carl Palmer as mentioned, and also played with Arthur Lee's Love for a short while. Other than these few facts, we don't know much more. An Internet search revealed precious little information.

GREGG THOMAS

Gregg played with a bizarre San Francisco power trio called Mint Tattoo, which cut one very obscure album for Dot Records in 1967. Shortly afterward, Mint Tattoo joined Blue Cheer en masse and recorded a couple of now-rare discs with that band. Blue Cheer's sound grew substantially softer with its new members. Gregg bore a facial resemblance to Carmine Appice.

DENNIS THOMPSON

Dennis Thompson is the hard-rocking drummer with The MC5 who stormed out of Detroit with a highly controversial LP on Elektra Records (the earliest copies featured singer Rob Tyner yelling, "Kick out the jams, motherfuckers!"). Later copies were cleaned up and although the band espoused revolution, drugs and sex, they were finished after their second album. The hype created by their manager, political activist John Sinclair, just didn't fly. By the time the band realized what was going on, it was too late and they split. The MC5 still play occasional dates with Dennis on drums.

ROB TOWNSEND

Rob Townsend was not the brother of The Who's guitarist (their names are spelled differently), but rather the drummer in the Brit band Family, who never gained acceptance in this country, despite some good records and dynamic live shows. Rob was a dramatic player, capable of thunderous fills and gentle timekeeping, often within the same piece of music.

CHRIS TOWNSON

Chris played drums with John's Children, the band that kick-started the career of Marc Bolan.

MAUREEN TUCKER

Maureen Tucker (third left) of The Velvet Underground.

One of the three female drummers in this volume, Mo Tucker played with The Velvet Underground, one of the most influential rock groups in history and Lou Reed's first notable band. The Velvet's music was dark and sinister, glorifying heroin addiction, homosexuality and transvestitism. They were part of Andy Warhol's troupe of avant-garde eccentrics for a while. Mo was supposedly rudimentally trained, but her no-holds-barred primitivism belied this claim. She was present when the Velvets regrouped for a short series of concerts in 1993 and has also recorded her own solo albums.

ROSS TURNEY

Ross played drums in the Canadian group The Collectors, which morphed into Chilliwack.

JOHN TUTTLE

John drummed with Fever Tree, a Texas band mistakenly associated with California due to their hit "San Francisco Girls," a truly memorable piece of psych-rock and an FM radio hit. John's playing was always on the money. During the course of their career, Fever Tree experimented with different types of sounds and John could always be relied upon to interject something appropriate.

JOHN VIDICAN

The band Kaleidoscope played "world music" long before the term existed, using an esoteric variety of strange stringed instruments coupled with the usual rock instrumentation of guitars, bass and drums. The band included David Lindley, who later worked as a sideman for Jackson Browne, Warren Zevon and many others. John Vidican was their versatile, imaginative drummer. You would have had to possess such qualities to play the band's music, which took in rock, jazz, Middle Eastern, folk, country and many other influences. The Kaleidoscope's four albums have just been re-released in a CD box set and their cult following remains strong.

JIM VOIGHT

Jim drummed with the Califorinia psych-rock band The Peanut Butter Conspiracy.

JIMMY WALKER

Jimmy held down the drum chair with The Knickerbockers from Bergenfield, New Jersey who hit the charts in late 1965 with the Beatles-inspired "Lies," a garage-rock classic. He came from the pre–British Invasion school of rock drumming and his playing exhibited the influence of the "twist bands" of the day. Jimmy gave up the drums and surprised a few people when he took Bill Medley's place in The Righteous Brothers. It was a partnership that didn't last long: not long after joining the group, singer Bobby Hatfield, the other original Brother, also left.

LARRY WALL

Larry's insistent sixteenth-note fills helped make "Keep On Dancing" by the Memphis-based Gentrys a huge hit. The band used to appear on rock TV shows and lip-synched the song with Larry playing an inverted washtub. Anything could happen in the Sixties.

MICKEY WALLER

His playing was so casual it could almost be considered sloppy, but Mickey Waller, who played with Steampacket and The Jeff Beck Group, and on all Rod Stewart's early solo albums, was one swinging rock drummer. Mickey's approach was based not on technique, but on feel, and he always succeeded in making the music groove, as it should. His playing on Stewart's rendition of Chuck Berry's "Sweet Little Rock 'n' Roller" is about as perfect an example as you could find of the early rock n' roll "in between" beat that combined a boogie-woogie shuffle rhythm with a straight-eight feel, not an easy accomplishment. Very few drummers do it better. Mickey became an in-demand session player in the Seventies.

JOHN IKE WALTON

John Ike was the lanky, blond Texan who handled drumming duties with The Thirteenth Floor Elevators during the height of their popularity in 1965–1966. He favored the use of his ride cymbal bell for timekeeping, and developed a distinctive style that other Texas drummers copied. John has participated in a few Elevators reunion concerts over the years.

BRUCE WATERSON

Bruce played with The Gestures from Minneapolis. Their best-known tune was "Run, Run, Run," which charted to number 44 nationally.

KEN WEAVER

Hardly an outstanding musician, Ken Weaver played with The Fugs, a loose conglomeration of Greenwich Village poets and musicians whose vulgar humor and song lyrics shocked some people in the mid-Sixties. The group's first two records appeared on ESP-Disk, a small NYC indie label, but they later inked a major contract with Reprise Records and tried to make themselves more acceptable to a wider audience. Live, Ken occasionally left the drum throne to deliver "sermons" about sex, drugs, politics or the police.

KEITH WEBB

You've probably never heard of Keith Webb, but you should have, for he was one of the best British drummers this writer has ever seen and heard. He played with singer-songwriter-guitarist Terry Reid from 1967–1971. The group was a guitar/organ/drums trio, which allowed Keith plenty of room to stretch his considerable chops on material like "Season Of The Witch," "Bang Bang," and Reid's originals. His drumming could be soft and subtle, with hints of jazz, or as explosive that of as another Keith…Keith Moon. I still listen to Terry Reid's old vinyl albums and marvel at the quality of Webb's drumming. I am dumbfounded as to why someone as talented as Keith Webb never went further in music. It's anybody's guess what became of him from a musical standpoint, but it certainly was the drumming community's loss. Keith still lives in England.

bang, bang
you're
TERRY REID

Keith Webb, far left.

DAVE WEBSTER

Dave played drums for The Music Explosion, an Ohio group that had a hit with "Little Bit O' Soul" in 1967. The band petered out quickly, but Dave's drumming, with its Keith Moon-like intensity and power, was impressive and exciting.

ALLEN WEHR

Allen Wehr played drums in a band called Morning Glory that recorded one album for Fontana Records, glorifying the lighter side of peace and love, circa 1967. It didn't sell and the group disbanded.

RICHARD WEISBERG

In 1968, MGM records tried to convince the record-buying public that the "Bosstown Sound" was the next big thing. It was nothing more than a clever publicity hype to promote a handful of bands from New England that the label had signed. The campaign was a flop, but one of the better bands amidst the brouhaha was The Beacon Street Union, whose drummer, Rick Weisberg, was a very creative player who knew how play with subtlety when the music demanded he do so. The Beacon Street Union cut two albums and broke up when the "Bosstown Sound" fizzled.

PAUL WHALEY

What Paul Whaley lacked in subtlety, he more than made up for in velocity and sheer attack. He was the original drummer with Blue Cheer, who came to national attention with their no-holds-barred version of Eddie Cochran's "Summertime Blues." Blue Cheer was certainly one of the first heavy-metal bands and Paul was indeed a very hard hitter. He used to wear thick leather gloves to protect his hands when he played. He left the band in 1970 and supposedly worked menial jobs. Blue Cheer still regroups from time to time and Paul has returned to their drum chair.

PAUL WHEATBREAD

With a name like that, you'd think he was a baker. Paul played with Gary Puckett & The Union Gap. It's no secret that session musicians were used on the group's records. Could Paul actually play? The band performed live, so we should assume he could.

ALAN WHITE

Alan White has been the drummer with Yes for decades, but started his professional career playing with Ginger Baker's Air Force, worked with John Lennon and Eric Clapton in The Plastic Ono Band, and has recorded or toured with Spencer Davis and Eddie Money, to name a couple. He is planning on recording his second solo album soon and has had a hand in composing some of Yes's music over the years. His web site is www.alanwhite.com.

ANDY WHITE

Andy White is remembered today as a busy British session drummer who played on The Beatles' first single, "Love Me Do." It seems that Beatles' producer George Martin felt Ringo Starr wasn't up to the task and White was called in. Ringo played tambourine. Andy also recorded with Tom Jones, Marlene Dietrich, Herman's Hermits, Billy Fury and many others. Today Andy still plays and teaches drums in northern New Jersey.

ALAN WHITEHEAD

Alan played with the British band Marmalade, who scored a U.S. hit with "Reflections Of My Life." The band is still together with two original members and tours the European oldies circuit.

BARRY WHITWAM

Barry played with teenybopper Brit hit-makers Herman's Hermits. Come on…don't laugh! Barry wasn't a bad drummer, although session musicians were used on many of the band's recordings.

RUSTY WEIR

You might remember Rusty as a guitar-totin' good ol' boy from Texas who had a hit in the Seventies with "Don't It Make You Wanna Dance," but he used to be the drummer in one of Austin's hottest Sixties garage bands, The Wig, who recorded the deranged classic "Crackin' Up" on Blacknight Records. He borrowed a few licks and tricks from John Ike Walton, but back then in Texas, who didn't? Rusty was a pretty fair rock drummer.

GARY WEISS

Garry played with Chicago's The Lemon Drops on their immortal Sixties punk classic "I Live In The Springtime." Unfortunately, Gary's drums were so poorly recorded as to render them almost inaudible.

KEVIN WESTLAKE

Kevin played drums with Blossom Toes, harbingers of the English psychedelic-rock movement.

MICHAEL WILDING

The Primitives were another in a long line of English R&B bands. With Michael Wilding on drums they produced some raving singles, none of which charted. The Primitives moved to Italy and reportedly did much better there than in their homeland.

TERRY WILLIAMS

He's been called the "King of Four/Four Time" and you might be hard-pressed to find a drummer anywhere with a better innate feel for rock 'n' roll music than Terry Williams. He had his first shot at the big time with guitarist Dave Edmunds in Love Sculpture, and then joined Man, a hippie band with strong tendencies toward San Francisco rock. Terry gained his real fame as a member of Rockpile and eventually joined Dire Straits when Rockpile broke up.

B. J. WILSON

Procol Harum's Barrie J. Wilson was without a doubt one of the best and most underrated drummers on either side of the Atlantic in the Sixties. He joined Procol Harum just in time to record "Whiter Shade Of Pale" and remained with the group until their demise in the Seventies. B. J. had played with the members of Procol Harum earlier in an R&B band called The Paramounts that gained some notoriety on the British scene, so he was no stranger to music. His drumming was solid and inventive, with dramatic fills and imaginative time patterns. Check out his work on the live version of "Conquistador" for an example. His use of the cowbell on the track "Whiskey Train" was equally fluid and clever. B. J. died in October 1990, but Procol Harum continues to this day without him.

B. J. Wilson, center, of Procol Harum.

DENNIS WILSON

Beach Boy Dennis Wilson's tragic story is one that encompasses fame and fortune gained and lost, a mysterious relationship with cult figure and convicted murderer Charles Manson, alcoholism, drug abuse, numerous failed marriages and an exceedingly violent temper. It's a long and complex tale that culminated with his drowning on December 28, 1983. Strikingly handsome, the embodiment of the tanned California surfer boy, Dennis was not an abundantly talented drummer by any means, but his simplicity suited The Beach Boys' music. He rarely played on the group's early records; Hal Blaine cut the sessions, and Dennis even gave up drums for a while after injuring his hand during a domestic dispute. The Beach Boys eventually hired a backup drummer and percussionist to play along with Dennis onstage. This writer witnessed the Wilson temper firsthand after a concert at Lynchburg College in 1971. At the end of the show, an enraged Dennis physically threw the band's percussionist off the stage. In his last days, Dennis made a few feeble attempts to straighten out his life, but it never happened. Broke and alone, he began borrowing money from friends and spent most of it on booze and dope. His final night was spent partying aboard a luxury yacht in Marina del Ray. Dennis dove overboard several times in cold water without a wetsuit and eventually didn't come up. Police found his body an hour later. The death was ruled an accidental drowning. Dennis was only thirty-nine, but the ravages of his lifestyle made him appear older than his years. According to his wishes, he was buried at sea. The Beach Boys, with only one original member, continue to play the oldies circuit. For a while, actor John Stamos sat in on drums with the group.

MICK WILSON

Mick Wilson played drums in the British band Dave Dee, Dozy, Beaky, Mick & Tich. They scored many hits in England and Europe, but never made a splash in the USA, and remarkably, they're still together with all the original members, no mean accomplishment these days.

RON WILSON

Ron Wilson played one of the most immortal drum solos in history: the one in "Wipeout." He recorded it in 1963 with his group, The Surfaris, and it was a huge instrumental hit. Every teenage drummer had to learn that famous tom-tom solo at one time or another. The beauty of "Wipeout" was that almost anyone could play it, and it remains a rock classic. The Surfaris soldiered on after Ron left the band, and he died in 1989.

DANIEL WOOD

Dan played with The Other Half from Los Angeles, who upset more than a few parents with their ode to drug dealers titled "Mr. Pharmacist."

DON WOOD

Don Wood evidently liked Bo Diddley beats and the drumming of Ringo Starr. He copied both exceedingly well in his band The Gants, who hailed from Mississippi. They came real close a few times to scoring hits nationally, but they always seemed to be bubbling under. After several singles and three albums, the band split, but like so many Sixties groups, they're back together and working.

JIMMY WRIGHT

Jimmy was a member of The Five Americans from Dallas, Texas. Their big hits were "I See The Light" and "Western Union."

ROBERT WYATT

A remarkable man and an interesting drummer, Robert Wyatt was the drummer in The Soft Machine, a British organ-bass-drums trio whose futuristic music sported influences from rock, free-form jazz and many other styles. They toured the U.S. with Jimi Hendrix in 1968, mystifying audiences everywhere. In the early Seventies, Robert accidentally fell out a window and was severely injured. Paralyzed from the waist down, he began playing keys and percussion instead, and developed his songwriting skills. Over the years, he has become a critics' favorite and continues to release the occasional disc in Europe, where he is well regarded.

DAVE WYNNE

Dave Wynne played with The Haunted, a legendary Canadian band, whose lone hit, "1-2-5" has become standard fare for Sixties-revival garage bands worldwide. Like "Louie Louie," it's one of those necessary songs to learn. The Haunted was the top-drawing band in the Montreal area for a while and it finally sputtered to their demise in 1970. They re-formed for one concert in the 1980's.

LUKE R. YOO

Luke R. Yoo was the name used by actor Don Grady (née Agrati), who starred in the hit TV show *My Three Sons* and had musical aspirations on the side. His band, Yellow Balloon, had a fluke hit of the same name. Influenced by The Beach Boys, their sound was all California sunshine and good vibes, and it was some of the most sickeningly sweet music ever committed to tape. The band ended not long afterward, but Don Agrati released at least one solo album later on.

PETE YORK

Pete York is still another British drummer who never got the credit he deserved. He was a jazz and R&B player at heart, and his playing was perfect for The Spencer Davis Group with Steve Winwood on keys, guitar and vocals. Their hits included "Gimme Some Lovin'," "Keep On Running," "Somebody Help Me" and "I'm A Man." Pete stuck with Davis after Winwood left the band, but the hits stopped, and he quit in October 1968. Pete remains in the music business today and is a well-established jazz drummer in England. He was a member of Rocket 88, the boogie-woogie big band run by Charlie Watts and Ian Stewart, and endorsed Rogers drums in the Sixties.

RANDY ZEHRINGER

Randy was guitarist Rick Derringer's brother and the drummer in The McCoys. His drumming on their first hit, "Hang On Sloopy," was fiery and stylized, with simple but effective tom fills between verse lines. Randy was definitely a cool drummer: he stood up when the band lip-synched on TV, was good-looking, played red sparkle Rogers drums and dressed in the latest Mod fashions. When The McCoys abandoned the teenybopper hit singles routine in 1968, their sound became more serious, with Indian and jazz influences creeping in. Randy made the transition seamlessly. In the early 1970's, they hooked up with Texas blues guitarist Johnny Winter and became his backup band, known as Johnny Winter And (supposedly, Winter didn't want to use the name "McCoys"). The McCoys achieved their greatest success in this new role and Randy apparently left the music business after the gig ran its course.

CESAR ZUIDERWYK (ZUIDERWIJK)

Perhaps the only Dutch drummer to attain true worldwide success, Cesar has been with Golden Earring since the late Sixties and he's still with the band, one whose personnel hasn't changed since the mid-Seventies. Although not Golden Earring's original drummer, he is the best known. His playing on the hit "Radar Love," and later on "Twilight Zone," was imaginative and hard-hitting. Cesar is also a noted showman. He used to leap over the drums at the end of the band's sets and his solos were always well thought-out. Golden Earring's web site reveals a full calendar of gigs booked right into 2006.

Pete York of The Spencer Davis Group, second from right.

Epilogue

This revision of *Great Rock Drummers Of The Sixties* is complete. It would have to be, because you're holding it in your hands. No more dumb jokes, I promise.

Hopefully, it won't take sixteen years to revise again.

By the way, it should be noted that *epilogue* is a perfectly acceptable spelling. I checked Webster's. Someone for whom I have very little respect told me it was wrong years ago. He was mistaken.

What you have now, in my opinion, is a much better product than you had in 1989: we have made the book more comprehensive, corrected mistakes, added a chapter and updated a boatload of information. If I had the luxury of unlimited time, I might succeed in adding a few more names or finding a few more mystery drummers, but as already stated, it is impossible to include every single drummer who played with a recording rock group in the Sixties. Hopefully, we've gotten many of your favorites this time. If we have omitted anyone, kindly let us know. There's bound to be a few.

To once again quote Ian Hunter, former lead singer of Mott The Hoople: "I've wanted to do this for years."

And finally, to answer a question asked by many: "Will you write a book on rock drummers of the Seventies and Eighties?" The answer is a definite no. It's not going to happen. The Sixties was my time, baby. I'll leave that project to someone else. I have other book projects in mind, so stay tuned.

DW Drummer Signing Off.